"*Dentistry's Business Secrets* by Dr. Ed Logan is a gift to dentistry. If you are a struggling or brand new practice, this book just might be the inspiration you need to help turn things around!"

Howard Farran DDS, MBA, MAGD
Founder and CEO, *DentalTown Magazine* and DentalTown.com

"In a well written and easily understood book, Dr. Ed Logan has answered in a practical way many of the most important questions about dental practice. The information in the book will be valuable to practitioners of all ages."

Gordon Christensen, DDS, MSD, PhD
Founder and Director of Practical Clinical Courses (PCC)
Co-Founder and Senior Consultant, CR Foundation, formerly CRA
Diplomate, American Board of Prosthodontics

"If you are a dentist who is ready to seriously grow your practice, *Dentistry's Business Secrets* will certainly help you reach your goals! Written by a real dentist who has "been there and done that," we consider this book a MUST READ for anyone in our profession!"

Dr. David Madow
Dr. Richard Madow
"The Madow Brothers," Co-founders, The Madow Group,
Creating Success for Dentists since 1989!

"Finally! A book that gives step by step instructions for operating an effective and efficient dental practice. Whether you are a brand new dentist or a seasoned dental professional, the systems outlined in this book will not only help you become more profitable, but will actually make your chosen profession more enjoyable. Don't just read this book, but implement the systems outlined in it and enjoy the success that follows. This book is a must read for every dental professional!"

Larry Mathis, CFP®
Author, *Bridging the Financial Gap for Dentists*

"*Dentistry's Business Secrets* reaches out to the dental professional on a personal and practical level, establishing common ground in our battle to achieve practice growth and success through the application of tried and true principles."

Bill Blatchford, DDS
President and CEO, Blatchford Solutions:
Dental Practice Management Consulting

"This is a must read for every dentist, no matter where you are in your career! Dr. Logan relates the principles of profitability that create successful practices in a very systematic approach, all the while showing you how to avoid the costly mistakes that so many dentists have endured."

Matthew Horne, DDS
Private Practice, Austin, Texas

"*Dentistry's Business Secrets* provides a wealth of knowledge based upon personal, practical experience. A must read for the new dentist and those reevaluating their own practices."

Stephen Lindblom, DDS
Redwood City, California
Adjunct professor,
University of the Pacific Dugoni School of Dentistry

"Ed Logan is a great business person who happens to be a dentist, and therein lies his value to us as his readers. *Dentistry's Business Secrets* is a game plan for turning your dental practice into a thriving business. One of the best practice development investments you will ever make!"

Eric Herrenkohl
President of Herrenkohl Consulting
Author, *How to Hire A-Players,* Expert author for Monster.com

"*Dentistry's Business Secrets* is a true compendium of business best practices they did not teach you in dental school. If you own a dental practice, manage a dental practice or are considering purchasing or starting your own practice, you need this book!"

Mark Kennedy
Managing Director, ETS Dental,
Professional Dental Placement Company

"Dr. Logan cleverly and humorously shares his personal anecdotes in a style that is honest and genuine, drawing upon his own personal successes and relating them in a manner that can be applied on Monday morning in your own office."

Michael Kling, OD
President, Invision Eye Care Optometry, San Diego, California

I have been a practicing CPA for 36 years. Our firm has a successful niche working with over 300 dentists and dental specialists. Dr. Logan has written a cook book that should be mandatory reading for all fourth year dental students. It would also serve as a great resource for those who have been in practice, no matter the length of time. This book covers every topic of concern to a dentist and almost nothing covered in the book is taught in dental school. Kudos to Dr. Logan

Bill Bender, CPA, PFS
Bender, Weltman, Thomas, Perry & Co, PC, CPAs
Member ADCPA

"I wish I would have had this book years ago! Most of this information I learned by trial and error (school of hard knocks). An informative and enjoyable read!"

Michael Bennett, DDS
Private Practice, Cape Girardeau, Missouri

"This book is a valuable resource that makes management at every level a whole lot easier. Do yourself a favor and keep Dr. Logan's *Dentistry's Business Secrets* within arm's reach on your desk!"

Donald Rooker
Director of Operations, Eye Care Associates of San Diego

Dentistry's Business Secrets

Proven Growth Strategies for Your New or Existing Practice

Edward M. Logan, DDS

AuthorHouse™
1663 Liberty Drive
Bloomington, IN 47403
www.authorhouse.com
Phone: 1-800-839-8640

© 2011 Edward M. Logan, DDS. All rights reserved.

No part of this book may be reproduced, stored in a retrieval system, or transmitted by any means without the written permission of the author.

First published by AuthorHouse 2/15/2011

ISBN: 978-1-4520-2570-4 (sc)
ISBN: 978-1-4520-2571-1 (dj)
ISBN: 978-1-4520-2572-8 (e)

Library of Congress Control Number: 2011900776

Printed in the United States of America

This book is printed on acid-free paper.

Certain stock imagery © Thinkstock.

Because of the dynamic nature of the Internet, any Web addresses or links contained in this book may have changed since publication and may no longer be valid. The views expressed in this work are solely those of the author and do not necessarily reflect the views of the publisher, and the publisher hereby disclaims any responsibility for them.

Dedication

This book is dedicated to my wife Katie; the coolest person I know, to my son Will; my new best friend and to my child on the way; whom I cannot wait to meet!

Acknowledgements

The work of this book was truly a family affair. I owe a debt of gratitude to my sister, Julie Thompkins, who was the inspiration behind the writing of this book, and to my mom, Linda Logan, who wielded her English teacher's red pen in the editing of this manuscript. With their help my goals for this book have been realized. Thanks ladies!

Table of Contents

Foreword xv

THE BUSINESS OF DENTISTRY

Chapter 1   What We Did Not Learn in Dental School 1

Chapter 2   Why You Need a Template for Growth and Success of Your Dental Practice 9

YOUR STYLE OF PRACTICE

Chapter 3   Should You Associate, Buy or Start a Practice from Scratch? 15

SETTING UP SHOP

Chapter 4   Choosing the Right Location and Practice Opportunity 33

Chapter 5   Office Design Decisions 43

Chapter 6   Before Your Doors Open 57

Chapter 7   Your Fee Schedule Determines Profitability 69

HIRING THE IDEAL STAFF

Chapter 8   Is There an Ideal Staff? 77

Chapter 9   Staff Skills, Duties and Expectations 83

Chapter 10   Fielding the Perfect Team 97

FIVE-STAR CUSTOMER SERVICE

Chapter 11   The Guest Mentality 113

PRACTICE MANAGEMENT

Chapter 12   Time and Efficiency for the Dentist.......................... 125
Chapter 13   Cost Controlling Strategies 151
Chapter 14   The Psychology of Dentistry...................................... 171
Chapter 15   Mistakes I Have Made 187
Chapter 16   Start Your Practice, Then Start Saving...................... 195

A DAY AT THE DENTIST'S OFFICE

Chapter 17   Treatment Planning for Case Acceptance 207
Chapter 18   Co-Payments, Collections and Financing................. 223

DENTAL INSURANCE MASTERY IN YOUR PRACTICE

Chapter 19   Insurance 101.. 237
Chapter 20   Insurance Participation Decisions............................. 251

MARKETING YOUR PRACTICE FOR SUCCESS

Chapter 21   Creating a Powerful Marketing Plan 267
Chapter 22   Internal Marketing Efforts 273
Chapter 23   External Marketing Efforts.. 293

INTERNET MARKETING

Chapter 24   Designing a First-Class Website................................ 327
Chapter 25   Getting Your Website Recognized (Search Engine
              Optimization) 351
Chapter 26   Social Media Marketing... 379

Chapter 27 Internet Toolbox 403

Chapter 28 Internet Glossary 409

CAN YOU REALLY DO THIS?

Chapter 29 A Success Story 415

Closing 421

Practice Management Resources for Dentists 423

References 425

Index 429

About the Author 439

Foreword

If you have taken the time to pick up this book, you are well on your way to taking your dental business, or any healthcare business for that matter, to the next level. Dr. Ed Logan's *Dentistry's Business Secrets* is one of the best practice development investments you will ever make. It serves to enhance our clinical education by revealing the essential business truths often overlooked in health professional training. Fortunately, we have this book to help us navigate the sometimes murky waters of creating a highly successful practice through putting in motion Dr. Logan's techniques for running "the business of healthcare."

Let me start by saying that I am not a dentist, but an optometrist. I have not spent the long hours of study required to obtain a dental degree nor exercised the discipline to master the delicate skills of restorative dentistry. I hardly know the difference between a root canal and the Panama Canal, or an amalgam filling and grandma's pie filling. However, as a healthcare professional myself, I do know this: most of us are ill-equipped to successfully run our own healthcare practices without a clear course of action. I am not suggesting that we are incapable of being good doctors, but rather that we lack the necessary skills to effectively manage the day-to-day operation of our businesses.

As optometrists, we experience a journey similar to our dental compatriots: four years of undergraduate education, four or more years of post-graduate training, loads of anatomy, physiology, pharmacology, all necessary to provide the care expected by our patients. For me, it has been a long journey of reading as many books as I could find on the subject of business, people management, sales and marketing. I have spent thousands of dollars on business consultants, newsletters and practice management seminars. I have joined consulting groups for the purpose of sharing ideas and key business metrics, participated in think tanks throughout the country consulting with owners of practices similar to my own and read every piece of literature I could find on the business of being an optometrist. In all, the single most valuable resource I have discovered has been learning from the successes and failures of my professional colleagues, adopting the business principles that have worked for them and avoiding those that have not.

Upon completing my residency, I was eager to start my career and begin utilizing the clinical skills and knowledge that I had accumulated through my years of training. I knew I wanted to be my own boss some day, but felt I needed to first master the clinical aspects of my profession. The thought of stepping right out of school and into the responsibility of running a business seemed quite overwhelming. Sure, I was confident, maybe even a little over-confident, with all that I had learned about the clinical aspects of eye care. I had passed all of the academic requirements to practice in my chosen profession and felt prepared. I had amassed an enormous amount of educational debt, like so many graduates today, and knew I needed to start working as soon as possible. I was ready to start "wowing" my patients with all my clinical expertise and brilliance.

As the shine began to wear off my new, freshly-pressed lab coat, and the day-to-day grind of providing patient care as an associate doctor began to set in, my desire to run my own practice and become my own boss began to emerge. I had seen enough of what I would not do in my own business by the doctors for whom I had worked, and felt that I was ready to venture out on my own. Although I had no real business experience or expertise, and certainly no training or qualifications to run a business, I took the leap.

Soon after purchasing my first practice, I recall naively asking one of my more seasoned colleagues, "Dan, what's the secret to marketing my practice and being successful?" I will never forget his reply: "Mick, nothing works, but you have to do something." At the time, I did not realize the wisdom in that comment, and quite frankly, I thought it was a fairly pessimistic attitude from someone who owned his own business. I soon realized, however, that what he meant was: *not one thing* works, therefore you have to do *something*. So I began my long journey of learning to run a business, of managing people and of becoming a better, more effective leader. It has been through this process that I have learned to *do something* to help my business succeed.

Ed Logan and I became friends many years ago and quickly discovered that we shared a passion for taking care of our patients, and, equally important, being successful in our businesses. Although our education, training and the services that we provide are dramatically different, we face similar challenges and obstacles when it comes to running our offices, managing our staff members, and growing our businesses. Since we first met, we have spent countless hours bobbing on our surfboards and soaring up and down the Southern California coast on our bikes discussing our businesses and the personal challenges and victories we have each experienced. We continue to share what works and what does not work, what we should be doing but have not yet done and what we have tried over and over again, but quite possibly never should have tried in the first place. We learn from each other's style, personality, experience and example. I am confident that this is the key to your success as well: sharing practical, real life experiences with your peers that can fundamentally propel and energize your business, just like it did ours.

In his book *The E-Myth Revisited,* Michael E. Gerber points out that a highly successful practice can grow into a highly successful business only when the doctor-owner begins to work *on* the business instead of *in* the business. Said another way, it is the difference between going to work as an *entrepreneur* and going to work as a *doctor*. Instead of spending our day solely on the needs of our patients, we need to also focus our attention on the needs of our business. So how do you achieve this? It is not easy, and there are no sure-fire answers.

In *Dentistry's Business Secrets*, Dr. Logan presents a straightforward, practical, no-nonsense approach to successfully growing and managing your dental business. Whether you are starting your practice from "scratch," or are a seasoned veteran in the business of dentistry, you will find a wealth of information rarely presented at dental seminars or in dental school. His unique insights and keen analytical perspectives are the result of years of experience in several different practice modalities. Dr. Logan cleverly and humorously shares his personal anecdotes in a style that is honest and genuine, drawing upon his own personal successes and relating them in a manner that can be applied on Monday morning in your own office.

By carefully following the proven templates that Dr. Logan presents here, you will begin to reap the rewards of success, enjoy watching your business grow, and save countless hours of time and money which might otherwise be wasted on costly seminars, newsletters and business consultants. I congratulate you on beginning or continuing the journey of working *on* your business instead of *in* your business. I encourage you to dig in, trust the principles presented here, and watch what can be accomplished when you apply these tried and true ideas. Being a healthcare provider is a lifelong journey. So too is being a business owner. Bridging these two journeys together can bring you a personal satisfaction that only those who attempt it can ever understand. Dr. Ed Logan's *Dentistry's Business Secrets* is a book to help make your journey a little easier. Enjoy the ride!

Michael A. Kling, O.D.

Dr. Kling is president and owner of Invision Eye Care Optometry, a private practice in San Diego, California. Dr. Kling has been an expert examiner for the National Board of Examiners in Optometry and is an Adjunct Faculty member of Southern College of Optometry. He is one of the founders and president of Refractive Management Services Corporation, a refractive surgery management company, and is a past Clinical Director for TLC Laser Eye Centers, now NVISION Laser Eye Centers, in La Jolla, California. He is a past-President of the San Diego County Optometric Society, has chaired various committees for the California Optometric Association (COA), and in 2000, was named "Young OD of the Year" by the COA.

THE BUSINESS OF DENTISTRY

Chapter 1

What We Did Not Learn in Dental School

Last month I was trudging through the task of cleaning out an old filing cabinet, finally disposing of unneeded paperwork. Since my office was beginning to resemble that of Andy Rooney, I concluded that this had now become a necessary chore. Blowing dust off a faded document, I realized I was holding my final transcript from dental school. I am unclear as to the real value in keeping this record so long, but I found myself in a state of nostalgia while reviewing it. Memories of dental school flooded my mind, mostly of good friends and good times, though some memories not so upbeat.

The transcript itself confirmed the primary theory behind the need for this book. I was not so interested in the grades earned in each class as I was in the types of coursework required of me. I concluded that of the 284 credit hours earned in four years of dental school, only four of those hours covered topics related to running a business. We netted nearly twice as many credit hours in embryology as we did in practice management. While I can attest that this information is pretty exciting to review when a couple is expecting a child, I hope not to be called to act as an obstetrician any time soon. I am daily called, however, to manage a dental practice.

The Master Clinician

Since less than two percent of our graduate school education covered themes related to business, it seemed essential to make this limited exposure count. Most of the course time, however, was spent learning how to work with a dental assistant performing four-handed dentistry. Business start-up, growth and management were given cursory attention, yielding yet again to the dental school's central imperative, training graduates for clinical excellence.

Dental schools are charged with the unique responsibility of adequately preparing all of us to deliver standard of care dentistry to millions of people. Their goal is to ensure that, clinically, we can all pass muster. I am sure our well-meaning instructors hold hopes that all of us who choose to will be successful in running a private practice. It is just not incumbent on them to assure that we will.

The MBA Dentist

The profession of dentistry is vastly different from other occupations requiring the skills of business management. Those acquiring upper-level positions in Corporate America receive training specifically in the acquisition of business knowledge and acumen. Business is what these people do. It does not matter much what specifically the business does that makes the job pertinent. Most highly trained business managers move from one position to another with the freedom and speed of Helio Castroneves. They are neither tied to one company, nor committed to any particular product or service. They are merely committed to the business of doing business.

My older brother is an ideal example of the dissemination of skills an MBA educated business executive might experience throughout a career. Very close in age, we completed graduate school at roughly the same time. Since then, my brother has held nearly a dozen different positions with companies ranging from Frito Lay to LoanSurfer.com, whose wave, sadly to say, has since crashed. At the inception of this book's authorship, he held the title of CFO at a mid-sized company, publicly traded on the NASDAQ. He has since graduated to yet another position, that of CFO of a private firm in a related industry. The fact that his professional career continues to be so fluid confirms the point being made.

I, on the other hand, have held one job, dentist. Since graduating from dental school many years ago, the thought of doing something else for a living has rarely crossed my mind. This stands to reason given the enormous time and energy sacrifice demanded from graduate school in the health professions. This is not to mention the grand debt load accumulated during this multi-year period of deferred gratification. Not only are we required to delay any potential earnings typically accompanying an educated person during this phase of life, but we are also asked to bring a barrel full of cash to the school in exchange for our education.

The typical dentist will then become further entrenched in debt by assuming a healthy new practice loan. This advance commonly includes working capital to help keep the craft afloat until calmer waters prevail. When I find myself complaining, however, I am reminded of the software engineer Samir's quote in the movie *Office Space*. When faced with the proposition that he might be required to work for the loathsome firm Initech for the rest of his life, he offered, "It would be great to have that kind of job security." We have chosen a great profession, one that can reward us handsomely for our hard work.

It never appeared strange to me to be in one occupation for life until I stopped to consider the flexible nature of my friends' work lives. The average American changes jobs every five years. I have one friend who boasts a total of 32 different occupations in the past five years, skewing the averages considerably. Even auxiliaries in our industry tend to exercise the ability to surf from office to office. It is not unusual to receive résumés from dental assistants and hygienists listing four or five different practice owners as prior employers. In fact, one of the occupational perks dental hygienists appreciate most is the ability to work when they want for whom they choose. It is also quite common for dental auxiliaries and front office staff members to change careers altogether.

Medical doctors are similar to dentists in terms of their long-term occupational commitment. This is easily understood given their extensive training, heavy debt load and even greater requirement of deferred gratification than that of dental professionals. Medical doctors are, however, much less likely to become encumbered with practice loans, as they assume the role of business owner with much less regularity.

A friend and family physician early in his practice related to me the various ways in which MDs elect to practice. He explained that the most practiced form of medicine, that within a small group, limits the upfront cost and serves as more of a blend between private practice and group practice. The next most popular form of practice is within a large organization, such as hospital, government or university employment. In this case, the individual doctor is shielded from the requirement to borrow money in order to start working. Going it alone by starting a private practice is the approach taken by less than one in six medical practitioners. Not only are a large percentage of medical doctors free from the burden of additional debt, they are also excused from the responsibility of running a business. The following data from the U.S. Department of Labor bear out these trends:

> Physicians and surgeons held about 633,000 jobs in 2006; approximately 15 percent were self-employed. About half of wage–and-salary physicians and surgeons worked in offices of physicians, and 18 percent were employed by hospitals. Others practiced in Federal, State, and local governments, including colleges, universities, and professional schools; private colleges, universities, and professional schools; and outpatient care centers. [1]

In contrast to the practice style numbers for MDs, the statistics for dental professionals are markedly different. According to the Bureau of Labor Statistics Occupational Outlook Handbook, 2006-07, there were 150,000 licensed dentists in the United States at the time of publication. The following excerpt emphasizes the overwhelming propensity for dentists to work as solo practitioners:

> About one third of dentists were self-employed and not incorporated. Almost all dentists work in private practice. According to the ADA, 78% of dentists in private practice are sole proprietors, and 14% belong to a partnership. A few salaried dentists work in hospitals and offices of physicians. [2]

While there is a growing trend of dentists who start out working for conglomerate practice management companies with multiple locations nationwide, the primary goal for most dentists is to eventually break out on their own. This typically means pocketing more of what you produce, but also imposes the responsibility to learn and put into practice the intricacies of running a business. Learning right the first time eliminates wasting time and money through trial and error in your own business.

As trained dentists, we tend to have only one shot at a career. Though some move on from this profession to others, most are committed to being dentists and doing dentistry. Accordingly, most dentists have accepted the commitment to running their own businesses. Investing sufficient time educating ourselves in the fundamentals of business administration is essential. We are owners, managers and administrators. If we do not know how to effectively manage those job descriptions, our businesses stand little chance of achieving maximum profitability. When we do invest the time and energy to acquire this business acumen, we position our practices for success, far beyond that of many or our peers. The dentist earning an *honorary MBA* is the one in charge of the profitable practice of the future.

The CEO Dentist

People often ask, "How many days a week do you work?" They are regularly perplexed by my response. "Seven days a week," I offer. What they are really meaning to ask is, "How many days per week do you treat patients?" Therein rests the confusion about running one's own health care practice. People outside the profession of dentistry commonly associate a four-day workweek with laziness and gluttony. I am routinely informed, "Oh, you've got it made!" I suppose they are right in a way, but not in the way they mean to imply.

There are those within our own profession who do not clearly understand what it means to work on the business as much as is necessary to position and preserve its place at the front of the pack. Within the scope of our four-day workweek, we may perform dozens of what are, in reality, very delicate surgical procedures. Comparisons might be drawn to surgeons outside dentistry who may operate only two days per week, treating as few as two patients each surgical day. Granted, the typical medical surgery can last much longer, and that which hangs in the balance may indeed carry greater significance. However, no other surgeons are expected to operate five or six days per week.

The fact is that dentists typically expend significant physical, mental and emotional energy each week which others might find difficult to appreciate. This expense takes a toll on the body and mind which we as dentists may not even recognize. Consider that the goal of a doctor operating at maximum capacity is to ensure that every available kernel of time on the schedule is occupied by a productive procedure. This permits little time to break away from the operatory, and less to manage the myriad aspects of the business outside of clinical dentistry.

How many other jobs do you know that fit this description? I am reminded of many of my friends who are able to complete their employment related tasks by working from home. I sometimes wonder how much of that time at home can actually be defined as *work*. Perhaps I am just jealous, but working from home sounds pretty good to me some days.

At the end of our four surgical days, we are often left with very little desire to participate in the management activities necessary to maintain the predominant ranking of a successful business. We might regard these duties as nonproductive, and therefore, of low priority. We are forced to perform the managerial obligations of a typical CEO in the margins of time we have away from the actual practice of dentistry. This creates the chasm into which many highly skilled clinicians fall in our profession. Within this void is where most of us perform *the business of dentistry*.

Given the time constraints we share as general dentists, it is imperative that we manage our businesses as efficiently as possible. I can think of no greater example of the CEO Doctor than a close friend and practice owner with whom I have shared strategic business ideas for many years. He loves manipulating spread sheets, attending business industry seminars and identifying the ways in which he can take his practice to the next level. In his free time, if he is not jamming with his upstart band, he is pouring over profit/loss statements. If you find that you would rather do other things with your time away from work, you would be well advised to become Dr. Efficiency in your practice management.

What This Book Has to Offer

Your experience with business courses in dental school may have been different from mine, and perhaps you feel your business training was adequate. The clear majority of dentists, however, admits to sharing a unified experience in school, and emerges feeling woefully unprepared for business life after graduation. It is all too common for me to hear from a dentist that running a business is a scary proposition, and that more training would be very much appreciated before venturing into it. My hope is that this book will serve to fill the void of business knowledge left after graduation from dental school. My desire is that you will find useful information you can immediately apply to your practice. Lastly, my goal is that this book will enable you to run a more profitable dental practice and continue to grow it to the utmost of your personal satisfaction.

If you are reading this book, you have identified a need to formulate a plan to help you take your business to the next level. You have fought a significant part of the battle. This book is intended to serve as a realistic representation of what results can and cannot be expected from any strategic growth and practice management program. I have knowledge of these results from having started three practices from scratch during my career, and implementing nearly all of the techniques described in this text. While keeping your expectations grounded in reality, I will share tried and true techniques which have resulted in rapid increases in new patient volume in each scratch practice.

I am not going to use phrases such as "practice explosion" or "tons of new patients guaranteed!" My desire is to under-promise and over-deliver, which are principles that also serve the health care professional well when interacting with patients. Though each practice is different from the next and no one can assure equal success for all practices, similarities abound. These parallels allow us to define methods proven to achieve results within almost any practice environment. I have labeled the guide to these methods a *template for growth and success of your new or existing practice*. I am extremely confident that by implementing this template, your business will experience rapid expansion, perhaps from its inception.

I intend to give credit for ideas where credit is due. Though I have blended concepts from years of learning, study and application in my practices into my own form, I wish to acknowledge the dentists and pundits originally responsible for these ideas. By drawing from an extensive network of practice owners, business managers, lecturing dentists and practice management consultants, this book offers decades of experience and expansive knowledge. This vast array of information is intended for immediate application to your new or existing practice, with the goal of lifting it to maximum profitability.

While certain chapters apply specifically to the doctor choosing to start a business from scratch, most of this book is intended for application in any existing dental practice. My goal is to provide valuable information which the practicing dentist can immediately put in motion to improve practice growth and profitability.

I have given you only the stuff that works so you can avoid wasting time and money through trial and error. Included is a chapter entitled Mistakes I Have Made, directing you away from those missteps that have fruitlessly caused me so much strife, wasted energy and expense. I provide a resource section containing practice management tools and marketing campaigns which can be directly put to practice. All the information is designed to guide you through doing it yourself, and getting started right away. I am enthusiastic and confident that you can apply the action steps outlined in the template for growth and success and lay claim to practice expansion virtually instantly. Let's get started!

Chapter 2

Why You Need a Template for Growth and Success of Your Dental Practice

When I began researching information on how to start and build my first dental practice, I was surprised to find that very few of the authors on this subject were actually dentists. These pundits were typically marketing majors, English majors, advertising specialists and occasionally dental hygienists. They could not fully relate to my situation because they were never wet-handed dentists. I was discouraged by their lack of understanding of the fundamental emotions and complexities of the job of health care provider. They had a product to sell but not a problem to solve.

Articles, journals and books written about running a business rarely address the unique needs of the individual dental practice owner. Ours is a highly specialized industry with very specific business requirements. When the literature is directed toward the individual dental practice there is little comprehensive attention given to the intricate details involved in growing an existing practice, and even less to starting a practice from scratch.

Much of the practice transition literature we receive is dedicated to purchase/sale arrangements, occasionally considering the topic of associating. There are consultants and brokers on seemingly every corner offering views on how best to take advantage of the dental transaction marketplace. There is an abundance of information available on how to buy a dental practice and more still on how to sell one. Why then is there a void in the literature and on the lecture circuit regarding the way in which dentists can profit from growing existing practices or starting and growing their practices from scratch?

The obvious answer is that there is no money in it for the proponents of these sales arrangements. The practice brokers certainly will not benefit from your starting your own practice. They will not benefit from your growing your practice to the point of requiring an associate. This book is intended to help fill that void and assist you in realizing your potential in the business of dentistry. The most experienced and knowledgeable people in the area of growing dental practices and starting practices from scratch are dentists who are busy doing dentistry and growing their practices.

When dentists are involved in lecturing, writing and disseminating information to the dental professional, it is typically in the form of *clinical* dentistry. While the importance of honing one's clinical skills during professional school cannot be overstated, learning how to intelligently manage the operations of the business can be argued to hold equal value in determining the success of your dental practice. The utilization of a template for growth and success of your dental practice will help remove the roadblocks that may be inhibiting you from reaching your potential in the business of dentistry.

Implementing the tested action steps will help allay the fears and uncertainties that may discourage you from starting your own practice. The template for growth and success offered in this book is multifaceted and begins with choosing a practice location, which cannot be overemphasized in terms of its importance to the success of any new business. This template incorporates information relating to office design and atmosphere, hiring and training staff, insurance terminology, participation and selection, fee setting, collection protocol, treatment planning and patient and account management.

The section on dental insurance in this book provides definitions and explanations to help you understand the alphabet soup of insurance terminology, a topic particularly foreign to me when I initially entered the dental marketplace. Typically this is an area of expertise acquired only through managing your business. An attempt is made here to help you start or advance your practice with advanced knowledge of the dental insurance industry and its potential impact on your career success.

Likely the most important elements of the initial and continued success of a dental practice are marketing and advertising. The dental marketing section in this book is exhaustive. It includes internal marketing strategies which focus on recall appointments, getting treatment scheduled, referral programs and staying in front of your patients with quarterly newsletters and seasonal reminders. This book outlines multiple external marketing techniques including the critical new resident mailer program and local advertising campaigns.

Arguably the most important piece of marketing information provided is that pertaining to website design, recognition and optimization. These seemingly esoteric terms define the wave of the future in terms of business marketing. If you are not on this wave, you are, to use a term from my surfing days in Southern California, caught inside. That is to say, the wave is carrying the tide, but you are not riding it and are about to be crushed by it. I have dedicated two lengthy chapters to this information, emphasizing its importance in the successful growth of the practice of the future. As I review the mountain of marketing materials I have accumulated over the last two decades, very little information exists that simply explains what dentists need to know to grow their practices through Internet marketing.

Marketing for dental practices, and for most products and services, has transformed greatly in the past decade as technology continues to move us toward receiving most of our information from Internet sources. We are currently living in an age where business advertising is defined by the Internet Marketing Revolution. The multi-billion dollar business Google is best known for being an Internet search company, though its extraordinary revenues come from advertising. It is therefore truly an advertising company.

Website presence and recognition are imperative to the maximal success of the growing dental practice. Proper site construction and positioning will determine the success or failure of your Internet marketing campaign. Today more than half of our new patients come from searching and finding us on the Internet. Of course, when I started practicing, none of my new patients even had the Internet.

The information and terminology contained herein can seem overwhelming and possibly too *techie* for most people working outside the world of information technology. I have attempted to simplify this language to help you clearly understand the decisions you will make on website design, maintenance and optimization. This information is invaluable to the achievement of optimal business recognition and capturing of the potential new patient population.

The practice management section of this book offers cost controlling strategies to effectively reduce your business overhead, allowing you to run an optimally profitable dental practice. Time and efficiency methods including scheduling for production and clinical material selection are detailed to assist dentists in maximizing our most precious commodity, time.

I offer strategies for staff training which assure control of your daily schedule, thereby reducing stress and promoting productivity. Business organizational skills are encouraged for those dentists not so enamored with the idea of running a business. This section also deals with the all too real but little discussed topic of professional burnout. I delve into the psychology of management, as it relates not only to that of your staff and patient population, but also to the area of self-management in the stress-laden workplace in which we as dentists operate.

The template delineated in this book also includes suggestions on paying yourself and saving for the future as well as possible ways in which to avoid the business mistakes I have made. The mistakes section is intended to immediately advance you years down the road in your business development by outlining avoidable pitfalls that have entrenched me during my years of experience in starting three dental practices from scratch.

This book concludes with a true story of the transformation of a dental practice neophyte to that of a successful business owner managing a highly productive and profitable practice. This account is intended to help allay the fears we all have when we go out on that limb of uncertainty and choose to hang our shingle. Starting, growing and managing a business with your name on the sign can be an intimidating endeavor, but it can also be the source of excitement, personal and professional growth and great reward! I hope to be able to relieve some of your uncertainty and provide real world solutions to your practice growth challenges with the template for success I present in this book. I know it works. I am excited to see it work for you!

Your Style of Practice

Chapter 3

Should You Associate, Buy or Start a Practice from Scratch?

When I was in dental school, I remember overhearing some older dentists reminiscing about how things used to be very different when they were starting out in practice. They explained how it was most common for dentists entering practice to simply *hang a shingle*, namely to place a sign out front and let the patients flow in. The voice speaking to Kevin Costner in the movie *Field of Dreams* comes to mind, "If you build it, he will come." Often misquoted as "they will come" the point is clear, when these dentists were open for business, the patients came in flocks.

This generation of professionals had little problem quickly establishing successful businesses in light of the supply/demand ratio of dentists to potential patients. These were the so-called Golden Years of dentistry; an era in which practitioners enjoyed untethered financial freedoms. Not only were marketing and advertising unnecessary, they were considered bad form.

As with any economic supply/demand disproportion, the pendulum began to swing back in favor of the dental patient seeking value. Margins began to squeeze and the field of dentistry became more and more competitive. Dentistry's hey-day of the 1970's gave way to the competitive landscape of the 80's and 90's. Not so easy now was it to hang your shingle and make a living. Marketing and advertising slowly entered the marketplace, eventually becoming nearly as commonplace as the dental license itself.

Doctors just out of school looked either to buy an established practice or to associate, thus defraying the debt of their high-cost educations while learning the business of dentistry. They perceived value in the practices they were buying, which were already up and running. Many of these new dentists may have underestimated the inherent costs of buying a practice, both in terms of financial expense and the sacrifice of freedom.

Quite often the price a dentist will pay for a practice is overly inflated because of the unrealistic value the selling doctor sees in the practice. This is understandable given the years of hard work and passion invested in patient care and practice growth. Most practices are viewed as an extension of the dentist's family and are therefore very difficult to relinquish. Not only will this passion be reflected in the price tag but also in the constraints placed on the entering dentist's practice philosophy and freedom.

This concept of practice freedom, though often overlooked, cannot be overstated. The mentality of most dentists I meet is one of individuality. When polling my classmates on the most common question in the dental school admission interview, "Why do you want to become a dentist?" the answer of greatest frequency was, "I want to be my own boss." Of course, this was likely not the most common way in which they answered the question in the interview. Clearly, health care providers have much deeper reasons than this for entering such a challenging yet rewarding profession.

Recalling my interviews at five dental schools spread across the United States, many reasons for entering the profession came to mind. Interestingly, all five interviewers asked me that very question. "I want to be in a line of work in which I can help people," I answered. "I like working with my hands. I still enjoy the learning process of continuing education. I like health care and am intrigued by human physiology." While these answers were all true, *I want to be my own boss* was also floating around in my head, but never making it to my lips. Remember, I wanted to get into dental school! The point is if we are being honest with ourselves, many of us will find that independence and individuality rate very highly on our personality profiles.

This individuality is a great asset when running one's own business, but can be an unfortunate liability when forced to adapt to a selling doctor's practice philosophy, which may vary tremendously from our own. This is an all too common problem with practice sales relationships. Imagine getting so far down the road in a sales agreement that it is too late to turn back, only to discover that you are not inclined to practice dentistry this way for the rest of your career. You may still be able to convert the existing patients and staff to your new style of dentistry, but it quite possibly will come with many months or years of undue frustration.

Benefits of Associating

After graduating from dental school, I worked as an associate in multiple practices for over four years. Unlike most of my friends who stayed local and either assumed Dad's practice, bought the practice of their former dentist or hung a shingle in their home town, I decided location to be of greatest importance. Deep in debt from having chosen to attend dental school out-of-state and thereby paying a whopping non-resident tuition, I needed to make money fast. I determined that dropping another few hundred thousand dollars to buy a practice was probably not the best way to initiate that process.

My story is by no means unique. Current figures indicate that many dentists are graduating with between $200,000 and $300,000 of student loan obligation. [3] We are forced to get to it and one of the best ways to achieve this is by working as an associate for an established doctor. Since there is no upfront cost to doing so, we are able to take a portion of our paychecks and immediately pay down our debt.

United States dental schools do a fantastic job in training us to be clinically knowledgeable, diagnostically capable and patient protective. We learn a lot about certain procedures and a little bit about virtually all of what we may see in practice. We perform procedures until we have them mastered to near perfection. We actually learn so much more about Anatomy, Pharmacology, Biochemistry and Histology than we will ever use. I realized how much I had forgotten when I dug up my embryology notes to see how my first child was developing en utero.

Despite what many clinically gifted students might express, what was deficient in school was training in speed and efficiency. It seems next to impossible to build clinical efficiency when we are allotted three hours to perform an occlusal filling. I recall two of those hours sometimes being consumed waiting for my rubber dam application to be approved by the instructor. This is not necessarily the fault of the dental schools, as they are often understaffed and unable to quickly serve as many students as are operating in the clinics.

Another limitation to tempo training comes as a result of the dental school's obligation to ensure that procedures are performed with top quality in mind. We are being trained to be accountable for the oral health of the general population, and that is a huge responsibility for the university. Suffice it to say, clinical speed is not top priority on the list of dental school instruction.

Working as an associate doctor serves the purpose of bringing a new graduate's clinical pace up to that which is necessary to operate in a productive practice. I value the associate arrangement as on par with the General Practice Residency (GPR). While less than ten percent of dentists pursue these residencies after graduation, the GPR has been shown to offer valuable polish to an attending doctor's clinical prowess. Most dentists, however, present company included, have had enough of the schooling process by graduation and are ready to get to work and make some real money.

Improving clinical efficiency comes not only in the form of enhancing swiftness of delivery, but also in that of sharpening diagnostic ability. It makes sense that this can only come with time and through experience. There is no way you can see in the four years of dental school all the things that you will see in practice. The more cases you treat, the more you will be able to eliminate time wasted trying to figure out how to treat them. Doing so within the comfortable confines of an associate arrangement reduces stress while promoting growth. Having the experienced doctor down the hall to consult when needed provides a great avenue of continued learning for the new dentist.

Even when we graduate with deftness of clinical skill, we may still lack the training necessary to properly employ the dental materials used in today's esthetic dentistry techniques. Nearly two decades removed from dental school instruction, I am still surprised at the lack of training the schools provide in the field of cosmetic dentistry. I understand the reasoning, however. These procedures are typically not deemed necessary and most often considered elective. Nonetheless, they are a major driving force in the success of today's dental practice.

This comes as a result of the overwhelming public demand for these services.

This deficiency in cosmetic dentistry training is reinforced whenever I interview or hire a new associate just out of school. New graduates are often very comfortable with oral surgery, pediatric dentistry, operative dentistry and fixed prosthodontics, but quite uncomfortable with cosmetic reconstruction. Though this is clearly a generalization and many new doctors possess skill in restoring these cases, I find that most of this knowledge comes with experience.

Shortly after graduation, I was very fortunate to have worked for a doctor noticeably gifted in the practice of esthetic dentistry. The definition of this form of dentistry applied not only to performing cosmetic reconstruction, but also to understanding the physical characteristics of the bonding materials we were using. Though I viewed my clinical education as more than adequate, I soon realized how much I did not know.

The practice owner encouraged me to attend a series of seminars presented by Dr. Ray Bertolotti, the inventor of the term Bondodontics. He told me that Dr. Bertolotti had much to offer because he was a wet-handed dentist just like we were, and very entertaining as well. The lecture series focused on the myriad applications of adhesion dentistry, the bonding characteristics of various materials and proper material selection based upon the procedure being performed.

Dr. Bertolotti publishes a free E-newsletter called the *Fifth Quarter Seminars Newsletter* which I highly recommend for dentists desiring to advance their knowledge of dental materials and adhesion dentistry techniques. His lecture series, *Fifth Quarter Seminars*, covers topics for the novice to the advanced Bondodontist, and operates in cities throughout the country and around the world. You can learn more about the E-newsletter and lecture series at www.adhesion.com.

As a clinical neophyte, I attended multiple lectures by Dr. Bertolotti, spoke to him personally and communicated through email. What I learned about the extensive applications of adhesion dentistry revolutionized the way I would practice dentistry from that point forward. Fortunately for me, this knowledge helped position the services I offered in my future practices in the sweet spot of patient desires. An older doctor I worked alongside used to joke with me about being what he labeled, "a chemical dentist." "People don't want that chemical crap in their mouths," he would laugh. I would respond, "People do want minimally invasive, esthetic and long-lasting dentistry." According to Dr. Bertolotti, a Bondodontist was able to "Give the patients more of what they want, and less of what they don't want."

Had I not first worked as an associate, I may have always practiced the way I was trained, never transforming my skills through this advanced learning. Associating offers benefits related to business ownership as well. Walking the halls as an associate doctor allows the new dentist to gain firsthand knowledge of how to and how not to run a business. How are we to obtain this vital information otherwise? Our options appear to be learning through trial and error, having an experienced dentist educate us on the subject or perhaps by reading a book on the topic. Trial and error learning in one's own practice can be expensive. Learning through observing someone else's successes and failures, however, is considerably less costly.

Since I did not know anything about dental insurance, scheduling for production, staff relations, billing or collections, I had a lot to learn. What I observed helped form my image of the type of practice I wanted to run and how exactly I wanted to run it. This knowledge was invaluable, and for me, it was free. In fact, I was getting paid for it. I recommend that any dentist choosing to associate should pay particular attention to the inner workings of the business. Watch, listen and do not be afraid to ask questions. Your boss may even discover that you have some valuable suggestions that just might make the practice more profitable.

Associate arrangements are not only for the new dentist right out of school. As a result of the recent decline in the stock market and real estate market, many older doctors are being forced to return to the workplace. Previously retired, they are now obligated to support personal living expenses by joining practices and again churning out the dentistry. New dentists working alongside these more experienced doctors would be well advised to garner as much knowledge from them as possible. They have already been there and they know the rules of the game. Most of these doctors are more than willing to share what they know to help ease the burden in any way they can.

Benefits of Purchasing a Practice

In business, there are many opportunities that present immediately and unexpectedly. In dentistry, this means that some circumstance arise forcing the hand of a doctor to sell the practice before desiring to do so. Nationwide, this happens several times per week. In this case, you can become, in a sense, an arbitrageur, get a steal of a deal and immediately take the reins of a practice for a fraction of its true value. If justification is needed, you are still helping the selling doctor out of a dilemma. Remember, you do not need to buy any practice, and therefore no one else is required to buy this practice either.

Another practice purchase opportunity that makes sense presents when the buying doctor owns a dental practice which is not currently operating at optimal capacity. The McGill Advisory defines optimal capacity as "being as busy as you want to be, doing the type of dentistry you want to do." [4] The McGill Advisory is a monthly newsletter for dentists and dental specialists that I have found to be of great value to my practice management and business management efforts. A local orthodontist has provided me a subscription to this newsletter for over four years now. In lieu of accepting the routine specialist bribe of Macadamia nuts and birthday cake, why not suggest a yearly subscription to The McGill Advisory? It may prove much better for your physical health and that of your business.

The following excerpt from The McGill Advisory article on running a profitable practice details the benefits of merging another doctor's practice into your own:

> Buy a Practice and Merge It into Your Own – As practice busyness declines, doctors need to remember that operating at optimal capacity should be their primary business goal. Accordingly, the fastest way to reach 100% of optimal production is to purchase a competitor's practice and merge it into your own. With one stroke of the pen, you can dramatically increase practice production and collections, and significantly improve your bottom line, with little risk. [5]

Though I agree with this article in principle, one stroke of the pen is always accompanied by a stack of cash backing it up. This expense is the little risk that the article references. A friend and dental school classmate recently did just this. His successful practice was operating near optimal capacity until he hired an associate doctor. Unable to quickly fill two dentists' schedules, he searched out ways to increase new patient flow. A local doctor forced into retirement was looking to sell as soon as possible. My friend was in the right place at the right time and had the capital to make this transaction work. In this type of situation, it makes good financial sense for a dentist to buy another doctor's practice.

The focus of this book is not to instruct you on how to buy or sell a dental practice. There are certainly numerous sources of detailed information covering both topics. This is not to say that there are not real benefits to buying another dentist's established practice. When Mom or Dad owns a successful dental practice, and son or daughter is an anxious new dentist waiting to take over, by all means get the transaction done. This is quite commonly the cheapest way for a young doctor to get a foot in the door of a profitable practice.

We once teased a classmate that the reason it was taking so long for he and his dad to close the practice transition was that they could not agree as to whether he would pay his dad $5 or $10 for the practice. These arrangements typically work out quite well for the entering doctor, while not so profitably for the selling doctor. There is obvious value in a parent's pride when a child inherits the blood, sweat and tears of the parent's creation. The younger dentist will be taking over the care of all the families of patients with whom the elder dentist has formed such distinct relationships. How appealing that is. It is important for the selling doctor to realize that, while appealing, pride usually fails to meet financial obligations. Therefore, the best practice transaction arrangement will equitably represent each party.

Most practice sales arrangements leave one party feeling as though money was left on the table. Seemingly contrary to logic, it has been demonstrated that the best sales agreement tends to leave the seller feeling that more could have been made from the deal, and the buyer that less could have been paid for it. This typically indicates that the price was fair and the needs of both parties were equally represented.

Buying a dental practice often presents the requirement to come to the table with a load of cash, and limits the freedom the purchasing doctor has in terms of practice ideology. I understand the purported benefit that taking control of a machine in motion by acquiring a doctor's charts provides. This makes sense to me only when the purchasing doctor makes money on the acquisition. Similar to acquiring equities or real estate, the money is made when you buy not when you sell. Even though it seems reasonable to fairly reward a selling doctor for years of hard work, it is not incumbent on a new dentist to buy any practice. Therefore, if the numbers do not appear quite favorable to you, perhaps there is another buyer better suited for this practice and another practice more suitable for you.

Benefits of Starting a Practice from Scratch

The frustrations and costs associated with so many failed and tenuous practice sales arrangements in recent decades have yielded a momentum shift back in the direction of new dentists starting their own practices from scratch. A study conducted by ETS Dental, an organization meeting staffing needs of the entire dental practice industry, revealed the following:

> While many industries were slogging through the "Great Recession," we have found that outside of a few saturated dental school cities, there are really no unemployed dentists. From 1975 through 1986, dental schools graduated literally thousands of dentists more than they have graduated over the past twelve years. Good economy or bad, this simply means that over the next decade, there will be a steadily decreasing population of dentists per capita. [6]

In light of these findings, it is apparent to me that this trend supports the likelihood that dentists can successfully forge out on their own. The pendulum appears to be swinging back in favor of the general dentist, which is a very exciting trend for us! Fewer graduating dentists means decreasing competition, thereby a reduced need to go out and purchase charts just to stay afloat. The benefits of opening your own office are numerous, offering a multitude of compelling reasons for any dentist to start a practice from scratch. The scratch practice serves to overcome the constraints on freedom and practice philosophy that are so prevalent in the purchased practice.

When managed properly, the scratch practice also reduces the initial outlay of expense a dentist will incur. It eliminates sales brokerage fees and the premiums paid for overvalued practices. With so many practices for sale in the marketplace, they are actually becoming devalued. Newly trained dentists these days are showing themselves quite capable of production levels very close to those of dentists in mature practices, often times exceeding those levels.

You are not the substitute teacher

When you buy a practice, its patients have chosen the selling dentist for a variety of reasons and have likely developed a loyal relationship over a period of many years. They may like the fact that the selling doctor does not aggressively treatment plan, never hurts them and is great with their kids. These patients may even appreciate the fact that the selling dentist has some gray around the ears or even no hair at all. They may have a gender bias, a college bias, a dental school bias, or if they live in my city, a bias for the particular high school the dentist attended.

As strange as it may seem, this is true. I am reminded of an inquiry from a particular new patient in my current practice shortly after selling my practice in Southern California and returning home to Missouri. "Where did you go to school?" he inquired.

Proudly, I replied, "The University of Washington in Seattle," assuming this patient had an interest in and knowledge of what I believed to be one of the leading dental schools in the country.

"No," he said, "where did you go to school around here?"

"Oh," I replied, "I went to Mizzou," thinking now that this guy wanted to bond with me about the recent resurgence of our one time 0-11 football team, the Missouri Tigers.

"No, no, I mean where did you go to high school?" he begged.

Feeling almost insulted and very perplexed as to why in the world this person would want to know where his dentist attended high school so many years ago, I offered, "I didn't grow up around here." My patient would not have recognized my high school. It would not have allowed him to put me into the box he had awaiting me. I was later educated on the fact that this was a very common question for people growing up and attending high school in St. Louis. Months later a fellow traveler seated next to me on an airplane inquired, "Where do you live?"

"St. Louis," I replied.

"Oh," she said with a wry smile, "what high school did you go to?"

Very witty was she. We were clearly famous for this curiosity.

The point is that the patients in a practice sale arrangement have not chosen you. You have chosen them. They have no initial loyalty to you. Their loyalty is only to the selling dentist and to the staff members with whom they have become so familiar over the course of so many years. Patients are typically more skeptical of a dentist buying them and assuming them in the practice sale arrangement than they would be if they were to leave their dentist and search out a new one on their own. This makes perfect sense given our natural human desire to be in control and to make choices for ourselves rather than to have them made for us.

Even the simplest changes can upset and frustrate many patients. "She told me I needed a new crown." "He told me I have a *disease* in my gums!" "She made my daughter use that nasty fluoride rinse and told her she couldn't eat or drink for half an hour." "He said I needed three of the fillings Dr. Jones put in replaced. He wants to take x-rays on me every year, too. I just wish Dr. Jones were still here."

Clinical philosophical differences are only one area where a patient being *sold* in a practice sale arrangement may become confused or discontent. "They made me pay before I left the office. Can you believe that? Dr. King always used to bill me." "I'm really upset that I can't get an appointment at 8pm like I used to. This is so inconvenient for me." "I can't remember the last time Dr. Perry raised his fees. This new guy seems to raise his fees every year!"

Starting your practice from scratch allows you to avoid these patient loyalty pitfalls which may inhibit you from implementing management tactics which are most profitable for your business. Starting from scratch provides a clean clinical palate for you to paint any way you so choose. Starting a scratch practice permits you to be the dentist you want to be without the restrictions of patient expectations formulated by "the way

Dr. Rooker used to do it." Starting from scratch allows you to begin fresh with the ideal patients in place…your own!

There are no wounds to heal

When buying a practice, you could be purchasing years of poor treatment by the prior practitioner which you will need to repair. In the case of dentistry, this means having to replace crowns or fillings in an untimely fashion possibly before insurance will cover the procedure. I am reminded of a colleague who bought a practice and soon came to discover the selling dentist's "commitment to whiskey, and not to his dentistry," as my friend related it. This resulted in quite a commitment on the part of the entering dentist to replacing substandard treatment for a period of years.

The costs associated with this level of retreatment cannot be accurately determined in the practice sale agreement. Additionally this pits the acquiring dentist against the selling dentist, and therefore against his loyal patients. Not only are you now the substitute teacher, you are absorbing time and material costs that are not recoverable.

Throughout my career I have worked as an associate in a variety of practices, at least eight that readily come to mind. These practices spanned from the small fee-for-service cosmetic dentistry practice to the behemoth factory machine HMO practice to the public aid inner city school program. While there is definite value in the learning experience one can garner while working as an associate, there is typically a lot less monetary value that can be acquired. This stands to reason because the income level of the business owner will comparatively dwarf that of the associate.

Experience has taught me that most dentists are quite skilled and very committed to delivering the highest quality dentistry and standard of care. The owner of the HMO practice I mentioned was an excellent clinical dentist. We are typically very well trained and possess the skills and clear desire to provide first-class clinical dentistry for our patients. However, there are marked differences among practitioners in terms of what they deem clinically necessary, acceptable or relevant. These clinical philosophical differences can undermine the trust relationship the acquiring dentist is so earnestly trying to nourish with the acquired patients.

One experience I had as an associate involved a practice owner dentist of advanced age. His patients loved him! He was their friend, confidant, psychologist, drinking buddy, neighbor, relative, baseball coach and Mr. Congeniality. One thing he was not was their treating dentist. He was so endearing that it was difficult for him to ever inform his friends that they needed any dentistry done, and in many cases redone. I marveled at how he would enter the room with a smile and a story, sitting down to chat for a while. He would then move his mouth mirror through the air for a few seconds thus waving the magic wand of healing over his patients, deeming them caries free. Can you imagine buying that practice? I was clearly the enemy when it came to his patients. I, after all, wanted to perform dental procedures on them and take all their money.

Dentistry is a tough profession. We are faced daily with patients questioning our intentions and feeling the pain of our bad news. It is difficult enough to develop trust with your own new patients. It is much more difficult to establish a trusting relationship with another dentist's loyal patients when forced to practically steal that trust away from them. You can avoid the financial costs of replacing substandard dentistry, and the rapport-severing costs of espousing a clinical philosophy different from that of the selling dentist, by having all your patients *choose* you. In the scratch practice, you are not the substitute teacher. You are the head of the class.

You determine office atmosphere, equipment, staffing, business model, policies and insurance participation

When considering purchasing a dental practice, make sure not to overlook the cost of making changes that fit your needs. If you choose to keep the staff members of the retiring practitioner, you will have to re-train them to your policies and business model. This task often proves particularly difficult and extremely expensive.

Just as the loyal patient is committed to the selling doctor, so too will be the existing staff. When you build your practice from scratch you begin with a clean slate, affording you the opportunity to select your ideal staff trained in the systems *you* choose. Their loyalties will be to you, just as will be those of *your* new patients.

Many times when a dentist is ready to sell the practice or retire, updates to the dental equipment and office décor have not been made in years, sometimes decades. The selling doctor has gotten used to the little nuances of the outdated equipment and has learned to deal with the problems they present. Keeping this aged equipment presents costs in terms of reduced production, inefficiencies and headaches created by things not functioning properly.

Replacing the antiquated equipment not only comes with obvious fiscal costs, but also with the time and energy costs of installation and training. These were likely not costs that were considered in the practice sale arrangement. If you are going to need to buy new equipment for your new office, why not buy it for your new scratch practice instead of for someone else's practice for which you have already paid? This eliminates the double-tax and provides you the opportunity to buy only the equipment you desire.

The vintage office décor and time-honored office atmosphere become yours through inheritance when you purchase an existing practice. The independence and individuality you may possess as a dentist can be reflected in the scratch practice when the time comes to express your commitment to quality and esthetics through your office design. In a practice sale arrangement, you have already paid for these things anyway. Why not pay for them in the form and fashion which define you and your new practice?

Office policy, business management, collection protocol and fee structure can vary widely from practice to practice. While dentists have obviously spent innumerable hours learning their craft, many often express their lack of training when it comes to running a small business. These things can all be learned, and this book attempts to teach specific protocols which equip the practicing dentist with the tools necessary to properly design, operate and manage a successful business.

Purchasing an existing practice means purchasing its existing protocols as well. This works well when the business is managed in an ideal manner. All too often, however, the systems in place lack ingenuity and limit the productive potential of the business. Inefficiencies exist, overhead expenses are out of control, collections are inconsistent and accounts receivable are astronomical. The financial and management costs involved in changing existing systems can be overwhelming. These costs are eliminated in the scratch practice. By starting your business with time-tested, productive, efficient protocols in place, you can achieve your goals years ahead of your peers who may be learning tough lessons through trial and error.

You are your own boss without compromise

While the amount of decisions may seem overwhelming to consider, the tremendous benefits of a work environment of your own choosing is well worth the initial time and energy invested in making these decisions. When buying a practice, the hours have already been set for you and there is a level of patient volume that may vary from your ideal volume. As an associate, the business owner decides how many patients you will see and even how much you need to produce, which at times can be unrealistic. In the scratch practice, your hours are your own. You decide the amount you want to work and the level of income you aspire to obtain. As a trusted colleague once explained to me, "Ed, the worst day I ever had working for myself was better than my best day working for someone else!"

The autonomy a scratch practice provides, coupled with the high cost of buying an overvalued practice, makes now a great time to start your own business and work independently. Would you like to be your own boss? Do you want to set your own hours? Do you want a clean slate with all the right systems in place for your ideal office? Would you like to control the costs the way you determine? Do you want to keep all the profits for yourself?

Do you want to start fresh in an office environment free from wounds that need healing, substandard treatment, underperforming staff members in need of replacement and unrelenting overhead? Would you like every new patient to be your own as opposed to your being the substitute teacher for the selling doctor's patients? Would you like to decide how much you want to work, when you will take your vacations and the level of income you aspire to obtain? Then what are you waiting for? Go ahead, hang your shingle!

Setting Up Shop

Chapter 4

Choosing the Right Location and Practice Opportunity

How Do You Choose a Practice Location?
You have probably heard the familiar adage "Location, location, location!" The importance of this principle cannot be overstated when considering where to begin your practice. Choosing a practice location is a complex decision. Many factors weigh into this determination. We must first decide where we want to live. Do we have the ability to move anywhere in the country, or are we committed to one location? Can we choose what climate we prefer and move to an area amenable to that preference? Do we enjoy fitness activities and the outdoors? Do we prefer the bustle of the city, or the peacefulness of a small town?

We are at times limited in our selection process by the area in which we live. We must evaluate how far we are willing to commute to work each day. We must determine what types of dentistry we are comfortable performing. Do we want to do a lot of dentures? Do we mind doing extractions or root canals? Are we capable of being a one-stop-shop when it comes to providing every imaginable dental service? If the answer to those questions is, "No," then we cannot elect to work in a small town far from any larger metropolitan area.

Do we enjoy working with children? Would we prefer to work primarily on adults or the aging population? Our answers can guide decisions regarding the type of community in which we choose to open our office doors.

I recall being on vacation in a small mountain valley town at the base of the Cascade Range in Central Washington State. I loved the area, the beauty of the jagged mountains, the deep green of the valley, the crisp, clean air, the smell of the Evergreens, the easy way of the people and the commitment to fitness and the outdoors of these locals.

I decided to have a look through the phonebook to assess my potential competition from other dentists if I one day decided to uproot to the Great Northwest. There was one dentist listed, but he was not even in the town in which I was staying. He was in yet another small town, miles up the road. The closest specialists were over 90 miles away. I thought, *What if I had a surgical procedure with which I was not comfortable? Would my patient really want to endure the long trek to the oral surgeon? What about root canals? I can do most of them, but can I do the difficult cases as ideally as the standard of care demands? Do I really want to do every procedure under the sun?*

The answers to these questions are different for all of us. They are, however, questions which necessitate honest responses before you can conclude where you ultimately desire to practice. Important factors such as your desire to live close to family and friends or perhaps to practice in your hometown may help determine your final destination.

Researching Demographics

If freedom and flexibility permit you to select a practice location from virtually any city in the country, I would encourage you to diligently explore the demographic data revealing the best places in the United States to practice dentistry. The facts, figures and statistics to which we currently have access can help swing the patient/dentist ratio dramatically in your favor. The most rapidly growing zip codes with the greatest new home construction, highest employment and new business development, reasonable cost of living and wage standards can provide cherry picking opportunities for the dentist opening a new practice.

There are a multitude of companies that can assist you in performing demographic evaluations, including assessment of the potential for growth of any location of interest. This demographic research is imperative in your search for the most lucrative practice locale. Many of my practice's external marketing programs rely heavily on this information to target and influence the population of potential new patients. Multiple links to companies offering demographic research data are provided as follows: www.freedemographics.com, www.quickfacts.census.gov, www.zipskinny.com, www.bls.gov/bls/demographics.htm and www.esri.com.

The demographic profiles obtained can provide local area census data relating to population, number of households, age, gender, income, education level, occupation and marital status. Home values, types of homes and the years in which the homes were built are readily available. Historical and projected annual household growth can be determined. One can even ascertain the type of transportation to work most commonly utilized and the average travel time involved in those commutes. A mean dollar value for various consumer expenditures can be identified and later employed in your marketing agenda.

Economic development information additionally provides yearly figures for population trends, residential building permits issued and labor availability. Property tax rates and major area employers are accessible as well. Knowing the type and number of intermediate and large corporations in your area can provide valuable business data. When considering a new practice, I use this knowledge to determine if the potential practice location is capable of yielding steady new patient flow and sustaining rapid and consistent growth.

Later in the business cycle, a practitioner can exploit this information to directly target the labor forces of these companies with specific marketing efforts. Learning the particular type of dental insurance each of the local companies offers its employees is highly valuable information when determining insurance participation for your practice as well.

Position Your Practice for Success

When contemplating location specifics, it is important to examine the amount of traffic driving by your practice, the convenience to residents in nearby neighborhoods, the number of similar practices and the growth of the area. Many practitioners make the mistake of merely considering the importance of drive-by traffic volume and how many competitors are currently practicing in the area. A much greater determinant of the future growth and success of a practice is the number of new families moving to the area.

I once opened a practice on a narrow street in the middle of a small neighborhood of homes where the drive-by traffic was minimal. In order to grow this practice I had to expend vast resources on marketing and advertising. Another soft cost I assumed was that of listing the office as an in-network provider with a number of PPO insurance plans. Though there is no initial outlay of funds to participate with these plans, there is the definite cost of lost production via the significant fee reductions the plans mandate. As my practice grew I was able to slowly reduce my PPO plan exposure, and was ultimately able to discontinue my plan participation altogether. My goal was to build the new patient volume through PPO participation and then return to a completely fee-for-service practice. I repeated this scenario with the opening of my next office as well. I will discuss in greater detail whether to PPO or not to PPO later in this manuscript.

After selling my practice in Southern California and returning to the Midwest, I began working a few evenings a week in the office of my childhood dentist. This generous opportunity afforded me by Dr. Jerry Fondren, a colleague I still consider a mentor, allowed me some time to make decisions about what I wanted to do with my next practice. My dentist's office was located in a very established part of the city with no new construction sites available. The vast majority of residents had lived in the area their entire lives and had been seeing the same dentist for years. I knew I would be fighting an uphill battle to attract new patients. The appreciation I had for my childhood dentist inspired me to go into dentistry, and though an outstanding clinician, even his practice still relies on new patient traffic after more than 30 years in business. Growing a practice from scratch in this area would have proved extremely difficult.

When selecting the space for my newest practice, I did not take for granted the benefits of location and drive-by traffic. The new office sits on a main thoroughfare which leads to several new neighborhoods and other local businesses. The speed limit is only 35 miles per hour on this road, so drivers have the time to take note of my signs. On average, I receive nearly 100 new patients a year from drive-by and walk-in traffic. Within the five mile radius of my address an average of 400 households of new families settle in each month. Additionally, the office is located adjacent to a pre-school. We therefore benefit from parents dropping in at the beginning or end of the day to make appointments. This is free advertising.

An outstanding orthodontist in my area has two locations. She provides the same high quality care, friendly staff members and warm environment at both locations and markets the offices similarly. However, one location is next door to my newest office where she takes advantage of all the benefits previously stated. Her other practice is hidden in a strip mall with the only visibility being from a 60 mph highway and from the small businesses located adjacent to her. This area is also more established and is not seeing the same amount of growth in new homes and residents. This practice is barely able to stay afloat while her practice next door to mine is booming.

Uncovering Practice Opportunities

Having selected the city in which you will live and work, you are now ready to explore business opportunities for your practice. You should now be seeking a way to capture the most lucrative practice opportunity via the most valuable allocation of resources. Many different forms of practice opportunity are available on the open market at any given time. A meaningful first step is to notify any and all local dental equipment and supply reps of your desire to open a new office, giving them a protocol which is ideal to your business desires.

These sales and equipment reps typically work for large companies that may be specific to particular areas of the country. However, many of them are nationwide. They tend to have inside knowledge of opportunities which may be hidden from the general population of dentists. I have found that the equipment reps are particularly willing to work hard for you in the beginning, as they are trying to win the account. They have more to gain because the profit of equipping a new office dwarfs that of supplying one. It is important not to commit too early to any one company, because you cannot be sure which source will present you with the ideal situation that suits your needs.

It is an unfortunate truth that many dentists wait far too long to begin the process of selling their practice. They procrastinate until they are past their prime, new patient flow has all but dried up, all the treatment plans have been completed, the office décor has become antiquated and the newest technology has passed them by. Dentists looking to purchase a practice are not interested in such an office. It is difficult to see the value in a practice like this and dentists starting out certainly do not want to pay the price the selling dentist believes the business to be worth. These practices therefore sit idly on the market for months and years, becoming less likely to sell as the days pass.

The unfortunate situation in which the selling doctor has now been placed presents a remarkable opportunity for a dentist looking to start a practice from scratch. Forced to salvage anything from the business, the retiring doctor becomes willing to negotiate tremendously favorable terms for the entering dentist. At times, the new dentist is not required to buy the practice, but may offer remuneration for some of the better equipment and supplies left behind. An agreement to assume the terms of the existing lease allows the entering dentist to begin immediately within the framework of a functioning dental office, thereby avoiding any production delays awaiting construction activities.

The new dentist can either immediately initiate marketing activities to obtain new patients for the business, or elect to make office décor, design and equipment upgrades before opening the doors to the practice. Often these upgrades can be made with limited outlay of time and expense. The lease assumption provides the new dentist with all tenant improvements left behind by the exiting doctor.

Equipment and office supply liquidation without the requirement to purchase dried-up charts provides the new dentist one of the greatest opportunities in terms of value. When probed specifically about this type of business prospect, a dental equipment or supply rep will likely have a number of suitors in mind.

Other such unfortunate circumstances are occurring on a daily basis in the dental marketplace. Dentists are practicing longer, many until the day they die. Untimely deaths sometimes befall dentists at the height of their careers. Their practices are often left with no one to take the wheel. Very commonly no discussion has taken place between doctor and spouse or family members outlining precisely what should become of the practice should this unfortunate event transpire.

Many doctors have not established a Trust nor do they have a Last Will and Testament clearly delineating the ultimate possession and future direction of the practice. Though unfortunate for the family, an opportunity exists for a dentist seeking to assume responsibility of such a practice. These practices can remain in probate court for months. Many times the surviving family is neither willing nor able to pay the taxes the probate courts impose. By the time a deal is struck, what may remain is a shell of a practice within which you can build your new practice.

There is inherent value in this type of transaction, and the practice remnants will likely be offered at a deep discount to market value. Again, dental equipment and supply reps may have a handle on which of these scenarios exists at any given time in your marketplace. Another source of information relating to these available practices may be local probate attorneys or real estate attorneys. Their contact information can be readily obtained via the Internet or through the telephone book.

I have reviewed practices compromised by a variety of factors including a doctor's untimely illness, litigation issues, emotional instability, inability to manage the books and employee embezzlement. Some doctors end up in bankruptcy court resulting from mismanagement of business or personal finances. Some have been helped along down this path by their spouses. They ultimately become forced to liquidate their assets at bottom basement prices. Someone is going to benefit from the inherent value therein. Why should it not be you?

These scenarios may seem rather harsh and unfair. Business is often a contact sport. Those that survive and prosper are typically those that are best able to minimize and control costs and locate and identify value. The executive in a hostile takeover bid is not attempting to put forth the most judicious offer considered equitable for both parties. The buyer is typically smelling blood in the water and trying to take advantage of a company which has been beaten down, whether fairly or otherwise.

I am not suggesting the approach should be to leave the selling party with inequitable remuneration for the hard work and investment bled into the practice. In truth, I believe it important to always be fair, honest and as friendly as possible when dealing in business. It rarely pays to burn bridges, but more importantly, there are certainly greater goals in life than to be the most successful business person in the game. I am merely stating that opportunities exist and an intelligent business person should be well poised to take advantage of them.

The most unlikely scenario presented itself when I was investigating potential locations to open my first practice from scratch. I was splitting time as an associate in three different offices while investing my free time in search of the ideal practice opportunity. I had alerted the local dental supply reps of my intentions to start my own practice, my only qualification being, "No HMO practices please!" My business philosophy was simple: Do everything opposite of the way my boss in the managed care machine was doing it.

I received a call from a local dental equipment rep informing me that an office fitting my described practice requirements may become available. This office was comprised of two dentists sharing space, each having operatories on opposite sides of the front desk. They shared the front desk, reception room, sterilization area, lab, file cabinets, supply room which housed the vacuum and compressor and even the doctor's office. As it turned out, they were sharing more than those things as well.

These two doctors were self-described best friends, going fishing together and taking ATV trips to the desert. Their families were close and their relationship went back years. They felt so comfortable with their friendship that they decided years ago to open an office together while keeping their individual practices separate. One doctor owned the building and the other simply leased space. For years this arrangement worked out quite well. At the time I was called in to assess the location, I was unaware of the reason behind its availability. I was put in contact with the leasing doctor and we scheduled a meeting.

Entering the reception area I was initially impressed with the floor plan, décor and general office atmosphere. I remember the feeling of excitement I had regarding the possibilities working in this office would afford me. I was ready and I wanted to start my new practice as soon as possible. *I can do this*, I thought. *I just need to work out the best deal and then I can get started running my own practice!*

If after thoroughly researching the business of starting a practice and assessing multiple locations, you get a feeling that, *This is it, this is the one*, you should not ignore this impulse. I had many practice referrals prior to this particular office opportunity leading me down paths I was not interested in traveling. I became frustrated by the sales reps' inability to understand what I was describing to them with respect to my ideal practice. They would supply me contact information for every type of practice except what I had explained, including large managed care affiliations and practice sales opportunities. That is why this one stood out as different. Finding the ideal location for starting your new practice may take some patience, but your persistence will greatly reward you.

Given the circumstances surrounding the practice availability, I was at the wheel in this negotiation process. I had no intention of buying the leasing doctor's charts and he had no intention of selling them to me. He was going to open and equip a new office just down the street from his current location, and expectantly take his patients with him. All he wanted was for someone to assume the lease and release him from the responsibility of honoring it.

We negotiated the purchase of certain dental equipment that would remain behind at a rate well below market value. I automatically acquired all his tenant improvements and office décor as a result of the lease assumption. I negotiated a rent reduction for the first six months while I was starting out and he agreed to cover the difference. There was really nothing else to discuss.

I decided to take out a small working capital loan to make minor office décor improvements, purchase some necessary dental equipment and provide a longer cash runway to get the business in flight. The loan I obtained for this practice was a mere one quarter of the amount I borrowed for my current practice. I had stumbled upon a golden opportunity not to be expected on the open market. Now all I had to do was implement my template for growth in order to have my new practice succeed. The problem was that I had no such template. I really had no idea how to make this work.

I read volumes of literature relating to business management and marketing. I learned about how to best compete for the coveted new patient. I attended seminars on how to treat your patients and staff. These lectures told me exactly what to say, scripting all my interactions. They taught me how my staff should answer the phone, how to sell veneers, how to treatment plan with my hygienist, how to hire and how to fire.

This information was all over the place. There was no pattern. There was no blueprint. There was only trial and error, and there was a lot of error. I discuss in subsequent chapters how to save money and time and how to eliminate unnecessary headaches by avoiding the same practice mistakes I have made. I anticipate that this information will put you much further down the road to success than I was when first starting out. I trust that the time-tested template provided in this book will allow you to gain valuable information which can be immediately implemented toward the success of your dental practice.

Once you have identified the city or town in which you will live, the particular practice opportunity you will pursue and the specific practice location you desire, you are ready to set up shop. This is an exciting time for you. You have done all the necessary research. You have the ability to succeed. Go get started making your practice a success!

Chapter 5

Office Design Decisions

Much of the discussion related to selecting an interior decorator is based upon the assumption that you will need to design an office environment from scratch. A good designer is also valuable if your existing practice space requires only upgrades and the creation of a new identity. Selecting a contractor for your project becomes necessary when you are making larger tenant improvements or are building the office from ground up.

During the location selection phase of your practice, you should consider the degree to which each type of opportunity will require planning, building and investment. Listed from most involved to least, these opportunities include:

1. Land purchased and plans drawn to construct a building to accommodate your new dental office
2. Space leased within a suite consisting of an existing foundation, frame and roof
3. The white-box in which the foundation, dry wall and ceiling are in place but which is otherwise a blank slate
4. An existing suite with completed tenant improvements, painted walls, finished flooring, doors and framed windows but which is not plumbed for dentistry
5. An existing dental office suite with completed tenant improvements in need of moderate to advanced overhaul
6. An existing dental office suite in need only of minor upgrades

There is one final practice type I have failed to mention. It is that of the mobile home converted into a dental office. I am unsure how this one escaped me, because it does exist in nature. I once dated a girl who worked in one such office. The owner of the practice had been in business for years, and this arrangement had worked out quite well for him his entire career. The dental assistant would set the lab cases out under a bush in front of the mobile home when the office closed at night, and the lab tech would pick them up on his scheduled run. Sometimes this girl and I joke about how simple our lives could be if we decided to practice dentistry this way. I know all these things because this girl later became my wife.

In certain situations, the decision concerning the particular office type may be already made for you to some degree. If you are able to negotiate the ideal business arrangement with respect to a white-box, for example, you may have to inherit the costs associated with building out this space. The costs related to those designs at the top of the list are not solely financial. If you have never been involved in the construction or wholesale remodel of a home, you may be dazed by the decision making process attached to these endeavors.

There is generally greater freedom offered by location opportunities requiring greater time and energy. Freedom is nice, but it comes at a price. My suggestion is to evaluate what is more important to you. Is it having the liberty to make all the decisions relating to your new practice environment or the time and expense savings incumbent with choice restrictions? The blending of the two typically yields the greatest return on investment.

I have started practices in three types of these scenarios. One practice existed within the environs of another dentist's office. I was responsible for nothing in terms of improvements, except to provide on occasion new dental material and supply technology and some minor equipment upgrades. Though this was excellent in terms of cost control, the office atmosphere may have been more suited to the established clientele of the practice owner.

The antiquated equipment and paneling on the cabinetry resembling that glued to the sides of my dad's old station wagon required some explanation from time to time as well. The sky blue wallpaper offered an attempt to brighten the claustrophobic, dimly lit operatories. Clearly this office offered me a low cost alternative to a more involved build-out. It allowed me to get up and running immediately, with no production loss resulting from construction delays. I lost no sleep deliberating over which pendant light matched which sconce and at what precise levels to hang them. I was, however, bound by the restrictions of someone else's sense of décor and office atmosphere.

Another scratch practice opportunity permitted me the freedom to make all choices relating to brand of dental equipment, style of cabinetry, colors of paint and arrangement of operatories. I did not have a blank palate on which to paint, as the suite design was already in place. I did however, have the liberty to coat the canvas with my own unique perspective of the ideal office environment. This scenario offers the greatest value of any type of scratch practice opportunity. It provides the liberty to create the atmosphere most reflective of your ideals and personality at a price well below the white-box scenario.

The third arrangement I engaged was of the form one tier more costly than the traditional white-box. My current practice operates in the suite of a free standing building, originally presented to me as an existing foundation, frame and roof. Though I was not responsible for the building's construction, the remaining decisions and accompanying expenses were mine to lament and rejoice.

This opportunity presented itself seemingly by accident. I was attending an Open House put on by a friend who recently started her orthodontic practice many miles from where I lived. As the drive out to her office wore on, I was selfishly regretting the fact that I had agreed to this long trek. My thoughts were those of a complaining child suffering through the drive on a family vacation. *Why am I doing this? It's so far from my house. She won't care if I don't show up. She probably won't even notice.*

Finally arriving at this tiny enclave that housed her office some 45minutes from home, I was unimpressed by the scarcity of homes and businesses surrounding me. *Why did she start her practice way out here? There's no life this far west of the city*, I thought. Not only did she start her practice here, she also planned and funded the construction of the building housing it. *What was she thinking?* I pondered in disbelief. *Well, I'll just pop in and offer my "congrats and best wishes" and then move on down the road back to where some people exist.*

My low expectations were checked at the door upon entering her office. *What a warm, welcoming, relaxing environment this is*, I reflected. The warmth exuded not only from the electric fireplace cleverly positioned adjacent to the operatories, but also from the polished wood floors, inviting colors and comfortable furniture reminding me of home. My thoughts turned to, *Wow! How did she do this*?

The entrepreneurial orthodontist gave me a tour of her accomplishment and then led me to the open suite neighboring her office. She had the building constructed with plans to lease this space to someone else, preferably another dentist. I gave a cursory glance inside, noting the dirt and gravel foundation and the cold, vacant emptiness of this suite. I did not waste a second trying to envision what could evolve within these walls. I certainly had no interest in driving all the way out here to start another practice, nor could I imagine parting with the funds necessary to give form to this barren landscape. Speaking of barren landscapes, where were all the people?

As with so many decisions in life, time has a tendency to change one's perspective. In this case, very little time was necessary to initiate this process. As my drive home wore on, I contemplated the residential feel and openness of her office. *There are so many windows. I love that!* I reflected. *What a cool place she has to go to work each day. It feels like you're not even at work. And again, there are all those windows. You could get the impression that you're outside all day and not cooped up in an infirmary. You could even put in skylights in order to watch the clouds float by. Patients would love that too!*

What was I doing thinking about patients? Was I seriously considering furnishing this muddy desolation with patients? Was this even possible? How much would this project set me back? How long would it take to complete? Where would I get the patients? Is this just another one of my grand ideas?

In order for any fanciful vision to take up residence in reality, it must be tested with empirical analysis. Thus began the stages of demographic research, fiscal valuation and target marketing possibilities. This opportunity, though initially dismissed as unimaginable, finally achieved high marks when examined under the microscope. It was something that eventually fit quite nicely within my risk tolerance scaffolding. It was a business idea that seemed to offer potentially very lucrative return on investment. It was an investment I finally became willing to make. The next step was to find a contractor to make this inspiration come to life.

Choosing a Contractor

Selecting the right contractor for your project is a decision of tremendous importance. The planning, decision making and construction phases of this endeavor will put you in a marriage with this person you may quickly want to annul. If you are able to secure the best available, however, you will be spared immeasurable financial waste and mental anguish. The right contractor may at first glance seem not to fit the definition.

Believe it or not, you should probably search out the guy who constantly bothers you about every nitpicky detail. You want the one who is most neurotic when it comes to even the most miniscule element of your office construction. You want to grow so weary of this guy, that you will not be surprised when he calls you on your honeymoon to ascertain where exactly you want the electrical outlets placed, six inches or eight inches above the countertop!

The alternative to such a thorn in your side is the contractor who is never available, does not own a watch, cannot seem to remember scheduled appointments and never writes anything down. This type of contractor, by the way, is the one most prevalent on the open market. He is the one you should not take to the altar or you may never make it home at night. His window of time will be "Anywhere between noon and 5 p.m." He is the Cable Guy.

Finding this diamond in the rough contractor is a challenge that might take some time. Start first by investigating which construction contractors the dental equipment and supply companies are keeping busy. Some contractors limit their businesses solely to dental office construction. I believe these to be the specialists you should look to employ. Ours is a very specific industry. The average contractor will not likely have familiarity with dental plumbing, vacuum and compressor lines and computer-equipped operatory requirements. Dental equipment, overhead lighting and operator ergonomics are items and concepts novel to the typical general contractor as well.

Hiring a guy in-the-know will save you incalculable time and energy. Interview several contractors to determine which one has the attention to detail you demand to complete your endeavor on time and to your specifications. Offer a bonus to be paid if the project is concluded by a certain date you have in mind. Suggest a graduated reduction in remuneration for every week the construction lingers past the agreed upon completion date. You need to be fair and include the stipulation that if circumstances delaying the project arise for which you are responsible, you will waive this provision.

Your contractor should utilize a leading-edge graphic design software program which permits you to view multiple permutations of suite arrangement. You will likely change the arrangement of equipment, furniture and even operatory positioning many times before you are completely satisfied. What the contractor wants to avoid is changing these things midstream. This encumbers the project with unnecessary delays.

Ideally, these issues will be resolved through software utilization prior to the commencement of any construction. More costs are associated with these in-progress changes, and they sometimes bear limitations. I remember trying to incorporate arched walkways into an already framed drywall overhang. This would have been best accomplished during the graphic design phase of the project. It cost me a bit more money and a lot more indignation from my neurotic contractor.

These general contractors typically do not do any of the heavy lifting themselves. They commonly have a crew they have employed for years who know their expectations, demands and procedural protocol. They are like the orchestra conductor guiding the direction of the vision. If you have the right contractor, you probably have the right crew. This is important because they are the ones doing all the work.

My contractor, for example, will fire a worker for not answering his phone by 5 a.m. That is the type of enforcement you need from your general, because you will not likely be able to get these guys to do much on your own. A good contractor will typically take about ten percent of the proceeds from the build-out. It will prove well worthwhile by eliminating the need to chase these guys around to do their jobs.

If you choose a construction project from the white-box on up the list, be prepared to have answers at the ready to every question imaginable. A good contractor will not act without your approval. This necessitates your understanding of what is going on at all times in your build-out. You also need to understand the questions themselves, which is no easy task in itself. Were you aware that the trestle pattern of the girders at the hip joint could inhibit the positioning of your skylights? I was not.

Do not expect the response, "I don't know, what do you think?" to be an acceptable answer to these questions either. I thought this guy should know more about this stuff than I did, so why could he not just figure it out on his own? At times I wanted to ask him if he thought the heated gutta percha technique was better than the vertical condensation approach to obturating root canals. Or, what would be the best way to determine biological width while performing an anterior gingivectomy? What do you think about that smart guy?

Clearly this guy got under my skin. He was my cross to bear for almost eight months, day and night, 24/7. I had to come up with answers to things I did not even know were questions. I considered changing my cell phone number to get rid of him. He would not leave me in peace until the final coat of paint was brushed across my walls. I was exhausted by the process. I swore off any home improvement efforts for many moons to come. I know that I am a dentist and expected to be particular, but this guy made me look like Pig Pen from *Charlie Brown*!

Did I mention what an outstanding result we achieved? Did I relate how often patients comment on what a stunning office environment we have? Did I explain how much I love the multiple dark wood framed windows and skylights? Did I describe the friendship my contractor and I developed subsequent to this tour of duty? Did I tell you that our families get together from time to time? If you desire the most esthetic, professional result, I suppose you want a guy like that. I hope you too can become friends with your contractor. I would not count on it though.

In contrast to the obsessive/compulsive general contractor, there is the guy who never shows up on time for a scheduled appointment. That guy is also the one who may never show up at all. Sometimes he may show up for awhile, and then in the middle of the project decide that he is done showing up altogether. Every time I would complain to my friends and family about my contractor's obsession with the insignificant, they would offer, "You're lucky to have a guy like that. Most of them never call you back." I felt anything but lucky at the time. In retrospect, however, I would suggest absorbing some of this incessant inquisition in order to arrive at the result you desire.

I have yet to understand the work ethic ingrained in these contractors who do seemingly whatever they want. They exist with no regard for their given word. I am uncertain as to whether they simply do not remember what was agreed upon, or if they intentionally disregard it. I am told that this behavior runs even more rampant in the home improvement industry than in commercial construction.

I once had a contractor install countertops in my kitchen. I made the mistake of paying him before the project was completed. Eight weeks and countless phone calls later, I was able to set up a time for him to complete the job. Fearing the worst, I left him a message the day before the appointment to assure him the key would be out back *tomorrow*, and that this would be the only day we would have available for several weeks. Returning from work on the day of the scheduled installation, I realized that the key was still in its place but the countertop was not. Had he forgotten the appointment? Certainly not, I confirmed it twice. I was once again reminded of my good fortune in finding the contractor I hired to build out my dental office.

Depending upon the type of practice opportunity you select, you will inherit varying degrees of investment in terms of money, time and energy. If you determine that you desire the greatest level of freedom in decision making, you will be faced with the requirement of contractor selection. You should interview, deliberate and choose wisely your partner for what may seem like an eternity. With the greatest risk comes the greatest reward, however, and with this you are likely to be able to create your ideal practice. Just hang in there along the way. That obsessive contractor may be the best friend you and your new practice will ever have. And yes, mine did call me on my honeymoon!

Office Atmosphere: There's No Place Like Home!

Creating a beautiful, comfortable and relaxing office environment will have an impact that cannot be overstated. If the office design and décor are ideal, they will be a constant source of internal marketing.

When designing and decorating my offices, I took pains (and believe me it was painful at times) to create a peaceful, warm and inviting setting. I wanted to avoid the typical medical office paradigm with its sterile look, feel and smell.

Patients often comment that they are put at ease by the more comfortable environment of an office that looks like a well-decorated home. A traditional medical office with its white walls, uncomfortable waiting room furniture, sign-in sheet and sliding glass window through which a stressed receptionist barely acknowledges people sets patients up to feel even more apprehensive prior to treatment. You can win patients for life simply by providing an environment that shows them you care.

My waiting room contains paintings, a small water fountain, faux painted walls, comfortable furniture from Pier One, an open arch into the front office area and several large plants. Skylights are positioned above the operatories so patients can relax while regarding the clouds, rain, birds and airplanes. Arched walkways welcome the patient down each corridor. A colleague in Washington State has a beautifully landscaped area of large flowers, bushes, plants and a waterfall outside his operatory windows. Strategic placement of multiple windows helps reduce the feeling of confinement associated with the typical medical office aura.

When contemplating your office design and décor, consider all of the senses. Reducing or muffling the sounds of dental equipment, lab devices and unhappy children can ensure a calming environment for waiting patients. Streaming music throughout the office will provide the patients with a distraction for their ears. Using potpourri, candles, fresh baked bread or cookies will help overpower the chemical smell that permeates so many offices. Providing a variety of current magazines, photography albums, procedure brochures, children's books and games and a *Before and After* picture album serves to entertain patients while they wait.

It is common on the lecture circuit to hear speakers opine about the importance of ensuring that all the waiting room literature is dental-related. While I understand the concept of focusing the potential buyer's attention on things you are selling, I do not reside in this dental literature only camp. By and large, people do not care about dentistry the way you do. True, you would like to be able to positively influence them in that direction, but this may be better accomplished with a more subtle approach. The old adage comes to mind, *You can attract more bees with honey than with vinegar.*

Dental treatment is perceived as vinegar by many people. You should consider yourself fortunate that they are even in your office. You will get to the treatment part. Let them relax a minute, unwind with their favorite magazine and get lost in the gossip if they so choose. When they enter the back office, nicely appointed *Before and After* framed photos of your cosmetic cases will subtly provide information about what you have to offer them. Marketing displays relating to whitening campaigns, brochures outlining the importance of sealants and photos of composite fillings replacing amalgams are more effectively positioned in the patient operatories. You will get the information to them. Just let *them* make their own decision to buy it. That's what they want to do anyway.

Many medical offices virtually wallpaper the reception area with policy signs. With their big bold lettering and construction paper background, these signs taped to the wall next to the receptionist are anything but welcoming. They outline policies regarding returned checks, late cancellations, co-pay collections, finance charges and cell phone usage. While patients need to be made aware of these policies, these signs do not lead to an inviting, calming atmosphere for patients as they await treatment. They can even lead to a barrier of communication between patients and the front office staff.

One day while traveling I peered through a dental office window to ponder the design and décor. Nothing stood out in terms of the office environment except the one and only item hanging on the wall in the reception area. It was a sign stating, *YOUR MISSED APPOINTMENT AFFECTS THREE PEOPLE; THE DOCTOR, THE EMPLOYEE and THE PATIENT WHO WANTED YOUR APPOINTMENT.* Though humorous and true, it does not go a long way toward engendering the good will of your patients. Unfortunately you are at the mercy of the patient to some degree, unless you have a completely booked schedule and no need for new patients. If that were the case, however, you would likely not be reading this book.

A welcoming, peaceful, nicely appointed office will make your job of selling dentistry so much easier. People typically equate this environment with a commitment to quality, cleanliness and attention to detail, and they value that. This alone will convert most people to committed patients of record.

The contractor who assisted in the design and construction of my most recent office confided in me that so many dentists do not understand the value created by spending just ten percent more on design upgrades. He primarily designs offices which elicit a commercial feel rather than a residential feel. As a result, those few that are conceived with a residential quality in mind really stand out to him and to the doctor's new patients. During our construction phase, John offered, "Ed, you're going to do really well here." Why not spend the extra ten percent on an investment that will yield returns for life?

Now that you have created a beautiful, relaxing office atmosphere, why not exploit it to the benefit of your business? You have already paid for it; you might as well put your investment to work for you. Prospective new patients need to be given the chance to step inside your unique office environment and experience its calming, domestic feel.

When we opened the doors to our newest office, my receptionist prodded me, "We just have to get people in the door to see this place!" Her thought was that the nature of the office design alone would attract potential patients. This is your greatest repetitive source of internal marketing. It is a fixed cost and its enormous return on investment cannot be fully captured.

Take every opportunity to show off your gorgeous new office to anyone who has interest. If designed properly, you will be amazed at how many positive comments you will hear from patients, supply reps, sales personnel, job seekers distributing résumés, USPS, FedEx and UPS workers, dental specialists, other dentists and virtually anyone who wanders into your office.

Take the initiative to get as many people through your office door as possible. You can accomplish this by having an open house, allowing community residents to walk through the office and meet the doctor and staff. They may perhaps choose to schedule an appointment as well. You can advertise your open house with pictures in the local weekly, on news channels, through distribution of flyers and with signs and banners.

Maximize your website by placing photos of the office throughout. Allow browsers to take a virtual tour of your office. You can get as fancy with this as you desire. Potential patients can get the feel of walking through the office via streaming video. This technique is employed routinely on real estate websites, giving the possible buyer the emotion of living in the house.

An additional benefit of the comfortable office atmosphere was never lost on me during the design phase of my projects. This is the fact that *you* have to be there working all the time. You may as well enjoy it as much as possible while you are there. I personally love the outdoors and would prefer to do dentistry outside if I could. Since this is obviously not a possibility, I always sought and designed office environments with an abundance of windows. I even voided the warranty on our building's roof in order to break through it and install skylights. While this is quite a perk for the reclined, vulnerable patient, it also provides me a distraction from the miniature, sometimes claustrophobic environment in which we focus each day, the oral cavity.

The archways atop the corridors and framed paintings of the European landscape and Mediterranean Sea give me the impression that I am on vacation, or at least that I may again be at some point. In my California practice the photographs were directed more toward giving me the feeling that I was surfing the ocean, or merely lying on the beach watching the sun set. You can create any environment that reflects your interests, and thus place yourself more at ease in the sometimes stressful environment in which we work.

The Interior Designer

There are multiple factors to consider when determining the need for an interior designer to help coordinate your office décor. Many doctors have a flare for home improvement, which can easily be translated into the fabrication of the new office. They may have in mind precisely what identity their ideal practice environment will adopt. They may know how to coordinate color schemes for the walls, carpet, wood flooring or stained concrete. These doctors might know how to tie in the dental equipment and cabinetry, and exactly what style of artwork best completes the aura. They may even be knowledgeable about which stores offer the best deals on all the necessary materials.

If you are one of these design savvy doctors, then you would probably be wasting your capital by hiring an interior designer. If you are like most of us, however, you may need a little help. You may be surprised by the number of decisions you will be required to make when designing an office. In the midst of your busy days, the answers to most of these questions might be, "I don't know," or, as time wears on, "I don't care!" A professional designer is paid to know and to care. The good ones really do.

Finding the right designer is critical to the success of your project and to your state of mind during the process. As is true with most small business relationships, word of mouth is the best way to secure a recommendation. In order for someone to supply you a referral, they typically will have had a positive experience with the worker. With the popularity of home improvement in our society, it has become increasingly more common for friends and family to have hired an interior decorator. These are obviously excellent sources of referral for you.

Dental office contractors, dental equipment and supply reps and even other dentists may provide outstanding leads in this area. Failing the ability to land a good designer from one of these sources, online searches often provide a diverse array of contacts in the profession of office design and décor. If you can remember where you stowed away your phone book, I suppose there might be some information in there as well.

I had the opportunity to employ the services of a good friend's wife for the design phase of my most recent project. In the past I had done most of this work myself. Though I had an overall impression of what I wanted, she assisted with this larger project to streamline décor decisions. She was an interior decorator by trade, though now taking time away from work while carrying her third and fourth child in the form of twins. She was gracious enough to lend her time and professionalism through this process, which endured until quite close to her due date. I felt badly for her as she wobbled around the flooring, paint and furniture stores with me, assisting in the decision making process.

In the end, you will probably have your ideas and the designers will have theirs. You will be the equipment expert but they may offer more expertise in choosing the proper upholstery and style of cabinetry. You will know how to make the office flow most efficiently but they may be better equipped to coordinate colors. You should know where the lab and sterilization area must go, but they may make suggestions as to the particular types of counter tops and sinks which will appear most attractive.

If you have the time and proficiency to make all the choices relating to the design and décor of your new office, you may be able to save some money by doing this yourself. If, however, your time could be better invested making other business decisions, I think it is wise to hire an interior decorator. This will ensure the beautiful, comfortable, relaxing office environment necessary for your practice to achieve its greatest potential. It will also relieve you of additional stress which you may not anticipate before you are engulfed in the process.

Seek a designer who comes highly recommended from a friend or family member, and compare rates to obtain the greatest value from this investment. You might be surprised by the incalculable return on investment provided by this hiring. Remember, creating the ideal office image is going to serve as a constant source of internal marketing for your practice. Avoid the mistake made by most dentists who underestimate the value of the office environment that speaks of quality, cleanliness and attention to detail. Patients clearly value those things. As dentists, we should too.

Chapter 6

Before Your Doors Open

Choosing a Practice Name and Proper Signage
Have you ever looked for a plumber in the phone book? If you are not lucky enough to have your own Joe the Plumber, you might have been forced to thumb through the Yellow Pages and throw a dart to randomly make a selection. You would naturally start at the beginning of the Plumber section, right? In the not so recent past, the rule of thumb for choosing a business heading was to select a name that began with the letter A in order to be the first listing in the phone book. The result was that so many plumbers were employing this strategy that *AAAA Plumber* became a choice as well. Fortunately, the Internet Revolution was born and the telephone book was laid to rest.

It is now wise to choose a business title that contains your city's name and your specialty in order to increase your website's presence in search engines. For instance, *Austin Family Dentistry* would be the best choice for an Austin dentist located in a neighborhood booming with young families. When first establishing your business, you will need to assess the names of other local offices to make sure you do not duplicate one that already exists.

All of my marketing pieces and patient materials list my name followed by *Family and Cosmetic Dentistry*, to clearly demonstrate my desire to provide quality general and cosmetic dentistry to patients of all ages. When patients refer their friends to a practice, they refer to the dentist's name and not the practice name. Therefore, ensure that potential patients can find your name in print advertising, online searches and on your signs.

Whenever possible within zoning laws, you want a sign at the street level which is sure to be acknowledged by drive-by traffic. Our practice also displays large signs on the front and side of the building. The side building sign accounts for much of our traffic from the pre-school next door. When designing or renovating your building, add signs on every side of the building that can be seen from the road or from other businesses.

Each sign should show some way to contact you or at the very least find you online. A large sign just stating DENTIST may attract a good amount of walk-in traffic, but it makes it difficult for those driving by to determine how to contact you by phone. Your practice name, or an easy to remember phone number or website address, will help patients find you quickly and easily. I have chosen to put my name on the lawn sign, my website address on the building front sign, and my practice name on the building side sign. This redundant signage provides the potential patient a clear knowledge of your presence and multiple ways to obtain contact information for your practice.

Recently, I decided to take advantage of the increased drive-by traffic that many of the newer area businesses afford my office. Taking note of the line of sight of the passers-by, I determined that I was squandering the chance to acquire countless new patients by failing to express my availability. I designed and priced two banner signs, one to be serve as a yard sign and one to display on my only remaining office wall yet devoid of signage. These signs were fabricated with a professional appeal, yet together yielded a cost of $130. The phrase *Accepting New Patients* caught the attention of a local business patron within one week of the sign's posting, and my practice had already earned its first new patient from this negligible investment.

What Hours Should You Work?

An excellent way to immediately build your patient base is by offering consumer friendly office hours. In our busy times, patients appreciate extended and weekend hours. This is especially true in suburban areas where long commutes to work make it difficult to visit the neighborhood dentist during the workday. Early morning and evening appointments are typically the first to book out in advance and to have a waiting list. If you are willing to work these hours, you will find marketing your practice considerably easier. Be sure to highlight these flexible hours in all advertising and on your website.

Experience has shown that patients often arrive late for these extended hour appointments, having difficulty getting out of the house in the morning or leaving the office in the afternoon. Be aware of this trend when scheduling these appointments. For the chronically late patient, state the appointment time 10 -15 minutes ahead of the actual scheduled appointment.

Weekend hours are in high demand for most career oriented patients, providing another schedule time that is quite easy to fill. However, Saturday schedules are often filled with cancellations and no-shows, as more exciting prospects than a visit to the dentist arise. You may find your staff staring out the window on a beautiful day while patients decide they would rather spend that day golfing, or, as was the case in my California practice, going to the beach. If you offer Saturday hours, you may consider requiring patients to make a non-refundable deposit ahead of time to encourage them to keep their appointments.

A cancellation policy and broken appointment fee can be of some benefit. However, this fee proves to be one of the most difficult to collect, especially from a new patient who does not show up for the initial appointment. I am reminded of a new patient marketing technique I picked up years ago at a management seminar. We were instructed to call all new patients the night before their initial visit, welcoming them to the practice. We were to ask if there was anything we could do to make the next day's appointment a more positive one. I promptly abandoned this technique when, on the second such phone call I placed, the patient responded, "Uh, yeah, don't charge me." She subsequently decided to flake her appointment the next day. *That didn't turn out the way I had planned*, I thought.

Offering highly flexible hours is a great way to quickly and affordably build a patient base in any dental practice. As is the case with creating a beautiful, residential office environment, catering to your patients' strong desire for non-banking hours serves as a constant source of internal marketing. Outside of the cost of giving up some of your mornings, evenings or Saturdays, this form of advertisement comes free of charge.

This type of marketing is similar to becoming an in-network PPO provider in that you can literally open your doors and let the deluge of patients flood in. Potential new patients assign nearly as much importance to early morning, evening and weekend hour availability as they do to whether or not your practice accepts their insurance. The difference between the two is that signing up for PPOs comes at the cost of lost production from the sizable mandatory fee reductions. You could do practically no other marketing and yet be successful by working these nontraditional hours. Today's frenetic lifestyle makes these appointments that valuable.

Finding a staff that is willing to work such nontraditional hours may present a challenge. The fact is, however, in today's suffering economy many people are just happy to be employed. Even when the economy is in full stride, those who are competing for dental office positions are not routinely in command of the negotiation process. You will eventually be able to secure a staff willing to work these hours. You simply might need to be somewhat more diligent in your search.

Whether you as the doctor want to work these inconvenient hours is another question. While working hours that accommodate the patient is great marketing, doing so will impact your daily routine. This is a sacrifice that tends to make sense in the initial stages of a dental practice, but may become less than worthwhile when you get up and running. If you do not mind keeping these hours indefinitely, you will likely find your practice teeming with new patients and their many referrals. On the other hand, I recall a dental school instructor once relating to me, "I didn't go to school for eight years to work Saturdays!"

How Should You Select A Dental Software Program?

When faced with so many initial costs in a new practice, it can be tempting to purchase the cheapest software available, since using the software will not be a large part of your job as the dentist. However, this decision can be costly if it does not allow efficient use of your staff's time. Poor software can permit patients or billing to slip through the cracks by not tracking overdue recalls, unscheduled treatment and overdue accounts.

Dental practice software prices vary tremendously, ranging from $1,500 - $15,000. The requisite yearly subscription fees range from several hundred to several thousand dollars. The software's associated features span from the most basic to the Cadillac of capabilities. When considering your purchase, look for software that:

1. Provides reports to monitor productivity, referrals, overdue recalls, overdue accounts payable, unfiled insurance claims and unscheduled treatment,
2. Contains a system of checks and balances, including a daily report of posted payments and adjustments matching the totals on the deposit slip and credit card settlement report,
3. Includes online training opportunities and a dedicated customer care team,
4. Delivers an easy to learn format that does not require hours of staff training time,
5. Offers time-saving features such as pre-filled options,
6. Allows electronic claim submission and the ability to email radiographs and
7. Is not encumbered with exorbitant annual update fees. This is where the software distributors make their money.

It is not typically necessary to buy the most expensive software, however. Many of the bells and whistles that drive up the price might not prove useful in your particular office setting. The most expensive software companies support high overhead costs for marketing their product and for the payroll of an extensive sales staff. This overhead gets passed on to you in higher purchase and renewal rates.

The major dental equipment and supply companies peddle software that tends toward the upper rung of the expense ladder. There are three programs which are the most prevalent in the industry. There is no debating that these three have outstanding capabilities, ease of use and upgrade potential. There is also no debating that you will pay handsomely for these greatly hyped features. Not only are the initial software purchase fees much higher than other more rudimentary programs, the yearly subscription rates are excessive as well. As with any form of technology, you need to determine if the benefits of owning the best in show is worth the expense you will incur. The businesses running at greatest efficiency with the most controlled overhead may not always be the ones purchasing the newest technology available.

I once utilized one of the big three software programs in a former practice. We currently employ a software program developed by a local company which contains all the aforementioned features for a fraction of the cost of the more highly touted programs. It is incumbent on any business owner to seek and implement value in order to attain the greatest bottom line. Be wary of what the dental supply houses are attempting to purvey. Seek out which software program will provide for the needs of your particular practice type at a price reflective of those needs.

What Should Your Daily, Monthly and Quarterly Reports Include?

Reports are not a sexy topic, but proper reporting can lead to greater collections and more attractive bank statements. Reports provide the best way to determine whether your internal marketing and collection efforts are working. Financial reports provide a check and balance to ensure that all money is being deposited correctly and that collections are being pursued in a timely manner.

At the end of each business day, the office manager should generate a Daily Report showing all the production and payments for that day. The office manager should then review the report for any omissions prior to submitting it to you. You should then analyze the Daily Report to confirm its accuracy before leaving for the day. This report helps to ensure that all treatment has been recorded. The daily report also totals the payments by type (cash, credit card or check). The numbers in this report should match the daily deposit slip and credit card settlement report, providing confirmation that all payments have been posted correctly.

Monthly Reports should be run as follows:

Patient Referral Report - Lists which patients were referred by other patients during that given month. We use this report to write thank you notes and reward patients for referring.

Referral Source Report - Lists the number of new patients who appointed in our office as a result of all referral and marketing sources other than patient referrals. This includes referrals by specialists, drive-by patients, walk-ins and responses to advertising. Depending upon your dental software program, this may be divided into multiple reports. We record a specific referral source for every new patient who walks in our door. This is the only way to determine with certainty which marketing efforts are valuable and to assign an accurate return on investment.

New Patient and Production Numbers Report- We use these figures to compare data with other months and years, in order to track progress, set goals and determine bonuses.

Accounts Overdue Report- We run two different types of reports to ensure we are catching all accounts that have gone more than 60 days without a payment.

Insurance Overdue Report- Most insurance companies pay within two to three weeks. Smaller companies can take up to six weeks. We run this report for any unpaid insurance claims that are more than six weeks old. We run a similar report that shows if any insurance claims have accidentally gone unfiled.

Adjustments Report- This displays all adjustments made to any patient account in the past 30 days. This does not include any payments, only write-offs. Adjustments are entered in by code to indicate why the adjustment was made. Running and reading this report is a very important step in setting up a proper checks and balances system. This is a report that should be heavily scrutinized in order to fend off the potential for staff embezzlement.

Quarterly Reports should be run as follows:

Overdue Recall Report- This report lists patients who have not had a recall in the last six months and who do not currently have a recall appointment scheduled. We send out a reminder postcard stating: *Our records show that it is time for your dental check-up. Please call our office to schedule today.*

Unscheduled Treatment Plans Report- This shows patients who have had a treatment plan created but have not yet scheduled for the treatment. We use this list to send a follow-up letter to the patient including an educational brochure on the procedure discussed during the treatment plan. During slow times in our office, we may elect to send out postcards to these patients offering a discount on the outlined treatment.

Billing and Collections Report - Our dental software keeps track of bills sent and can produce a billing report. We take an additional step and keep a spreadsheet of information about who received a bill, when it was sent and why the patient was billed. Our goal is to figure and collect accurate co-pays at the time of treatment so as to avoid billing. This spreadsheet indicates the reason why we were unable to fulfill this goal for a particular account and provides accountability to continue seeking this goal. Our spreadsheet also contains a list of patient accounts that have been sent to collections and why this step was necessary.

Finally, a Patient Criteria Report can be a source of useful information for marketing purposes. We run reports to determine how many patients live in a particular zip code, how many patients are on certain types of insurance plans and how many patients are no longer active? As an aside, instruct your staff never to mark a patient inactive in your computer system unless they are certain the patient has moved away or switched dentists. Do not mark patients inactive simply because they have not come in to the office recently. This would prevent the patient from appearing on the overdue recall report and from receiving the newsletter, both reminder tools used to encourage patients to return.

Knowing the proper reports to run and the function each report performs will help your practice reach its optimal levels of production and collection. This uninspiring topic should not be ignored by the dentist desiring to run the business instead of the business running the dentist. An additional benefit of timely reports is the hedge they provide against embezzlement. The smart practitioner will thoroughly review each report for accuracy and then have the office manager fax all reports to the doctor's accountant. Many times, the assumption alone that a third party will be reviewing the numbers will serve as a major deterrent to staffside sub 2embezzlement.

Equipment and Supply Decisions

As professionals trained in the delivery of clinical dentistry, most equipment and supply decisions are a matter of personal preference. After having worked with materials for many years, we have developed familiarity and comfort with many and dissatisfaction with others. If you share my continuing education experience and redefine how you practice dentistry, material selection may require more investigation. Many of the pundits on the lecture circuit provide detailed lists of products and manufacturers which support their techniques.

The most popular avenue for fulfilling equipment and supply requirements comes via the major dental supply houses. Available companies vary by region and are all very similar in terms of price, service and supply options. For example, in Southern California I used JB Dental, in St. Louis I used Henry Schein and Benco and in Washington State I used Burkhardt Dental and Patterson Dental. Each company offered similar pricing and customer service. Though certain companies offer exclusivity on particular equipment types, these contractual agreements are rare. This creates a free-market environment allowing you to make buying decisions based upon cost, value and preference.

Certain dental merchandise is sold exclusively through companies independent of these larger chains. Ultradent, for example, develops and distributes a line of multifunctional materials and supplies. I have found many of these products to be very useful in cosmetic dentistry techniques. Tin Man Dental and Danville Materials have been valuable suppliers of materials used in adhesion and esthetic dentistry. Dentsply Tulsa Dental, Sterngold and Microcopy offer excellent customer service and exclusive product alternatives.

A multitude of small companies compete by manufacturing and retailing specialized products only available through them. I have had success purchasing from these companies, as they are motivated to provide the best product at a competitive price. Many times they formulate products which are materially equivalent to their high-priced competitors. The list of companies I have mentioned by name is by no means exclusive. Attending continuing education seminars and further defining your method of delivery commonly yields a list of independent suppliers that can support your needs.

With so many competing suppliers and material choices, how do we determine what to buy and from whom to buy these items? One highly effective method is to research dental equipment and materials by attending a lecture sponsored by CR Foundation. [7] One such seminar supplied me the reference guide, *Cutting-Edge Products for Clinical Excellence,* outlining hundreds of product choices and contact information for the particular company manufacturing or supplying each product. I consulted this list for many of my initial material choices in my current practice and continue to revisit it from time to time. This outline simplifies the initial ordering process by centralizing a vast network of manufacturer contact information in one source. It also serves to reinforce all the materials you will need to complete every dental procedure you will be offering in your practice. The least beneficial time to discover that you need a dual-cure cement on hand is when the post is ready to be cemented.

In addition, CR has an annual *Outstanding Products – Buying Guide* that highlights the best materials reviewed by this independent non-profit group during the previous 11 months. This Buying Guide also lists the top products in almost every category of dentistry. The goal is to provide dental clinicians a listing of the products that will make their practice faster, easier, better, and potentially more profitable.

Gordon J. Christensen Clinicians Report, formerly *CRA Newsletter,* is a periodical edited by Dr. Gordon Christensen, a pioneer in dental industry research. The following is an excerpt from the *Clinicians Report* website describing its attributes:

> Available since January 1977, each 4-page *Gordon J.Christensen CLINICIANS REPORT*° (formerly *CRA Newsletter*), contains concise reports on multi- and single product evaluations identifying their advantages, limitations, clinical usefulness and testing manufacturers' claims. Clinical information is obtained from a volunteer team of actively practicing dentists who use their expertise to compare new products against those they currently use. Clinical data is also obtained from controlled clinical studies. Scientific data is collected by *CR* scientists in their labs in Provo, Utah, and from various other lab

facilities where they travel as needed to access equipment and expertise. *Gordon J. Christensen CLINICIANS REPORT*® is printed monthly in 9 languages and is circulated in over 90 countries worldwide. The English version is also in electronic format. [8]

Clinicians Report offers an online subscription option with full search and cross referencing capabilities of the past 30 years of *CR* test results. This provides doctors the ability to search specifically for any product they are considering and consult issues related to its testing. When opening my current office, I ordered two years of back issues of *CRA Newsletter* and made purchasing decisions based upon my research. This is a very practical tool as it eliminates manufacturer bias and reports only those findings of our professional peers. CR Foundation courses and information about the monthly Gordon J. Christensen *CLINICIANS REPORT* are available at www.cliniciansreport.org or by phone at 1-801-226-2121.

Dental supply houses can offer assistance with decisions related to major equipment purchases. Different dental chair designs and manufacturers provide varying styles appealing more to some dentists than others. Certain operatory configurations and delivery systems suit particular styles of doctors. In the chapter entitled Time and Efficiency for the Dentist, I address operatory design for efficient flow of patients and staff. Proper equipment selection to improve ergonomic delivery of clinical dentistry is also addressed. An experienced equipment rep can walk you through the advantages and disadvantages of each type of unit. Equipment sales associates can also help determine the variety of auxiliary equipment best matching your needs.

Another option one might consider when making large equipment purchases is interviewing an independent equipment specialist. These individuals typically bill on an hourly basis, sometimes offer substantial discounts and purportedly have specialized knowledge of the particular equipment they market. They commonly manage the ordering, installation and maintenance of this equipment. Results vary depending upon the specialist a dentist hires. Some equipment specialists are required to travel long distances to service your office and many bill for the commute. At times it may be difficult for them to obtain the parts necessary for repair. Though I have found value in employing the services of certain independent specialists, I have also enjoyed the reassurance that the big dental houses provide.

Even the major dental equipment retailers come with a high price tag for hourly maintenance. I am often reminded of a cell phone conversation between a maintenance technician servicing my equipment and his employer. I overheard him boasting about how much revenue he had produced that day in hourly service billing. Though I realize that his is a business too, I would rather assume that his primary goal was to assist dentists struggling through a full schedule by restoring their faulty equipment. I would not suggest openly discussing with your patients the thousands of dollars you produced that day.

After many years of experience running a practice, I realize the value in learning the intricacies of my own equipment and how to properly repair it. This extends all the way down to changing light bulbs. Certain employees are savvier than others when it comes to diagnosing office malfunctions and making minor office repairs. More routinely, however, I am apprised by my staff of the fact that, "It just stopped working, Doc." Most days I am thereby called to become *Mr. Fix It* in one form or another. It does not pay to call the equipment technician every time something "stops working." Applying your diagnostic skills to that of your office inventory will save you immeasurable expense over the years. I find that more often than not, there is a simple reason that something stopped working and not that it is in need of sophisticated maintenance or replacement. The power cord and reset button come immediately to mind.

I graduated dental school without ever having seen a dental office vacuum or air compressor. In fact, it took me several years as an associate before I even knew what they were. Who would have thought that they were the driving force behind all the dentistry I had provided to that point? The more you investigate the configuration and functioning of your office and equipment, the more you will be able to stay on schedule when something simply stops working.

Given the enormity of decisions related to the initial equipment and supply order, it pays to consult resources to assist with this endeavor. Professionals abound willing to help you make these choices. By researching in advance, you can avoid the partiality present in those hoping to sell you products and services.

Chapter 7

Your Fee Schedule Determines Profitability

You might be surprised by the latitude you have in the selection of your fees. Your fee schedule is a great determinant of the yearly production levels your practice will be able to attain. You can only provide so much dentistry while operating at maximum capacity. This is defined as the greatest amount of work you are capable of rendering in any given workday. I think it is best for you to decide at what level of maximum capacity you wish to operate. It will not be 100% for everyone. If your practice is operating at this level, your production will now be limited by your hourly fees. This is an often overlooked calculation, though it is simple arithmetic.

Though it is true that you can increase practice production by working smarter, not harder, dental procedures carry time and energy limitations. You should do all you can to improve your efficiency in delivering services. This includes performing quadrant dentistry whenever possible, scheduling for production to ensure the most productive procedures get priority and referring out procedures at which you do not particularly excel. Even when these things are executed to perfection, you are still limited by time in terms of the amount of service you are able to provide. The adage, *Time is money,* is never more applicable than it is in the field of dentistry.

You should attempt to define an hourly rate of production which you desire your practice to realize. You should then determine how long it will take you to perform each procedure. You can then set your fees accordingly, ensuring that your desired hourly rate of production is met based upon this calculation. Assuming you are operating at optimal capacity, this should be a goal that is realistic and achievable.

If your schedule is full, you can very nearly predict what your gross receipts will be for the year. By controlling and calculating your overhead percentage, you will be able to arrive at a very accurate estimation of the amount of money you will take home each year. Again, you are able to control this to a large extent by setting your fees consistent with the income level you desire.

I understand how this might appear as an unrealistic scenario, as most of us would like to make more money for what we do. I concede that there are definite limitations to what people will pay for dental services, but they are typically not as stringent as you might assume. Most dentists never find out what those true limitations are, because they are hesitant to raise their fees for fear of losing patients.

I cannot assure you that no patients will be lost, but if all the other aspects of the template for success are in place, you will likely lose far fewer than you think. Patients have chosen you for a reason. You do not necessarily want them to choose you because you have the lowest fees. My experience has revealed these shoppers to be the most disloyal patients out there, the patients I do not want in my practice.

I have a friend whose motto is, "I want to be the *every man's dentist*." This is to say that his fees are set to attract as many patients as possible to his practice. My friend has been rewarded well in his business. He works very hard and his time demands are especially high. If this is the way you wish to practice, I highly encourage you to do so. From the standpoint of business efficiency, however, this is not the ideal practice strategy. You will see more patients, assume more overhead, increase stress levels and limit the profitability of your practice.

These things are all the necessary result of the *Time is money* rule. More important than the factor of money in this equation is the contention that when time and materials are compromised, so too will be treatment results. Some dentists excel at producing high volumes of dentistry in a fast-paced environment. Though experience and clinical efficiency strategies have made me faster than many, the extremely high volume practice is not for me.

It is a respectable notion to want to be every person's dentist. I simply strive to provide the best dentistry I can to every patient I see.

We provide significant amounts of dentistry at no charge or at greatly reduced fees for those I consider to be in need. The feeling of good will the health care provider can experience at times has always exceeded the rewards money has ever been able to give me.

When it comes to the selection of a dental office, patients rarely choose based upon price alone. They consider multiple factors such as consumer friendly office hours, friendliness of doctor and staff, appearance of a clean and contemporary office atmosphere, convenient location and whether the doctor takes the time to answer their questions. A doctor who seems to care and is easily trusted will influence new patient decisions much more than a low crown fee. Offering patients these advantages will allow you great flexibility in the determination of your fee schedule.

Do You Need A Scientific Fee Analyzer?

The establishment of a fee schedule is best accomplished with the help of a scientific fee analyzer, which displays compiled data from insurance companies. These data outline fees that are routinely charged by participating doctors, segregated by zip code. Consequently, the listed fees could be below the true average, as some practitioners only submit their agreed upon PPO fees in order to avoid the aggravation of write-offs. The zip code segregation provides you with accurate information about fees charged by your neighboring competitors.

Fees are assigned a percentile rating based upon the percentage of dentist submitted fees that fall below them. For example, if your submitted fee is assigned the 80th percentile, it means that 80% of fees submitted by other doctors in your area are below yours and 20% are above yours. It will be your decision as to what percentile you wish to apply when establishing your fees. My advice would be to utilize the maximum fee percentile you can assign without losing patients resulting from exorbitant fees. It may require some trial and error to most accurately make this determination. This uncertainty is largely reduced however, by not exceeding the 95th-100th percentiles. The utilization of a fee analyzer in this case is invaluable.

Companies providing dental insurance to their employees commonly purchase plans which reimburse based upon a chosen percentile of dentist submitted fees. The specific fee information is derived from an insurance company database based upon actual claim forms submitted by dentists. If a company wishes to be generous to its employees, it may purchase a plan that reimburses up to the 90th percentile. This means, for example, roughly nine out of ten dentists in the employer-based zip code will provide preventative services to the employees at no out-of-pocket expense. If, however, a company decides to be somewhat stingier with its benefits, it may purchase a plan reimbursing at the 70th percentile. In this case, the patient will owe money for a cleaning at some three out of ten offices in the area.

The insurance company will refer to its reimbursement level as UCR, no matter if it reimburses at the 90th percentile or the 70th percentile. The plan the insurance company has sold contains a predetermined reimbursable rate of UCR, which stands for Usual, Customary and Reasonable, set at whatever percentile has been agreed upon and purchased by the employer. This is why there is no standard UCR, and why any insurance company that attempts to convince your patients that its UCR is the actual UCR for your area is misleading them. Most employers are cost-conservative and make efforts to control their overhead when it comes to dental and medical benefits. Therefore, many dental insurance plans are purchased at lower percentiles. This is why your fees may commonly exceed what is reported to you as UCR. (UCR is further defined and explained in this book's section on *Dental Insurance Mastery in Your Practice*.)

An added benefit of the scientific fee analyzer is the ability it provides to determine at what percentile each insurance company is reimbursing. We commonly review the EOBs (Explanation of Benefits) we receive from insurance companies. These forms denote how much of your assigned fee is being paid and what portion is considered above UCR.

If, for example, you are charging $70 for a procedure and virtually all insurance companies are reimbursing that full $70, your fee is most likely at a very low percentile ranking. If, however, your submitted fee is $110 and the insurance companies are reimbursing based upon $85, you know that the UCR at that percentile is $85. You can then locate $85 on the fee analyzer to determine which percentile ranking this fee represents. This information becomes invaluable when attempting to provide accurate co-payment estimates for your patients, a topic I discuss in greater detail in later chapters.

I purchase fee analyzers from a company called The Udell Webb Leadership Institute (www.webbdental.com). Dr. Webb is a dentist who has taken the initiative to teach other dentists how to prosper from information previously held exclusively by insurance companies. His analyzers provide information pertaining to every routinely billed dental procedural code. [9] Each code lists fees reflecting charges submitted by area dentists in the 50th, 75th and 95th percentiles. This information allows dentists to select a particular fee for each procedure based upon the value they perceive their services to hold. Such spoon-fed information provides the doctor confidence that the chosen fees will not be exorbitant nor will they be undervalued.

Fee analyzers range from $300-$500 and are updated annually. If implemented properly, this expense is recovered almost immediately. Though I can think of no reason for a doctor to elect not to purchase a fee analyzer, most doctors are not even aware they exist. Instead, they are seemingly grasping at straws when selecting their fees. There is a science behind this strategy, and any practice owner aspiring for efficiency should consider utilizing the fee analyzer when determining procedural fees.

Colleagues who have started practices in surrounding areas can give you guidance on fees as well. As with other cost of living differences, medical fees vary greatly by region. If you practice in the Midwest, do not expect to be able to charge the same amount as your friend in California or New York, even though you are doing the same work.

Do not under any circumstance set your fees by the PPO fee schedules! These fees will average only 40-60% of what your actual fees could be. Accept these fees only when you are an in-network provider for a particular insurance plan, as you are thereby mandated to set your fees at a particular level. Otherwise, you are free to set your fees wherever you choose.

How Often Should You Raise Your Fees?

Over time, you may find that you need to modify your fees based upon patient feedback, equipment and supply prices or overhead costs. Routinely raising fees by 3-5% every 10 months has many advantages.

When implementing this adjustment, raising every fee by the same percentage across the board is beneficial. I would suggest not wasting time and energy attempting to adjust each fee separately, perceiving possible negative reactions from patients and insurance companies. These perceptions are usually much worse than reality. The adjustments typically go unnoticed by patients, but serve to add significantly to your bottom line.

Raising your fees every 10 months gives you an additional fee increase every five years above what a typical yearly increase would provide. Set a reminder on your scheduling software when your next fee increase should occur. Since it is very difficult to institute large fee increases to make up for lost time, doctors who do not raise their fees annually commit themselves to greater overhead percentage and lower profits for the remainder of their careers.

It is commonly recommended to raise your fees 5% across the board in order to keep pace with inflation. This fee increase helps defray the costs of investing in new technology for your office and rising payroll expenses. On average, operating costs for the typical practice are advancing at a rate of 3-4% annually. In order to maintain or improve profitability, practice fees must be raised above that level.

Being mindful of the economy at large, go easy on fee increases in times of economic downturn. A 3% increase will normally keep pace with inflation during these periods, as overall growth and spending will wane. Though some practitioners will continue to operate with apparent immunity to any recession, most will find practice volume to slow in accordance. The goal is to take the patients along for the long haul, so absorb some of the recessionary pain with them while striving to keep them in your operatories.

In determining your fees, do not underestimate the value of the efforts you have made to create a unique dental environment for your patients. They value that, and therefore, so should you. You are taking pains to provide high quality care and a comfortable encounter. It takes time to provide exceptional clinical care and service. Low fees and high volume encroach upon that time. Being rewarded for your efforts will allow you and your business to continue to satisfy your patients' desires and expectations for the best dental experience available.[10]

HIRING THE IDEAL STAFF

Chapter 8

Is There an Ideal Staff?

The most important thing to keep in mind when choosing your staff is that the ideal staff is really an ideal *team*. I have always found this to be an overused, somewhat corny cliché, but my experience has borne out its truth. When I think of a team, I envision a group of athletes doing something they love, conforming to the ideals of their coach. The best are able to minimize their importance for the ultimate success of the squad. Though professional athletes may not fit this description, the goals of the team do not center on monetary reward.

It is rare to find staff members who are motivated more by the ideals of the team, than by their own remuneration. You cannot expect them to be. This is not their practice and they almost certainly would not be coming in if they were not getting paid to do so. Would you? Do not feel slighted if so many employees throughout your career do not feel as strongly about your practice as you do. They may enjoy dentistry. They may feel rewarded by taking care of people. They may appreciate your office environment and the quality of care you provide. They may be grateful for the way you treat them with respect. They may even like you, but they are coming in to get paid!

What it means in dentistry to be an ideal team member is to possess the desire to do whatever is necessary to ensure the efficient flow of the daily schedule. This means having the willingness to perform a task that is "not my job," when the demands of the day call for it. The lines between job descriptions become very faint for the ideal staff. They will all be cross-trained and will know that their varied abilities are valued. They will not be lazy nor complain when called upon to do something they would rather not do. We all do things each day in the workplace that we would rather not do. The ideal staff understands and accepts that this is part of the job.

Your ideal team will be composed of people who get along well with others. They will be friendly, hopefully funny, and liked by their co-workers and by your patients. They will like you and you will like them. They will not harbor jealousy toward other staff members. They will be comfortable with themselves, diligent and intelligent, and will enjoy what they do. These people will not gossip and will not slander. They will add to your day, not siphon the life from it. They will simply come to work, do their jobs, and not complain when asked to also do the jobs of others if necessary. Finding these people is a tall order. They are out there, however. Uncover them and you will field your ideal team.

The successful dental practice is founded on the assumption that patients are going to like the people in the office. As simple as it sounds, this is the key foundational ingredient in your business plan. If you are starting your business from scratch without any patients, this is especially important. Certainly, your office needs to look nice, your service needs to be top notch, you need to be able to painlessly deliver the clinical dentistry to the standard of care, but most importantly, you and your staff need to be liked!

Upon graduating from dental school, I took a position as an associate in a large, managed care practice. There were more than twenty employees and four dentists. I remember my boss telling me one day that his staff was not important to him because he could fire one today and hire an identical one the next day. It reminded me of the Bill Cosby stand-up routine in which he tells his disobedient son, "I brought you into this world, I can take you out. It makes no difference to me. I can make another one that looks just like you!" In my youthful naivety I found my boss' statement to be rude and thoughtless, one I would never utter when I became fortunate enough to run my own practice. I really could not believe the insignificance he assigned to his staff members. How could he care so little about the people who labored so diligently for him each day?

Now, many years and multiple staff members later, I am finally beginning to understand the motivation behind his sentiments. There is a middle ground, and I am not saying that staff members should be marginalized. Though I have had the luxury of employing some excellent, motivated, bright and diligent workers, the average worker would have tossed me aside just as my boss would have his staff. There is very little loyalty in the workforce, and much less predictability in the lives of your staff. If circumstances present that make another offer more appealing, make home life a more immediate necessity or make work less appealing or even unnecessary, your ideal staff member will suddenly quit the team.

There was a time when I had the perfect blend of employees in my practice. I had a college educated, extremely intelligent front office manager. I employed a highly skilled hygienist with advanced clinical abilities and a soothing, pleasant demeanor that patients loved. The chair-side assistant I hired took pains to make sure everything I wanted was performed systematically and without the necessity for micromanagement. Not only were these employees gifted in their abilities relating to their job descriptions, they were also quite comfortable operating as a team. I cannot recall an incident of reported disdain or dissention among them. We all got along fantastically and we considered each other friends. It was truly fun to go to work.

I always knew the day would come when that team would be dismantled, and I knew I would likely never find such a cohesive unit again. Almost simultaneously, the requirements of life called each of them. Two returned to college for graduate degrees, one becoming a teacher, the other studying to become a nurse. My hygienist was pulled away by family obligations, and then there was one. Only the practice owner remained and it was time to start seeking the squad of replacements.

This is a common scenario in the business of dentistry. You have to be nimble and your feelings need to remain somewhat distant when it comes to your staff. I am not suggesting you adopt a cold attitude toward them, but merely that you understand that staff member departure, which will occur, is not personal. It is life, and that is business.

The best dental office staff members typically have the shortest half-life when it comes to their employment in your office. Most commonly they are overachievers, making a brief stop for the moment to secure some income while they ponder their next life achievement. Many are working part-time while they are in school. Their education routinely leads them to another profession, an advanced degree or possibly to becoming a dentist themselves. They are hard workers, intelligent and easily trained. They retain what you teach them and can apply this knowledge immediately. They are called to higher things. They may aspire to one day be the boss, not the employee.

The search for the ideal staff needs to be tempered with some reality, despite what some practice consultants might have you believe. Some suggest that you should be as patient and as diligent as possible, for as long as is necessary to avoid settling for mediocrity. They implore you not to compromise! The truth is, unfortunately, that most candidates applying for the lines of work you are offering did not typically set the curve in their chemistry courses. They were not regularly on the honor roll, and may have never received their high school diplomas. The dental assistant position, for example, is one which requires little or no education, with certain responsibilities being permitted merely through on the job training.

This is a delicate topic because here we are forced to evaluate others in a manner different from ourselves. The candidates for employment will not be similar to your peers in terms of academic efforts and accolades. As a dentist, you have been surrounded by overachievers who have typically done very well in school. They try harder, work smarter and are more diligent and persistent than others you may have encountered. Your expectations of yourself are very high. Your expectations of others, therefore, may be higher than is reasonable. As important as it is to hire the ideal staff, you may want to keep your expectations in check.

It is not uncommon for the applicants you will interview to have no college credits whatsoever, and almost never will you receive a job application from a college graduate. The pay that accompanies these positions typically relegates the employee pool to solely include high school educated prospects. Even the best front office employees routinely achieved that status through promotion from the back office. Most front office staff members in dentistry are there because they learned dentistry through assisting. Since we are typically smaller business owners, we cannot compensate on a level that competes with other managerial position employers. The highly skilled, educated businessperson is going to elect to join a larger company in exchange for the greater wage and benefits. We are left to sift through the applications for employment that remain after all the good jobs are taken. Do not be discouraged when assembling the ideal team becomes more challenging than the pundits profess.

That being said, the ideal staff is out there. It is not easy to find, however. I later present the rules to follow which outline the processes of advertising the positions, interviewing, trialing the candidates and ultimately employing your discernment to select the perfect hire. Each one plays an important role in the success of your business. Each one helps form your ideal team.

Chapter 9

Staff Skills, Duties and Expectations

The All-in-One Dentist

A few years after dental school, I got in touch with an old friend and former classmate. In catching up he described to me the practice of one of our classmates. Apparently, when anyone would call the office, this doctor himself would answer the phone. When patients called they would be greeted with, "Thank you for calling Dr. Potosi's office, may I help you?" We got a laugh out of this, revisiting some humorous stories about our friend from dental school.

Though amusing to most, Dr. Potosi was clearly trying to control his overhead. He had become The-All-in-One-Dentist. Given the nature of the scratch practice he was establishing, success is sometimes achieved through any means necessary. Cost control is a highly effective method for extending the runway from which your practice is attempting to take flight. The All-in-One Dentist eliminates the need for hiring decisions and payroll expenses in the beginning when cash is tight. Of course, most dentists are not excited to perform the duties of supporting staff members.

As entertaining as I thought it was to hear Dr. Potosi answering his own phone, circumstances bore the same destiny for me in the years to come. After having sold a business and taking some time away from dentistry, I decided to open another practice with the goal of keeping things simple. I was weighing other opportunities at the time and I really had no intention of taking up permanent residence in this practice. The idea was to control the overhead, stay nimble and allow the ability to jump ship when the necessary time arrived. Prior to getting married, much of my life was played out in this fashion.

I did everything. I greeted the new patients, took their x-rays, developed and mounted their x-rays and did their cleanings. I learned once again how to perform scaling and root planing. I set up and sterilized the operatories. I assisted myself in four-handed dentistry with my own two hands. I ordered supplies, scheduled recalls, collected payments, printed receipts and generated insurance claim forms for the patients to submit. The only thing I would not do is answer my own phone. I was never able to get the amusement of Dr. Potosi's situation out of my head.

So, in keeping form with my tight-walleted protocol, I hired my sister to answer the office phone for me. She answered the calls via cell phone, scheduled the patients and then emailed me about when I would be working. This was truly the skeleton crew of dental office staffing. At one point my sister-in-law suggested that I also offer to take the patients out for coffee after their dental appointments. "Do you have anything going on right now? I've got some free time, why don't we go down to Starbuck's?"

Though this is definitely not the ideal way to practice dentistry, the example is offered to show that this can be done. If strategized properly, your dental practice should never make you feel like you are behind the eight ball. Do not let your overhead spin out of control, add staff members as you can afford them and hire with the ideal team in mind.

Front Office Manager

The front office manager will provide the prospective patients their first impression of your office. It is therefore crucial to the initial growth and success of your practice to hire the right person for this position. The front office manager is also the first position you will need to hire. As a cost-conserving measure, you may elect to do your own cleanings and work without an assistant for a time as your practice grows. You will not, however, be able to also perform the job duties of the front office manager.

Sometimes dentists starting new practices will hire a dental assistant to serve as both the receptionist and chair-side assistant when patients and revenues are limited. This may make sense as a short term solution, but this dual role will eventually lead to phone calls going unanswered and patients being ignored. These two consequences can spell certain death for a new practice in its infancy.

Though it may seem obvious to doctors that the front office manager will largely shape the initial feelings and ideas a patient has about their office, most of them fail to hire specifically with that idea in mind. It never ceases to amaze me how many medical and dental offices are staffed by grumpy, stressed out, unpleasant front office managers. Recently returning from a day of doctors' and specialists' appointments for her child, my sister wondered aloud, "How much do you have to pay a receptionist to smile every once in awhile?" This was particularly salient to me as it typically requires a lot to get under her skin. It is crucial to hire someone for this position who is friendly, professional and not easily distracted or stressed.

Duties of the front office manager are multifaceted and include answering phones, scheduling patients, checking insurance benefits, greeting patients, handling new patient paperwork and data entry. A front office manager operating alone may be additionally required to assume the tasks of ordering supplies, maintaining the files, writing thank you notes, requesting x-rays and accomplishing numerous other duties that arise throughout the workday. If your office does not employ a separate business manager, the front office manager will assume the duties of insurance claim filing, co-pay determination and presentation, payment collection, marketing and billing.

Your front office manager must be able to multi-task, as attention will be divided among several things at the same time. While the office manager is calculating a co-pay or presenting a treatment plan, a new patient may walk in while another patient may call. The ideal candidate can handle multiple duties at once while maintaining calm and not making the patients feel like they are an annoyance. This employee also has to be capable of keeping track of details in the midst of these chaotic times.

Hiring an office manager with previous dental office experience will provide a smoother initiation. The experienced employee will not need training in the basics of dental terminology, including tooth numbers and surfaces, procedure names and coding. Most applicants for the office manager position were at some point dental assistants, having now progressed to the front office. This back office experience will come in handy on busier days when their cross-training can be exploited to assist with operatory set up and sterilization. Most employees appreciate the willingness of the front office staff to don a pair of gloves and lend a hand where help is needed.

However, if you have the time to train someone on this information it might be wise to consider hiring someone with a college education but no experience in your particular field. This will help you avoid having to re-train the employee and break habits or expectations that may have developed in another office.

If at all possible, hire for intelligence as well. This may seem self-evident, but it is often overlooked in the interview process. Since the requirements for a personable, multi-tasking front desk employee are tantamount, delving into a candidate's intelligence may become secondary. This often proves difficult to assess in an interview as well. My experience has borne out that if you hire for intellect, you will be spared innumerable hours of micromanagement, repetition in training, lost net profit resulting from mathematical errors and recurring headaches.

It is impossible in an interview setting to know for certain if a candidate will be a good fit for your office. Unfortunately, it is also difficult to provide a working interview for this particular position since it requires so much initial training on software. Calling multiple references is critical when making this hiring decision. As with all the positions you hire, begin the employee with a 60 day probationary period, after which you will review whether this is the right fit for your office. While letting an employee go is always a difficult task, it is much easier and less of a legal risk if it can be done within the trial period.

Dental Assistant

Nowhere is it more important to hire a team player as it is for the position of dental assistant. This is no place for the prima donna. This person will serve as the glue that keeps the team working together as a cohesive unit. This logic may seem counterintuitive when viewing the office manager as the person actually managing the practice. The fact is, however, that the guts of what happens in a dental practice takes place in the back office, not the front office. That is where the commodity is being exchanged in the business of dentistry. That is where your production is being generated. The level of efficiency of your schedule will be largely determined by the abilities of your dental assistant, and your level of production will fluctuate accordingly.

Training classes for this position vary from a twelve-week course to a one-year program. Depending upon state laws, some dental assistants who have completed extra training are permitted to perform expanded functions such as placing fillings, packing cord, taking impressions and seating crowns.

Some dentists decide to forego hiring an assistant who has gone through schooling and choose to provide on the job training (OJT) instead. This can be accomplished if you have the time available in your schedule, the patience needed to teach someone and a dental assistant with the ability to learn and implement new tasks efficiently. A primary benefit of this training is the freedom it affords to instruct the assistant in your precise needs. This provides doctors with new practices the liberty they commonly seek in running their own business. The OJT dental assistant will not have to break habits created while in training or while working in another dental office.

Many dentists find it more beneficial, however, to hire someone with at least a basic knowledge of dental instruments and the anatomy of the mouth. An assistant skilled at the delivery of clinical dentistry will save you valuable time in training. Hiring an experienced assistant will also allay the initial frustration of having to do much more of the clinical work yourself. Additionally, if you choose to hire someone with no training or education in dentistry, that person may quickly discover distaste or dislike for the dirty work involved in dental assisting. In terms of the new practice dental assistant, my advice would be to hire someone with basic dental knowledge and then train this new staff member in your protocol while on the job.

Personally, I have done well with hiring the dental neophyte who possesses no knowledge of the field of dentistry. When afforded the luxury of interviewing a larger pool of applicants than merely those with dental assisting backgrounds, I have been able to hire for personality traits that I know will make the employee a better assistant. I appreciate being able to train an open-eyed newbie the ways of our profession, in just the manner I deem appropriate for my particular office environment. Old habits are hard to break and even more difficult to replace. I realize this luxury will come at a cost, but to me it has been worthwhile when I have been able to identify and hire the right person for the job.

The pay scale for the dental assistant will be graduated based upon experience. The neophyte rewards you with the lowest cost and the most flexibility. The assistant with basic knowledge of the field of dentistry will demand only slightly more in salary. The Certified Dental Assistant (CDA) with years of experience comes at a higher cost. The Registered Dental Assistant (RDA) with certification will expect a greater wage and the Expanded Functions RDA will demand a salary similar to your own. Though an exaggeration, your practice will need to be extremely busy in order to make this hiring decision worthwhile. I have hired assistants on all rungs of the ladder, and I have found the most value in the OJT assistants who have been properly selected.

An ideal dental assistant candidate will be comfortable talking with patients and answering questions. The assistant will need to be able to comfort a patient before, during and after procedures. The ability to cross-train with the office manager's duties is also essential. This will provide back-up on the phones and in the front office when the office manager is busy or absent. In essence, you need a hard working, motivated, personable, intelligent and informed person to ideally fill this role. I encourage you to take the time to interview thoroughly and to be highly selective. These hiring decisions will go a long way in determining the ultimate success of your practice and the level of peace of your daily life.

Dental Hygienist

Initially, you may be able to do your own hygiene until your practice gets busier. You will not likely do this job as skillfully as a dental hygienist, primarily because you will not likely enjoy this work. There may be a dentist out there who takes pleasure in filling the role of dental hygienist, but I have yet to meet one. We feel over-trained for this job, when the reality is that we are typically under-trained for it. Registered Dental Hygienists (RDH) and in a handful of states,

Licensed Dental Hygienists (LDH), take pride in their work and enjoy the freedoms afforded by their profession.

If you start from zero, you should initially do your own hygiene. Performing your own hygiene allows your practice to grow while sparing you the exorbitant overhead expense of having a hygienist on the payroll. An additional benefit of performing your own hygiene is the ability to get to know your patients and establish a rapport with them. This relationship is critical to the growth of a practice in its infancy. Almost every dentist I know who started from scratch played hygienist for a while.

For patients with minimal restorative needs, the dental hygienist may play the most important role in a dental office. My six-year-old niece is convinced that the dental hygienist is the *real* dentist since all I do is count her teeth while my hygienist cleans, x-rays and treats her teeth with fluoride. Of course, one staffing obstacle is that many dental hygienists would tend to agree with my niece's sentiments.

The ability to locate and hire the ideal hygienist for your team is controlled by multiple factors. As of 2008, there were 301 accredited dental hygiene programs operating in the United States, many of which are associated with dental schools.[11] Dentists trained in schools without hygiene programs may be at a disadvantage when it comes to their knowledge of the dental hygiene profession. They may not be aware of the varied educational requirements necessary in each state to become a dental hygienist, which can range from three years of schooling to a Bachelor's degree.

Most hygiene school applicants are required to complete at least thirty hours of prerequisite courses, including Anatomy and Physiology, Microbiology, Pharmacology, Medical Terminology and basic Chemistry. Dental hygiene students are then required to train in an accredited program which bestows either a hygiene certificate or an associate's degree upon completion.

Forty-eight of these schools require a Bachelor's degree for completion and seventeen schools offer a Master's degree as an available option. The advanced Master's program is typically required for dental hygienists aspiring to enter the fields of research, education or administration. To obtain information about dental hygiene programs in your area, and to possibly assist you in hiring the ideal hygienist for your practice, visit www.adha.org.

In 2008 there were more than 174,000 hygiene positions held in the United States. [12] Since dental hygiene is a multi-location profession, there are likely considerably fewer hygienists than this in practice. Most hygienists are employed in dental offices, though some hold positions in medical clinics, public school health programs or social work environments.

Dental hygiene is one of the fastest growing professions and it is estimated that in the next ten years, approximately 63,000 new hygiene positions will be filled. [13] This figure represents a 36% increase from current levels, far outpacing the averages for other occupations. Acceptance to hygiene school is becoming very competitive and high academic achievements are required for admittance. This, coupled with their high demand and flexibility, serve to position hygienists in the driver's seat when it comes to the negotiation process with dentists.

Each state has different protocol for the examination and certification process necessary for dental hygiene licensure. Many board exams provide licensing capability in multiple states. These are called Regional Board Exams. Some states allow for licensure by credential, permitting the hygienist with experience practicing in another state to obtain a license in their state simply by passing an ethics or state law exam. You should become familiar with the licensure requirements of your state, and you should request that the candidate's license be presented at the outset of the interview process.

There appears to be no additional benefit in hiring a dental hygienist with a Bachelor's degree as opposed to a RDH or LDH without this degree. Any dental hygienist who is licensed to practice is perceived to have received similar and adequate training in the field. The clinical and interpersonal skills necessary to excel in the dental hygiene profession seem to be independent of additional undergraduate education. I would not suggest paying more for a dental hygiene candidate touting this degree.

While it may be argued in some circles that certain schools provide a higher level of training, key factors in selecting the ideal hygienist for your team lie outside this criterion. Though clinical expertise is essential, it is a difficult standard to measure in the interview process. Possibly more important to the initial growth and success of your practice is the ability of the dental hygienist to befriend and bond with your patients. Working interviews will effectively provide information about the candidate's clinical abilities. Your interview skills and discernment will be tested to provide the necessary information about the candidate's personality and interpersonal skills.

Since your dental hygienist will likely be the team member spending the most time with your patients, it is the hygienist the patients must most like and trust. I cannot accurately portray the number of times in my career a patient has recounted an experience with a dreadful hygienist. Dental hygienists are sometimes depicted as sadistic, rough and unfriendly. Not to be too insensitive to the unfairly criticized hygienist, dentists are often characterized in this fashion as well. Patients sometimes lament that their previous hygienist "hurt me" or "lectured me." In fact, I would wager that an uncomfortable relationship with one's dental hygienist is the most common reason offered for a patient's switching dental offices.

Imagine the possibilities that employing a friendly, soft spoken, likeable dental hygienist open up to you. Hiring a person possessing the opposite traits of *Helga the Hygienist* or *Bloody Mary*, as some patients have so named them, will provide you the opposite results. Since patients are already expecting the worst from their hygienist, someone who merely does not fit this negative image will garner their attention. Someone who speaks and acts in an entirely positive manner will shake their foundation! Patients love a hygienist like this. They will love your practice because of it. They will keep coming back, and they will refer their friends and family to you as well.

Patients will form a deeper relationship with their hygienist than they will with you or any other member of your staff. The ideal dental hygiene candidate desires to form those relationships with your patients. In fact, that is why many hygienists begin their careers in the first place. Your hygienist will connect your patients to your practice.

Employing a hygienist whom patients enjoy seeing will help your business in a number of ways. A friendly, professional hygienist whom patients respect will provide:

- A reduction in the number of cancellations and no-shows your practice experiences.
- An increase in the referrals your practice receives as patients will share with their co-workers and neighbors the exceptional service they received.
- A healthy recall program which provides stability to your practice in good times and bad. If a patient just experienced wonderful treatment at the hands of a hygienist, it will not be difficult to make a six-month follow-up appointment.
- Increased production as a result of the trust your patients have in your practice.
- Decreased managerial stress, freeing you up to be a more productive dentist and a happier boss.
- Team unity as co-workers will not resent the elitist, aloof hygienist sometimes encountered in dental offices.

I highly recommend at minimum a one-day working interview with any hygiene candidate you are seriously considering hiring. Obviously, checking references is important, but nothing can replace the opportunity to visualize the hygienist at work. A working interview is not an exact representation of the potential employee's work habits and personality, as the candidate will be on best behavior during this time, but it often affords the opportunity to expose certain red flag behaviors. Friendliness and enthusiasm should be evident in the first interview with a dental hygiene candidate for employment. If you are creating a family dental practice, it is important for the hygienist to have patience and gentleness with children as well. Ensure that the working interview schedule contains a variety of ages and patient types to give you the best idea of how this candidate interacts with patients.

As strange as it may seem, I do not consider experience to be an assured asset when it comes to the ideal dental hygienist. I routinely receive résumés from hygienists touting themselves as the most knowledgeable in the field. They graduated from hygiene school in 1932 and have practiced in every state in the union. As routinely as I receive them, so too does the waste basket. This is not to say that some experienced hygienists will not fit well within your practice; they just are not for me. They may not be for the scratch practice either.

The new and growing practice is dynamic. Systems are new and may require revisions through trial and error. Hard and fast rules of the past may not have a place here. As the business owner, you need the flexibility to make the rules and change them as you see fit. Though being open-minded to the suggestions of a well-meaning staff is at times very beneficial, your practice is not a democracy. Re-training employees set in their ways puts in place a hurdle you do not have the time to clear. Unless they are clearly open to the new and different philosophies you have for your business, the experienced hygienist is better suited operating in the experienced practice.

The dental hygiene candidate just out of school, however, is yours for the molding. Yours is the only practice philosophy this hygienist has known or will know as long as this staff member remains in your employ. Though the training will initially require a bit more time and energy, time is one commodity you will have in the beginning. Money is a commodity in lesser supply, and the novice hygienist will require less of it. There will be no habits to break, no dogma to overcome and no resistance to your requests. This is still a professional trained in dental hygiene. This is *your* hygienist.

Keep in mind that these recommendations come only as a result of my experience in practice. I am sure that there is a tremendous supply of experienced dental hygienists who might be highly beneficial in growing a practice from its inception. This type of hygienist must be willing to adapt habitual modes of operation to your practice philosophy and protocols. The experienced hygienist must also have the welcoming personality to establish friendly relationships with the continuous supply of new patients that your new practice will require. These personality traits are independent of time and experience in the industry. Many have gregarious, kind, warm and inviting personalities which bode well for the relationships you will need to foster. If you find an experienced dental hygienist possessing these traits, the knowledge and experience brought to bear could actually serve as a positive force in growing a new practice.

As is the case with your crown fee, the wage demanded by hygienists will vacillate wildly depending upon the practice zip code. When practicing in Southern California over a decade ago, I paid my hygienist $45/hour. In Missouri, the average hygiene wage is around $30/hour.

An island in the Puget Sound in Washington State boasts an average salary for the dental hygienist of $110,000/year. I have a colleague in a Seattle suburb that pays his Restorative Hygienist over $140,000/year. These specially trained hygienists can account for significantly greater production by placing fillings, impressing and cementing crowns and anesthetizing patients for the doctor. They definitely earn their wages in a bustling practice. They are not, however, typically recommended for the newly formed scratch practice.

Information on expected rate of pay for hygienists and other job titles in your area is readily available online through websites such as www.payscale.com and www.cbsalary.com. I often pay staff at the high end of the pay scale. I do not consider staff salary the place to be pinching your pennies. You should diligently seek and interview for the ideal hire and then pay a wage just above what might be expected. This will engender a feeling of good will from your staff and will promote their diligence and loyalty. You can still be cost conservative here by hiring a hygienist just out of school. This candidate will not expect a wage equivalent to that of the hygienist serving a fortieth year of duty.

Hygienists are typically the highest paid employees, and rightly so. They are the only staff members who can actually produce for you. While dental assistants can sell dentistry, their productive abilities end somewhere around the level of whitening tray and mouth guard fabrication. This limitation is eliminated when you hire a dental assistant with expanded functions credentials. Front office staff can peddle products and influence the scheduling of treatment, but they cannot perform any of the actual production. Hygienists can carry their weight and should routinely out-produce their wage. Good hygienists will produce amounts double or triple that of their remuneration. It is therefore critical to be selective in the process of hiring your dental hygienist.

Apart from you as the dentist, your dental hygienist will be your best earner. Interview and hire wisely here and you will reap returns on this investment for years to come. This person will be trained in the clinical delivery of dental hygiene, but other skills and characteristics of this team member will bear equal if not greater importance to the ultimate growth and success of your dental practice.

Business Manager/Treatment Coordinator

As your business grows and you are able to afford another staff member, hiring a treatment coordinator who also serves as your business manager is a wise decision. This team member's responsibilities include: calculating patient co-pays, presenting treatment plans, educating patients, coordinating marketing efforts, managing the staff, generating financial and patient reports, administrating payroll and posting payments.

In the early stages of a new practice, the need for this position will not be that evident. As the practice grows and the receptionist becomes busier, a dedicated treatment coordinator will profit you because the patient will be given one-on-one attention without distractions while the treatment plan is being presented. This time and attention allows the patient to ask questions and to be educated on the particular treatment needs outlined. Patients are considerably more likely to make an appointment for treatment if they are given this kind of personal attention.

The treatment coordinator also organizes treatment with specialists by writing a brief referral explanation, sending x-rays and helping to coordinate the appointment for the patient. After treatment by a specialist has been delivered, the treatment coordinator should call the treated patients to inquire about their recovery and to schedule the next phase of treatment in your office if applicable. The treatment coordinator sends a follow-up letter and thank you note to referring specialists after a new patient is seen in the office. In this role as a coordinator of specialist care, the treatment coordinator also has the opportunity to grow referring relationships with area specialists.

A business manager who handles your staffing needs and complaints provides a buffer between you and the staff which can serve to eliminate confrontation. Staff members can take up their requests and complaints with the business manager who can sort through these conversations to determine which problems require your involvement. The business manager will oversee and safeguard that the staff is handling patients in the way desired by the dentist.

Hiring a business manager who devotes time to marketing can be a critical factor in how quickly your practice grows. You will quickly learn that you do not have the time to care for your patients, oversee the development of your practice, train your staff, maintain the finances and spend time researching new marketing ideas. This is a position that can help to pay for itself by attracting new patients and encouraging those patients to appoint for treatment. Establishing an effective marketing plan and hiring an employee who can oversee it are imperative to the rapid growth of your practice. The employment of a business manager, one who is dedicated to the continuous implementation of a successful marketing strategy, is a necessary expense which will render a substantial return on investment.

Chapter 10

Fielding the Perfect Team

Where Do You Find the Right Staff?
The position available and the level of experience desired will determine where to start looking for a new employee. If seeking to hire a dental assistant or hygienist fresh out of school, your best choice would be to contact the employment offices of the local hygiene and assisting schools. These offices will post free ads for you as a service to their students. Most schools host employment fairs in the spring as well.

When seeking experienced dental office staff members, the myriad of dental sales reps that frequent your office can bestow a wealth of information. These reps have a firm grasp of what staff members are coming and going in other offices. Sales reps develop familiarity with the efficiency and personality of the office staff, given their repeated visits during business hours and through the supply ordering process.

In fact, the sales reps tend to possess more intimate knowledge of the individual dentist than you might expect. I recall once hanging out with a number of these reps following a local seminar. I was the only dentist in the group, but by the gossip they were slinging, you would not have known that our profession had even one representative. I felt like I was surrounded by a group of journalists from *US Weekly* or *OMG!* They did drop names, but most often they referred to these doctors as, "My Account." I, of course, wondered what my reps were spilling about me, as their "Account."

This experience reminded me of time spent with a group of pharmaceutical reps in Southern California. There is no room for naivety when considering what sales reps are saying about you, but no doubt, they are saying something. By and large, that is what they do. Do not be surprised if their statements lack accuracy. I think it best to take caution in what you share with them. Your words might be exploited when discussing their Accounts.

Most local newspapers provide an online listing of their classifieds section. In my city, it is actually cheaper to pay for a print ad which will be automatically added to the website, rather than to pay solely for the online ad on the newspaper's site. Your classified ad will garner much more attention online than it will by being buried in the print of a newspaper. Besides, does anyone read the newspaper anymore?

If Craig's List operates in your city, it provides a wonderful service for attracting prospective employees. With the exception of major markets on the East and West Coast, you can place a classified ad on www.craigslist.org free of charge. In the larger markets, you may be required to pay a small fee for this service. Though associate dentists rarely respond to Craig's List ads, I have hired my last two dental assistants through this site. One concise ad garnered me over a dozen résumés in little more than one weekend. Candidate responses to Craig's List ads online also provide the hiring dentist insight into the level of professionalism of each applicant. Many respond to your email address in the manner in which they would text message their friends, using no capitalization or punctuation. These respondents' résumés quickly make their way into my Trash Folder.

You may choose to post your employment ad online through one of the major job search websites such as Monster.com or Jobster.com. The fees involved may be prohibitive for the wage level of the position you are offering. Certain employment sites such as DentalWorkers.com and iHireDental.com restrict their focus to jobs in our profession. I would start with the free listing websites first before assuming any expense to secure your ideal staff. Since your search is local and the wage you are able to offer is not going to be competitive in national recruiting, it pays to seek first word of mouth referrals from colleagues, co-workers, friends and relatives.

If you are in a competitive market for office staff members, they may be interviewing you more than the reverse. In this case, another great thing about creating the office environment that stands out above the rest is that you will be first in line when it comes to courting the ideal team. A beautiful office and warm, welcoming atmosphere can help sell the job to the candidate for you.

Staff Benefits

There are three primary reasons to offer staff benefits to your employees. One is simply that you desire to be benevolent to those working for you. Another is to take advantage of the maximum monetary tax deferral through a qualified benefit retirement plan. Still another is to lure good hires in a competitive staffing market. The ideal team will commonly seek practices providing more than an hourly wage. There are many types of benefit packages you can offer your employees, depending upon to what degree you wish to supplement their pay. You may elect to offer retirement plans such as a 401K, Defined Benefit Plan, Profit Sharing Plan, Simple IRA or SEP IRA Plan and match a predetermined percentage of each employee's deferral amount.

You may incorporate in the pay package employee inclusion in a group health plan, or decide to pay a portion of an employee's individual insurance premium. Vacation pay, sick time and staff bonus programs should all be factored into the employee's pay scale, and revealed to them at the time of hire. This serves the dual purpose of creating staff member awareness of their true hourly pay and alerts you to the actual dollar value you are expecting in return for the employee's services. Staff members can compare the actual wage you are offering with other offers they may be entertaining.

Staff Bonus Programs

Agreements rewarding staff for outstanding effort are quite popular with employees and can benefit your company financially as well. The costs associated with such arrangements will vary depending upon the structure of the program instituted and your staff's ability to achieve certain predetermined levels of productivity. Philosophies abound on how exactly to incentivize staff members for their accomplishments, and numerous bonus plans result all with different compensatory goals in mind.

The real reason to implement such a bonus program has less to do with fiscally rewarding your staff than it does with increasing your bottom line. Though your employees may not view this the same way you do, the wage upon which you have agreed should already be considered fair compensation for hard work. The true goal of any bonus plan should be to promote staff awareness of certain financial objectives and encourage performance beyond these levels. You must first determine values for production, collection, accounts receivable, overhead and profit above which you view your business to be "overachieving." These targets should be somewhat difficult to attain, but not impossible, or you risk staff discouragement and abandonment of the additional effort you are trying to promote.

New patient volume incentive plans

One highly effective and easy to implement bonus plan is executed by rewarding front office staff for increasing new patient volume. An example would be to compensate $10 for every new patient per month scheduled in your office beyond the 30th new patient. Busier practices can elect to enforce higher minimum numbers of new patients. There is virtually no greater way to influence your bottom line positively than by increasing the new patient flow of your practice. I currently utilize a form of this bonus program in my practice and it continues to yield highly positive results.

Collection incentive plans

Another program is based upon the principle of rewarding staff for increasing the monthly collections of your practice. This collection incentive pay plan considers that while practice production is important, it is the collections value that forms the basis of your profitability. You start by determining practice collections for the preceding 12 months. Using this value as a baseline, your staff members will now receive a 12% bonus to be divided evenly among them, for any amount collected above this level. The payouts are calculated on a monthly basis and distributed quarterly. When monthly practice collections fall below the baseline, this negative value will roll forward. For example, if you miss your goal by $2,000 one month, you will start off the next month $2,000 down. Staff members are thereby encouraged not to *throw in the towel* early on in a bad month, as they will need to make up this amount by quarter's end before receiving any bonus.

For the collection incentive pay plan to work efficiently, you should recalculate the base level every six months. This allows you to maintain pace with inflation and current practice collections. Other cost increases should be factored in as well. Every 12 months, consider a ten percent increase in the cost of doing business and add that to the collections base. Additionally, consider the increase in payroll costs for the prior year and add that to the base level. This protects you from paying out bonuses for efforts consistent with stagnant practice growth. Fully disclose to staff members how these numbers are being calculated prior to plan implementation. Remember, while you need to protect yourself from overpaying for status quo efforts, employees need to feel as though they can realistically reach these bonus levels or your plan will most certainly fail.

Production incentive plans

Another bonus plan that gets the entire staff involved is one based purely on production goals. For example, if your practice produces $4,000 on any given day, each employee becomes eligible for a ten dollar stipend. In order to realize this bonus income, the practice must produce $70,000 for the entire month. If this monthly goal is not accomplished, all eligible daily bonuses will be forfeited. When the practice produces $850,000 in any given year, each staff member will earn an additional $1,000. The extension of the daily goal to a more long-term objective again reinforces continued diligence from staff members even in times of business stagnation.

Hygienist incentive plans

A hygiene department bonus plan can be established, thereby directing the incentive to the faction of your business more responsible for practice production than any excepting restorative dentistry. It is estimated that diligent hygienists should produce roughly triple their wage. Therefore, identify that level as the baseline for your bonus plan. This amount includes any radiographs taken but excludes exams performed by the doctor. Any day your hygienist achieves production above this level, you pay out an additional ten dollar bonus. Graduate the bonus as the daily production increases. For example, at each $80 increment of production above the bonus level, an additional $5 will be awarded. Establish monthly and yearly goals for your hygienist as well, determining the bonus levels by tripling the monthly and yearly wage. Achieving monthly goals should be rewarded with an extra $100 and yearly goals with an additional $1,000. Instituting these long-term goals maintains staff focus and encourages perseverance even in the face of missed daily objectives.

Résumés

In your classified advertisement, be sure to ask applicants to email or fax their résumés and references. Résumés allow you the opportunity to take a first glance into an applicant's attention to detail, work experience and education. You will be surprised by some of the résumés you receive. Several years ago, I placed an ad for an *experienced* dental front office manager. Of the 20 applications I received, only four of the applicants had any experience in a dental office. One of the women had only worked as a cashier at a candy store. While her previous work experience may have helped send more patients to the dental office, she clearly did not have any dental front office experience.

My staff has joked about the idea of publishing a book filled with some of the comical résumés we have received. It never ceases to amaze me how many people seeking employment do not take the time to proof-read and perfect their résumés. Job experience and education are ignored if the résumé contains typos and clearly demonstrates lack of attention to detail.

Below are examples of résumés submitted to my practices over the years. No modifications have been made to the content, except for the elimination of the applicants' names and contact information:

> hi im a dantal assistant i got out of school last june and ive been   looking for a job in the field i would love to work at your office afew days aweek and i live close hope to hear from you soon and thanks for your time

To this I responded:

Dear (Applicant),

Not to be rude, but I would like to make some suggestions that might assist you in terms of securing employment. When you send an email or a résumé to a professional's office, it is always good to use appropriate spelling, grammar and punctuation. You need to pay attention to these important details if you expect a potential employer to take you seriously. There are so many errors in what appears to be the one sentence that you wrote to me that I cannot consider this a serious job application. For your benefit, I would suggest not communicating to health care professionals, or anyone for whom you are hoping to work, in the manner in which you might text message your friends. I hope I have been of some assistance to you with respect to your search for employment.

Good luck and best regards,
Ed Logan

I Ii,
I am seventeen and i would live to work as a dental assistant I live in the area. When I graduate I want to go into dental hygiene but need to figure out if I would like it first. I have never worked in a dental office before but would love to be trained. I am very absorbent with information and would love to lean. I'm a extremely friendly and outgoing girl how loves to put smiles on others faces. I was just curious what the hours were on wensdays and the mondays and fridays.
Thanks Alot.

I am in school for dental assistant i'm learning charting right now i would to be hands on i'm very dependable, hard worker and fast learner if i sound like something you may what you may call or e-mail me thank you for taking the time reading this

Summary of Qualifications:
Work well in fast pasted environment. Will maintain professionalism at all times.

> Dear Sir or Madam:
> Please except my resume in compliance with your request for the open position.
>
> I am detail orientated and can work with very minimal supervision. I have a very strong work ethic and look forward to a new challenges.

While we have all been responsible for undetected typos, the total lack of professionalism displayed in many of today's résumés seems to speak to the quality of work these applicants might perform. The world is now one dominated by quick communication, text messaging and absence of attention to detail. Unfortunately for these candidates, dentistry is a profession that requires detail and attention at all levels.

In contrast to those résumés with total lack of credibility, are those I receive when interviewing for the position of associate dentist. Many of these résumés have made me feel like a real underachiever when comparing my accomplishments with theirs. In fact, one applicant had so many varied experiences and previous professional job descriptions that my wife and I questioned whether the résumé was even authentic. My next thought was to wonder why this person would desire to lower himself to the position I had to offer him of associate dentist. This doctor had served as a pilot, naval officer, engineer, chemical researcher, owner of an ethanol production company and even a mortician. To post his entire résumé here would consume the remainder of this book.

Checking References

Many employers do not take the time to check references or verify the facts posted on résumés. Job seekers are aware of this tendency and may exaggerate or falsify information. Calling references can involve a game of phone tag, especially when you are trying to reach another dentist for a reference. However, this is a step that must be taken.

Most applicants will not want you to contact their current place of employment because they have not yet given notice of their departure. If you are highly confident in a potential candidate, you can check the older references first. You can then offer the job on the condition that you will be contacting the applicant's current employer for a reference once notice has been given and prior to the start date in your office.

The following is an excerpt from The McGill Advisory newsletter, highlighting the ways in which checking references for potential employees have changed in recent years:

> Traditionally, doctors have relied on potential candidates to supply job and personal references for them to check. Now, more dental practices are using online resources to do background checks and expanded checking using references not supplied by the potential new hire. Many practices are following the lead of other businesses by performing Google and Yahoo! searches of a candidate's name as a routine part of the new hire process.
>
> Moreover, professional networking sites such as Linkedin.com and Jobster.com are making it easier for employers to get in touch with those who have worked with job candidates in the past or know them personally. These sites, where people create online profiles and then link to professional colleagues who are also members, can be used to find mutual connections that doctors can contact for information. Many doctors even check to see if there are mutual connections with a candidate on Facebook.com and MySpace.com, the popular social networking sites.
>
> According to a March survey of The Ponemon Institute, a privacy think tank, 35% of hiring managers now use Google to do online background checks on job candidates and 23% looked people up on social networking sites. About one-third of those web searches led to rejections, according to the survey. Doctors often find that potential new hires post risqué photographs and provocative comments about drinking, recreational drug use and sexual exploits on these social networking sites. Practices are using these searches to find out

about a potential candidate's lifestyle to determine if it violates the core values of their practices. [14]

Interestingly enough, I had recently employed similar research techniques to learn more about a potential candidate just prior to reading this article. The results were consistent with the one-third that led to rejections. This candidate had a MySpace listing that was not privatized. His page revealed photos of drinking games played with fraternity brothers, which in and of itself was not a deal breaker. His profile offered more information about his motivation, "I'm all about the M. F****n' Paper Chase!" You will need to determine for yourself what values you would like your employees to bring to work with them. I am not particularly concerned with what this guy wants from his life, and I do not judge him for his desires. I merely think it is best to represent yourself professionally in arenas which may be evaluated by potential employers to make first impressions. A word to the wise for those dentists just out of school and looking to associate, it is always best to privatize your profile!

The Interview Process

Unfortunately, most hiring situations occur in the midst of time constraints and, on occasion, in an emergency situation requiring an immediate hire. You may feel that you need to hire the first person to successfully complete an interview without cursing the former dentist or using the words "totally" and "like" in every sentence. As much as possible, take your time and research as many candidates as is feasible. Remember, you may spend more wake time with your staff than you will your own family.

When allotted adequate time, the interview process can yield exactly the loyal employee for whom you are searching. One innovative interview technique was described by a practice owner on www.DentalTown.com, an interactive website providing dentists real-time professional information from peer dentists. The doctor described conducting an interview with eight candidates in one room, two of whom were actually current employees of his practice. The potential hires were asked to complete a number of standardized exams, including personality and IQ tests. They were encouraged to openly discuss their thoughts and answers with one another. The two mice in the field, of course, reported back to the doctor on which applicant they would hire if required to do so.

I found this technique simple yet ingenious, as it is a measure of true character more than it is a test of numbers and letters. I have always wanted to provide a standardized math test to front office candidates but never felt comfortable doing so. You can present a wide variety of assignments during the interview process, provided that they fall within the realm of the applicant's legal rights. Simply determine the skill set required for the position available, and test specifically for a candidate's strength in those areas.

If you receive a high quality résumé, you may need to contact the applicant quickly in order to avoid losing this candidate to another office. Some initial phone interview questions concerning availability and work experience can help to eliminate candidates and conserve time. When we last hired a front office manager, my business manager conducted phone interviews with eight applicants. She narrowed the field to three for face-to-face interviews with me. The phone interview is an effective time saver and a valuable step in beginning the interview process.

Our resource section includes candidate interview and applicant reference questions with space provided for you to record answers. The list is divided into initial questions to ask during the phone interview and follow-up questions to ask during the face-to-face interview.

The Employee Manual

At the time of hire, each staff member should receive a copy of your Employee Manual. This handbook details office policy relating to employee expectations and responsibilities. Included should be descriptions of dress code, job responsibilities, hours worked, vacation and sick pay, employee benefits including bonus programs and grounds for termination. Have each staff member sign a form indicating receipt of this manual and keep a copy in your employee file. Our Employee Manual can be accessed through the Practice Management Resources for Dentists section at the end of this book.

Hiring Mistakes

What do you do when all your due diligence and efforts to hire the ideal staff member backfire and you are left with an employee who makes you dread going to work each day? There is no perfect employee, just as there is no perfect employer. However, there are definite deal breakers when it comes to keeping an employee on staff. Do not hesitate to release an employee who is making your work life more difficult and less enjoyable. One such example is the staff member who seems to be a professional energy sapper. These people can quietly suck the life out of you and your practice.

My brother's role as CFO of a large corporation makes him responsible for the management of many more staff members than the typical dentist would ever be. He once explained to me that in every instance in which he terminated someone's employment, he wished he would have done it sooner. As dentists, we tend to care about people, perhaps more than we should at times.

We do not drift toward confrontation and we, like many people in management positions, do whatever we can to avoid uttering Donald Trump's famous edict, "You're fired!"

Again the example of buying a home or other tradable equity seems applicable; you make the money when you buy, not when you sell. When you hire correctly, you make money by avoiding the re-training costs associated with employee termination. When you hire incorrectly, no amount of training will help this person become the employee you desire. You will be forced to explain to a poor hire the same principle multiple times. It will become clear early on that certain employees will not assimilate new information and directives without repeated coaching. This type of person needs to be let go, and sooner than later.

The same standard can be applied to the energy draining staff member who persists with a sour attitude all day after earning a reprimand. This business is difficult enough without emotional drama following you around throughout your workday. The best way to deal with this type of behavior is to avoid it altogether. An astutely managed hiring process will help you along this path.

Once an employee has made it past the initial 60 - 90 day probationary period, it becomes more difficult to end employment without demonstrable reasons. I am reminded of the television show *The Office* and the manager Michael Scott's disdain for Toby, the H.R. employee he so desperately wanted to fire. Michael's boss insisted that the employee could not be fired without cause. Michael's retort was that he had *cause*, "It is beCAUSE I hate him!"

Your employee handbook should outline reasons for immediate termination, and grounds for dismissal within a warning period. It should also clearly delineate the dress code for your practice. I continue to be amazed at what some people believe to be appropriate fashion for a professional office environment. Our employee manual outlines the following behaviors that may result in immediate discharge:

- Conviction under any criminal code or law
- Falsification of information given for personnel records
- Insubordination, including but not limited to refusal to do assigned work that the employee is capable of doing
- Inability or neglect in the performance of duty, or neglect in the care of property
- Repeated and unexcused failure to notify the Business Manager of absence from work
- Theft or attempted theft of property
- Working under the influence of alcohol or illegal drugs, or possessing the same on the property of the practice
- Violation of established safe working procedures
- Neglect of HIPAA privacy practices established by the practice.

It is smart practice to document any behaviors or actions that are inconsistent with the expectations you have for your employees. Maintain a file for each employee in which you record these missteps. Whenever possible, if the error affects or involves another employee, have that employee initial the record as well. The employee file should also contain a record sheet listing positive performances to be referenced during job evaluations and bonus discussions.

Candidates for employment enter your office with their best foot forward. They can deceive even the most discerning of interviewers. They may even give the appearance of intellect through the masking agent of confidence. They may present in sheep's clothing while aspiring to embezzle you for all you are worth. These things may easily go undetected in an initial interview setting. They will, however, be less likely to go the distance if you have an extended working interview and trial period in place. Do not esteem yourself higher than that of the deceivers. They are professionals, just as you are a professional.

Five-Star Customer Service

Chapter 11

The Guest Mentality

Arguably the most productive way to grow your dental practice is by providing over-the-top customer service. Striving to achieve first class customer service in your office requires time, energy and commitment, but can yield greater returns on investment than any other form of practice marketing you may choose. Patients by and large remember more about the way they were treated by the doctor and staff than the way their treatment actually went. They are much more likely to refer friends and family to a kind, caring and friendly practice than they are to the cold natured health care practice with which we are all too familiar. Getting your staff members on board with this philosophy is imperative, and it all starts with getting them to understand it.

Dr. Tom Orent, owner of Gems Publishing, USA (www.GoldAutoPilot.com), is a dentist who has pioneered ground-breaking ideas on the dental practice customer service front. I have had the good fortune of attending one of his 1000 Gems Seminars, speaking with him personally, emailing practice management ideas with him and purchasing and employing many of his helpful teaching tools in my practices. In his publication, *Getting to Yes, Fast!* Dr. Orent, also known as *The Gems Guy*, details the importance of creating a guest mentality with each patient. He advises, "From the moment a patient walks through your door, until the time he/she leaves your office, pretend he/she is a guest in your home." [15] He adds, "Case acceptance is not readily improved by learning the proper closing techniques. The *close* starts from the minute they enter your practice—perhaps even before." [16]

While there are numerous ways in which to achieve this standard, it is clear that a capable staff and committed doctor are mandatory. As every person is unique, the technique tends to be more successful when individual personalities are taken into consideration. Some people are clearly uncomfortable taking their shoes off when they enter your home, while some who are not, perhaps should be. Too many words can be a turn off for some, whereas certain people seem to thrive on constant conversation. Standardizing the new patient experience is a good way to assure predictable staff behavior, but I have found customization of this procedure to be of greater benefit. One thing is certain; people enjoy it when they are treated as unique and relevant. So roll out the red carpet and assume the role of Dr. Hospitality!

The New Patient Phone Call

Handling the prospective patient's initial phone call with warmth and friendliness is of paramount importance to converting this person to a patient of record. This is the first item of training for any of our new personnel. Our phones are answered with a greeting of "Thank you for calling Dr. Logan's office. This is (name of employee.) How may I help you?" This is in contrast to the terse greeting extended so commonly in dental offices, "Doctor's office." My staff is trained in the importance of patience and understanding during this primary contact. Later in this book's insurance section, I discuss what information needs to be gathered during this phone call. However, we try to make this an easy process for the patient and not an interrogation.

At minimum, one rollover phone line should be available to ensure that patients are rarely, or, ideally, never greeted with a busy signal or voice mail message. Our staff staggers lunch breaks in order to provide phone coverage during a period of time when potential patients may have a respite from work. We forward our business line to a cell phone when the office is closed during regular business hours and a have a staff member answer these calls. We therefore have live phone coverage nine hours per day, five days per week. This is certainly far more than industry standard, but one new patient will prove considerably more valuable than the payroll costs you assume by keeping the phone covered. The telephone is the most valuable commodity of a growing dental practice.

During the initial phone call, we request the new patient's address in order to mail the patient forms, our most recent newsletter and some pertinent office information ahead of time. This simple step helps patients feel more acquainted with our office prior to their first appointment. We also use the patient's name in conversation to lend a more personal touch to the first inquiry phone call. Toward the conclusion of this call, we point patients to our website to download our new patient forms. This is yet another effort to help patients feel more comfortable with our office before ever walking through the front door.

It is common in marketing literature to suggest asking no questions of the potential new patient during the initial phone call. This is proposed as a means to endear the caller to your office by making the preliminary encounter smooth, efficient and pleasing for the new patient. After all, this person called you. Why should the patient have to answer a bunch of your questions? Perhaps the patient called to have you answer a few questions.

I am typically under time constraints when I place phone calls during the work day. I am generally in need of information quickly and do not enjoy being first interrogated before receiving the opportunity to submit my first question. The *20 Questions* game the gate keeper is required to play has always appeared to me as a road block in the way of our potential business relationship. Therefore, I am not opposed to training your staff member to kindly greet the new caller and then act as a catcher's mitt and information provider, responding to the patient's inquiries. After all, the primary goal of the new patient phone call is to get the patient scheduled. This is what the patients want as well, so why not provide it for them?

When I am greeted in this helpful manner, I am always surprised and impressed by this additional effort, as it is rarely delivered. This effort is atypical and stands out to the potential customer. Even if they are shopping around during the initial phone contact, patients may remember your kind, welcoming receptionist when it comes time to finally select one of their possible suitors. Do not burn bridges while pitting your office against patients by placing your desires to obtain information above their desires to do the same.

A modification to this zero questions technique is providing the caller all the information requested first, and subsequently gathering small amounts of data necessary for the efficient flow of the new patient appointment. This information might include the patient's contact information in case necessary schedule changes present and insurance information which allows you to obtain a pre-estimation of benefits for the patient. We have found this blended technique for handling the new patient phone call to be the most efficient and effective for our office. The patient will still feel valued and welcomed, and the staff will acquire the information necessary to make the new patient experience smooth, accurate and professional.

What's in a Name? Properly Greeting Patients

Front office employees should greet patients by name when they first walk through your door. If the employee is currently on the phone or with another patient, an attempt should still be made to greet patients and let them know they will be accommodated right away. This may sound like common sense, but the vast majority of medical offices do not treat patients in this manner.

I am reminded of sitting in the waiting room of my family physician's office when a woman walked in frantically informing the receptionist that she thought she was having a hypertensive attack. The receptionist told her to have a seat and someone would be with her shortly. We were the only two people in the waiting room and I observed this lady squirming in her chair as the time rolled by. Five minutes elapsed as I listened to the receptionist gossiping with a co-worker about someone else's life. I watched them file their nails and chat as the patient fidgeted nervously. Finally, the patient approached the window and asked if she could come in and have someone take her blood pressure. I was relieved that I would not now be called upon to administer CPR to one of my medical doctor's patients in his own office.

Though this true story may represent an extreme example, similar anecdotes involving the medical office witch-ceptionist abound. Given the fact that it is far more common for these employees to be aloof, cold and unfriendly, your efforts to train a staff to interact in the converse manner will not go unnoticed. When attempting to establish an insurance independent dental practice, it is mandatory to adopt an attitude of caring and concern for your patients. This practice philosophy falls under the auspices of internal marketing and will, over time, generate consistent patient referrals and a tremendously loyal patient base. Obtaining these two results should be the primary focus of your overall marketing campaign.

Insist that your receptionist makes every effort to remember family members' names and engage in conversation while your patients wait. This will help to put nervous patients at ease and lend a family atmosphere to your office. Have the front office manager make notes on the daily schedule regarding a patient's interests and family members' names to ensure that all staff members can make the patient feel important, valued and remembered. Include a dedicated page in the patient record that documents information unique to that patient, like the fact that he is fluent in Russian or that she was a competitive equestrian in her youth.

People tend to be fonder of their name than any other commodity they possess. This is true even if they would have rather been labeled something else at birth. This particular designation has accompanied them through every occasion in their lives. It was exclaimed during the first reprimand by their mother, pronounced by their teacher on the first day of school, whispered by their first girlfriend and recognized on graduation day. Their name is their identity. Remember it and you will go a long way toward remembering the name of a loyal patient for life.

Puttin' on the Ritz

Certain businesses simply rise above the rest in terms of the first impression they impart. Their business philosophy is clearly to place customer satisfaction above all else. These companies hire with this idea specifically in mind. The average worker applying for employment in these businesses will never be invited back for a second interview. To gain employment here you need to demonstrate drive, ambition and, most importantly, an outstandingly positive and energetic attitude. A sense of humor, wit and an inviting personality all come as prerequisites to join the workforce of these top companies as well.

Companies that come to mind are Southwest Airlines, Nordstrom and the Ritz Carlton Hotel. Employees here are trained to meet and exceed all customer expectations with every encounter. Flight attendants for Southwest Airlines can sometimes be mistaken for stand up comedians, helping to reduce some of the common anxiety related to flying. A sales associate at Nordstrom will walk around the length of the counter to hand you the bag containing your purchase, rather than merely handing the bag across the counter. She will stand beside you, smile warmly and thank you for your purchase. An employee at The Ritz will escort you to the restroom in response to your simple inquiry as to its whereabouts. Dr. Orent, in his pursuit of five-star customer service, recommends taking staff field trips to Nordstrom and The Ritz Carlton, in order for them to experience the guest mentality you are trying to portray in your office. He suggests taking your staff to The Ritz for lunch, and requesting to sit in a library or coffee room for an hour or so after lunch. Dr. Orent contends that, "The minimal cost involved will be repaid a thousand fold, once your staff perceives the extra special feeling; the aura of The Ritz!" [17]

These customer friendly businesses stand out because most companies seem to completely ignore the importance of customer service. In fact, many appear to make efforts to disregard the customer altogether or provide the impression that the patron is being a nuisance or otherwise unwanted. I am reminded of the airline incident experienced by Ben Stiller's character in *Meet the Parents*. After having endured the incessant typing and exorbitant fee offered by the flight attendant, Greg, R.N. is forced to wait in a line consisting solely of him. Finally, following the flight attendant's demand to check his carry-on luggage, Gaylord Focker snapped. All consumers have a tipping point. Try not to allow poor customer service to take them there.

The ignorance on the part of most businesses offers you the opportunity to attract new customers simply by bestowing at least a reasonable level of service. After having trained staff in this customer service philosophy at multiple practice locations, I am still amazed by how inept most businesses are in this area. I am at times offended by the lack of attention given to the consumer in many business environments. I recall a statement related by a former dental assistant, after having trained and worked in my office for several years. She confided, "Now when I go into other businesses I really notice how poorly the staff treats the customer. I get a bit frustrated because I feel truly disrespected! There clearly is a difference in the way we treat our patients."

Patients notice this difference too. They appreciate it, respect it and genuinely desire it. They will continually revisit the customer friendly business and they will refer friends and family members to such an establishment. They will satisfy the goals for which your entire marketing campaign exists, to obtain a base of loyal, repeat customers and a continuous flow of new ones.

New Patient Paperwork

Allowing patients the opportunity to complete the necessary new patient paperwork prior to their initial appointment provides a smoother transition when a new patient walks through your practice door for the first time. This can be accomplished by mailing new patients the paperwork in advance and maintaining a page on your website offering New Patient Forms to be downloaded and printed out. Many patients comment on the convenience and time savings this affords them considering their busy lifestyles. This is yet another simple step that distances your practice from other dental offices, reconfirming your commitment to offering a smooth, efficient appointment experience.

Whether new patients bring the completed forms with them or complete the paperwork in your office, thank them for taking the time to do so. The required completion of extensive forms containing redundant informational requests presents one more road block to the comfortable rapport you wish to establish with your new patients. As much as possible, keep the length of these forms to a minimum, while accurately gathering all the data necessary for the health and proper care of your patients.

New patient paperwork should include contact information, insurance data and a medical release form. Also, you will need to provide a HIPAA statement and obtain a patient signature acknowledging its receipt. Our new patient forms, accessible through the Practice Management Resources for Dentists section at the end of this book, include a page encouraging the patient to perform a Smile Evaluation. This tool allows us to subtly engage the patient about potential cosmetic interests, without judging them on apparent imperfections. It can also serve to stir up interest for these services and educate patients on what might be available for them in our office. Our smile evaluation form includes the following questions:

- Are you dissatisfied with the appearance of your smile?
- Do you have spaces or gaps between your teeth?
- Do you have old fillings or dental work which you perceive to be unattractive?
- Are your teeth (please check the following that apply): chipped, protruding, crowded or misshapen?
- If you could change one thing about your smile, what would it be?
- If we could offer you a simple and inexpensive way to whiten your teeth, would you be interested?
- How would you like your teeth to look in 15 years?

This simple Smile Evaluation allows an opportunity to engage the patient in conversation about possible cosmetic procedures, educate on dental hygiene for a life-long, beautiful smile and discuss the possibility of replacing old amalgam fillings. If a patient is able to complete this form at home, either through the new patient mailing or by downloading the forms from your website, more time can be spent on seriously considering this Smile Evaluation. You will have plenty of patients who provide humorous answers to the open-ended questions, particularly question #7. While most middle-aged patients respond, "Like they did when I was 20," our more mature patients often express, "Not in a cup," or "I'll be dead by then!" When asked if he was dissatisfied with the appearance of his smile, one patient responded, "My wife is."

Our forms also capture a dental history. This addition extends to our patients the impression of our care and concern for their individual experiences and inquiries, as well as their overall comfort. More important than anything this form can provide us is what it provides the patient in terms of the initial relief of dental anxiety that accompanies so many patients entering a new practice. Our dental history form includes the following questions:

- Do you feel nervous about dental treatment?
- What can we do to alleviate your nervousness?
- Have you ever had a bad experience in a dental office?
- What can we do to make this experience better for you?
- Do you have sensitive teeth?
- Does food trap between your teeth?

- Do you think you have active decay or gum disease?

A number of comical responses to question #4 above have provided some levity to the day at times. Among others, "Vodka," "Beer" and "Dancing bears" come to mind.

Practice Management

Chapter 12

Time and Efficiency for the Dentist

I began my college career majoring in business, mainly because I had no idea what I wanted to do with my life. After a couple years of padding my GPA, I decided to make a U-turn and attempt to gain admission into dental school. This redirection obviously required quite a heavy load of science courses in my final two years of undergraduate work. Accumulating the necessary credit hours of chemistry, physics and biology, I graduated with a major in psychology and minor in biology. I never forgot, however, the most important lesson I believed to have learned from my earlier business classes, that of time and efficiency.

I recall being fascinated with the time and efficiency studies major corporations conducted in order to achieve maximum productivity. *Touch each document only once, thoroughly absorb it and assimilate it to ensure that no time is wasted revisiting this text. Do things right the first time so you only have to do them once. Never retrace your steps.* Millions of dollars were spent on these studies, and apparently the companies funding them found value in their investments.

We know that perhaps in no other profession is the adage, *Time is money*, more appropriate than it is in dentistry. We can learn a lot from the studies on time and efficiency. The more we learn about efficiency in the practice of dentistry, the greater productivity we will be able to achieve, the less time we will waste while at work and the less stressful our days will become. The more we are able to apply that knowledge, the more profitable our businesses will ultimately be.

Dr. Efficiency

The CEO Dentist is in no way a workaholic. I am not advocating more time spent at work. This is borne out in this chapter's discussion of the low overhead practice operating productively on a three-day workweek. Producing high volumes of dentistry can be important to revenue flow. More important to profitability, perhaps, is learning to collect what you produce and to limit your overhead. When these things are not accomplished, where is the importance of producing the dentistry? Is it an exercise in futility? Is it fruitless labor?

My strongest memory of fruitless labor resulted from a weekend at my in-laws. My wife's father is a melon farmer, taking pride in being completely self-sufficient. Spending summer weekends at the farm typically requires turning vines and picking melons. Having no childhood experience with farming, most of the process seemed very foreign to me. Since I am not afraid to get my hands dirty, I jumped right in. Prior to marrying his daughter, I had to earn my mettle on the family farm. One weekend the home's septic system became clogged, and nothing would flush. The congestion was in the underground pipes which were supposed to drain out into the field.

While other people in a similar situation might have called a plumber, my father-in-law called his son, who conveniently owned a backhoe. Having no idea where the actual blockage was, we dug randomly into the earth, hoping to cause an outpouring of stench. When all we got was drizzle, we attempted to manually open the floodgates by digging with our hands. More drizzle. We dug for hours. It seemed to me that we were digging much too far downstream, given that no significant drainage was occurring on this end. Being new to the family, knowing little about melon farming and less about unearthing septic pipes, I dug on. Finally, I suggested that maybe we should take the backhoe up the hill and dig closer to the source.

With one punch of the backhoe into the ground, Mount St. Helens erupted and trips to the restroom returned to normal. If there is one thing I know about, it is how to work efficiently. I was glad to have been able to throw my skill set into the mix to get this problem solved. Though your problems as business owner will not typically be so foul, you will be called to maximize your time and eliminate efforts that bear no fruit. Dr. Efficiency is a master at maximizing time whenever it becomes available, both clinically and executively.

You are Master of the Ship

Just as controlling costs is important to maximizing business profits, efficient use of your time at work is imperative to generating optimal revenues in the most compressed period of time. This resourceful management of your occupational schedule not only assists with cost control but also supplies additional hours for you to enjoy activities away from work. Time and efficiency applications are not only important to clinical procedural management, but also to the management of your business. This in many ways can be considered to be your own self-management with respect to running your practice.

Though certain responsibilities can and should be delegated to a capable front office manager, many dentists under-appreciate their roles in efficiently managing their businesses. The more involved the dentist, the more assured the business owner is that systems are operating optimally and that money is not slipping through the cracks. The more attention the doctor is able to devote to the specifics of the business itself, the less the dentist will be required to cut teeth in order to make the same living.

I often hear dentists express, "I don't like running the business. I just want to do dentistry." While I can appreciate this sentiment, when minimal consideration is given to the business aspects of the practice, maximal dentistry will be required solely to keep the business afloat and the dentist's lifestyle supported. In the untimely event that producing large volumes of dentistry is no longer an option, it would certainly behoove the doctor to have had some awareness of where the profits have gone.

Fortunately, business management is a skill we can learn and improve upon, just like any other. As with dental procedural efficiency, over time doctors can identify those things which make them more proficient with respect to time allotted to business related tasks. Learning to exploit the time one has away from patients to hammer out business tasks is of highest priority. Since dentists tend to run their practices in the slim margins of time in which they are not treating patients, efficient use of this time is a must. This way, while at work and reviewing profit/loss statements, you will not become too disheveled when the office manager pulls you away to interview a dental assistant or fix the compressor that just stopped working!

Get Organized!

I can think of very few occupations in which the laborer is responsible for job accountability in perpetual five minute intervals. Dentists are notorious for attempting to fill every kernel of open time in their schedules. They feel they are not being as productive as possible if they are not continually whipping around the office. Contrast this with the cubicle employee working for the average corporation. Peter Gibbons from *Office Space* summed it up best, "I probably put in about 15 minutes of real, actual work in any given week."

Working to improve organizational skills often helps doctors become more efficient at conquering business tasks. At any point during the day, your desk will be covered with items of varying importance. Determining their order of importance, and tackling that which holds the most value in its completion will ensure greatest productivity. As one busy ophthalmologist running a multi-doctor practice once framed it up, "The important stuff always makes its way to the top of the pile."

My wife never understood why leaving some portion of clothes sticking out of the dresser drawers seemed to bother me, or why I arranged my shoes one next to the other in the closet. Fortunately for her, she is clutter blind. Not so lucky, I tend to notice the defects in our imperfect world. A good friend of mine, an optometrist running his own business, once described to Katie his feeling, "When I see clutter, I think, *clutter*! I have to first organize my surroundings before I can work in them." She later confided in me that his statement made her empathetically think; *Aw, now I know how Ed feels*.

While obsessing over clutter control clearly inhibits efficiency, organizing your workplace is mandatory to the effective management of your business. Some doctors are naturally skilled in this area, while others are noticeably more challenged. Delivering clinical dentistry efficiently requires clear organization of thought in order to replicate procedural sequences in the most productive manner. Likewise, running one's business profitably entails this same dedication to organizational thought. We can all improve our skill in this with time and effort. The more we are able to approach our workday with reproducible patterns which are thought through in advance, the more smoothly the day will progress and the more likely we will be to stay on schedule. It is not such a bad thing to keep your thirst for organization in check, however. Taking care of our first child has made me realize that my house will never be free from clutter again. Somehow I have become okay with that.

Scheduling for Production

A comprehensive review of a patient's day at the dentist would not be complete without a discussion of how the patient got on the schedule in the first place. Whether the staff is dealing with a new patient phone call or appointing an existing patient for treatment, exercising control over the dentist's schedule is a must. The most productive offices schedule for production. When patients are tucked into openings at random, you risk working a completely full day with relatively low productivity. While being busy is important, being productive is imperative.

The best way to ensure productivity is to guide your patients into the slots most beneficial to your practice. It is of great benefit to schedule the most challenging and more productive procedures in the morning hours. This not only assures that the day's labor will be fruitful, but that the doctor will enter these demanding situations with the bucket of energy being most full. Have your staff leave these blocks of time open until productive dentistry assumes them. If these slots remain unoccupied two days in advance, attempts should be made to fill them with any available treatment, including consults and emergencies.

Early morning and evening hours are always the easiest to fill. Therefore, train your staff to first offer the more difficult to schedule time slots to patients. When patients are encouraged to choose from one of two available appointment times, for example, 10 a.m. and 2 p.m., they will typically make arrangements to be available at these times. Only when patients refuse to schedule or these challenging appointment times are occupied should a staff member offer the most valuable time slots to your patients. These prized times can be filled more easily at the last minute.

We request credit card information from each new patient scheduling an initial appointment. Though this may serve to turn some people off to our otherwise welcoming office environment, it does protect us from the overhead burden of a failed appointment. This protocol also apprises patients of the inherent value of the appointments they are scheduling. I am relatively lenient on a patient who has a valid excuse for missing an appointment, and I even credit the understandable, "I'm sorry, I forgot!" excuse. Of course, when it happens again, I am a little less forgiving. I am more concerned with the patient who blatantly disregards our business needs, or disrespects us altogether.

We offer email reminders one month in advance of a scheduled recall and request that the patient confirms receipt of this contact. We reinitiate the reminder two days prior to the appointment to ensure against patients overlooking their commitments. With today's technology, unless a true emergency arises, it is virtually inexcusable for a patient to fail an appointment without at least 48 hours' notice.

Below is a list of 10 suggestions for daily schedule control offered by the editor of *The Profitable Dentist* newsletter (www.theprofitabledentist.com), Dr. Woody Oakes, a pioneer in dental practice management, taken from his book *The Winning Combination*:

1. A year in advance mark off all holidays, vacations or other times you will be out of the office.
2. Be aware of other trends throughout the year, and plan accordingly. For example, you may want to work extra days to accommodate your preschool checkups.
3. Patients should be *guided* into those times which are best for you.
4. Fill the block times first (maximum production procedures). It should not bother you to have the block unfilled for Thursday if today is Monday.
5. Once the block is filled, you can schedule the busy work around it.
6. Always try to fill the hard-to-fill times first; the popular appointment times can easily be filled with short notice.
7. Ten-minute time units are more productive. It is necessary for you to determine how much time is required for each procedure to schedule properly.
8. Remember that the doctor cannot be two places at the same

time. He can, however, do a denture adjustment while another patient is getting numb.
9. You would be wise to maintain a call list in case of no-shows.
10. It is sometimes difficult to work in emergencies, but all emergencies should be seen that day. However, you should try not to make a good patient wait for a toothache patient who comes in every five years. Sometimes emergencies can be seen at the end of the day or just before lunch. This is a problem in all offices, but you should never turn down an emergency patient. At least get the patient into the office. [18]

Scheduling for production is of utmost importance to the efficient flow of your practice. This can mean different things to different dentists. Scheduling for the dentist's actual time in the operatory as opposed to the full time a crown prep procedure will take, for example, exposes the wasted time that is otherwise hidden. This method allows you to fit more procedures in per day by knowing exactly how long the doctor will be needed in each operatory. Performing the most involved procedures in the morning when energy levels are peaked aids in reaching daily production goals while supporting accuracy, quality and attention to detail.

Scheduling quadrant dentistry on multiple teeth reduces subsequent appointments for the same procedures and limits the number of times patients require anesthesia in the same area. Sterilization expenses, staff time with respect to set up and break down and costs associated with arranging appointments and collections are all preserved. Patients of course appreciate fewer injections and less time away from home or work.

Strategically placing exams, consults and emergency evaluations in the afternoon allows the doctor to *wind down* toward the end of the day. When reviewing the daily schedule before work, the doctor can feel encouraged to invest ample energy in the morning to complete the more difficult procedures, knowing that a cooling off period is coming after lunch. The ideal schedule contains 80% of daily production in the first half of the day and 20% in the second half. Efficiency is increased and profitability enhanced when doctors tackle the more challenging procedures with a full tank. Exercising this control over the schedule also serves to relieve one of the impression that the practice is running the doctor.

Though jumping from chair to chair is a common practice in dentistry, it is not always the most efficient or productive use of one's time. Working on one person at a time can be highly productive if properly planned. If your hygienist is still involved in a recall prophy at the time you are available to perform the exam, it is often beneficial to do the exam when the time best suits you. This not only prevents the hygienist from unnecessarily waiting for you while you complete a procedure (which all hygienists love, of course), but also eliminates later interruptions at a more inconvenient time when you may be involved with other business management tasks. This practice of efficiency helps to ensure that patients are not made to wait and that your schedule remains on time.

Practice management consultant Cathy Jameson (www.jamesonmanagement.com) offers the following suggestions:

> Limiting stress needs to be a goal in your practice that receives the attention and commitment of everyone on the dental team.
>
> The person responsible for the appointment book must have the ability, the education, the time and the desire to make each day successful.
>
> A month that is made up of evenly productive days will be less stressful than a month that is full of high-and low- income days.
>
> To determine your monthly goal:
> --calculate how much it costs to run your practice per month;
> --add to this the amount of salary and compensation you desire;
> --add a percentage of planned profit.
>
> Total these three areas to determine the amount of

revenue your practice needs to produce every month. This is your monthly production goal.

A daily goal provides the dental team with a means to monitor progress and determine if the practice is on or off course.

The idea is to have 12 equally productive months in the year so that you do not get to the end of the year and wonder how your practice fared financially. [19]

Office Design and Equipment Choices for Efficient Flow

Design to avoid bottlenecking

When designing your office first make a mental image of the eventual flow of patients through your practice. Envision areas of potential staff and patient bottlenecking and construct your office to avoid them. Ergonomic equipment choices and wide operatories permit freedom of movement for both patients and staff. Operatories with an open entrance and a pass-through at the foot of the chair allow smooth flow of traffic. Organize equipment and supplies to be within arm's length of doctor and staff while working. Design your office to reduce the number of steps a provider is required to take to get from one destination to another.

My current office design incorporates a pass-through sterilization area, open on each end and devoid of doors. When one staff member enters from the left, the other exits to the right. Not only does this design serve to increase efficiency, but also to reduce the stress associated with a claustrophobic work environment. The sterilization cabinets were designed with openings in the counter tops to discard sharps and waste without having to touch handles or open doors. The sink is positioned in between the contaminated area to its left, containing the ultrasonic cleaner, and the sterile area to its right, supporting drawers for clean instruments and tray set-ups. The natural flow is to discard sharps and waste on the left first, place instruments in the ultrasonic then the autoclave, then bag and set up clean instruments to the right. The omission of this seemingly apparent design element invites multiple daily traffic jams, compromising office efficiency.

Our laboratory was intentionally positioned out of the path of travel of any patient or other staff member not requiring entrance into the lab. A tavern style swing door was installed to facilitate opening and avoid handle contamination from dirty gloves. The doctor's office is positioned out of the flow of traffic and can be accessed via a back entrance. This reduces bottlenecks and eliminates that uncomfortable walk of shame through the waiting room in the eventuality that the doctor arrives late for work.

Design for ergonomics

Though many dentists express discontent with European style delivery systems, I enjoy the ergonomics and efficiency of clinical delivery these units offer. This design allows you to position the handpieces and instruments over the patient's chest, permitting easy access and rapid delivery. While some doctors contend that the proximity of equipment to the patient's body may be a source of anxiety, I have yet to hear that complaint from a patient in over of decade of experience using these systems. Operatory cabinetry should be designed with openings in front and back, allowing access to preassembled procedural trays. Any operatory design that reduces the requirement to bend, twist or reach will help the dentist and staff stay healthy and practice longer, with more fluidity and greater efficiency.

Digital radiography

Digital radiography is perhaps the most time-conserving product introduced to dentistry in over a decade. The immediacy with which we are able to capture, view and store images dramatically reduces waste in the form of time, materials and maintenance. The purchase of a digital panorex machine has brought me closer to realizing a dental equipment expenditure that actually pays for itself than any other. Patients love having the ability to visualize their x-rays larger than life, virtually instantaneously. I love the fact that all exam and recall appointments requiring radiographs are nearly 20% less costly to my business in terms of time allotment alone.

There is no lag time for film processing, no processor to purchase (a large expense), no messy developing liquid (which quickly expires) and no films to mount. I have yet to encounter a film processor that lived beyond the tender age of three without major reconstruction being necessary. Its early demise typically occurs in the middle of a busy day when x-rays are absolutely necessary to complete the day's procedures, particularly during the molar root canal you are doing at the time.

We have no time to waste in our work environment. Everything is scheduled in small increments of time and if something happens to delay a procedure, our whole day gets pushed behind. You know the stress that accompanies being behind all day and making patients wait far too long in your reception area. Digital x-rays help relieve this burden. They can even help you catch up when you are running late. They are immediate!

Though some digital x-ray systems require you to scan the films for a short period of time, the more efficient systems do not demand this. We use a digital panorex and three different sizes of intraoral sensors, all requiring no developing, scanning or processing. Patients routinely comment on how much more comfortable the sensors are than traditional films which tend to pinch tissue with their sharp edges. I continue to be amazed at how quickly the entire x-ray process is completed. Once the staff has learned the nuances of the technique, there is really nothing to it.

While time and efficiency benefits are merely one of the myriad advantages to employing digital radiography, there still remains resistance from some dentists. There seems to be a learning curve with digital x-rays, and each system is vastly different from the other. I find that when comparing even the highest quality digital film to processed film, the contrast of traditional film allows for better diagnostic clarity. Others may disagree with that assessment, and technology will certainly improve with time, but other indisputable advantages of digital film abound. Digital x-rays clearly demonstrate less radiation output. We recently had our machines tested and they were found to emit no measurable radiation. Patients appreciate that, as do I given the fact that my staff members and I are the ones on location all day while x-rays are being taken.

Virtual reality glasses, TVs and headphones

We utilize VR glasses in our practice primarily for anxiety reduction, but also for the procedural efficiency they afford us. Having televisions or music headphones in each operatory serves these purposes as well. The distraction a patient can find in a dramatic movie or a favorite tune creates an amnesiac quality with respect to the passage of time. When we are in another operatory checking a hygiene patient, our entertained restorative patient will not mind so much that we are gone for a few minutes. Given that responses to open-ended questions and idle chit-chat cut into our allotted procedural time more than anything else, eliminating these things just got a whole lot easier.

Having offered the use of virtual reality glasses in my practices for a dozen years, I can think of no greater patient pleaser that I have been able to provide. "It's like I'm not even here" "I can't hear the drill or see what you're doing. I love that!" "Wow, that crown was fast! Time just flew by with these glasses on." These glasses make an efficient appointment appear even more so to the patient.

We hang VR glasses in each operatory in clear view of the patient. You can purchase various types of these glasses on www.iglasses.com. The price will vary depending upon the quality of the glasses. I would encourage you not to try and save money by selecting the cheapest pair. Theses glasses will be assuming significant wear and tear, and you want them to hold up over time. You can, however, conserve money by purchasing inexpensive DVD players to support the VR glasses. We bought several portable DVD players for $40 each and positioned one in each operatory. We have a laminated list of movies, some in 3D, from which our patients can choose. We also encourage them to bring their own movies if they so desire.

Though the benefit of having patients wear the VR glasses is huge, you often have to press the issue to get them to do so. Most parents know that using the glasses on their children will provide a great distraction. Convincing adults to use them, on the other hand, is not always such an easy task. I have my dental assistant almost insist, unless the patient is completely against the idea. After the initial "No, that's alright," response we find so common, my assistant offers, "Are you sure? They are really good at taking your mind off the appointment.

You can't hear the drill going and you don't have to look at the doctor's instruments."

Patients typically do not understand their value until they give the glasses a try. They certainly do not appreciate the reduction in your stress and amount of time sacrificed chatting. Nor do they grasp your increase in productivity through efficiently delivering the dentistry. The manner in which we offer the glasses almost assures their acceptance. More than nine out of ten patients wear them during restorative procedures.

I am reminded of a colleague who has the glasses sitting in his operatories, but does not use them. I inquired, "Do your patients love those things, or what?"

"I never really use them," he responded.

"What?" I inquired. "Why not?"

"I don't find that my patients have much interest in them," he answered.

"Have you ever encouraged your patients to try them out?" I asked. "Do you even ask if they may be interested in them?"

"No, not really," he laughed.

Though it may seem tedious to get this system going, using the VR glasses will save you time and money and create the *Wow* factor in patients that even your best internal marketing can ever hope to achieve. You have to press on through the initial patient resistance though. You have to at least ask!

Two-way radios for efficient communication

Many large practices have found great value in the use of radios which permit doctor and staff communication while eliminating the time wasting necessity to *walk to talk*. On a recent tour of a local orthodontist's office remodel, I had the opportunity to see this technology in action. This doctor's practice is so expansive that before he installed this new communication system, the need for his staff to ever exercise outside of work appeared minimal. The command center in the back room housed a collection of wires that, when assembled together, may have spanned the many miles from his practice back to my office. Given my less than positive experiences with computer system installation and networking in my office, I shuttered to think of all the brain power invested to coordinate this lattice. Fortunately for this orthodontist, he had hired the right team of skilled professionals to pull this off for him.

The radio communication in this doctor's office was accompanied by a video monitoring system with cameras and screens in nearly a dozen locations. Staff, patients and associate doctors were continually being observed while performing their tasks. The visual component of this complex was intended to facilitate doctor/staff communication by apprising the doctor of when he was needed in the treatment rooms. Though this is a great tool for communicative efficiency, staff members willing to relinquish their privacy to this degree may require additional compensation.

The benefits of this type of system are plentiful. It obviously reduces disruptions to the natural flow of the business. It allows staff members to announce patient arrivals, the need for hygiene exams, emergency patients added to the schedule, the presence of sales associates and return phone calls holding without ever leaving the comfort of their work stations or operatories. Certain doctors are utilizing a system called Vocera (www.Vocera.com), which appears a good alternative to two-way radios. There is no doubt that these systems improve efficiency in the dental office. I just had a hard time getting past the 1990's Bobby Brown concert headsets the staff was required to wear around the office.

Clinical Efficiency and Material Selection

When working multiple restorative operatories simultaneously, procedural time management and proper delegation of duties becomes imperative. As doctors gain experience, they typically learn how to most efficiently perform procedures. This generally means never allowing down time while awaiting patients to get numb or materials to set up, nor having the doctor perform tasks which other personnel are qualified to complete. The most important clinical efficiency skill a dentist can master is how to take full advantage of any wait time by performing other tasks which will eventually be necessary to complete. In other words, eliminate all wasted time.

Capitalize on wait time

When scheduled procedures incorporate both the upper and lower arches, anesthetizing the upper arch first allows the doctor to begin treatment in the maxilla while awaiting mandibular arch anesthesia. A capable dental assistant can preserve time during a fixed prosthodontic procedure by loading a silicone-based preoperative impression with temporary material in anticipation of final impression removal. This pre-operative impression will ideally be captured while awaiting patient anesthesia, further maximizing potential down time. This impression can be stored for the potentiality that a patient loses a temporary and requires a re-fabrication.

Eliminate unnecessary procedural steps

Another important way in which we can conserve time is by learning which steps in our method really have no reason for being there. A true master of efficiency will only perform actions absolutely necessary, without compromising clinical integrity. I am convinced that if you polled any of my former dental assistants, you would find me left wanting in this area. Though I know I should, I still have problems obeying their request to "Stop dinking around, Dr. Logan!" I am also quite certain that even though I may believe it to be so, there is really no material improvement in my work when I mess around searching for perfection. In fact, our work may be better when we just do what we know how to do and get out of there. The business strategist and aptly labeled *Father of modern management*, Peter Drucker, may have put it best when he stated, "There is nothing so useless as doing efficiently that which should not be done at all."

Trial and error

The most sweeping dental efficiency cost savings comes with clinical experience through trial and error. Dentists learn by practicing what works for them and what does not. I have found that trying to be the hero by attempting feats never before described in the literature usually results in more trouble than it is worth. There are reasons we are taught to do things the way we are. Certainly, we can learn new techniques and improve our clinical prowess through continuing education, study and practice. I make every effort to operate in the most clinically efficient manner possible. I make an even greater effort to learn from the history of my clinical practice missteps. The more we can eliminate the costly steps in our procedures that bear no fruit, the more efficient doctors we become. I try to keep in mind Albert Einstein's definition of insanity: "Doing the same thing over and over again and expecting different results."

Isolate and visualize adequately

Isolating multiple quadrants with a rubber dam or Isolite (www.isolitesystems.com) can enhance the dentist's ability to treat numerous teeth without oral structures inhibiting vision. The Isolite system advances the concept of the rubber dam by not only providing isolation, but illumination and aspiration as well. This system allows isolation of maxillary and mandibular quadrants simultaneously, along with retraction of the tongue and cheek. It includes a bite block for patient comfort and enhanced access. It continually aspirates fluids and oral debris and delivers bright intraoral illumination. The Isolite system seems ideal for the doctor assuming the role of All-in-One Dentist, as it consumes many functions of the dental assistant. It also comes in handy when the doctor is called into the office after hours to single-handedly treat an emergency.

Visual magnification in the form of loupes or magnified eye glasses is the closest thing to a mandatory purchase for clinical dentistry that I can imagine. Unless your vision is that of Albert Pujols, your dentistry could also likely benefit from the enhanced clarity that magnification affords. Many companies compete for your business in this arena. I have both OraScopic 3.5x and Designs for Vision 2.5x glasses, having used the latter pair since dental school. I can think of no other investment in the area of dentistry which has offered me such longevity. My OraScopic lenses are accompanied by a fiber optic headlamp. Increased visibility supports efficiency because, when you can see something clearly, you can do it right the first time and eliminate the need to revisit your work. Many of these manufacturers purport an added benefit of ergonomics related to their products. I have yet to find the pair of glasses which allows me to sit up straight with my head up and eyes facing straight forward, while still permitting me to visualize the operative field. I am open to suggestions.

Utilize auto-mix and fast-set materials

Appropriate clinical material selection can augment procedural efficiency as well. Doctors adept at working expediently can take advantage of certain fast-set impression, bite registration and temporary materials. Auto-mix materials dispensed from guns reduce time, material waste and clean up procedures. Use of a temporary cement such as Systemp from Ivoclar that comes out 100 % in the temp, leaving no cement residue to clean up from the prep not only expedites the try in process but also eliminates the need to scale vital dentin. This may save additional time by reducing the need for anesthetic. Consider mixing a small amount of Vaseline in with the temporary cement for preps with adequate mechanical retention.

Dr. Scott Perkins has developed a series of instructional videos and clinical aids stressing efficiency through utilizing time which may be ordinarily wasted. His *15 Minute Crown Prep* technique arranges the necessary steps in this procedure in the most efficient manner possible. Dr. Perkins contends that it is not so much about doing things quickly as it is about using your time most effectively. He emphasizes the use of timers to ensure that you are staying on pace during the procedure. This effectively reduces my most inefficient clinical tendency, dinking around. These timers are pre-programmed to give an audible alert when, for example, materials should be set up or anesthesia should be profound.

Dr. Perkins has also designed a countertop holster for storing the multiple auto-mix guns he recommends using in his videos. He stresses the importance of fast-set and auto-mix materials, most of which come in guns of some type. I have employed Dr. Perkins' gun holster and *15 Minute Crown Prep* video, and discussed with him the magic of his techniques. He shared with me in one conversation the reliability of his *15 Minute Molar Endo* technique, though I have yet to embark on this mission. I do not think many of the endodontists to whom I have referred have done so either. Though I have not been able to match the speed of Dr. Perkins, the pace at which I am able to render restorative dentistry has increased through efficiency to a point of my own satisfaction. Anyone can do this. You just need to eliminate the waste.

Six-handed dentistry

Most people talk about four-handed dentistry as the ideal method for efficient delivery of restorative dentistry. Contrary to the adage about too many cooks in the kitchen, the more hands you have in the mouth, the faster you can be. Oral surgeons are masters of six-handed dentistry. While the surgeon has two hands in the mouth, one assistant aspirates and maintains the airway and another passes instruments to the doctor. If you ever observe or assist other types of surgeons at work, you will notice a number of people in the room assisting with the procedure. The sooner the exposed patient can be sealed from the external environment and brought off sedative anesthesia, the better. Clearly, efficiency is of utmost importance here.

While a properly trained dental assistant can assure continuous preparation of involved teeth through adequate evacuation and mouth mirror cleansing, who is handing you the materials and instruments? I am almost certain you can envision a time when you were required to wait on your assistant during a procedure. How many times do you suspect having two more hands would have reduced your stress and allowed you to complete your procedure more rapidly?

The obvious resistance to six-handed dentistry arises from the additional payroll necessary to accommodate two more hands in the operatory. Since the dental assistant typically occupies the lowest position on the salary totem pole, an efficiently scheduled, productive practice will be readily able to afford this addition. The doctor's time is worth so much more, and when forced to wait on an assistant, that valuable time is unnecessarily wasted. Give six-handed dentistry a try and see how fast you can be. You may have to go home early, or possibly cut back your weekly work schedule. And what a shame that would be.

Whether you choose to operate with two assistants or one, it is your responsibility to train these employees on how to make your visit to the operatory most efficient. This requires communication, feedback, time and energy on your part and willing and capable participants on their part. Before long, a skilled and motivated dental assistant will have the restorative heart of your practice banging on all cylinders.

A good assistant will take personal responsibility for the successful, expedient completion of your restorative procedures. This ideal team member will have your room set up correctly before you make your entrance. You should be able to sit down, focus your eyes on the anesthetized teeth and never have to look up until you are finished. Practicing consistency in terms of your procedural sequence allows the assistant to anticipate your needs. When you are haphazard or inconsistent, you cannot expect an assistant to follow your train of thought. Efficiency in the restorative operatory comes with proper coaching and replication of a predefined order of actions.

An example of this dental assisting efficiency taken to the extreme came to me when I was just out of school and practicing as an associate. Most of my experience with dental assistants to that point had been with those salaried workers in dental school who would occasionally drop by the operatory to assist me with shade selection. I remember thinking; *I don't need you to help me pick out a shade. I need someone to suction for me so I can use my mirror!* Suffice it to say, we were doing most of our own assisting. Expecting very little from this temporary assistant my boss had hired, I entered the operatory. It turned out that this assistant received her training in the military, and this training immediately stood out as vastly different from that of those on the dental school dole. She had my patient lying back in the chair, mirror and explorer in her hand, waiting for me to get to work. I was initially so disheveled that I did not know quite what to do. "Looks like you're ready for me, huh?" I uttered. "Yes sir, Doctor," she replied. I was glad to finally be out of dental school!

Delegate, delegate, delegate!

Laws vary from state to state with respect to which procedures your auxiliaries are allowed to perform. Some states such as Washington permit restorative hygienists to do much of the dentistry that does not involve diagnosis and cutting teeth. I have a friend who disclosed to me several years ago that he was paying his restorative hygienist $120,000/year. Listening to his staff spin stories about what a mess he was on days she was absent from work, she certainly appeared worth every penny to him. I suppose going to work for him was a completely different adventure when he was the one who actually had to do the dentistry!

Many states are quite liberal when it comes to procedures allowed to be performed by expanded functions dental assistants. Most states permit the registered dental assistant to take on a wide range of functions. Many states allow placement of rubber dams and sectional matrices, staining and glazing CERECs, trying in partial and complete dentures, taking preliminary impressions, performing in-office bleaching and fabricating night guards. You should hire with the idea in mind that you are going to allow your dental assistants to do everything they are permitted to do by law. It would behoove you to become comfortable with delegation of duties if you ever hope to carry your practice to the level of optimal profitability.

Do Not Micromanage

Since you are the boss, you are in high demand throughout the day. Staff members left unchecked will run every imaginable detail by you for approval. Questions arise that could be addressed at a later time, or could be self-explanatory if the team member were properly trained. When addressing important responsibilities or making significant calculations regarding your business, you should be left uninterrupted unless a true emergency arises. It is your responsibility to inform your staff of the importance of this time to the business. What the staff commonly considers an emergency very rarely warrants immediate attention.

Train your staff members to keep a log of the questions and concerns they feel require your attention and present them to you twice daily, at lunch and at the end of the day. Many times this empowers staff members to ascertain the answers on their own, eliminating the disruption of your productive work pattern. It is completely inefficient for you as the business owner, manager and dental provider to also serve as the sounding board for every perceived "emergency" in your office. By outlining this behavior in the beginning and defining for your staff members the importance to their employment of your being allowed time to complete these tasks, you can assuage the perception that you are aloof and unapproachable.

One of the best approaches to staff management protocol I have found is outlined in the book, *The One Minute Manager*. [20]One fundamental concept this book offers is that staff micromanagement is one of the least effective means to inspire exceptional performance. When employees are conditioned to expect that the boss will swoop in and save the day whenever they become entangled in a difficult project, they will wait for the boss to do so. They will never feel encouraged to seek the solution on their own. They may also feel intimidated that an incorrect decision will invite interrogation and punishment.

The One Minute Manager, on the other hand, is more detached than most employees find comfortable. This manager is no manager at all, in the traditional sense of the word. The employees are given responsibility to do their jobs on their own, because these are their jobs, not those of the manager. After the initial period of fright and discomfort dissipates from the mindset of the employee, real progress can be made. This progress has been shown to be far more advanced than that of the micromanaged employee. The definition of a good employee is one who embraces this level of autonomy after the shortest period of anxiety.

Though certain staff members are not interested in much more than the paycheck, motivated employees can achieve remarkable levels of personal growth through this process. It is as if they are the boss. They are expected to perform as such, as if their decisions are important and critical to the company's success. The best employees find deep value in this type of management. Typically, after a period of disdain and resentment for the boss, an all-star staff member who really gets it will end up appreciating the One Minute Manager, and desire to work for no one else.

When hiring, keep in mind the need to seek out the personality type that is able to handle this kind of management. The ideal candidate will do well with very little management at all. This candidate will reward your practice with fewer headaches for you and greater productivity for your business. In the words of the business management theorist Peter Drucker, "Most of what we call *management* consists of making it difficult for people to get their work done."

Multi-Tasking

The idea that you might be able to conquer tasks more efficiently through multi-tasking may be overstated. The literature shows that concentrated focus on one job at a time yields greater results than attempting to assume multiple responsibilities at once. That is not to say that there is not some value in possessing the unique skill of multi-tasking. To watch my office manager answer two phone lines, talk to a patient standing at her desk, calculate and collect a copayment and answer my questions simultaneously is a feat to behold. I can do about one of those things at a time. The problem is that mistakes are made much more often when our attention is redirected from the task at hand.

I like to think that I can do one job very proficiently when I am allowed to focus, completing the task before moving on to the next important assignment. When I am distracted during numeric calculations, for example, the speed with which I can get back into the numbers is arrested. I am most efficient and accurate when completing a solitary task uninterrupted as opposed to when I am forced to juggle many chores simultaneously. Though many people pride themselves on their ability to multi-task, the reality is that most doctors are more productive when handling one endeavor at a time.

The Morning Huddle

The morning huddle is a concept promoted by most dental consulting groups as a necessary event in the daily schedule of a dental practice. Many dentists purport gaining productivity from this routine. While I do not dispute the professed significance of such a meeting, the morning huddle has never been a staple in any of my practices. I believe the important benefits of any sunrise gathering can be realized by addressing issues on the spot, throughout the day. Like the immediate discipline of a house pet leaving behind evidence of improper behavior, this method permits less time to elapse and creates less likelihood that addressed items will be forgotten. While it is the doctor's responsibility to review charts before treatment, doing so early enough will allow any necessary discussion with staff regarding productive efficiency.

Any time a meeting is scheduled, hourly staff pay is increased. There is obviously no chance of producing any dentistry during this period of time, so you are already starting out in the hole. You will need to recover in potential lost production the hourly rate you paid your staff to clock in early, simply to break even. Since there is a chance that no more production will be recovered using this method than by addressing patient issues just prior to their appointments, there is the potential to lose money by assembling morning huddles. Your time

The Three-Day Workweek

Operating your business within the framework of a more condensed schedule can yield maximal productivity in fewer hours and fewer workdays. I am reminded of a statement offered by my childhood dentist, "I can produce as much in 25 hours per week as it would take most dentists 35 hours to produce." The data bear out that dentists operating within a highly efficient, compressed work schedule tend to be more productive and ultimately more profitable. Dentists utilizing a three-day workweek often out-produce those laboring four or even five days per week. The explanation for this is that these three-day practices are operating more efficiently. There are fewer openings in their schedules, and waiting lists of patients help to ensure that. Schedule compaction not only fosters greater hourly production, but also enhances profitability by reducing overhead.

The elimination of additional payroll hours and associated variable costs can reduce overhead and directly flow to your bottom line. Less time at work permits periods of rejuvenation necessary for most dentists to side-step the all too frequent reality of occupational burnout. A dental school instructor related an anecdote of once dining with colleagues, each sharing numbers of annual practice production, each trying to out-boast the others. On the contrary, my friends and I often try to outdo each other by actually scheduling the fewest number of workdays per year. Net income being equal, the true victor in terms of practice success may be the dentist achieving this income result via the fewest labor hours invested.

Operating your practice on a three-day workweek offers multiple variations of workday selection, provides patients with multiple appointment time options and helps prevent workplace boredom. For example, a doctor may choose to work Monday, Tuesday and Wednesday of one week and Wednesday, Thursday and Friday of the next. Vacation time can be worked into the six-day chasm between weeks, eliminating the necessity to close the practice for an entire week. When the doctor elects to open early on Monday and Friday and close late on Tuesday and Thursday, patients will always have convenient scheduling options.

Patients can choose appointments on any day of the week, early in the morning, over the lunch hour or after work, even though the practice is only open three days any given week.

Another option for the doctor is to open the practice the same three days every week. Whether the doctor chooses M-W, T-Th or W-Fr, the resulting five-day break between patients regularly seems adequate to reduce professional burnout. The downside to this type of regularity in the schedule is the difficulty it imposes on patients to find convenient appointment times. Any three-day workweek also encroaches on a doctor's ability to treat dental emergencies in a timely fashion. For these reasons, a doctor may elect to open Monday through Thursday one week and Tuesday through Friday the next. This schedule affords the doctor a four-day weekend every other week and permits patients to be seen in a prudent manner through convenient appointment times.

Taking Care of Yourself

Certain activities away from work, such as getting adequate amounts of sleep and exercise, tend to make us more efficient as well. To help combat the high stress level accompanying our occupation, these often neglected elements in life are mandatory. For most of us, the goal of entering health professional school was never to achieve hypertension and otherwise poor health. If we live our work, we leave little time to work on our own wellbeing. If attaining the greatest wealth is not the primary objective, operating efficiently can supply us the time to focus on ourselves, our family and friends and whatever else we deem important in life.

Most dentists have been trained to be efficient in life by virtue of the time demands placed on us throughout the schooling process. We have learned to make the most of every available fragment of time. As time has passed, I feel like this practice of efficient time management has extended to virtually every aspect of my life. Some doctors possess more of a propensity for efficiency than others. The more efficient the practice operation, the more profitable the business will be and the more time away from work will be afforded the doctor.

When I was a kid I brainstormed a number of gadgets that would help me save time in performing tasks that I did not particularly enjoy. Since my brother and I always joked with our dad that he made us start cutting the grass at four-years-old, I had a lot of time to work on efficient lawn mowing techniques. A particular annoyance to me was the morning blare of my alarm clock, which was positioned well below my bunk bed and therefore out of my reach. I designed a contraption that allowed me to turn that blasted thing off without ever leaving the comfort of my warm bed. While my brother aptly coined my inventions *lazy devices*, I tended to view them as *time savers*. I perceived no worth in fruitless labor then, and as a dentist, I see even less now. It's not that I'm lazy bro, it's just that I want to conserve my precious time!

Ten Steps to Improve Productivity and Reduce Stress

At times I am left to ponder, *If it weren't for all these patients, I could probably get some work done around here!* Below is a summary of an article in the McGill Advisory offering techniques for effective time management that dentists may find valuable in their practices and lives:

1. Analyze how your time is presently spent.
2. Prioritize to be effective.
3. Plan your day to accomplish your priorities.
4. Learn to delegate.
5. Practice saying "No".
6. Get plenty of exercise and sleep.
7. Complete difficult tasks first.
8. Stay focused on one task.
9. Establish clear goals and agendas for meetings.
10. Utilize idle time effectively. [21]

Employing well-trained staff members with written job descriptions and an understanding of your ultimate goal of practice efficiency also goes a long way toward assuring your practice operates like a well-oiled, productive machine. There should be virtually no eventuality that has not been considered and accounted for with respect to managerial protocol. It is absolutely possible to run a practice wherein the patients do not wait, and hence the waiting room is more aptly deemed the reception area.

The efficiency you practice in your managerial and dental procedural efforts translates into happy, satisfied patients. There is no accurate way to determine the productive value of managing a practice which is so consumer friendly that it is often unrecognizable as a doctor's office. The response from patients when your hygienist greets them at the door upon arrival, "Oh, I can't believe you're ready for me already!" will become commonplace. These patients translate into treatment acceptance, appointment confirmation, new patient referrals, ultimate business solvency and practice sustenance. The only negative effect you may encounter is a patient's discouragement from being provided inadequate time in the reception area to complete that juicy article in *US Weekly*!

Chapter 13

Cost Controlling Strategies

For a profession viewed as one of the most ideal ways to make money, it is amazing the depth of the financial bunker in which we find ourselves when starting out in dentistry. More than 80% of dental school students are obligated to receive substantial student loan assistance in order to achieve graduation. Considering the great cost of today's professional education, coupled with the debt likely assumed during undergraduate programs, one might presume that cash would simply start raining down on us the moment we leave school. On the contrary, most of us are required to more than double our postgraduate debt load in order solely to open our practice doors to the public. This is true whether a dentist decides to purchase an existing practice or simply to start a practice from scratch.

In dental school I remember thinking, *It doesn't really matter how much money I have to take out in loans while I'm in school. I'm going to be able to pay it all back right away because dentists are loaded!* I was not alone in this thinking. One of my classmates was in the habit of visiting our university's student loan officer virtually every time the adjacent Cascade Mountain Range received another dusting of snow. The woman responsible for funding his ski trips eventually realized his intentions and sentenced him to the student loan penitentiary. After his relegation, this poor guy barely found the funds necessary to complete his education, confirming the moral of the story in *The Boy Who Cried Wolf*.

I, on the other hand, was fortunate to be in good graces with our university's student loan disseminator. I was far away from home, encumbered with out-of-state tuition and in legitimate need of these funds. I was therefore afforded the freedom to add to my mounting debt veritably without regulation. Though this was a welcomed incentive allowing me to explore the many facets of the Great Northwest during my four years of dental school, this extended vacation came with an interest rate accruing by the minute. Upon graduation, I recall a classmate confiding, "I wish I would have been able to do more of the things this part of the country has to offer in these past four years." I barely understood what she was talking about with this statement. I felt like I had done it all by year two!

Though I do not regret taking my Sallie Mae-funded dental school adventures, someone would eventually have to pay for them. I think anyone who knows me would confirm that I have never been a reckless spender and unrealistic about financial responsibilities. Dentists can and do pay off their student loans, and typically go on to make good livings. The degree to which dentists exercise the discipline necessary to limit that which goes out will ultimately determine how quickly they attain solvency, and desirably, financial independence. This can be defined as the place in life wherein there is no further fiscal necessity to go to work. Or, as Jerry Seinfeld eloquently put it, "I don't have to do anything I don't want to do anymore."

While I am not sure that the primary goal in life should be to get to a place where one does only that which one desires, financial independence affords the option to do whatever is determined to be worthwhile in life. If it is dentistry, good on ya mate, go do dentistry! If it is ministry, forge on with ministry. If it is spending time with your family, nurture those relationships. If it is playing in a band, break out the 80's headband and start rockin'. If it is competing in an Ironman Triathlon, train hard! If it is farming, you can retire like my father-in-law and cultivate the earth.

Given the levels of negative net worth most doctors assume by day one, it is incumbent on them to discover the means by which to control costs and limit additional liabilities in their practices. One of the biggest reasons very few doctors ever achieve financial independence is their failure to effectively implement cost controlling strategies in their practices and in their lives. Even if your desire is the same as one colleague related to me, "I want to work so long that I die with my handpiece in one hand and my mirror in the other," you may want to plan for the eventuality that this will not be possible. If spending is never controlled, almost no amount of money that dentistry can afford will be sufficient to sustain your lifestyle indefinitely. While we make good money, we are not professional athletes, nor are we rock stars. Despite the appeal, it is not always advisable for us to try to live like them either.

Fixed Costs

There are certain business related costs which are fixed, and those which are variable. Many fixed costs can be negotiated and controlled up front by a shrewd businessperson. For example, if you do not own the building in which you practice, wise lease negotiation is a must. Equipment selection and tenant improvements should be performed with an eye toward value, longevity and functionality. These costs will often be wrapped up in a business loan or lease, and should not be dismissed without adequate contemplation. The business note will come with an associated interest rate, which should be negotiated down to the absolute lowest percentage possible. This is money out of your pocket and into that of a broker, so spending the time to obtain the best rate will ensure that your hard work is rewarded.

Business expenses which are fixed and recurring comprise the majority of the practice overhead in a dental office. Do not assume that you cannot influence and determine what these costs will be. Consider using staff members to research some of the expenses we have discussed and present the options to you. Taking the time to shop, compare and negotiate fixed cost items up front will pay dividends for your efforts every day of every month of every year.

Business Loans

This same fortitude in price shopping can be applied to loan securitization for the purchase of your practice property, if you are so inclined. Brokers have access to a daily rate card which they use, along with other factors, to determine the interest rate you will pay for the loan on your property. It is in their fiscal interest to assess a percentage rate higher than the lowest possible rate for which you qualify. Brokers are often paid a kickback in the form of a yield spread premium, reflecting the difference between these two rates. There is no need for you to pay these spreads, which can amount to multiple thousands of dollars per year.

It is in your best interest to negotiate your loans or leases with multiple lenders and various brokers. My brother the CFO prides himself on the endurance he displays by contacting roughly 20 different lenders before arriving at the lowest possible interest rate. He believes his vigor to be rewarded when he successfully shaves a mere 1/16% off the lending rate. While most of us might despise the thought of producing such a tedious effort, my businessman brother admits, "I actually enjoy doing it." The fact that I have yet to secure a note at a rate equivalent to any of his loans reminds me that these efforts can be quite fruitful for the doctor willing to enlist the time. Keep in mind that you can request that your broker show you the daily rate card to assure you are truly receiving the most ideal rate. You can also visit www.bankrate.com to compare interest rates from various lenders across the country.

There are a whole host of garbage fees that accompany these loans. Many times these can be reduced or eliminated altogether through the skills of a dynamic negotiator. When lenders desire your business, they may be willing to provide you the most favorable terms for your loan. It is often simply a matter of requesting that these application, processing, underwriting and document preparation fees be removed from the loan agreement. It can also be beneficial to ensure that no prepayment penalties are included in the loan. If at any point in your practice life you are in the mode of debt reduction, you may desire the freedom to eliminate your practice loan via an early payoff.

Business loans can be structured with various periods of repayment. Consulting your accountant early in the negotiation process is important in order to determine the most beneficial terms of the note for purposes of tax deductions. Sometimes paying back the loan in five to seven years provides a more rapid path to debt reduction and thus potential financial independence. Though I am neither a certified financial planner nor an accountant, and I recommend consulting professionals in order to assist you in your financial decisions, I believe debt reduction proves invaluable to a dentist's fiscal peace of mind.

Insurance Premiums

Other negotiable fixed costs can be found in insurance premiums for policies that most dentists purchase to cover themselves for a variety of potentialities. Finding the right agent who is willing to assist with multiple policies sometimes affords the greatest reduction in premiums across the board. Ensuring that the policies you are comparing are identical in coverage, rate shopping can potentially save hundreds, even thousands of dollars per month.

Payroll

Payroll costs, though sometimes varying from period to period, can also be considered fixed expenses. The cost savings in this category will be achieved at the time of hire for each staff member. While a valuable employee should be remunerated fairly, some room needs to be allowed for traditional raises and bonus income. If you start out with payroll costs that are out of control, you stand little chance of later reeling them in. Additionally, hiring right the first time will make you money by eliminating re-training costs associated with staff turnover.

Your payroll will also include any staff benefit programs you may choose to provide. Retirement benefits such as Profit-Sharing Plans, SEP-IRA's and 401K Plans are all valued by loyal employees. Keep in mind that the amount you will reward each staff member may be closely related to the individual's rate of pay. It is therefore important to be mindful of the pay scale upon hiring, as offering these plans automatically increases an employee's hourly rate. Electing to cover staff members with a group health insurance policy, or absorbing a portion of your employees' health insurance premiums are both excellent motivators for potential hires. Calculating total remuneration to include these benefits and disclosing real hourly wage to your staff members is important, as most employees do not regard these benefits as part of their earnings. It is likewise important for you as business owner, as it provides acute awareness of this very considerable overhead expense.

Payroll company fees vary widely, as do their services. I have had the unfortunate experience of sifting through multiple payroll companies in order to uncover the one that makes the least number of errors. Having become extremely frustrated with a local company that charged very little but provided even less, I moved on to one of the largest companies handling payroll in the United States. Although the monthly fee was triple that of the small guys, this payroll behemoth made just as many mistakes. It became routine for me to learn of costly tax errors having been made, requiring multiple staff hours on the phone to resolve.

My staff frequently relayed the payroll company response, "We only help you process your payroll, and it is up to you to check everything we do to ensure its accuracy." I decided yet again to jump ship to another payroll service provider, hoping once more that a smaller company would grant more intimate service. Fortunately, my current payroll company has stood the test of two years' time, offering reasonable fees while providing excellent customer service. An added bonus this company affords is a user-friendly online payroll system, thereby reducing the additional payroll costs associated with its implementation.

Our payroll company also handles the administration of the practice's 401K plan. The unique benefit herein is the immediate communication of the bimonthly payroll amounts to the 401K administrator. This absolves my staff of the responsibility to coordinate transfer of employee earnings values to a third-party administrator. It is amazing how often this additional step yields inaccuracies and frustration. Lest I represent this as a completely faultless marriage, it remains all too common for me to receive tax statements informing me that the payroll company has made yet another error or omission.

An alternative to hiring an outside company to process your payroll is to manage this responsibility in house. Software programs abound which facilitate every detail including calculating wages, breaking out retirement plan amounts, insuring bonus plan compensation is accurate and even printing checks. This last step can be avoided by offering direct deposit of earnings into an employee's bank account, which I have found to be a major staff pleaser. As I am also an employee of my corporation, I too appreciate the luxury of one less trip to the bank. When your practice is in its infancy, time may be a more available commodity and processing your own payroll can help to reduce your overhead. As more patients invade your free time, however, you may want to look to an outside source to relieve you of this burden.

Utilities

Office utilities present fixed costs which most dentists might assume non-negotiable. Though you may be limited in your ability to negotiate gas and electric prices, telephone and Internet service costs can commonly be conserved simply by making the request. Cable, telephone and Internet service providers often offer discounts to bundle your package and utilize their companies exclusively. From time to time these companies may market lower prices to new customers than current clients are paying for the same services. It has always behooved me to call them to task on these offers and thereby reset my monthly billing to reflect these new, lower prices. One phone call to my telephone and Internet service provider reduced my monthly bill by one-third.

Office Cleaning

If you have your office cleaned and maintained on a weekly basis, interview several cleaning companies to establish the most reasonable price for trustworthy service. Prices and end product differ tremendously among cleaning companies so it is wise to seek referrals from area businesses when selecting a company. Companies that clean other offices in your area may offer a discount, as including your office could fit conveniently within their schedules. It is important to review the company's insurance policies and security procedures before making this decision. Remember, a total stranger will have access to your building when it is empty. In order to remain HIPAA compliant and employ additional security precautions, we keep our files in a separate room that is locked at night. A locked filing cabinet can serve the same purpose.

Recurring Marketing Expenses

Certain marketing expenses are recurring and can therefore be considered fixed costs. For example, if you have chosen to increase your office visibility by listing your practice on the Internet dentist locator, www.TheDentistSearch.com, you can make a decision regarding the level of value you wish to obtain from your listing. A Gold Listing will afford you the greatest visibility and recognition with the search engines and therefore position your practice above the listings of most of your peers. Most marketing programs will offer a variety of product options from which to choose based upon your marketing budget.

Practice marketing and advertising expenditures are similar to lab costs in that they carry the potential to generate high volumes of revenue as their values increase. Practice management literature routinely points to 4% of production as a standard target for a monthly dental marketing budget. Though I have found this number to be a bit excessive in my practices, I do find value in continually positioning the practice in front of the consuming public. As a practice matures, these costs can be reigned in and more narrowly defined. For example, striving toward the goal of utilizing Internet marketing as the primary source of advertising can provide the greatest returns while reducing the overhead percentage assigned to marketing.

Variable Costs

Many expenses in dentistry are variable costs, and can thus be controlled to a greater extent than those which are fixed. Much of this control is played out by the exercise of restriction in terms of product and service purchases. Plainly, if you want to completely eliminate costs in this arena, do not make these purchases at all. While this proves to be a far too simplistic and ultimately unrealistic measure in a healthily productive dental practice, it illustrates the degree to which a dentist has control over these expenses. At the opposite end of the spectrum is the dentist who buys whatever anyone is selling because it is pitched as either "the next great thing" or "absolutely necessary for the success of the practice."

Dr. Jumper vs. Dr. Keeper

One of the few business lectures I received in dental school taught me the lesson of Dr. Jumper vs. Dr. Keeper. Dr. Jumper is the dentist who becomes enamored with every little pearl marketed to the practice, every piece of new equipment, new technology or new gadget that is promised to return millions. Consequently, Dr. Jumper leaps into these purchases and becomes the new best friend of any sales rep within a hundred miles. This becomes quite costly until the time that Dr. Jumper, if that time ever arrives, finally realizes that *if it sounds too good to be true, it probably is.*

In contrast to Dr. Jumper, Dr. Keeper is the dentist who one might consider Old School. This doctor is the one who never updates the office décor, never changes any techniques in response to more efficient technology and never buys anything the sales reps are selling. Dr. Keeper resists the temptation to buy into anything new or different even when doing so would greatly increase the productivity of the practice. This also proves quite costly because from time to time certain things come along, for example, computers, which can tremendously enhance business revenues while significantly mitigating overhead. If Dr. Keeper were able to clear the hurdles of discomfort and intimidation, the resulting net income from the office upgrade would reward greatly for this fortitude.

One of my patients described her former dentist's office in which the equipment was held together by duct tape. The duct tape dentist is a good example of a Dr. Keeper. While there are clearly innumerable practical uses for duct tape, dental office repair in plain view of skeptical patients is not one of them.

The idea here is to be neither Dr. Jumper nor Dr. Keeper. The tenet expressed to us was that we should become dentists falling somewhere in between these two doctors. My proposal would be to become Dr. Analytical. This dentist blends the best qualities of both doctors while leaving behind those characteristics that inhibit practice growth and prosperity. Dr. Analytical effects cost control by determining whether purchasing the new product, service or fancy piece of new equipment will do one or more of the following things:

- Make the doctor more money
- Make the doctor more efficient
- Make the doctor's job easier
- Make the doctor's job more enjoyable
- Provide patients a necessary service otherwise unavailable

If none of these benefits is present, the sales rep should be allowed to peddle those products down the road to Dr. Jumper.

Dental Supplies

Certain variable cost items are necessities in any dental practice. Although you will definitely need dental supplies every month, you are not at the mercy of the supply reps in terms of what and how much you purchase. It is useful to establish a monthly budget for supply expenses, just as one would for personal living expenses. For example, you can train the staff member responsible for placing supply orders to limit monthly expenditures to 4% of practice production, or whatever value makes sense in your practice. If your practice produces $50,000/month, you would provide this staff member with a $2,000 cap on monthly dental supply orders. Office supply expenses can be predicted and controlled in this manner as well. It is apparent how these costs can spin out of control when there is no accountability placed on the fiscal quantity of these orders.

Dental Laboratory Costs

Dental laboratory costs will vary from month to month as well. This is not a variable cost, however, that you should aspire to limit. While you can benefit from controlling costs by testing the work of various labs and negotiating rates among them, there is net income upside to incurring a high lab bill. Typically, fixed prosthodontics performed in quadrants yields some of the greatest returns in terms of production and net income. As these procedures come with inherent lab work, it is commonly a good indication of a successful practice to have a higher monthly lab bill.

Computer Maintenance and Repair

Many computer industry companies offer monthly service contracts in which dentists pay in advance for a predetermined number of maintenance hours. In this scenario, the computer related cost would become a fixed expense. While I do not recommend entering into such a potentially wasteful agreement, I definitely would suggest negotiating the costs down to the most equitable level acceptable to both parties. Considering the designation of the dental practice as a relatively small business, I prefer to handle computer maintenance and repair on a variable cost basis.

Research potential computer companies by asking for referrals from other area businesses or patients *before* you need to use these services. Unfortunately, I can speak from painful experience about the importance of knowing how you will handle a computer problem prior to its occurrence. The time when all of your operatories are full with patients and your computer server crashes is not the ideal to be researching computer companies.

Patient Referral Programs

Throughout my career I have experimented with various means by which to encourage existing patients to refer their friends and family members. While clearly the most effective way to achieve this is to provide caring, trustworthy, honest and painless service, some patients seem to require a bit more prodding. I consider this an internal marketing expense, one which varies monthly depending upon its success.

Persuasive methods range from providing movie tickets or sending small gifts to the referring party, to simply offering cash as an incentive. The most business-wise plan I have employed involves posting a credit of $25 to a patient's account for each new patient referred to our office. This assures that any amount you dole out must come back to you in the form of accepted treatment plans or preventative dentistry. This is industry standard for large retailers and is referred to as *store credit*. One current patient has been storing up credit for years now in hopes of affording that long sought after cosmetic dentistry she so desires. Whatever plan you choose to institute, you are guaranteed more new patients with every payout, thus ensuring the lifeblood of your practice.

Networking Gift Programs

While blatant purchasing of referrals is generally left to the dental specialists, this variable cost can be of some benefit to the general dentist as well. Networking gifts around the holidays are so common that I recommend providing these at alternative times of the year. Since you as a general dentist will be on the receiving end of most of these fruit baskets, anything you can do to bring attention to your practice from area specialists will stand out.

Network gifting is not limited to our profession alone. You can gain traction in local companies having large employee populations by providing free goods to the entire corporate payroll. We have had good luck reaching out to area businesses such as MasterCard and CitiBank.

Be sure to incorporate contact information, including your website address, on all items you dispense. Engraving your practice name and phone number on free toothbrushes is mandatory.

The same gifting can be done at area schools. We have designed coloring books specific to dentistry and offer them to children in local elementary schools. We include them in a take home bag containing other kid-friendly items. The goal, of course, beyond providing fun for all ages is to get your practice contact information in front of the parents. Network gifting like this is an inexpensive form of external marketing which can produce considerable returns on investment.

Sometimes the time for giving will appear quite clear to you. I recall a single mother in a former practice who had extensive decay and a less extensive ability to pay for her treatment. We filled the cavities over time, and one day she shared with my employee that she was having trouble affording groceries and basic needs for her family. I sent a staff member out to pick up some essentials at the supermarket and offered them to her at the end of her appointment. She cried with gratitude, and that became payment in full on her account.

Staff Bonus Programs

A detailed description of various staff bonus programs is found in this book's section, Hiring the Ideal Staff. These programs, though clearly in place to bring your business greater profitability, are considered a variable cost to your practice. Since the expense will be different each payroll period depending upon the productivity of your practice, there is no clear way to predetermine these expenses. When the programs are designed properly, however, the additional expense will be more than accounted for by the supplementary revenue they create.

The Low Overhead Practice

There are clearly different kinds of successful practices. There are those that dentists run and those that run dentists. There are high powered, multi-operatory, multi-dentist, fast paced, extraordinarily productive machines and there are laid back, highly efficient, minimally staffed, cost controlled, bottom line focused dental businesses. The personality type of the practice should reflect that of the dentist running it. As no dentist is identical to another, neither should be the identity of their practices. Certain Type A personality doctors seem to require very little sleep or relaxation and thrive on activity and action. These dentists may desire to prep every tooth in every possible mouth requiring treatment. They will be quite comfortable producing as much dentistry as is achievable.

Many dentists want to produce as much as possible because they believe that this is the path to the greatest income. While this is true in an astutely managed, cost controlled practice, it is not always the case when considering net income after expenses. Regularly overlooked is the value that lies in the practice that is leisurely paced, cost controlled and efficient. It is okay if you do not want to operate at maximum capacity, but rather at a volume more suited to your temperament. As in other areas of life such as parenting, academics and athletic training, it is best to limit the time you spend comparing your practice to those of other dentists. Each individual's personality and drive are unique and this needs to be considered when determining personal desires for your practice and life.

Most practice management information leads us to believe that we as dentists need to work as fast and as hard as possible in order to achieve maximum production. What they do not share with us is the toll this effort may be taking on us and on our bodies. If you are comfortable sinking all your energy into making money, then the ends may justify the means. If you are not, however, do not be made to think less of yourself because you want to run a moderate yet efficient practice. You can still be largely successful by becoming very mindful of business overhead and practice profitability.

In fact, the data bear out that moderately sized dental practices tend to control costs better than peer practices producing either minimal or maximal volumes of dentistry. A 2008 study of 160 dentists by the Academy of Dental C.P.A.s member company Bender, Weltman, Thomas, Perry and Company, P.C. (www.bwtpcpa.com), collected data on collections versus overhead expenses for 142 practices. [22]The study revealed that practices collecting less than $400,000 had an average overhead of 88.7%, excluding officers' salaries, pension and profit sharing. Practices collecting $400,001-$600,000 reduced average overhead to 75.5%, and those with collections of $600,001-$1,000,000 posted an overhead average of 68.5%. Above this revenue point, overhead percentage began to rise again. Practices collecting $1,000,001-$2,000,000 averaged 70.6% overhead, and those with collections greater than $2 million recorded overhead of 72.1%.

What these numbers indicate is that at very low levels of practice collections, overhead will outrun your efforts to control costs. This is true because of the mandatory nature of fixed expenses that all dentists are forced to shoulder. As practice collections increase, the revenues will eventually outpace these expenses, thereby reducing the percentage of profit that overhead swallows up. This particular study seems to reveal a relative sweet spot for practice collections, at least as it relates to maximal return on energy invested to be productive. For some practices, producing amounts above this level may require a marginally less efficient control of overhead. It will more reliably require a greater investment of time and energy to do so. Clearly, pure profit will still be greater, but will come as a marginal return on investment. It is a personal decision as to the value of that additional return for each dentist.

Keep in mind that every dollar you spend running your business is another dollar you will need to earn simply to break even. Be wary of the salesperson who informs you of the pedaled product, "It will pay for itself." In all my years in practice I have yet to witness anything I bought actually doing the dentistry for me. Nothing, of course, except the occasional hired associate dentist. Many people do not seem to consider the cost of labor as an important factor in the equation of business profitability. I believe this is a cost that should be considered at least as relevant as a highly expensive piece of new equipment. When you make the purchase, you are required to work it off before you can even get back to par.

A friend and colleague recently spent $20,000 upgrading his computer system solely to establish compatibility with the newest version of the software his practice was running. I am sure he was told that this conversion would "pay for itself" in two years or so. Another friend shared with me that his new office expansion caused him to "owe seven creditors hundreds of thousands of dollars for the rest of my life." Both of these dentists have very appealing offices and will more than likely recover these investments at some point. However, I am quite certain that none of these upgrades will ever pay for themselves.

The dentists' consistent labor is what is going to be called due in order to settle these debts.

The minimally staffed, fee-for-service practice operating at 50% overhead is given little attention in the world of dental consulting and practice management. The assumption is made that dentists want to be as productive as possible, this at the expense of all else. Why is it assumed that all dentists want to be as busy as they can be? Perhaps it is because we are known to carry such extreme debt loads associated with merely existing as dentists. Possibly it results from the angst we feel when an operatory sits open during a scheduled workday. The truth is that those operatories sit unoccupied on Saturdays and Sundays when most dentists do not schedule patients, and typically at least one more day each week. Why are we any more at ease on those days, when most of our overhead remains, excepting hourly staff pay and minimal utility expenses? Why are we any more relaxed about our open dental chairs when we lock the doors at night and go home?

Or perhaps the notion that we need to produce as much dentistry as is feasible is instilled in us by the dental equipment and supply companies that profit when we purchase the most expensive luxuries dentistry has to offer. They know dentistry is expensive, so they can charge us extraordinary amounts to produce it. This creates the circular necessity to do so even more. Dentistry is still a multi-billion dollar industry. The dental equipment and supply companies are sharing in quite a number of those billions.

Maybe the impression of maximum effort is seeded in the perception that dentists are overachievers and workaholics. After all, dentists have been required to excel through diligence and perseverance in order to achieve their status as doctors. Conceivably, outsiders consider us driven to succeed my any means necessary, and define success as owning the practice that produces the greatest annual revenues. It is also reasonable to assume that this perception is there because it is so often true.

This mindset of ultimate productivity may stem from our culture's desire to make as much money as possible in what we do for a living. While I am not begrudging those espousing this belief, I do contend that this goal can come at a cost. If there are other things you value in life greater than the maximal productivity of your practice, you can still pursue them while running a highly profitable business. The rules of cost control and efficiency bear much greater importance in these skeleton crew practices that hope to compete with the behemoths. The reason they can compete at all is the fact that what matters most in terms of profitability is not production, but net income after expenses. Unfortunately, too many dentists pay little or no attention to this reality.

Consider a practice that produces $100,000/month with a 75% overhead. Contrast this with the practice producing $50,000/month with an overhead of 50%. The result is $25,000/month in net income in both practices. Which $25,000 would you prefer to earn? You have to believe that the $25K in the larger practice has come at a greater cost in terms of time and energy. In fact, assuming equal fees and identical procedures, this cost is exactly twice as great. This is the cost of labor that is so often ignored. Personally, I have better things to do with my time than doubling my workload to account for wasteful spending.

The same equation applies even when a dentist churns out $200,000/month in hopes of outrunning the little guy. This high speed doctor operating at 75% overhead will still need to pump out twice as much dentistry as the tortoise at 50% overhead, just to reach the finish line dead even. I am rarely impressed by production levels. I am, however, impressed by profitability. You cannot outrun your overhead. You can control it, however. When you do, that additional productivity goes straight to your bottom line.

Overhead control takes as much concerted effort as producing large quantities of dentistry. It starts with an understanding of how overhead is calculated, and an awareness of what yours actually is. Do you know what your practice overhead is? If you feel uncomfortable with business math, it may prove highly beneficial to hire a financial planner, a bookkeeper or an accountant who is willing to take an active approach to managing your overhead. Practice management firms abound willing to assist to this end. Be mindful, however, that any expense you incur in helping you crunch the numbers goes directly to increasing your overhead.

If you are reasonably proficient in math, you can perform these tasks yourself with the help of simple programs such as *QuickBooks*. Profit/loss statements can even be generated on something as uncomplicated as an Excel spreadsheet. Regardless of the means, calculating a realistic representation of the viability of your business is mandatory to achieving maximum profitability in your practice. Larger corporations would not consider walking blindly through their financial statements. We too own for-profit businesses; therefore, we should not be any less familiar with our numbers than is big business.

Though mature practices can definitely benefit from restructuring aimed at overhead control, the new dental practice is in an ideal position to gain tremendously from this focus. The low overhead business can easily become an achievable reality in the scratch practice by becoming defined as such from the outset. The most effective way to control overhead is by limiting the number of staff members you are required to pay. This type of skeleton crew practice is often the ideal way to achieve maximal profitability. Though this is a contrarian view, I have witnessed the successful replication of this template in multiple practices.

The skeleton crew practice demands greater attention to detail in terms of tracking practice statistics, analyzing marketing returns, reviewing charts and maximizing efficiency. In return for these efforts come the benefits of fewer staff management concerns, reduced labor costs on the part of the doctor and greater pocketing of that for which you have worked so hard. If someone operates the type of business that generates revenues while one sleeps, it makes sense to do whatever possible to sell more widgets, for example. If you do dentistry, however, the cost of labor is a necessary consideration.

The success of such a tightly staffed practice is predicated on the hiring of highly skilled, efficient team members. Scheduling longer procedures of productive dentistry on your best patients can permit the employment of only one dental assistant. Collecting at the time of service and choosing not to participate on multiple low reimbursement insurance plans will allow you to succeed with only one front office employee. A gentle, congenial hygienist can engender trust and ensure consistent revenues by minimizing failed appointments and by convincing patients that your treatment plan is the best available.

As strange as it may seem, as a practice matures there are even greater opportunities to reduce staff overhead. A doctor can choose not to accept assignment of benefits for most insurance plans. This means that patients are ultimately responsible for submitting their own insurance claims and receiving reimbursement from their insurance companies. The risk herein is the potential loss of patients to the lack of convenience that your office is providing them. Many people, of course, are unwilling to pay the full fee up front and then wait for checks from their insurance companies. Since most dentists do accept assignment of benefits, patients will easily be able to find a new dentist who is willing to do so. If, however, you are not inclined to do any dentistry without assurance of payment (aside from that which you have chosen to perform on a charitable basis), this type of practice may be an option for you.

So much of the dental literature entices us to believe that we should all strive to achieve our dream practice, which is commonly defined as that which pumps out the greatest volume of dentistry. If I had a dollar for every time I have heard the description "dream practice" over the years, I would be comfortably living another dream at this point. I for one have never once had a dream about any of my dental practices. I am just not sure whose dream this definition represents. Is it the dream of the practice management consultant? Is it that of the practice broker? What about that of the dental equipment and supply rep?

Certainly we all want to operate successful practices; otherwise we would be pursuing other lines of work. What is underrepresented is the fact that not all of our dreams are the same. I have a friend whose office houses sixteen operatories and races in and out of four hygiene rooms throughout his day. I recently read an article in which another dentist acknowledged a similar sixteen operatory practice as that for which we should all strive. I am pretty sure he even used the term "dream practice" to describe such an environment. I am not sure about you, but that sounds less like a dream to me and more like a nightmare.

What we need to consider is the reality that every one of us starts each workday with a bucket full of energy. Some days begin with your bucket being more full than others, of course. Certain dentists draw from a deeper bucket and thrive on high paced, very busy environments. Nonetheless, as the day progresses, the contents of the bucket slowly pour out into your patients, your staff and your business until very little remains for you. If your dream is to enlist all of your energy into the maximal production of revenue, then the sixteen op practice might be for you. If it is not, however, you should not be made to feel like your dream is any less relevant than that of the high volume doctor. The dream practice should, therefore, be redefined to assume a less universal designation, as this will mean something very different to each of us.

As with any practice management technique, cost control can be taken to an extreme. My father-in-law, for example, reuses his coffee grounds. My grandfather-in-law removes all the batteries from his clocks, remote controls and radios before leaving on vacation. We can spend more time tripping over the pennies than that time is ever worth. However, running a profitable, cost controlled, minimally staffed, efficient practice is a real possibility. This can free you up to do other desirable things in life for which you might have otherwise not found the time. You can make your practice into what one of my revered dental school instructors lauded, *a means to an end, not the end in itself.*

Chapter 14

The Psychology of Dentistry

The Psychology of Management

Do patients know they are actually being *managed*? Do staff members realize they are continually getting managed as well? Do you understand that all these people require management in one form or another in order for you to achieve the ends your practice dictates? Every clinical procedure demands a detailed psychological management process. Some dentists are clearly better at this than others and some dentists do not even realize this need exists. This process begins with the patient's first phone call to your office, continues when the patient arrives at your door, heightens while the patient takes a seat in your operatory chair and continues through the time the patient's head rests on the pillow that night. Your ability to forge improvements in this facet of your health care delivery will ultimately result in reduced work-related stress and increased profitability of your practice.

To be clear, I am not insinuating that the people surrounding you throughout your workday be manipulated, just managed. As the general dentist business owner, you are the CEO, the manager and the technician. Although you can hire appropriately to delegate some of the staff-related management responsibilities, you are ultimately the person accountable for patient comfort, reassurance and trust. These personal elements must be possessed and practiced in order for the health care professional to succeed in business. I can think of no more poignant example of this than the profession of dentistry, wherein the patient anxiety level is at its peak.

While most dentists engulf themselves in the study of the physical and biological sciences during their undergraduate years, I chose to adopt the field of Psychology as my major. Though I minored in Biology and completed the obligatory Physics and Chemistry courses, I found it compelling to learn about the ways in which the mind formulated thoughts and expressed them through actions. Realizing the extensive psychological component of the practice of dentistry, I thought this background would aid in the pursuit of my ideal practice. Though I cannot state with certainty that my particular education has elevated me beyond the skills of any other dental provider, I do find this knowledge helpful throughout the day when dealing with staff members and clientele. If anything, it is useful to recognize what is happening, why it is occurring and how to effectively negotiate the situation.

You do not need a degree in Psychology to learn and understand the basic principles of human mentality. A less than fortunate sequella of practicing dentistry is that it sometimes puts us in contact with people at their absolute worst. I have observed the personality characteristics of certain individuals vary dramatically depending upon whether they are seated in an operatory chair with mouth agape versus when I encounter them in any other fashion in the general public. This stands to reason given the heightened level of anxiety and perceived total lack of control they have over the situation at hand. Add to this the financial strain imposed on them by the high cost of dental procedures for which they have absolutely no desire to pay. How often are we pleasantly informed that there is categorically no other place that our patients would want to be less than here seated in our dental chairs?

And who is in charge of managing the doctor? Are you aware that you are constantly called to manage your own thoughts, words and actions with respect to the manner in which you are perceived by your staff and your patients? Often the most difficult management process I encounter throughout my workday is the exercise of effective control over the language that emanates from my mouth. Most commonly I find that the most fruitful form of self-management I can institute is the prohibition of the thoughts having taken root in my mind from ever exiting my lips. The tested edict, *The less you say, the better,* proves itself here yet again. When we say nothing, there is a zero percent chance that our words will be misinterpreted. This does not, however, ensure that our thoughts and attitudes will not be misconstrued by the patient's perception.

"No Offense Doc, but I Hate Dentists!"

We are continually being examined through heightened awareness by anxious, apprehensive and sometimes slow to trust patients, as well as skeptical staff members who may question our intentions. Since perception is reality, we need to be mindful of how these opinions may form and be proactive in controlling them. While I am not recommending walking on egg shells in your office and quelling every thought that enters your mind, I believe it useful to carefully consider how controversial conversation might be interpreted by someone other than yourself. This is clearly more important during the initial stages of the doctor/patient or doctor/staff relationship.

Once we have a more defined perspective of the personality characteristics of the individuals with whom we interact in the work environment, we can more freely relate to them. It is important, however, to bear in mind that our identities as doctors position us as targets for legal action, whether founded or otherwise. Unfortunately, our best friends as we have once perceived them, can ultimately levy the blindside blow that leaves us reeling. It may prove less than cynical in business to amend the old adage to read, *Hold your enemies close and your friends closer.*

A seldom discussed truth in our profession is the degree to which this commonly expressed *hatred* can become indoctrinated into our own self-perceptions. There are many reasonable explanations for our repression of these feelings. Most of us desire to be perceived as stronger than we are. We are the doctors. We are the ones in control of every situation. Patients and staff members look to us for stability, not fragility. No one wants to show weakness, and we as health care professionals are even more representative of this reality.

Further, it is not in the interest of those marketing products and services to dentists to discourage us from the continued practice of our profession. I am reminded of a recent lecture presented by a dental consulting firm in which the speaker encouraged us to practice dentistry with continued intensity for as many years as possible. "I don't want to see you ever retire. I love this profession!" This statement, coming from a middle-aged dentist who had not practiced dentistry in over a decade.

Professional Burnout

Self-deprecation is not an uncommon theme with dentists who have been in practice for over ten years. Though many dentists continue to love and enjoy dentistry the same way they did the first day they entered practice, there is clearly a high incidence of burnout in our profession. After pouring time, energy and emotion into their practices year after year, the shine may begin to wear off the apple. The initial excitement which accompanied dentists into their new careers is often replaced with cynicism and reality. This is a tough job, make no mistake. Most dentists experiencing these feelings of doubt and discouragement are often pushed further into the abyss by assuming they are the only ones dealing with these frustrations.

Just attend a sizable continuing education lecture and look around the room. It sometimes saddens me to see the expressions on the faces of so many dentists. There appears a look of dissatisfaction and learned helplessness that Pavlov's dogs would likely have appreciated. The problem is no one talks about it. If this is happening to you, you are not alone. A big step in the right direction is to open up to a colleague you can trust. You might find that this dentist may be experiencing the same burnout and stress that you are. This person may also be very relieved to finally have someone else with whom to share these sentiments.

Study groups exist that can serve to lessen the impression of isolation experienced by the dental professional. One colleague related to me that The Seattle Study Club had helped him overcome his feelings of professional burnout. This particular club has groups in many cities throughout the country and covers a variety of topics in dentistry. The ADA sponsored New Dentists Group, with branches in multiple U.S. locations, offers the recent graduate an opportunity to meet and befriend cohorts less than ten years out of school. This simple interaction with, and shared experiences of, your colleagues can help to reduce the career exhaustion expressed by so many dentists.

What I have observed to cause professional burnout in the overwhelming majority of cases is the dentist's inability to control costs.

This root cause is evident in both personal living expense and business overhead expense management. Dentists are thereby forced to earn significantly more than their desire to work permits. Therefore, not only must they delay retirement, they are forced to perform more procedures on greater numbers of patients, working more hours and more days just to stay afloat. This, coupled with additional staff headaches, repair and maintenance necessities, daily business annoyances and patients who insist that they *hate you*, is all enough to drive anyone to occupational discontent.

While we may understand that our patients truly mean "No offense Doc," and that they really do not hate *you*, we are continually called to dispel these statements and to resist the inclination to take them personally. Some dentists are unmistakably better at this than others. I am reminded of a dental school instructor who, after hearing a student apologize for a classmates' lambasting of his teaching style, offered, "You must be mistaking me for someone who cares", or a slightly more profane variation of that statement.

Certain people do not care at all what others think of them. Many doctors care too much. Some argue that the best doctors are those who care the most. This may position them as better for their patients, but perhaps not so great for their own well-beings. Dental school did not prepare us for this expression of hatred from our patients. I never considered that I would be the source of tremendous fear and the target of disdain owing solely to the occupation I had chosen to support me. I was too busy perfecting my clinical skills and being excited about my future. There is an art to tempering our concern and compassion for others while continuing to practice our profession with peace of mind. This skill can be honed with time.

Considering the depth of negativity we encounter in our profession, it is incumbent on us to consider the positive statements that patients offer more often than the negative comments that are levied. If we are doing things right in our practices, there will certainly be an abundance of positive accolades on which to focus. It does not tend to take much to stand out from the crowd in the environment in which we work. Establish your practice as one that people praise, and ponder these compliments often.

Dentistry's bronze medal position behind flying and public

speaking as society's most feared experience is merely one of the challenges we face in our professional self-management. The perfection expected when performing multiple microsurgeries, the management of a sometimes difficult staff and the concomitant demands of serving as CEO of a small business combine to make up a normal day in the life of a busy dentist. It is understandable that our profession consistently ranks toward the top in terms of job related stress. To quote an elder colleague in response to his wife's loving inquiry, "How was your day, honey?" "Dentistry is the toughest job in the world!"

Again, the problem is that no one seems to talk about it. Dental school does not educate us on the potentiality for professional burnout. Many dentists may resist exposing their stress and frustration to colleagues for fear of presenting their practices as less than stable. We all have the same burden of self-management demands each workday. We all have days that are better than others and those that just seem to position our profession as the toughest job in the world. It is alright to feel uninspired to do energetic cartwheels in anticipation of your next workday. If you do, then you are among the truly fortunate. If you do not, you are certainly not without company. Do not be discouraged by the cheerleaders on the sidelines who might have you believe you are somehow wrong by failing each day to exclaim ours as the greatest profession in the world. While there is no doubt that dentistry can be a tremendously rewarding occupation, we would be remiss in neglecting to represent the difficulties that sometimes accompany our chosen vocation.

The Patient You Want to Lose

Patient selection is another often overlooked aspect of the effective management of a successful dental practice. As dentists, we seldom think of ourselves as the ones charged with selecting the patients who will patronize our practices. After all, the patients are the ones who will be selecting us to serve their dental needs, are they not? In many ways there is no avoiding that patients will be searching you out to become their dentist of choice. Notwithstanding, the extent to which you are able to fashion the thoughts and attitudes of those requiring your services will ultimately determine what type of dental practice you will be managing.

As we are all aware, there are many different types of people out there. There are grateful, gracious and kind people and there are those who are more self-serving. There are loyal, true and honest people and there are those who commonly fail their scheduled appointments and then fabricate stories about why this happened, again. There are those who are trusting and those who are skeptical. There are those who are always on time and those who are on their own forms of time. There are those who refer other patients to your office and those who may be very happy with their experience in your office, but will not share that with anyone. In the beginning, you may be more inclined to serve all these types of clients, as the requirements of a practice in its infancy might dictate. As your practice matures, however, you may find it more appealing to encourage the business in the direction of your own desired practice personality.

For example, if you hold your practice to the principle that patients will not be made to wait, you may wish to dismiss a notoriously tardy patient from your client base. If a patient habitually fails appointments or consistently refuses to have necessary treatment performed, you may elect to provide referrals to other dentists who may not consider this behavior to be as great a disruption as you do in your practice. The same principle can be applied to patients who are routinely confrontational with the doctor and staff. You should provide dismissed patients the names of and contact information for multiple area dentists who might serve their oral health needs. Be sure to take all measures necessary to ensure that you are not engaging in patient abandonment.

The idea of patient dismissal is controversial, one that finds practitioners on both sides of the debate. A friend of mine heard another dentist postulating a yearly protocol in which each staff member is encouraged to write down the names of five patients they would like to see dismissed from the practice. In this doctor's office, an interesting result of this exercise was that very commonly the names on each staff member's list shared a striking resemblance. Many times, he explained, all five names were identical even though the staff members had no prior knowledge of who their co-workers would be implicating. This experiment reveals that most often it is not the staff nor the doctor who is biased against individual patients, but the patients who bring this verdict upon themselves.

The friend describing this program to me began his career as an associate working under an older doctor. The more experienced dentist was not at all supportive of this annual staff exercise. His contention was that, "We are here for the patients, not the other way around." There are clearly two vastly differing philosophies here. My friend landed on the opposite side of the fence, finding the notion of tailoring his practice to those who respected his services highly appealing. Though I have never formally implemented such a program in any of my practices, I have often simulated the technique by asking staff members to verbalize their proposed list of five to each other. I have to admit, this little diversion nearly always yields results similar to those of the initial examiner. I never seem to have much difficulty coming up with my list of five either.

My wife recently related a conversation with a friend who called a dentist's office in anticipation of becoming a new patient. The receptionist inquired as to what type of dental treatment the patient expected she would need. My wife's friend responded, "I'd just like to come in and find out if any dentistry needs to be done, and to have my teeth cleaned." The staff member then replied, "Oh no, you won't be getting your teeth cleaned tomorrow, but you can come in for an exam and we'll see if we want to keep you as a patient". While there may be better ways of saying this, the message was clear; we will be interviewing you, you will not be interviewing us." This particular exchange stands out because it is obviously not the traditional the *customer is always right*, approach we hear preached in so many practice management seminars. Either the practice owner here is operating at optimal capacity and not interested in growing the business or is simply highly selective with respect to the style of practice that takes form.

Just as it is a goal to eventually achieve freedom from spending valuable time marketing your business, it is also appealing to reach a point of practice maturity that permits customization around your own practice philosophy. This might reasonably entail identifying and selecting those best suited to become loyal patrons of your practice. If you exercise diligence in efforts to satisfy your patients, it may behoove you to enlist only those patients who possess the capacity to be satisfied.

We have all encountered patients who, no matter the lengths to which we go, are never quite fully enamored with what we have done for them. As a friend and colleague once put it, "If you give these patients a finger, they will take the whole hand!" This is the person who has no respect for your time, lambasts the work of former dentists, does not value quality dentistry, is incapable of being satisfied and is argumentative with your staff. Such discontented patients might find themselves on the annual list of the staff member five. If you and your staff offer over the top customer service with a friendly, caring demeanor, the patient who is rude and offensive in the face of these efforts might exit your office with some walking papers as well. If you work hard to respect the time of your clients and strive to schedule only as many procedures as you can realistically perform within a given timeframe, the door should not be held open for the patient who does not afford you the same respect.

Some people will come up with the most outrageous explanations for why they failed their appointments and decided not to call to inform you. "I can't bring my daughter in because I'm taking care of a little baby." Unaware that this person, our patient in her late 50's, had a little baby, my receptionist inquired, "Whose baby?" "My daughter Mary, my little baby!" Mary, by the way, is 22-years-old.

The Patient You Want to Keep

The patient you want to keep is easily identifiable. This person is reliable, loyal, trusting, compliant, reasonable, grateful and possibly also someone who refers similar individuals to your practice. Though not necessary to the efficient flow of a successful business, this ideal patient might even present as friendly, enjoyable and perhaps even humorous. This person's agreeable personality will be as effortless to recognize and just as simple to categorize as the patient you want to lose.

It is alright not to serve the roll of every person's dentist. Most of us work very diligently to be respectful, professional and disciplined and to provide clinical dentistry of the highest quality. For those who do not appreciate and value these efforts, there is likely another dentist willing to put up with this negativity each day in exchange for the money.

Your practice will ultimately take the shape, personality and character of the patients it serves. This statement has no basis in demographics, but in the quality of the characters comprising it. What I am describing is a niche practice in which the provider desires to work daily in an environment which supports mutual value and respect. This ideal atmosphere reduces stress while increasing the enjoyment of the work experience.

Since this is merely one paradigm in which to operate a dental practice, these character assessments may mean little to some readers. If aggressively enhancing the paper chase is the greatest goal, then it is of minor consequence what type of customer the business serves. Character and practice personality can be ignored as long as each client presents with adequate financial means by which to remunerate for services rendered. As we are all in the business of profitability, I do not take exception this practice persona. I am simply pointing out that your practice will assume a particular identity, whether by design or by default.

At times, successfully navigating the waters buoying the difficult patient proves to be more rewarding than caring for the needs of the compliant customer. Though without doubt more challenging, this endeavor often yields greater satisfaction than the work we can complete with relative ease. Experienced dentists can hone their skills to triumph over almost any circumstance that may present in the course of a workday. Repetition, trial and error and learning from history can all add arrows to your quiver to prevail over taxing situations which once seemed uncontrollable.

Conflict Resolution

Despite your best efforts in achieving the trusting, hospitable atmosphere so desirable to the general population, there will present certain patients and situations that disrupt the calming environment you have painstakingly striven to create. When circumstances arise that position the patient against the practice, your ability to excel in the area of conflict resolution will set your practice apart from the traditional doctor's office. Since we know that most disgruntled patients are those with balances on their accounts, we must be mindful of this in our discussions with them. Though dissatisfaction with clinical services provided is at times the point of contention, most often people are upset with you because they owe you money.

Whatever the reasons patients may be frustrated with the goods and services provided by your office, more than anything else, people typically just want to be heard. The best thing you can do initially is simply to listen to them. Even when you feel like needing to bite off your tongue while doing so, it will pay to be patient and consider their statements for a moment. When a doctor takes the time to resolve a conflict in favor of a discontented patient, that patient will commonly become a satisfied, referring customer for life.

Exercising skill in the art of conflict resolution can serve to quickly turn a negative situation into a positive one. Though your staff should be trained in how to assuage patient concerns for most scenarios, involved cases are always better resolved by the doctor personally. Many times patients simply feel the need to express their opinions and they want you to hear them. When conflicts are addressed properly, dentists can win patients for life. A common psychological principle is being played out here, as people tend to bond with those who listen to their problems and adjudicate in their favor.

I am reminded of a procedure in which my associate dentist extracted four primary teeth on an eight-year-old boy as requested by his orthodontist. The teeth did not submit without a fight, and neither did the little boy. There was screaming and wailing and probably some sweat pouring from both doctor and patient. Though I was not present for this procedure, I was brought into the fold through a letter I received from the child's mother. She forwarded copies to both the treating dentist and the referring orthodontist.

This parent was clearly not happy with the manner in which the extractions were performed. She also questioned the orthodontic necessity for the removal of these primary teeth. When calling to check on the child, we tried our best to listen to the mother's discontent, and listen we did. Then, in a stunning turn of events, this disgruntled parent referred me three new patients the following month! With all my time in dentistry, I did not see that coming. I was just happy not to get a letter from her attorney. Instead, she was still sufficiently enamored with our practice that she felt comfortable sending her friend and her friend's two little boys to our office. The two young boys, however, were more than mildly concerned that they would have to go through the same procedure as their little friend!

The opportunity to overcome an obstacle is at times a welcome diversion from a stale workday. Too many of these, however, can exhaust the fervor of even the most ambitious dentist. You can limit your exposure to these hurdles by restricting your patient population to only those amenable to your style of practice.

Patient Perceptions in Cosmetic Dentistry

There is perhaps no other facet of our profession more reliant on patient satisfaction than that of cosmetic dentistry. Success in this field depends not only on clinical ability but also on an eye for esthetics. Therefore, it becomes imperative that the dentist's idea of what appears appealing is consistent with the patient's expectations. I have completed so many of these cases that I often feel like I can take on demanding procedures without concern for a client's sometimes unreasonable desires. Because I enjoy a challenge, I have at times overlooked the importance of patient selection while instead focusing on case selection. Unfortunately, these two things are occasionally mutually exclusive.

In today's dentistry we have materials at our disposal that allow us to perform remarkable feats that were clearly not achievable two decades ago. Smile design techniques and proper material selection permit results that are predictable and time-tested. We can now place beautiful restorations that are strong, durable and affordable. However, even with these fail safes in place, not every lady can be made to look like Halle Berry and not every man will end up resembling Brad Pitt. When patients seek the unattainable, it is required of us to temper their expectations with reality.

While most patients can be wowed with our esthetic dentistry prowess, a handful can never be satisfied. The cosmetic consult can serve to weed out these potential clients before they become a career long headache. Listen carefully to how these patients respond to your questioning. The cases I typically forego are the ones in which the patients are dissatisfied with prior work that appears nearly flawless. In these cases, I believe the imperfection to be with the candidate's expectations and not with the actual dentistry.

Even when I think I might be able to make subtle improvements, I realize that I may not be able to change a patient's perceptions. As opposed to hard selling cosmetic procedures by expressing "How great you're going to look!" I instead try to under-promise and over-deliver. Dental consultants may disagree with this approach and suggest that I might be leaving production on the table. I would rather select cases wisely, and gently instill the idea that the patient received so much more than was ever imagined.

The Psychology of Happiness

While it is inaccurate to generalize about that which makes people happy, there are similarities among us with respect to contentedness. Unfortunately, those things for which many people strive in business do not seem to offer ultimate satisfaction. Though chasing the dollar can be an enjoyable competitive sport for some, it often leaves us weary and short on time for other activities we value more. When managed intelligently, money can serve as a reliable source of liberty and comfort. It is only a source, however, not an object of comfort.

Studies reveal that humans consistently point to non-monetary things as the true source of their happiness. Time spent with friends, family and loved ones, enjoying activities in nature, doing things for others, faith based activities and relaxing on vacation all rank highly on the list of human enjoyment. When used as a vehicle to pursue things that make us happy, money can be a good thing. When we are consumed with its accumulation, however, it may not be worth the struggle.

While it is not for me to determine what it is that you should do with your money, there are certain principles of money management that can assist with keeping more of what you earn and thereby achieving greater freedom. With respect to psychology, it really comes down to tailoring the way we think about money. The results of a recent study of 70 millionaires performed by Jeff Lehman, author of *The Frugal Millionaires*, were posted online. Some interesting truths from his post follow:

> Frugal millionaires are unique thinkers when it comes to spending money:
> 1. They can easily delay their need for gratification when purchasing;
> 2. They do not like wasting anything (especially money);

3. They make living below their means painless;
4. They are resourceful in getting what they want by carefully timing their consumer purchases;
5. Their sense of self-entitlement is highly minimized and;
6. Spending is OK with them...depending on what they are buying (think: appreciating vs. depreciating assets).

These millionaires keep more money than they spend, that is why they are rich. Key Point: They do not view shopping as a sport. They shop efficiently and spend their time doing more important things with their lives. [23]

We tend to use the word rich in our society rather loosely. The definition of this word will be different for everyone. I am reminded of a consistent childhood lesson offered by my father, "Being rich has nothing to do with money, son." In addition, simply having a million dollars serves little purpose if one is leveraged to the hilt. Of greatest importance to me from this study are the millionaires' common threads of deferred gratification, living below one's means and the absence of self-entitlement. Sheryl Crow probably put it best through the lyrics of her popular song *Soak up the Sun*, "It's not having what you want, it's wanting what you've got."

The frugal millionaire may view money as simply another tool employed to achieve financial independence. This person would not tend to agree with the bumper sticker philosophy, *Whoever dies with the most stuff wins*! If the sacrifice involved to obtain all that stuff prevents you from enjoying any of it, where is the value in it? When our spending habits are out of touch with our earnings, we are then forced to endlessly chase our debt. When we are able to rein in spending and live below our means, we can live free of the restrictions imposed on us by that debt.

It may appear easy for those with money to talk about not focusing on it, while those with less may have a more difficult time living this way. There is certainly value in being privileged enough to not have to constantly worry about money, and this good fortune cannot be overlooked. However, people of varied income levels can benefit from controlling their mindset with respect to spending habits. I am pretty sure that almost everybody can spend all of what they make. The real challenge is to restrict ourselves from doing this, thus relieving us of the burden to constantly earn. Learning to be happy with what we have allows us to overcome this challenge with the least resistance. Then we might say, *Whoever lives with the most peace wins.*

Chapter 15

Mistakes I Have Made

No practice owner is immune from making mistakes in business. We all at times are forced to step out in faith with our ideas in hopes of dropping foot on solid ground. Unfortunately, business decisions are riddled with trial and error experience. Many times we find that our strides toward terra firma land us in quick sand. As entrepreneurs, we are necessary risk takers. With greatest risk comes greatest reward. Do not be discouraged, however, when those risks work out in favor of the house and not the gambler.

Radio Advertising Mistake

Given my understanding of the public's opposition to sitting through radio commercials, one might assume I would have been able to avoid the enticement to purchase one of these ads. Unfortunately, the sales pitch was greater than my ability to resist what I knew to be a risky investment at best. When I started my first practice, a friend convinced me that I needed to get my name out there and the best way to do that was to broadcast it over the airwaves. *Great idea!* I thought. *I want everyone to know my name.*

I began the process of interviewing numerous radio advertising sales reps, looking for the company with the most affordable package that would provide my practice greatest visibility. Most seemed very expensive and the first few reps appeared to present a very bland message. They were droning on about rate sheets, time slot positioning and demographics. I was unimpressed and on the verge of abandoning the project when Cody stepped foot into my office. He showed up with a large 1980's boom box on his shoulder and a big bright smile on his face. After informing Cody that I had already met with a number of other radio advertising reps, he took an imaginary bat from his shoulder and swung as if warming up for his pitch.

This guy made quite an impression on me, and he was about to get paid for it. Cody pressed play on the diesel of a tape recorded he was toting, and the sound which came out was a music jingle he had created specifically for my practice. I was hooked. *I'm going to be on the radio!* I thought. *I'm big time now.* All that was left to do was agree to the details and sign the contract. Little did I know that what remained of the process was for me to bleed lots of money for very minimal return on investment.

My spot ran numerous times on multiple days. I had my staff trained and prepared for the new patient explosion that was about to occur. I considered getting another phone line to accommodate what was sure to be an influx of calls during the times of day the spot was running. Not only were the calls few and far between, but the type of patient showing up for the complimentary consultation the ad promised was seldom interested in actually scheduling the dentistry I had to offer.

Young and inexperienced in business, I considered this a lesson learned. This learning experience did not come cheaply, however. I probably should have realized when I was at the radio station handing over that first big check what the manager of the station already knew. He took the check, looked at me and offered, "I hope this works out for you." Suffice it to say, someone made money on this transaction and it was not me.

Video Marketing Mistake

I embarked on perhaps my greatest marketing endeavor while managing my practice in Southern California. I decided that it was a good idea to create, produce and distribute a professional video advertising my cosmetic dentistry expertise to both existing patients and the general public. I was further convinced of this inspiration by the professional video editors who maintained a vested interest in the completion of the project. Featuring the NFL's San Diego Chargers' cheerleaders, The Charger Girls, I embarked on my own version of Hollywood's *Extreme Makeover*. The fact that two of these ladies were already patients afforded me the opportunity to feature their squad in the production. I encouraged/demanded staff participation, and invited select patients to relate positive anecdotes pertaining to our office. I, in turn, provided testimony concerning my youthful struggles with the imperfect smile.

This was a colossal undertaking, in terms of time and expense. I hired a producer, an editor and a camera man, and met with them often. I purchased the rights to an 800 number and paid a professional to brainstorm a jingle incorporating the number to stream throughout the video. I wrote the script narrating the 15 minute video, but needed to hire someone to smoothly deliver the monologue. I settled on a local radio personality whose fee was an affordable two bleaching trays along with whitening gel. My staff members, of course, charged me for their time while my patients participated out of the kindness of their hearts, and possibly for the promise of one of those most prized coffee mugs I would send to my referring patients.

The videographers set up shop in the reception area, and their people and equipment consumed much of the balance of my office space. Those not being filmed laid in wait, everyone crammed into my personal doctor's office. There we were; patients unacquainted with one another, staff members and me, all stuffed into this tiny room, heating up before our shot at 15 minutes of fame. Now that was comfortable for everyone!

The editing process was a project in itself. I hired a friend with a flair for the artistic to rearrange and assimilate the hours of footage we had captured. My buddy was admittedly a bit of a disjointed eccentric, so the project took a little longer than I had anticipated. Viewing the initial cut for the first time, I saw smiles flying all over the screen and heard blaring music in the background. We had some pretty serious rearranging to do. I grew so weary of the whole thing that I finally sent a staff member as proxy to finish the editing process for me. I needed someone to represent our ideas or the finished product would have looked more like a music video on MTV than a health care provider's advertisement.

When the project finally wrapped, I was left to determine how many video copies to produce. I decided that 500 was a nice round number, so the outsourcing company I employed to reproduce them handed me a bid. This firm would be responsible for box cover design and manufacturing as well. Yes, I did say box covers. This venture concluded just in advance of the DVD revolution's swallowing up of the video market. This meant that my 500 copies were going to be processed on video film compatible only with the video cassette recorder. The Charger Girls made the cover, and as an Aussie friend of mine would later say, "They were quite bully for that."

Nearly one full year after this notion of video marketing took root in my mind, twenty shipped packages teaming with my new cosmetic practice destiny landed on the office doorstep. The next step was to get these promotional jewels into the hands of the population of potential esthetic dentistry candidates. We mailed them to new patients, distributed them to existing patients, provided a display rack for their advertisement and sent them to new residents in our community. In the end, I am pretty sure that the only people who ever viewed that 15 minute video through its completion were my relatives during one holiday visit, and perhaps The Charger Girls.

The most significant obstacle to viewership turned out to be the free time necessary to devote to watching a video on dentistry. Dentists sometimes have trouble with this time commitment, let alone the average individual having minimal interest in the subject. The most poignant reminder of this fact came courtesy of comments offered by an existing patient, "I got your video, thanks. I haven't gotten around to watching it yet. I want to. I'll probably just wait until I come home one night really drunk and pop it in then. I'll let you know what I think about it." Perhaps my family would have derived more pleasure from my video had they also assumed his preferred viewing state.

I am reminded of the marginal success of this advertising project each time I move to a new home. The many remaining boxes of unopened videos always accompany me, yet I am unsure as to the reasoning behind this. I guess I will always have them as a constant reminder of my 15 minutes of fame. My young niece seems to enjoy the video with her uncle's face on the box as her favorite bedtime movie. At least when I do relocate, these boxes are prepackaged and sealed, providing one less hassle on moving day.

Television Commercial Advertising Mistake

Refusing to accept defeat through the apparent failure of my video marketing project, I attempted to reclaim some of my investment through television commercial advertising. Having already paid for the original shoot, radio personality monologue and catchy jingle, I thought I could certainly recoup the expense with the flow of new patients TV commercials would provide my practice. Plus, I could not let that witty contact number, 1-800-NICE SMILE, go to waste!

The television stations were happy to accommodate my desire to fight this battle to the finish. They provided my own personal advertising associate to help me determine the best ways to reach my target population. She helped me establish what content was ideal to extract from the video, what time slots were most appropriate to position my message and how many commercials per day to run.

I dissected the video into 30 and 60 second spots. I also provided the original 15 minute version to be used for infomercials as well. I submitted these segments for air on weekday afternoons and late at night. In return, I received minimal new patient inquiries. These calls came mainly from the unemployed sitting at home watching reruns of Judge Judy, or those coming home after a night out at the bars convinced that a bright new smile would help them connect with their desired mate. None of these patients were interested in paying for my services, however.

Apparently I failed to factor in that attempting to recapture my initial investment would require an investment of its own. I should have known from watching the Super Bowl that TV advertising was the most expensive form of marketing available. Yes, I had the piece already produced, but the spots came with a lofty price tag of their own. As I should have learned from my experience with radio advertising, someone was going to make money on this transaction and it was not going to be me. Big market advertising comes with big overhead expense and thereby marginalizes return on investment. Though perhaps not the intention of the rapper when he stated, "Mo money, mo problems," Biggie had it right when it comes to radio and television advertising.

Edward M. Logan, DDS

Computer Company Selection Mistake

The importance of choosing a local company to install your computer system cannot be overemphasized. When starting my most recent scratch practice, I decided to try and save some money by acting on a friend's referral and employing a small computer firm based in California. The price seemed right and I figured myself a fool not to retain these guys to provide and connect my entire network of computers. Given that my new practice was being built upon dirt floors within wood beamed walls, not in California but Missouri, made the process a bit more complex.

The owner of the company conceived all the plans and even recommended building the computers himself. While I was busy counting the dollars in savings, I was being blinded by the additional costs lurking behind the initial bid. I decided to ignore the fact that if anything ever went wrong with these computers, the installer would be unable to drop by, quickly evaluate and resolve the issue. After flying him in from San Francisco and watching the project and associated expenses extend far beyond the estimates, one might think I would have recognized the error of my ways. Still calculating that my costs would come in well below the local company bids, I allowed him to press on.

After absorbing the fees to rebook the return flight to the Bay Area for the second time, I assumed I was finished bleeding cash for this mistake. Not long after the wheels touched down at S.F.O., however, my brand new computers sequentially began to fail. Since these were state of the art, hand-built systems, no one seemed to know where to obtain replacement parts for the computers or how to go about repairing them. The company owner and system designer did little to help resolve our issues. He seemed rather to be best equipped to add fuel to the burning flames and exacerbate the problems. It became clear to us that he considered our I.Q.s to be sub-computer guy. This was not initially obvious to us, as he did not seem to speak any version of English with which we were familiar. Although at least two of my staff members speak technical jargon, his level of communication appeared deliberately aloof.

We were continually being offered the excuse that airborne dental debris must be entering the computers and destroying them. When that failed, he informed us that the brown-outs from local electrical surges were causing the hard drives to crash. Realizing this company would be of no assistance, I was forced to enlist an area specialist to rescue my practice from the computerless dark ages of dentistry. An untimely crash of the server, which appeared large enough to support a NASA mission, prompted an emergency run to the computer repair company of last resort.

Even these high cost technology experts could not recognize the components of this system, so I was forced to abandon the idea of using a server altogether. The fruitless information provided did not come without the price tag associated with this company's failed efforts. Slowly but surely, I was going deeper in the red for my decision to go with the cheap guy. The nightmare experience I had with this operation prompted me to envision a new tag line for this company; *Providing complicated solutions to simple problems!*

Save yourself some aggravation and overhead expense by interviewing various local computer companies and choosing the one with whom you feel most comfortable. My suggestion would be to utilize the big dental equipment and supply company you will be using for most of your business needs. This company will have a vested interest in maintaining your happiness and thereby keeping your business. Dental industry vendors are much more familiar with the system requirements of a dental office than the average computer firm. They are also considerably more likely to stay in business in your area, and not decide to move the company to Portugal like the guy who built and installed my computers did!

Chapter 16

Start Your Practice, Then Start Saving

Eat, Drink and Be Merry!

The thrill of bringing your business to solvency and beyond can be overwhelming. While riding the wave of a profitable practice, we can be easily lulled into believing that things are always going to be this good, despite what we do to ensure it. Many pundits use this uncertainty to scare us into believing we need outside services to maintain our dominance. My perspective is that when most dental practices reach a certain level of inertia, they will continue to reward the hard working dentists for many years to come. The truth is, however, many practices recede in value, volume and profitability resulting from a combination of factors.

Compared to most professions, health care in general is relatively recession resistant. Dentistry, in particular though, can encounter rough waters at times when the economy is weak. Our profession has undergone a transformation from one in which the primary revenue source was insurance based treatment to that of a more elective procedural based business. This shift has been positive for practice production volumes when the economy has been steady, but can cause production to fall off normal levels when consumer spending stalls.

With the average yearly maximum benefits most dental insurances provide a patient being between $1,000 and $3,000, simple math reveals that much of our income must be made outside of these limitations. The fact that these reimbursement limits have increased little, if at all, since the 1970's, supports dentistry's necessary swing to a more elective industry. While we can rely on the possession of dental insurance to get patients in our doors, we cannot count on it to sustain our practices. Revenues independent of dental insurance reimbursement average greater than 50% for many practices. We therefore depend upon our patients to fund our lifestyles.

When people are forced to cut costs, one of the first things to go is elective treatment. Compound that with the job losses associated with a recessionary economy and your practice now consists of more patients without dental insurance or discretionary income. It is imperative that you as a small business owner remain nimble enough to fund your expenses during these unanticipated, yet all too common, periods of interrupted growth. Cost controlling strategies and overhead mitigation is essential to withstanding the effects of declining practice production. A well instituted plan of routine saving throughout your career is another protocol crucial to keeping the business ship righted in this trying environment.

The whimsical nature of our country's economy is but one of the elements responsible for stagnant practice growth. The issue of professional burnout cannot be overlooked as our practices mature. When a dentist's perception of the practice as a dynamic life enhancement is altered, profitability can suffer. It takes a concerted effort to keep one's practice at the front of the pack. When we identify other aspects of life to be more important than the job itself, our former levels of maximal production may become unachievable. This in and of itself is not necessarily a bad thing. We need to be mindful of this potentiality and prepare for it accordingly.

Unexpected illness or injury can disrupt practice production and sometimes arrest it altogether. Though disability insurance and business overhead insurance distributions can assist when these unfortunate circumstances present, they often include lengthy elimination periods. When they do begin to provide disbursements, the amounts are rarely sufficient to sustain us for extended periods of time. Since we *are* the company, we are the ones responsible for supporting ourselves when times are tough.

After many years in practice, some friends and colleagues of mine have begun to discuss these issues in more detail. It seems almost taboo among dentists to admit their insecurities with respect to income saved. Most of us get caught up in the *earn-and-spend* mentality and feel little need to break this cycle in view of our lofty incomes. One colleague finally gathered the nerve to initiate an email thread about saving and retirement planning. The resulting banter, though amusing, further illustrated the immense need for this type of discussion. When a particular dentist responded, "I want it all right now, I'll worry about the future later," I could not help but laugh. Of course that is what so many aspire to do. Eat, drink and be merry, for tomorrow we die.

This dilemma is by no means specific to dentists. For the year preceding the writing of this book, the savings rate of the average American was in fact negative. This means that thanks to our ability to secure more credit than we can afford, we actually spent more money than we earned. The current economic recession has injected some reason into the budgets of our citizens, and the average savings rate has jumped to an astounding 5%. This demonstrates that saving money is not an unreachable goal. It should not take a crisis, however, to bring it to fruition. It does take, on the other hand, a well conceived plan and a dedication to remaining committed to its implementation.

(I am neither a certified financial planner nor a CPA and I have no formal financial or accounting education outside of that which I have pursued on my own. I recommend seeking the advice of professionals when it comes to all retirement, financial and tax planning. The financial planning and tax information I am offering here and throughout this book are nothing more than my opinions based upon personal study and experience. This information should not be considered as expert advice in these areas and may not be applicable or beneficial to your particular situation.)

Investing for Retirement

It has proven beneficial to me to take advantage of my retirement plan to the maximum extent possible with respect to tax law. Certain plan types are more beneficial to some dentists than others, depending upon the ages of the doctor and staff, number of years the business has been in operation and the amount of money the doctor is willing and able to commit. Funding your retirement plan regularly can yield substantial benefits over time. Certain tax benefits apply to qualified retirement plans, and should be discussed with your accountant to determine which plan is best for you.

If you are willing to invest the time, have a penchant for numbers and genuinely enjoy learning about taxes, investing and financial planning, there is a lot you can discover on your own. Information is available which will allow you to steer your own ship, if you are so inclined. While I still believe financial and tax professionals to be necessary in assisting with the process, the more you know, the more equipped you will be to bring suggestions and make decisions which are in your best interest. Though some creative and dedicated financial planners are out there, I have found very few experts who care about my money the way I do.

If you are intimidated about investing, disinterested or simply lacking the time to investigate your investments, a professional can be of great value to you. Though returns are important, a key element to making money when you are not at work is establishing a routine dedication of funds to whatever form of investment you choose. Dollar-cost-averaging, which results when you invest at specific time intervals, has been shown to outpace many other forms of investing. This strategy allows the investor to take advantage of price fluctuations, and thereby additional gains, by purchasing equities, mutual funds, etc., when costs are lower. The idea is that you make investing a regular, consistent application of funds to your retirement piggy bank, which can be defined as whatever diversification of investments you and your financial adviser have chosen.

Your Business as a Means to an End

A primary goal of starting a for-profit business is rarely to employ any means necessary to support the business, while ignoring the business owner's needs altogether. Though the dental equipment and supply industry will never restrict you from reinvesting all your returns back into the practice, it is rarely beneficial to do so. Once you have wrapped up your loan or lease for the initial practice purchase, property purchase, office build-out or office beautification, you should start focusing on yourself. This is not always a popular notion with dental industry vendors or consultants who may encourage you to continue to "put your money back into the practice for maximum growth." While this reasoning is common among small business owners, I think that it comes with frequently disregarded limitations.

Is it really in your best interest to continue to invest the majority of your resources into office improvements for the first seven to ten years of your practice? Have you not just spent a pile of money getting the place up and running? Were you not pretty happy with the decisions you made in designing and equipping your client-centered office? Is it really necessary to improve upon these things already? I find it more rewarding to the bottom line to garner as much value out of those initial purchases as possible. Consider a seven year note on your tenant improvements; what sense does it make to pay for something again during the repayment period for which you are still paying?

Do not be lured into believing that what is newest is always best, and that you are behind the times if you do not purchase it. Be Dr. Analytical and determine for your particular practice if that fancy pearl is really going to pay for itself like you are being told. Maintain confidence that your well contemplated buying decisions will pay off and do not keep buying things because of uncertainty. You are not in business to support the lifestyles of the equipment and supply reps. You are in business to support yourself, your family and anyone else you have determined to warrant your financial assistance.

Neither are you in business to support the business per se. The business is there to support you. The business is there to allow you to feed the pig, so he can ultimately feed you. It is not there to prevent you from keeping anything for yourself or from ever achieving retirement. Remember, the business is a means to an end, not the end in itself.

Debt Reduction

There is looming debate over whether reducing one's debt serves as a true form of savings. After all, as one retired dentist once informed me, "Taking on debt is the American way!" While this statement may be true, the reasoning behind it may not be so beneficial. Since most debt comes married to an interest rate, even when taking into consideration the advantages of tax deductions, you may be losing money by carrying it. Whenever I have presented various debt structuring alternatives to my accountant, he has always advised me not to consider taxes as the basis for assuming debt. When interest is deductible, you are still commonly paying the majority of it after taxes. When people claim, "It's a write off," the assumption seems to be that the full value of the investment will be recoverable as a dollar for dollar reimbursement.

This really only means that one's taxable income may be reduced by that amount, not that one will see all that money back at the end of the year.

It seems logical to pay off debt when the potential rate of return on that money, if it were to be invested, is less than the debt's interest rate including tax deductions. It also stands to reason that first paying off the highest interest debt including tax deductions is fiscally beneficial. I always evaluate the true interest rate which accounts for tax deductions when contemplating which debt to pay off first. You can calculate exactly what percentage return you are guaranteed by paying off this debt. If other forms of investment cannot guarantee you this return, or if you are unwilling to assume the risk that your investments might underperform, paying off debt may interest you.

Reducing one's debt can serve purposes other than providing guaranteed investment returns. It can afford the dentist liberty from being inextricably bound to the practice. The less you owe, the less you are required to labor to get back to par. Assume your personal living expenses and office overhead, excluding debt, remain stable; when your debt is paid off, your practice production levels can drop consistent with the monthly debt payment amount without negatively impacting your current lifestyle. This means that, if you want to, you can work less. Or, if you so choose, you can maintain production levels and simply take home more money or invest the additional monies in your retirement account. It also means that if an unfortunate eventuality occurs restricting your ability to produce, you will not be as encumbered with debt.

Financial advisers often point to the importance of saving and investing regularly, sometimes ignoring debt reduction in the process. While I do agree that habitual investing is a great way to plan for the future, reducing debt is another important piece to the savings puzzle. An opposing argument might be the following: if in lieu of saving you have dedicated all your available income to reducing debt, you may not have anything to show for your efforts if you are forced to quit working. Most debt will not be forgiven, however, when such a regrettable circumstance presents. Another argument is that the magic of compounding returns can provide substantial amounts of money in the future when monies are invested early and often. This reasoning represents the time value of money. As everyone has differing financial goals and expectations, careful consideration must be given to your specific financial situation when making these decisions.

When I started my first practice, I was looking for the ideal space in which to set up shop. One dentist posted an ad in a dentistry specific newsletter detailing space in his office that was available for another dentist to lease and occupy. Since I was in the *How Do You Choose a Location?* phase of my start-up practice, I dropped by to meet the doctor and evaluate the office space. This dentist was an amiable guy, but the location was too small to support future growth. The thing I remember most about this doctor was his expressed view on debt accumulation and repayment scheduling.

The dentist was probably in his early forties and leasing a space with five operatories. He had recently remodeled his addition and assumed a loan to fund the construction and tenant improvements. He told me about a nervous habit, an eye twitch, that he had recently developed resulting from the stress of the architectural project. This dentist then shared with me his ultimate comfort, however, in the fact that he had an entire 33 years in which to pay back the note! While I could appreciate the lower monthly payments that intrigued this doctor, I was not able to understand his willingness to commit himself to this endeavor into his mid-seventies.

Personally, I do not want to owe anyone anything for that long. I realize that, by necessity, it is sometimes unavoidable to carry debt into our golden years. However, the business cycle is often shorter than the life of a home, for example, and the loans accompanying businesses should be more concise as well. Though I was just starting out, I was a bit intimidated by the thought of engaging myself to this profession for such a seemingly endless period of time. I really felt troubled for this guy, and committed myself not to allow this circumstance to befall me.   If you plan to work as many decades as it takes for the handpiece to drop from your hand, I applaud you for your perseverance. Many dentists have expressed such a love for the profession that they levy the claim, "I'm never going to retire!" Personally, I love playing sports, competing and being outdoors. If I could do those things for a living and get paid for them, I would probably never look to retire either. I would not, however, plan my finances around the assumption that my body would hold up to do this forever. Though it is never appealing to think about our eventual limitations, as distant as they may seem, it is a reality that most of us will not be able to do dentistry forever. The faster you are able to become debt-free and unbound by the necessity to command a high dollar income, the more freedom you will have to do what you want to do, simply because you want to do it.

Pay Yourself First

Although reinvesting revenues back into the business, and clearly a certain amount is necessary, has been shown to increase production and practice valuation, doctors must first pay themselves or the ultimate gain is minimal. A more accurate representation of the value extracted from starting, growing and managing a business is the amount which has been put away. Selling one's practice has proven to provide less of a nest egg and more of an income supplement. One retiree confided in me recently, "There's no such thing as a nest egg!" The growing number of dentists coming out of retirement in recent years and back into practicing dentistry speaks to this reality. Unfortunately, many of these doctors have saved too little, watched their investments disappear through recent stock market erosion or maintained personal living expenses that outpaced retirement savings.

When determining what it means to have the business support you, consider not only the money it takes to fund your current lifestyle, but also what remains to sustain you down the road. I view every dollar saved as one dollar closer to freedom from the necessity to do what I do for a living in order simply to live. If I want to do dentistry for the enjoyment of it, then so be it. If I want to do it for my patients, then what a great way to do it! If I want to do it because I am clinically gifted, my patients love me and I like the identity of being a doctor, then these are all respectable motivations. If I have to do dentistry for the money and none of these other elements exist, then I am in a very precarious position and perhaps driving the fast lane to professional burnout.

Foremost in my mind is the lesson of deferred gratification I learned in a high school sociology class. Dentists have been conditioned to excel at deferred gratification by the necessity of their extended educations. Regrettably, this application of restraint often gets tossed out the window as soon as that first big paycheck hits the account. While we all like to enjoy the fruits of our labor, sometimes it becomes necessary to force ourselves to consider our futures. When we do save, we must resist the temptation to liquidate our investments whenever something more immediately pressing presents.

This scenario will replay itself repeatedly, with the first instinct being to access the savings coffer. This is quite possibly the biggest savings mistake a dentist can make. The notion is, *There is so much money in that retirement account, and I won't be needing it for such a long time.* This is the misconception that so commonly results in undermining the most well strategized investment plan. The consistent, habitual dedication of funds to your retirement account is to wealth accumulation what leaving the money in that account is to your future financial stability. As science and technology improves, we are living much longer than we were even in the very recent past. Since retirement income projections are now being calculated based upon a 100 year life expectancy, we need to plan for the encouraging eventuality that this expectation is realized.

A Day at the Dentist's Office

Chapter 17

Treatment Planning for Case Acceptance

Getting Treatment Scheduled

Your success in getting patients appointed for treatment identified through the examination process will be largely determined by that of the internal marketing protocols you have in place. In as much as possible, try not to allow a patient with a treatment plan to exit your office before scheduling an appointment. At the very minimum, assure that the patient leaves with educational brochures, a financial arrangement for the outlined treatment and contact information for your office.

Employing a dedicated treatment coordinator to explain the health benefits of treatment and the related financing options will greatly increase the likelihood that patients will appoint for treatment. This individual time allows patients to ask questions and permits your staff to educate them on the planned procedures. If no such treatment coordinator exists, it is mandatory that the hygienist, dental assistant or, ideally, the doctor supplies this individual time to each patient.

It is highly beneficial to distribute written information to your patients explaining particular procedures in detail. It is an unfortunate truth that much of the information related to patients during treatment planning discussions will be forgotten by the time they reach their driveways. Additionally, everyone has different learning styles. Patients who learn best by reading rather than listening will especially benefit from treatment brochures. Through the perusal of a brochure, a parent or spouse can be educated and reassured about the impending dental treatment a patient anticipates receiving. Brochures should be readily accessible and offered to each patient during treatment plan discussions. Smart Practice has a variety of high quality brochures detailing many of the most common dental procedures. These brochures can be personalized with your office contact information as well as a message from you.

Promoting Cosmetic Dentistry

Cosmetic dentistry lends itself to photography as the principal means by which to impart its message. Most dentists these days perform much of their dentistry in a cosmetic fashion, whether they consider themselves to be cosmetic dentists or not. This is borne out by the increasing popularity of tooth-colored restorations and all-porcelain crowns. Any practice can enhance the value of its patient base by increasing patient awareness of the esthetic improvements dentistry has to offer. This can be maximally achieved through the use of digital photography, most notably of your own patient cases.

The utility of digital photography in dentistry is multifaceted. We currently capture pre-treatment and post-treatment images of all patients receiving involved cosmetic care. I maintain an archived portfolio of photographs reflecting treatment performed for even the most minimally involved cases. Select cases reflecting various procedural options such as veneers, implants, composites, whitening and all-porcelain restorations are displayed in a *Before and After* section on our website. By accessing the website on the operatory screen, we are able to show patients cases bearing resemblance to their own. Illustrating the successful results of your work on patients receiving similar treatment establishes confidence in your abilities and enthusiasm for improving their smiles.

We have taken the additional step of displaying these pictures in a photo album kept in the waiting room, and in frames mounted on the walls throughout the office. We keep a second photo album available in the operatory area to be quickly referenced when discussing treatment options with a patient. By drawing from an extensive portfolio of photographed cases, you enhance your ability to schedule a wide variety of cosmetic treatment plans for care. A third album composed of testimonials from excited, satisfied patients can serve to stimulate patient emotion and encourage treatment.

Equally fundamental to a patient's likelihood to schedule esthetic treatment is the doctor's ability to impart a feeling of excitement concerning these procedures. Every patient likes to feel important and a dentist's expressed enthusiasm serves to reinforce this impression. A passionate dentist will enhance a patient's anticipation of the expected beauty of the treatment outcome. The most effective method of ensuring a high treatment plan acceptance rate is enlisting patient involvement in the decision making process.

Certain questions are effective in drawing the patient into the aura of excitement, while serving to eliminate many routinely expressed barriers to treatment. The most obvious hurdles to the scheduling of dental procedures are time, money and the expectation of pain. A valuable approach would be to suggest, "If we could find a way to work within your budget, would you be interested in this type of dentistry?" I also like to put the patient at ease by simply inquiring, "Are you concerned that there might be some discomfort involved with this procedure?" To encourage patient imagination I ask, "What do you desire your improved smile to look like? How do you think that new smile would make you feel?" Often I will ask, "Are there any other barriers preventing you from scheduling at this time?" When I feel as if I have successfully overcome these impediments, I always offer, "When would you like to have this treatment performed?" At times I might inquire, "Is there some special event for you this year during which you would like to reveal this new, beautiful smile?"

It is imperative that you provide the patient the opportunity to procure the treatment you have spent so much effort presenting. "When would you like to have this done?" is an inviting, non-confrontational query that demands a reply. Even if the response is, "Never," at least you have afforded the patient the option of scheduling today. So many times doctors, in their desire not to offend, omit this most essential step and thus ensure that no treatment gets appointed. If you are confident that you can improve a patient's smile, you have the technology and the patient is inspired to proceed, what is the harm in asking if the patient is ready to go? Perhaps we do not have because we do not ask.

I once attended a lecture by Dr. Steven Poss, an expert in esthetic dentistry, in which he advised the use of a cosmetic brochure tailored specifically to an individual's practice. He entitled his brochure, *What is a Smile Lift?*, capitalizing on society's desire for appearance-related procedures. I called and asked him if I could use the same tag line for my own brochure. He graciously agreed and I created a professional color brochure enhanced with *Before and After* case photos of my work. I position displays of these brochures on countertops and in operatories, in plain view of patients receiving treatment plans. I have also used these in mailers to specific demographics of households and hand them out to anyone inquiring about esthetic dentistry. These brochures are beneficial in explaining the details of cosmetic care and revealing the potential results in living color. I was later reminded of my gratitude toward Dr. Poss when I saw his larger than life ad on a billboard in Nashville while attending a Colts/Titans NFL game.

Promoting the excitement for cosmetic dentistry does not stop when the case is completed. Ultradent makes a convenient *Before and After* photo mount which I distribute to my cosmetic patients one month after case completion. I mail these images to patients at their place of employment to capitalize on visibility from co-workers, assuming patients are inclined to reveal that they had work done. This is an inexpensive way to encourage referrals for this rewarding type of dentistry that can be so profitable.

Dr. Bill Blatchford, a dentist and practice management consultant (www.blatchford.com), advises developing patient desires for treatment through questions that begin with *w* and *h*. He suggests asking "What do you expect from us?" and then telling patients how you can give it to them. He proposes that what patients want from their esthetic dentistry is for it to "look good, feel good and last a long time." He further recommends that to get patients over to your side and trusting your treatment plan, you must ask them about their favorite subject; themselves!

As a youth I struggled with the lack of dignity that accompanied an unappealing smile. Believe it or not, I was relatively unaware of what could actually be done to improve my particular situation. I must have considered my condition to be beyond correction. Though routine orthodontics and a few facial composites ultimately provided me the smile I began showing with pride, I had no concept of how quick, simple and affordable such treatment was going to be.

The possibilities were made visible to me through a cosmetic dentistry brochure I perused one afternoon while waiting in my general dentist's reception area. I was inspired enough to ask the dentist during my recall exam if such treatment options could be applicable to my case. His enthusiastic explanations excited me to the tipping point, and less than 18 months later I was sporting a new esthetic smile for life.

With the increasing predictability and popularity of porcelain veneers and all-porcelain restorations, the *perfect smile* can now be obtained in much less time than was true for my case. This improved timeliness is yet another benefit of today's cosmetic dentistry technology that we need to be sure to relate to our patients. My dentist employed two simple internal marketing, treatment scheduling protocols that ultimately resulted in a case closure and my extreme satisfaction with the treatment results. Had he not provided educational materials indicating the availability of these procedures in his office, and displayed the passion and enthusiasm for delivering them, I may have ultimately taken my business down the road.

Soft Tissue Management Programs

The treatment planning information shared to this point has been limited to certain patient interaction philosophies effective in assisting dentists to win patients for life. Dentists are extremely well trained in the clinical and diagnostic aspects of their profession. It seems, therefore, presumptuous to suggest ways in which a comprehensive clinical treatment plan should be outlined.

There are many companies promoting soft tissue management programs marketed to maximize your hygiene production. Some of these programs position the hygienist as manager of the hygiene department, encouraging the hygienist to run the department like a business. Many establish production goals and sell products and services in association with the periodontal treatment plan. Often times these programs are very aggressive, placing nearly every adult on advanced regimens. While these programs do not disappoint in their promise to produce income, they need to be monitored to ensure that the standard of care is being accurately represented.

I have yet to adopt one of these plans in any of my practices. I know I am leaving money on the table and I do not begrudge anyone who elects to implement one of these protocols. When properly executed, they are good for the patient and the practitioner. I have just been more comfortable over the years utilizing my own clinical judgment in treatment planning. You will need to determine if one of these programs is right for your practice.

Scripting Your Communication

Theories abound concerning the proper protocol for the new patient exam and initial rendering of the treatment plan. There is a wealth of consulting firms purporting the merits of scripting all verbal communication in the dental office. Virtually no word can exit your mouth except that which has been predetermined by some firm to elicit the most favorable response from your patient. This type of scripting has been very successful in the world of big business franchising. The worker at McDonald's is required to solicit, "Would you like fries with that?" or in the days preceding the scathing documentary, "Would you like to Supersize that?"

Large corporations are required to hire and train huge labor forces which are subject to rapid turnover. It is incumbent on them to have a repeatable template inn place to utilize in their training programs. The scripts have also been shown to induce the most buying of their product or service and provide a predictable measure of staff performance. They can be, however, quite impersonal. I do not dispute the effectiveness of scripting in the dental office environment. Most dental practice consultants make efforts to give a friendly, personal tone to their scripts. They may, however, fall short of establishing the true, more intimate relationship necessary between patients and their health care provider.

Though I have attended countless seminars and recorded volumes of notes on the topic of scripting, I have never effectively implemented such a protocol in any of my offices. When I have made the attempt, the words sounded very awkward coming out of my mouth. The only words that have ever sounded natural coming from me were my words, unscripted. Perhaps I would never have made a successful politician, but I do not think that is what people are looking for in their dentists. They are seeking someone they can trust.

Establishing Trust

There are many avenues to obtaining patient trust during the new patient exam. Each dentist will need to determine which protocol best suits the practice. One method is to have the friendly, compassionate hygienist greet and seat the patient. After initially getting to know the patient, inquiring about and listening to the patient's concerns and expectations, the hygienist captures x-rays and preliminarily evaluates the patient. The hygienist may point out areas of concern and offer possible treatment alternatives which the doctor might discuss.

The hygienist then introduces the doctor to the patient and openly relates the patient's expressed concerns, and the treatment possibilities previously outlined. Dr. Tom Orent labels this action "passing the power," suggesting that it reinforces in the patient's mind everything that has been discussed thus far. [24] This simple step affirms to the patient that concerns were heard and will now be addressed. In contrast to the all too frequent transfer from one customer service rep to another in which all particulars are lost, the patient will not be required to repeat everything that has already been tediously related.

Having comforted the patient with the gentle handoff of authority from the hygienist, the time has now come for you to take the stage. It is not for me to teach a dentist how to be trustable, caring and personable. My best advice would be to be yourself, because patients can easily detect when you are not. Studies have shown that patients whose dentists show concern and empathy have less anxiety, a greater perceived quality of care and a higher level of satisfaction. Patients tend to accept needed dental services from doctors that they identify as likeable and caring. Unfortunately for most in our profession, patients believe that few doctors fit this description.

Fortunately for you, a tremendous opportunity exists to win over the skeptical patient population simply by being friendly, listening to patients and making them feel comfortable. In fact, these factors may hold more importance in your practice success than any component of clinical superiority you may possess.

Certain interactions which have proven beneficial in solidifying the doctor/patient relationship may be helpful to consider. When greeting the patient for the first time, a smile is always perceived as a positive thing. A handshake and the use of the patient's name seem obvious but are important in initiating a bond of trust with your patient. Laughter is universally accepted as reassuring, and a compliment is something people do not receive often enough in our impersonal society. Simply listening to your patient will engender good will, the only cost being time. Of course, the cost for some patients in this regard is much greater than for others!

If you merely listen to your patients, you will be doing far better than most doctors. The subject most people know best and that which they like most to discuss is themselves. Therefore, indulge them. Ask questions about them and write down their answers so you will be able to revisit those conversations later. If you want to relieve your patients' communicative discomfort, talk about them. They know a lot about that subject! Talk about yourself only if they ask specific questions relating to you. This will happen less often than you think. When it does happen, it tends to make an impression. Patients who take the initiative to inquire about you personally are typically very comfortable with themselves and truly want to know about you. Indulge them as well. You will enjoy talking about you from time to time too, I suspect.

Bonding with Your Patients

In as much as is possible without appearing disingenuous, make an effort to establish a friendly bond with your patients. When you try too hard, the attempt at friendship seems false. I like to establish common ground with patients by asking about what they like to do, where they are from, where they live and work. If you are able to establish the, "*I'm just like you* mentality," according to Dr. Tom Orent, it is far easier to establish rapport with a patient. [25]

Examples in my practice may look as follows:

- Though my practice is located in a western suburb, I grew up in a working class area of the city. Whenever I have patients from this area, I will relate to them that my dad owned the bike shop in Old Town. I am still amazed at how many people remember that old shop, and that there are even some who remember my dad taking care of them.

- When I have Spanish speaking patients in my office I attempt to converse with them in Espanol. I confide in them that I spent time in Costa Rica and also tried to hone my skills while living in San Diego. I then ask forgiveness for the way I may be butchering their language!

- Whenever a fellow runner, cyclist or triathlete occupies my dental chair, we easily discuss our former races and more often than is necessary, the finish times in which we were able to complete these events.

This list will be different in your office than it is in mine, of course, but the principle remains the same. It is easier to share with patients things they may not want to hear when the dentist is already perceived as a decent person. In order to do this we need to learn to understand the differences in people and how they want to be treated. For purposes of the doctor/patient relationship, Dr. Walter Hailey may have put it best when he stated, "The Platinum Rule—*Do unto others as they would want to be done unto,* supersedes the Golden Rule." When we establish common ground, we confirm that we too, though doctors, are real people. When we establish a bond with our patients, we are not immediately the enemy, but someone who may actually have their best interest in mind. We then establish ourselves as likeable.

I was recently reminded of the benefits of this doctor/patient bond while on vacation. Last spring my wife Katie trained for the Rock and Roll Marathon to be run in San Diego in early June. Upon arrival in Southern California we picked up our shuttle, which consisted of a seldom driven pickup truck left for us by a close friend in the airport parking lot. Given that I was only running support for this particular race, I was in the mood for a much needed diversion from work at this point. I was happy to find that the truck started on the first try, which was never a guarantee for a vehicle that only saw the freeway when we came to visit. I was not quite as excited, however, to hear the CD that was playing in this antique when I fired it up. Some psychologist was waxing on about the many ways in which doctors are getting sued these days. *Oh man!* I thought. *The last thing I want to hear right now is how I might be getting sued back home while I'm out here on vacation.*

I began to envision the certified letter awaiting me at the office when I returned home.

My first impulse was to eject this killjoy and get on with my escape. As is the case with a B movie that regrettably catches your attention and prevents channel surfing, I could not seem to quell the message being delivered. I had to admit, this guy seemed to know what he was talking about and yet he did not appear to have it out for me. He was actually developing protocol which would assist doctors in our efforts to avoid getting sued. The premise was that it did not particularly matter what a doctor said when dealing with a patient, but the tone of voice employed that served as the primary predictor of an impending lawsuit. The studies he quoted offered evidence that even a doctor's clinical ability carried little significance in terms of the propensity to become entangled in legal battle.

The CD's narrator, Malcolm Gladwell, [26] related a study which followed two subsets of doctors, those who had never been sued and those who had been sued at least twice. [27] Dr. Levinson recorded hundreds of conversations between doctors and patients. She found that the non-sued doctors spent more than 3 minutes longer with each patient, and made orienting comments such as, "First I will examine you, and then we will talk the problem over," or, "I will leave time for your questions." Statements such as these seemed to set the patients at ease and ensure them that they would be able to ask questions should any come to mind. These doctors were more likely to engage in active listening, using statements such as, "Go on. Tell me more about that." They were also much more likely to make jokes and laugh during their consultations. There appeared to be no difference in the amount or quality of information offered between the two groups of doctors. The difference was solely in the way in which these doctors talked to their patients.

Another researcher and psychologist, Nalini Ambady, further dissected Levinson's recordings, focusing only on the conversations between surgeons and patients. [28]Dr. Ambady utilized two 10 second slices of dialogue a surgeon had with two different patients, leaving a total of 40 seconds for evaluation. Utilizing voice scrambling software, the researcher was able to disrupt the doctors' words, rendering them indiscernible. The software removed the high frequency sounds which allow us to recognize words, leaving only a garble. This garble preserved intonation, pitch and rhythm, but erased content. Dr. Ambady had judges assign ratings to the remaining slices based upon warmth, hostility, dominance and anxiousness. Using these ratings alone, she was able to reliably predict which surgeons got sued and which did not.

What is interesting about this study is that the judges had no background knowledge about any of the surgeons they were evaluating. They did not know the skill, experience or training of these doctors, nor the particular procedures being performed by them. What is even more compelling is the fact that the thinnest slice needed to predict a lawsuit was one revealing the tone of dominance by the doctor. Those surgeons appearing to sound dominant were typically found in the sued group and those less dominant and more concerned occupied the non-sued group. With the mood of the conversation still available, the researcher was able to determine what tone of voice appeared to allay patient aggression and that which seemed to invite it. According to Mr. Gladwell, "It comes down to a matter of respect. The simplest way that respect is communicated is through tone of voice, and the most corrosive tone of voice that a doctor can assume is a tone of dominance."

Analyses of malpractice lawsuits confirm that clinical mistakes are a poor predictor of whether a doctor will be sued. Patients are not inclined to file suits solely because they have been harmed by substandard medical care, but because this inferior care was accompanied by poor treatment on a personal level. Patients filing lawsuits tended to feel rushed, ignored or treated poorly by their doctors. Doctors failing to take time to explain what happened, to answer the patient's questions and to treat the patient like a human being are far more likely to be sued. Reliably predicting whether a doctor will be sued has most to do with knowing the relationship between the doctor and patient. According to a leading medical malpractice attorney, Alice Burkin, "People just don't sue doctors they like." [29] Though perhaps inapplicable to the patient pursuing a frivolous lawsuit, most people trust and confide in doctors who project an amiable persona.

I got on with my holiday with a little less trepidation, realizing that aside from attempting to deliver the best clinical care I was able to provide, I simply needed to give my patients a reason to like me.

That's not so difficult, is it? I thought. If you can engender trust in your patients and if they truly like you, your chances of gaining treatment plan acceptance are outstanding. As uncomplicated as it sounds, not only is being likeable the modus operandus of a doctor hoping to avoid litigation, it is the primary means by which to ensure a thriving, successful dental practice!

Communicating Effectively

Omitting certain dialogues and behaviors from your treatment planning process will go a long way in securing a trusting patient:

- Do not criticize.
- Do not complain.
- Do not interrupt.
- Do not argue.
- Do not criticize other dentists' work.
- Do not be arrogant.
- Do not lecture patients or *yell* at them.

In terms of the doctor's communication with the patient, it is less about what you do and more about what you do not do. The statistics are clear in revealing that most people who leave a dental practice are doing so because they do not like something about the dentist. The most common complaints among disgruntled patients are that the dentist is arrogant, lectures them or criticizes other dentists' work. I have found that the doctor/patient relationship shares similarity with that of the officer and the arrested, as anything you say can and will be held against you.

Though sometimes as dentists we may deserve the criticism, many times these customary patient complaints come as a result of our words being misconstrued. A small percentage of patients seem to be Negative Nelly's and no matter how you attempt to deflect their pessimism, they exhibit the desire and ability to corner you with your words. I, at times, feel challenged to teach them the error of their ways, and have on occasion been successful at outwitting them with reason. This is not typically the case, however, because they are the professionals here. It is generally more effective to say nothing, let their negative statements hang in the air, and possibly initiate an understanding in Negative Nelly that these words are a bit amiss. As my hygienist points out, "The less you say the better."

In contrast to the behaviors and discussions you wish to avoid when communicating with patients, those perceived as constructive include:

- Always begin the relationship in a positive manner.
- Give compliments as much as possible.
- Talk about patients' interests and lives.
- Show interest.
- Use the patient's name.
- Make every patient feel special.
- Be encouraging.
- Smile.
- Talk about things you have in common.
- Be enthusiastic about the treatment you are offering.

Respecting Your Staff

Another important factor to consider is the patient's perception of how you treat your staff. During the treatment plan process you should show respect for your hygienist. The same esteem should be given your dental assistant throughout every restorative procedure and the front office staff at the time of checkout. Even during times of high stress or in light of a staff member's obvious mistake, care should be taken to never let them see you sweat. Patients have heightened awareness of every detail occurring around them in the stressful environment of the dental office. Do not give them anything to put them over the edge.

Make an effort to compliment your staff in front of your patients. This will solidify your humility in their minds. Use *please* and *thank you* as common courtesy during four-handed dentistry. Patients admire and respect doctors who show value to the people who support and assist them. They see the doctor as a real person and they appreciate that.

Educating the Patient

Treatment plan presentation will vary in methodology from clinician to clinician. Conversion success rates are not always consistent with the type of methodology implemented. One thing being clear, however, is that it is imperative that the clinician effectively communicates how having the outlined treatment completed will benefit the patient.

Experience has taught me that most new patients are skeptical that the dentist is there to *take my money*, and are leery of aggressive treatment planning on the first visit. I do not refrain from comprehensive treatment planning and I always make sure to completely inform the patients of their needs. I just do not feel the need to sell them the entirety of an overwhelming treatment plan on their first visit. I educate them and encourage them to select the treatment that I know is best for them. They need to trust me before they will buy what I am selling.

Teaching through Technology

There are numerous ways in which a doctor can help patients to understand the need for their proposed dental care. Properly educating patients is a critical component of successful treatment plan presentation in today's dental office environment. Countless teaching aids are marketed to assist dentists with this endeavor. One of the more simplistic modes of educational communication includes offering written information explaining recommended treatment in the form of brochures. Video communication through a streaming educational DVD running in the reception area and on a flat screen TV in the operatory caters to a different style of learning.

Use of the intraoral camera and other diagnostic equipment such as a laser cavity indicator not only educates your patients but gives them the impression that your office is on the cutting-edge of technology. This idea can be further reinforced by developing a practice video and streaming it on your website. This video can also be used as a marketing tool both online and in hard copy format. Utilizing a digital x-ray system speaks volumes to your patients about your commitment to keeping your office up to date and technologically savvy.

Almost certainly the greatest benefit of offering digital x-rays is the patient's perception of them. As a patient once commented, "They really increase the cool factor of this place." We have a computer monitor mounted on the patient chair that we use to show patients their x-rays while discussing the treatment plans. The images are huge in comparison to traditional films, and they are immediate! Doctors can magnify calculus and interproximal decay. Patients can see what you see. Their dental needs are clearly visible to them, larger than life. What more education do they really need? Seeing is believing.

Handling Criticism of Other Dentists' Work

Many patients will take a seat in your chair and begin bashing the last dentist whose chair supported them. Some even confide in you about their levying a lawsuit against that unfortunate dentist. I am always amazed at their lack of realization that you are not hearing, "My former dentist was horrible!" but instead, "I'm going to sue you too!" I typically send Lawsuit Larry down the road to the next confident dentist.

At times during our exams we encounter dentistry that falls below the standard of care, and we are presented with a dilemma. Though it is incumbent on you to point out the areas that require attention, this should be done with the greatest possible degree of humility. It will not pay to take the seat of judgment against your colleagues, particularly when your patients suggest having had a positive relationship with them. People like to hear that the dentistry they have in their mouths is of high quality. Therefore, if it is, by all means apprise them of the fact. They will appreciate it. If, however, it is less than ideal, simply assign a treatment plan that will improve it.

Did the Patient Like You?

All the educational material in the world that dental supply houses package as things you simply cannot live without, are not worth a penny if you are unable to establish patient trust. In the end, that is where it all comes down. Have you been an effective communicator? Have you listened to your patient? Have you expressed care for your patient and concern for your patient's needs? Did your patient like you? Did your patient trust you?

If the answer to all these questions is *Yes,* patients will believe the needs you have expressed to them. Other factors certainly affect whether patients will schedule treatment, but the answer *No* to these questions will guarantee that they will not. I recall a former discussion with a practice broker and consultant in California who insisted she could transform an impersonal dentist into someone every patient would desire to see. I debated, "You can't teach people how to be trustable, personable and likeable. They either are that way or they are not." She replied, "Yes, but I can teach them to pull their masks down when they are talking to their patients!"

I suppose it is the little things that can be modified and adapted to present our patients a likeable, trustable dentist. This is the type of doctor from whom patients are looking to buy treatment. In the end, *you* are the one who is selling the treatment and from whom they will buy. It is not the educational material that sells the dentistry, nor is it the high-tech office in which it is delivered. It is not the fabulous treatment plan coordinator you employ to do just this. It is you as their doctor establishing yourself as someone they trust. It is you being a person that they like.

Chapter 18

Co-Payments, Collections and Financing

Checkout Procedure and Treatment Plan Estimate
Following the initial hygiene appointment and every recall appointment thereafter, make every effort to schedule the six-month dental check-up appointment prior to the patient's dismissal. I explain the importance of this step further in the chapter on internal marketing. If the front office staff appears busy, hygienists and dental assistants should be able to make this appointment chair-side. This will ensure that a patient does not slip out the door without scheduling the recall appointment. Have the patient fill out the recall postcard to be mailed a month prior to the appointment, and provide a reminder card to be taken home.

Checkout can be a busy time, especially for the new patient with an extensive treatment plan. As discussed in the section on hiring, if you are able to employ a dedicated treatment coordinator, this process can be much more harmonious. As the dentist is completing the new patient exam, the staff member responsible for calculating co-payments should be finalizing the treatment plan estimate for presentation. Software allowing the hygienist or dentist to enter a computerized treatment plan is ideal for expediting this process. The treatment plan is now easily accessible to the treatment coordinator. If this software option is not available in your office, the hygienist should submit the treatment plan to the treatment coordinator as quickly as possible.

While the treatment plan estimate is being calculated, offer the patient educational materials relating to the treatment outlined. If the treatment plan is substantial, offer the patient a seat in the consultation room while everything is finalized. You should provide the patient a detailed breakout including co-payment estimates for each procedure. Be sure to explain that listed co-pays are only estimates based upon the limited amount of information the dental insurance company provides. Inform the patient that the co-pay will be collected on the date of service.

For extensive treatment plans involving multiple quadrants, it may be best to initially provide an estimate for the most involved quadrant only, so as not to overwhelm the patient on the first visit. The treatment coordinator should explain to the patient that an attempt is being made to simplify the process, but that this treatment plan does not include all diagnosed treatment.

If the patient requires financing, discuss your office's payment plan options at this time. These alternatives may include extending credit through a third-party financing company such as Care Credit, automatic monthly billing of credit cards or electronic drafts from the patient's bank account. Ask the patient if there are any questions at this time and make every effort to get the treatment scheduled before the patient leaves the office. Treatment is much more likely to be scheduled while the patient is in the office than if the patient waits to call for an appointment. When patients viewing the treatment plan at the front desk suggest, "Let me think about it," usually they have already "thought about it," and they have typically decided to "forget about it" as soon as they leave your office.

As thoughts of their dental needs submit to more important necessities when patients exit your door, it is imperative that your practice has protocol in place to follow-up on patients with outstanding treatment plans. Our dental software allows us to keep record of treatment plans pending, thus ensuring that we, like our patients may have, do not overlook necessary treatment. Follow-up phone calls, emails, postcards and incentive notices can be utilized in intervals of one week, two weeks, three months and six months in attempt to schedule this outlined dentistry. We sometimes offer 15% off outstanding treatment plans in times of practice stagnation. Of course, when patients indicate to us that they understand their needs and will address them when they are ready to do so, we do not pressure them further.

Co-Payments and Collections

It is imperative to strive for the collection of accurate co-payments on the date of service. Most offices choose to bill after receiving insurance payment. Some make an attempt at co-pay collection simply by calculating a percentage of the total fee assessed. For example, if the crown fee is $1,000, the office manager may collect 50%, or $500, from the patient. This assumes that the patient's insurance will remunerate at 50% of the actual fee, when insurance plans more commonly pay 50% of their own UCR crown fee. This fee will almost always be less than your fee for a crown. If the insurance company's UCR crown fee is $800, for example, you have left $100 on the table, and will now be responsible to chase that money down from your patient.

Most patients believe that the estimate they have been given and the co-pay they initially submitted reflect the actual balance that they will owe. I know how I feel when the auto mechanic provides me an estimate prior to dismantling my vehicle and then surprises me a much larger bill after the work is completed. I understood at the time that I was being given only an estimate, but my frustration at receiving such a high bill quickly overwhelmed that understanding. In order to get my vehicle back, I will need to pay this higher than expected bill. Patients react in a similar manner when opening the bill from your office reflecting what their insurance did not pay. They generally believe they have already paid what they owe and that you are now overcharging them. This belief is further compounded when they receive the EOB from their insurance company explaining how your fees are remarkably higher than UCR.

Patient goodwill is only one reason why it is so important to collect accurate co-pays at the time of service. It is very expensive to set yourself up as a billing service when your profit results from operating as a dental office. We make efforts never to bill, but unless you position your office to charge patients the total fee up front, thus requiring that the insurance company reimburse them, billing will become necessary in certain instances.

Even with the best efforts to establish accurate co-pay estimates from all information available, the patient will nonetheless, at times, be left with a balance remaining. The collection cost associated with attempting to secure debt owed you is incentive enough to diligently pursue the calculation of precise estimates. An additional motivation is that people tend to pay their dentist last, after all of their perceived to be more important bills have been paid. Importance is generally assigned in view of which bills carry an enforceable finance charge, or which might encroach upon a person's standard of living if not paid on time. Most dental office billing protocols do not place dental practices under this umbrella.

It should be your belief that if you do not collect the balance at the time of service, there is a distinct possibility that you will never collect it. If you are eventually able to secure the debt, you will have done so at a greater cost than had you been successful in initially acquiring payment. At the very least, there will be the cost of a stamp and some payroll for the staff to create, print and mail billing statements. At the most, there will be the cost of numerous phone calls, billing statements and collection agency fees. The greatest costs, of course, will be that of not getting paid at all and possibly losing a patient who is disgruntled by the bill.

I once worked in an office in which the policy was to collect 20% of the fee charged for fillings, no exceptions. No attempt was made to accurately calculate what the patient's particular insurance might pay. Insurance remuneration varies wildly from plan to plan. Most insurance plans reduce the posterior composite benefit to what would be paid for an amalgam filling. Some plans have exclusionary periods within which your patient is only eligible for benefits on select procedures. All plans have maximum yearly amounts they will pay for services rendered. For restorative procedures, a numeric deductible is commonly due from the patient prior to insurance reimbursement. Furthermore, UCR will be dramatically different from one insurance company to the next.

There is virtually no way that collecting 20% will result in a balanced account following insurance company reimbursement. Your fees will not match those of the insurance company, you have not accounted for the patient's deductible and you have not considered whether the patient's insurance even covers this procedure. You do not want to follow this model and end up chasing payments for months, sometimes years after service was rendered. Patients should be told at the time the estimate is given that their co-pay is expected at the time of service. Though some patients will need to adapt to the idea of relinquishing their co-payment at the time of service, this step prevents arguments and possible loss of patients resulting from their subsequent receipt of a sizeable, unanticipated billing statement.

I insist that my staff members make every possible effort to factor in deductibles, maximums, UCR and percentages to create the most accurate estimate possible. You may face resistance from your staff. They may even claim it is impossible to calculate an estimate with accuracy. After all, most medical and dental offices simply collect a fixed co-pay or a percentage of the assessed fee, then bill the patient once insurance payment is received. Every time my staff members become complacent in this step, they quickly realize the burden of chasing down patients to collect the bill.

My staff has also learned with drama the ramifications of failing to collect the patient's entire co-payment at the time of treatment. I recall one afternoon while relaxing at lunch with my wife, I answered a call from the office on my cell phone. "Dr. Logan, can I call the police?" exclaimed my receptionist.

I made an attempt to calm her, "What's going on? Why do you need to call the police?"

Apparently, the mother of one of my adult patients was in our office making a scene over a bill her daughter had received. My receptionist believed her safety to be threatened.

"Yes, you can call the police if you feel uncomfortable", I said. "Ask the lady to leave or you will…" The perpetrator had already exited the premises, apparently familiar with what it meant to have the cops called on her.

Another recent occurrence took place on a Saturday night while entertaining friends in from out of town. We were about to go out for dinner when my cell phone rang. The voicemail, a destination reached by navigating a pathway from the office answering machine to the doctor's dental emergency number, involved another concerned parent. The concern was not about any true dental emergency, but about a billing statement received that exceeded the original estimate. The message was long. My patience was short. This was a bill that the patient truly owed. My office manager had already explained this to the parent at infinitum. The problem was that she had failed to accurately determine what the insurance would cover prior to treatment. Now this had become my problem on Saturday night.

One final anecdote occurring very early in my career alerted me to the fact that patients really do not enjoy paying their dental bills. While buried in operatory 6 of 14 in the HMO machine of my youth, I was pulled out to "Come take a look at this!" Through the only window in the office, the front door, I observed a patient picketing our practice. She was actually holding a sign and a blow horn. This patient was disgruntled about her bill and she wanted every patient walking into the office to know about it. Freedom of speech notwithstanding, my boss's connections with the local cops got her quickly, though less calmly, escorted away.

A colleague and mentor once told me, "It's not about you. It's always about the bill." He suggested that the patients who put up a fuss about anything are almost always the ones with a balance. You can avoid their disdain and your own dismay by not allowing patients to acquire a balance. This is accomplished by charging them an accurate fee up front, thereby eliminating the necessity of a bill. Patients will be happier with you if you do not bill them, and you will be ensuring payment by doing so.

Staff members routinely comment on the falsity in a patient's statement, "I will mail that to you this week." Experience has yielded that you can never predict which patients will default on payment. Even the new Mercedes Benz owner who befriends your staff and has been treated in your office for years may not pay unless you collect at the time of service. They are not going to mail it to you this week. They are going to wait until you call them again, thereby permitting *this week* to become *next week*.

Calculating estimates accurately is made particularly difficult by the wonderful world of UCR. However, it is possible over time to predict UCR for certain treatments, and many insurance companies will reveal to you by phone their UCR fee for a procedure. We keep a UCR chart of what insurance companies routinely pay for various procedures. Each time we receive an EOB, we record these amounts in the chart to aid in calculation of future co-pays.

After the treatment coordinator reviews the financial arrangement with the patient and prior to treatment, require the patient to sign the treatment estimate. The signed treatment plan should contain the disclaimer that it is only an estimate and that the patient will owe any difference that results after the insurance company has submitted payment. This statement should also inform the patient that a finance charge will be assessed on overdue accounts. The actual financial arrangement that we use in our practice can be accessed through the Practice Management Resources for Dentists section at the end of this book.

You should be acutely aware of the collection percentage in your practice and review it on a monthly basis. Since collection and production do not necessarily run parallel to one another, you may have either a collection deficit or, at times, a collection surplus. This means that it is reasonable to expect your collection percentage to be greater than 100% for certain months. As a result of the lag in insurance payments for treatment already rendered, it is more common to realize a collection percentage less than 100%. However, the closer you are able to bring collection in your practice to the dollars you produce, the less labor and overhead you will expend in order to live the same lifestyle.

Our collection percentage in an average month will hover around 99%. We very rarely send patients to collections because we collect payments in our office. I would estimate that less than .01% of my patients ultimately require collection proceedings. This ratio stands in stark contrast to a practice in which I once associated. I recall inquiring of the office manager at the beginning of my employ what the collection percentage in the practice was. She starred at me with a confused look and then realized she needed to come up with a number, and fast. She stated it to be, "Around 93%." She seemed quite pleased with that number too. You should not be so pleased with a collection percentage of that order in your practice. It would behoove you to have the real number more at the ready in your mind as well.

In treatment planning, I recognize that dental emergencies often necessitate treatment on the patient's first visit. I also understand that in terms of productive efficiency, it is sometimes beneficial to provide restorative treatment on the day of the patient's initial exam and treatment plan. It is my belief, however, that scheduling a separate restorative appointment from the new patient exam is ideal in building a trusting relationship between doctor and patient. I am not out to snatch up every scrap of production as soon as it presents itself. I am, rather, in it for the long haul. I want a patient for life.

Scheduling a separate restorative appointment also ensures that the patient has been presented, has signed and purportedly understands the financial arrangement set forth. When patients appoint and show up for their restorative appointment, it means they have developed a certain level of trust in you. This rapport makes for a more comfortable restorative procedure and a patient with reduced anxiety. This, to me, is even more important than the proper understanding of the financial arrangement. This is what will keep the patient coming back and referring other patients to your practice.

Patient Financing

In an optimally productive schedule, you will be doing quadrant dentistry, the cost of which will routinely exceed the limits of what most insurance companies will reimburse on a yearly basis. Most people have not factored costs for your dental care into their monthly budgets. We know that the average American has a negative savings rate, and therefore is not sitting on a pile of cash poised to become that of the dentist. Your goal should be to help patients find a way to afford the treatment they need.

Patients appreciate financing options, especially when considering more extensive treatment plans. In fact, many times the decision to proceed with treatment is hinged on the patient's ability to obtain financing. People typically make monetary decisions based upon what they believe they can afford on a monthly basis. Total cost generally becomes secondary if you are able to provide the patient an accurate breakout of what will be owed each month. This is how most bills are paid, so it is easily understood and factored into a budget. Your staff should be adept in calculating what a patient's monthly expenditure would be given a specific time period selected for repayment. Online calculators from financial websites such as www.bankrate.com make this easier.

My office has attempted multiple in-office financing plans. These include accepting a series of checks to be deposited each month, keeping a credit card or bank routing number on file for monthly billing and offering extended financing at a fixed percentage rate. While each of these plans appeals to patients and may increase the likelihood that they will appoint for treatment, there is inherent risk associated with any in-office financing plan. Automatic monthly billing of a credit card or bank account is the safest measure. Nonetheless, patients can still renege on these agreements by cancelling credit cards, going over their limits or closing bank accounts. When allowing extended payment plans you will be operating closer to optimal capacity, but you will also be doing some dentistry for free. Not all payment arrangements will result in your actually getting paid.

Recalling the McGill Advisory's definition of optimal capacity, being as busy as you want to be, doing the type of dentistry you want to do, you will need to decide if the cost of your labor is an acceptable sacrifice to operate your practice at this level. When I was a younger dentist, it most certainly was. Now, however, I will tend to leave some money on the table. My office has established stringent guidelines with respect to whom we will offer in-office financing, but even with this higher level of scrutiny we have found that over 50% of patients will miss payments when given an in-office financing option. At this point in my practice's development, we very rarely offer an in-office option.

My experience has taught me that the best way to offer financing is through a third- party financing company such as Care Credit. This is especially true during uncertain economic times when patients' pocketbooks are uncommonly squeezed. Care Credit offers nearly immediate approval which can be accomplished while the patient is still in the office. Care Credit's website offers a payment estimate tool which can quickly provide patients with monthly payment calculations. Finance charges are based upon the amount charged and the length of the financing program.

At the time of this writing, Care Credit's available promotions were as follows:

Payment Term	Patient Finance Charge	Fee Charged to Dentist
6 Monthly Payments	0% APR	5.9%
12 Monthly Payments	0% APR	9.9%
18 Monthly Payments	0% APR	13.5%
Extended Payment Plans		
24 Monthly Payments	14.9% APR	5%
36 Monthly Payments	14.9% APR	5%
48 Monthly Payments	14.9% APR	5%
60 Monthly Payments	14.9% APR	5%

You can determine which financing options you wish to offer your patients. You do not have to offer all the available plans if you wish to limit the finance charge you will be assessed. For balances less than $1,000, we extend only the 3 month financing option. For balances exceeding $2,000, we will offer the 12 month financing option. We do not hesitate to offer the Extended Payment Plan options because we are assessed a finance charge of only 5%. Patients are much more reluctant to select these plans, however, as they are charged our full fee plus a 13.9% finance charge.

A clear drawback to offering third-party financing plans is that you will forfeit some revenue to fees. Some patients will be wary of opening another credit line and prefer to set up an in-office payment plan if possible. Financing companies have tightened their belts and do not offer as much credit as they once did, so your patients may not be approved for the entire amount they are seeking. However, if the financing company has checked the patient's credit history and is hesitant to extend credit to your patient, your office would be wise to follow suit and not offer a large in-office financing plan. The benefits of immediate payment in full and avoiding the necessity to chase down payments and filing collections claims overshadow the cost of participating in these plans. Consider too the costs involved when a patient elects not to proceed with the treatment you have outlined.

When determining whether to offer in-office financing plans versus third-party financing options, realize that you will likely leave some money on the table with either decision. More money will go unrecovered, however, with in-office financing plans than will be the case with third-party arrangements. The regularity with which a patient will default on your trusting payment arrangement will outpace the fees you will assume with any third-party plan. Therefore, it is my recommendation to offer these third-party financing plans and to encourage your staff to promote their use with your patients.

If your staff members are concerned that these plans will cost the business money, they will be hesitant to offer them, even when the plan's availability will determine whether or not your patient will pursue treatment. It is helpful to establish for your staff clear guidelines for when to offer these plans based upon the estimate amount and the patient's willingness to pay for the treatment through another source.

Offering third-party financing is an excellent way to market your practice to families without dental insurance. These families are generally aware of their dental needs, but the high cost of dental care sometimes prevents them from seeking treatment. The fees you will incur by granting such financing will be readily recovered by caring for the dental needs of a fee-for-service family of patients.

Another way we seek to assist our patients in getting the treatment they need is by offering a 5% discount on patient payments over $500, if paid at the time of service by check or cash. This incentivizes patients to settle their balances early, saving us the cost of billing and eliminating the risk of payment defaults. Everyone likes to save 5% and we find that this option is selected often. No such discount is extended to patients paying by credit card, as we already assume a fee from the credit card company for processing these payments.

During trying economic times, most dentists do not operate at optimal capacity. Offering a variety of extended financing options is one way to move your daily schedule in that direction. Though patients tend to prefer in-office financing, third-party arrangements in which you get paid the entire balance up front carry much lower cost in terms of risk. Doctors operating an immature practice with the ambition of growing the production as quickly as possible should offer both forms of financing options. Doctors desiring to ensure payment for services rendered should elect to extend only the third-party payment option. Doctors already operating at optimal capacity will perhaps not be reading this book!

Dental Insurance Mastery in Your Practice

Chapter 19

Insurance 101

I can think of no other area in dentistry in which so little time is spent educating the newly trained dental professional than it is with dental insurance. It is incumbent upon the nation's dental schools to assure that each graduate achieves an adequate level of clinical expertise before bestowing the title of dentist. Given the time limitations of the dental school curriculum, it is understandable that the business management aspect of dentistry is often overlooked. Where business instruction is provided, dental insurance education is given little more than a cursory glance.

Dental insurance companies have become masters at keeping their information shrouded in secrecy. It is uncertain as to whether most dental school instructors even have access to enough information to relate to their students. If the modus operandus by which most dental practices process insurance is any indication, very little formal education ever transpired. Though the subject of dental insurance is admittedly mind numbing, the importance of its understanding is immeasurable to the optimal profitability of your dental practice. Master it and you will be miles ahead of most of your colleagues and on your way to establishing a practice with minimal accounts receivable.

Dental insurance can be extremely confusing for the dental patient, not to mention for you, the health care professional. Confusing as it may be, it is imperative that you as business owner familiarize yourself with the intricacies of the insurance plans your patients tote through your office door. This truth was borne out in a letter recently presented to me from a local periodontist, which listed over 46 insurance plans with which his practice participated. Understanding the most common insurance terminology and the ways in which dental insurance differs from health insurance will help ensure the greatest collection percentage. Most insured patients have a very limited understanding of their insurance plans and benefits. Patients assume that their dental insurance will be much like their medical insurance, typically outlining a well-defined co-payment and not involving a myriad of reasons for reduced or denied payments.

It is of no benefit to the insurance company to provide transparency in terms of the information it is willing to reveal to you or your patients. The unknown will go unchallenged, and perhaps the claim will be allowed to go unpaid. The patient will be pitted against the dentist, because the insurance company has proclaimed itself to be on the side of the patient. Almost inexplicably to the doctor, the actual provider of health to the patient, the patient will most commonly believe the insurance company.

While I maintain that understanding personal insurance benefits is ultimately the responsibility of the patient, front office employees must have an advanced knowledge of insurance benefits to maximize payment and collect accurate co-pays. We have designed an insurance brochure which we use in our practice to assist patients in deciphering the alphabet soup of insurance terminology. We distribute this brochure to each patient after the new patient exam. We find that these written explanations considerably conserve staff time and help eliminate patient misperceptions about what their insurance might cover. Our insurance brochure can be accessed through the Practice Management Resources for Dentists section at the end of this book.

An observation of the typical dental practice yields that training in the science of insurance benefits and remuneration is woefully inadequate. By collecting a standard, invariable co-payment, an assumption is made that all insurances are created equal. The fact is, however, that similarities among insurance companies are the exception, not the rule. We know this by the existence of innumerable differing UCR fee schedules among insurance companies. This is not surprising given the reality that insurance companies are in business to profit. There is clearly no fiscal benefit for them to provide full disclosure to office staff with respect to their fee schedules.

There are dentists on the lecture circuit who proclaim the insurance company as the enemy! A clear goal of these health care professionals is to even the odds by revealing the cards the insurance companies are holding. They do this by exposing anecdotes related to them by ex-employees of certain insurance companies. One particular revelation is the assertion that standard protocol in some companies is to scoop the initially submitted claim forms into the trash can. This effectively delays processing until follow-up efforts have taken place.

Since I have never worked for an insurance company, I cannot speak to the validity of this claim. I have learned, however, that more correspondence seems to get lost in the mail when sent to insurance companies than with any other mailing destinations I have encountered. The availability of electronic claims submission significantly reduces the possibility of the excuse, "We never received that claim."

Dental insurance companies will try your patience at times. They will find a way to deny your claims based upon the most miniscule of reasons. Commonly these explanations are not reasons at all, but merely stall tactics made in an attempt to buy time, or in hopes that your staff will overlook the claims and fail to resubmit them. The net effect is that they will never have to reimburse for these claims, resulting in greater profitability for the companies.

Stall tactics abound and include assertions such as, "Our dental consultant cannot read the radiograph that was sent." It is quite common to learn, "We find no need for placing a crown on this tooth, as it can be restored with a direct restoration." Of course they have found no need for a crown. How could they be expected to diagnose the defects in that tooth from so many states away?

You will be disrespected. Your clinical judgment will be challenged. Your treatment planning will be contested. Your intelligence will be insulted. Getting angry is easy. Getting paid is true victory. You need to establish your office as one that understands these tactics and insists on prompt, accurate payment. We get paid. So can you.

This *us against them* mentality may never be eradicated completely, but dentists can take measures to assure prompt, accurate payment from the insurance companies by implementing defined collection protocols. This starts with educating yourself on insurance company jargon and the technical aspects of insurance company operations. You must establish familiarity with these intricacies in order to teach and supervise your staff in this area.

A well-equipped staff armed with knowledge on par with that of the insurance companies will help circumvent delayed, denied and unprocessed claims. This will help narrow the production/collection chasm prevalent in so many dental practices, making your practice a more profitable, efficient business. So, back to school you go. Welcome to Insurance 101.

Insurance Benefits Checklist

We check insurance benefits within a day or two of a new patient's initial phone call. This is a critical step necessary to inform patients ahead of time whether they will owe a co-payment during the primary visit to your office. Most dental practices are not in the habit of taking the time to collect these valuable details. Staff members commonly offer resistance to the thought of a requisite extended hold time anticipating the representative from the monolithic insurance company to pick up the phone. This complaint is amplified by the fact that obtaining this information is mandatory for each patient who walks through your door. It is imperative to insist that this process is carried out for every new patient, every time.

Encourage your staff members that in performing a little extra work up front, they will be eliminating countless headaches later on in the patient management process. Encouraging to you should be the fact that by completing a simple benefits checklist worksheet, you will be ensuring your practice a much higher percentage of total bills paid, a lower accounts receivable balance than the vast majority of dental practices and fewer disgruntled patients.

Many of the major dental insurance companies offer online benefit information. The systems for Met Life, Cigna and Delta are very user-friendly and provide most of the necessary information prior to a patient's initial visit. Encourage your staff to explore and exploit online benefit information, thereby reducing the hair tugging hold time that will otherwise be forthcoming. This conserves payroll expense and provides written proof of a patient's benefits.

To help facilitate the information gathering process, our practice has created a benefits checklist worksheet which the staff completes for each new patient. The worksheet includes the following information to garner from the patient during the initial phone call:

- insured's name,
- date of birth, names and birthdates for other family members who will be seen in our office, thus extending the offer to schedule other family members at this time,
- social security number,
- group number and insurance company's name.

The worksheet also includes a place to record data gathered during our initial phone contact with the patient's dental insurance company. We record the date insurance was verified, the insurance representative's name and answers to the following questions solicited from the insurance company representative:

- deductible and maximum amounts, as well as how much of the deductible and maximum have been met thus far that year,
- percentage breakdown for each level of treatment,
- whether the benefits are on a calendar year/benefit year/contract year,
- frequency allowance and last date of cleaning, exam, x-rays, sealants and fluoride,
- if periodontal and endodontic treatment are considered basic or major,
- if there are any waiting periods,
- replacement frequency for prosthodontics,
- if night guards are covered,
- if full mouth debridement is covered and during what period and
- if composite fillings are downgraded to amalgam fees.

This may seem like a lot of information, but it is extremely helpful and time efficient to get all the answers you might possibly need the first time you call the insurance company. Otherwise, your staff will spend valuable time on hold waiting for an insurance representative when the patient is in the chair and you are in need of an answer straight away.

Insurance Benefits Definitions:

Deductible - The annual amount a patient must pay prior to receiving any insurance benefit for the treatment. Many insurance companies do not apply a deductible to preventative appointments. The deductible may differ depending upon whether the dentist is in-network or out-of- network.

Maximum Benefit - The annual dollar amount of benefits an insured patient receives. This amount varies but falls typically within the $1,000 - $3,000 range. Once an insurance company has paid the defined maximum amount, the patient is responsible for the rest of the dental costs incurred that year. Patients are sometimes surprised to learn that this maximum benefit includes the costs of preventative appointments. Sadly, these yearly maximums have not migrated significantly from their levels in the early 1970's. It remains unclear how the insurance companies have been able to get away with what stands as an obvious disregard for inflation.

Waiting Period - The time between an insured member's plan enrollment date and the date on which the covered person becomes eligible for services. Waiting periods are most common with crowns, bridges, dentures and implants.

Missing Tooth Clause - The dental insurance industry's equivalent to a pre-existing condition. This clause states that the insurance company will not cover any treatment for the replacement of a tooth that was missing prior to the beginning of coverage.

Insurance Levels of Service:

Preventative Services - Typically include exams, x-rays, cleanings, fluoride and sealants. Preventative services are often covered by insurance companies at 100%.

Basic Services - Typically include fillings and may include endodontics, periodontics and oral surgery. Scaling and root planing is commonly characterized as a basic service. Basic services are often covered by insurance companies at 50%-80%.

Major Services - Typically include crowns, bridges, inlays, onlays and dentures. Major services are commonly covered by insurance companies at 40-60%.

EOB Definitions:

EOB (Explanation of Benefits) - A statement sent to a patient from the dental insurance company explaining how much was paid to the provider of care and why certain charges were reduced or deleted. The provider of service also receives an explanation of benefits attached to the payment for services. EOBs are notorious for being difficult to decipher and could be defined as *extraordinarily obtuse benefits*. Every insurance company utilizes a different system for designing EOBs and defining the terms used within them. Some of the most common terms are defined below:

Allowed Amount - The maximum payable fee for a particular procedure established by the insurance company either through UCR (see definition below) or by network contract.

Benefit Amount - The percentage amount the insurance company will pay for a procedure based upon the schedule of benefits offered by the patient's insurance plan.

Complete/Full Mouth X-Ray Series - The practice of combining the fee for a panoramic x-ray with the fee for any other x-rays taken on the same date of service, thereby reducing payment for the actual x-rays taken.

UCR (Usual, Customary and Reasonable)

Usual, Customary and Reasonable (UCR) is among the most dubious monikers in the dental industry. UCR refers to the fee that an insurance company is willing to pay for a particular procedure. Every insurance company uses a different formula and a different set of criteria for determining UCR. Most companies base UCR on the geographical region, the cost of living in that region, fees submitted on dental claim forms and surveys conducted by the Health Insurance Association of America (HIAA). The determination of UCR is not regulated by any agency, and insurance companies are free to decide on UCR in whatever manner they choose. In our area, UCR can vary among insurance companies by over 100%.

A patient visiting a dentist who is not in the insurance company's network of providers must pay the difference between the UCR amount and the actual charge. UCR creates difficulty in calculating accurate co-payment estimates. Many insurance companies will disclose their UCR rate for a particular treatment over the phone. My office has taken an additional step and created a chart to track UCR fees from returned EOBs or via UCR confirmation by phone. Your staff may fight this step, but if you fail to account for UCR and merely collect a co-pay based upon a percentage level, you may be left to bill a patient hundreds of dollars not covered by UCR. Not only might you find this money hard to collect, but you also risk losing patients who were not given a clear idea of what they might owe and who now experience sticker shock following treatment.

A disturbing trend in our field is the intentional pitting of the patient against the treating dentist by certain dental insurance companies. UCR plays a major role in this sanctioned event. While every individual dentist is entitled to a unique fee schedule, many in the insurance industry are attempting to convince their members that theirs is the one and only accurate usual, customary and reasonable rate for dental procedures. This is quite clearly not the case. Patients are more inclined to trust the information supplied by their insurance companies, in whom they have a vested interest to believe. Many times these companies, if not altogether verbally, implicitly position the dentist as one who charges exorbitant fees, those much higher than the geographical UCR. It is our job to educate our patients on the erroneous nature of these accusations. I have been less than successful in this endeavor when I attempt to accomplish this with any degree of arrogance. Remember, your patients will naturally side with their insurance providers. It is for you to gently endear them to your way of thinking, which in this case is the right way of thinking.

Amalgam Downgrade - Specifically in the case of composite fillings, when an insurance company pays only the reimbursable fee for amalgam fillings. Insurance companies that downgrade composite fillings, and most do, only pay a percentage of the amalgam fee, not the composite fee. The patient is responsible for the difference between the composite restoration fee and the amalgam fee. Make sure to factor in amalgam downgrades on co-payment estimates! This is one of the most frequently overlooked adjustments occurring when a staff member calculates what a patient will owe for a filling. Clearly, not all fillings are created equal.

Alternate Benefit - A treatment that an insurance company employee who lacks a degree in dentistry deems as more appropriate than the treatment actually performed by the dentist. In other words, the cheapest level of care possible to fix a given problem. For example, an insurance company may reduce the claim to the cost of a gold crown rather than an all-porcelain crown if the gold crown is less expensive. The insurance company will in fact change your submitted code reflecting the treatment actually performed to the one which more economically benefits its firm. I am unclear how that can be considered legal, but provided that I do not have the degree of an attorney, I will not attempt to encroach upon their space. I would find it a nice gesture if the dental insurance companies would extend my fellow dentists the same courtesy.

Coordination of Benefits - When a patient has coverage through more than one dental insurance company, the companies coordinate their payments to ensure an overpayment does not occur. After the primary dental insurance company has paid, the secondary insurance will subtract this amount prior to making its payment. Patients often assume that if they have dual insurance, everything will be covered at 100%. This is typically not the case, especially if the primary insurance already paid more than the secondary insurance's UCR for a procedure. In this case, the secondary insurance will not contribute any further reimbursement. It is the responsibility of the front office staff to dispel the presumption that patients will be receiving 100% coverage at the time of service and to inform them that the remaining balance will be their responsibility. For larger treatment plans, we collect at least a small amount from the patient prior to billing both insurances.

Patient Responsibility/Due from Patient - The amount the patient owes the dentist. This amount does not calculate any payments that were made at the time of service.

Basics of Insurance Claim Submission

If you choose to submit insurance claims as a service to patients, every time you perform a procedure for which you are entitled payment by an insurance company, you are required to submit an insurance claim form to the payer. This form is standardized in dentistry and includes a section for the procedural codes and a description of the services provided. Space is afforded the doctor to script a narrative outlining the reasons necessitating the performed treatment. Many insurance companies request that additional information, x-rays or documentation accompany these claim forms.

You will not be required to submit such a form if your practice does not accept assignment of benefits from the insurance companies. Under this arrangement, the insurance companies will pay your patients directly, and your patients will be responsible for paying you your charged fee. In this case, you need only provide the patient a printed statement detailing the procedures performed and their associated codes. The patient will then forward that form along with an insurance claim form to the insurance company for payment. The only exception to this rule of insurance companies paying dentists directly is found with Delta Dental insurance. In certain states, Delta Dental refuses to pay the dentist but will reimburse the patient for services rendered. This is true even when the dentist does not accept assignment of insurance benefits for the practice's patients.

Insurance companies are beginning to reduce the number of x-rays demanded for claim processing. Crowns, bridges and root canals are the main procedures that routinely require that an x-ray accompanies the claim. It is commonly necessary to submit both full mouth x-rays and full mouth periodontal pocket charting with a claim for scaling and root planning. A few insurance companies no longer request x-rays for any procedures. Your front office manager should become familiar with the requirements of each insurance company in order to expedite the processing of claims and ensure timely payment to your office.

Expected payment time on a claim will range between two and four weeks. Claims submitted online are processed more quickly. Several major insurance companies encourage direct deposit into your bank account which serves to accelerate the payment process. One concern about selecting direct deposit is that a paper copy of the explanation of benefits often times does not accompany the payment. The EOB can only be accessed online, requiring the staff member posting payments to print out these EOBs to keep in patient files.

Our office has been uneasy about the possibility of missing an EOB online and not crediting a patient account accurately. Additionally, direct deposit does not allow the matching of posted payments with a daily deposit slip and requires checking the bank statement for every individual deposit. Certain banks charge an activity fee for the large number of deposits made via the numerous individual direct deposits. We have chosen not to employ insurance direct deposit in order to keep our system of checks and balances in place.

Expected payment time and actual payment time may vary tremendously. You will quickly learn which payers are notoriously delinquent and which submit payments in a timely fashion. The goal is to get paid as rapidly as possible, because as is the case with a crime scene, the longer the case goes unsolved, the less is the likelihood that it will ever be so. Insurance companies are notorious not only for denying claims, but also for delaying payment indefinitely. They know that the more an employee is made to linger over a claim, the greater the probability that the employee will ultimately overlook its hanging in abeyance or forget about it altogether.

It is incumbent on you as a boss to instill in your employees the highest level of diligence in collecting on each and every claim. It should be made a matter of pride to not fall prey to the postponement ploys of the insurance companies. You are entitled to that money, you earned it and therefore you should ensure that you get it! Interestingly, after establishing your office as one that demands to get paid, insurance companies tend to fall in line and exclude you from the list of practices they bully around.

Insurance companies highly recommend pre-authorization, also known as pre-treatment estimates, for larger procedures. Pre-treatment estimates do provide a patient with knowledge of the exact amount the insurance company will pay and the amount the patient will owe. They also provide reassurance that the proposed treatment will be approved.

The disadvantage to these pre-authorizations is the delay in treatment and scheduling they necessitate. It can take over a month before an estimate is returned. By this time dental disease may have progressed, or the patient may have forgotten about the importance of this procedure altogether. I always prefer to avoid the pre-authorization step if at all possible. It has been considered an insurance company stall tactic, and many times it results in no treatment being rendered, and therefore no payment being required of the insurance company. Met Life offers a real time pre-treatment authorization online for some procedures, but not for those requiring x-rays.

Whatever form of claim submission you implement, the collection of insurance monies receivable will, for the majority of practices, be one of the most critical staff training components of the business. You can do a lot of things as a dentist. You can be the best diagnostician, the greatest communicator and the most skilled clinician. You may be capable of providing the highest quality dental care much faster and more efficiently than your peers. You may be the most gregarious, friendly and endearing health care provider available. You may even possess the most astute knowledge of business exceeding that of most in the field of dentistry. You are not, however, likely to be in charge of collecting on that which you have produced. It is crucial to diligently train your staff in the importance of properly gathering data, submitting accurate claims and tracking their status through the mandatory destination of payment in full.

Electronic Claim Submission

Filing claims online can save time and money. This is especially true if your dental software is encoded with specific electronic claim submission programs. Electronic claims are processed for the insurance companies by third-party merchants. Most vendors providing electronic claim submission charge a specific fee per claim submitted. This fee accounts for the cost of postage, printing and processing. Some dental insurance companies absorb this fee and offer free electronic claims through a vendor. It makes economic sense for insurance companies to do so, because the process of receiving claims electronically significantly reduces their required staff time and associated overhead. This trend mirrors that of large firms reducing staff size via assigning tasks to online technology rather than to personnel.

We have found Claim Connect at www.dentalxchange.com to provide the simplest process for filing claims and the largest number of insurance companies for which they offer free claim processing. Claim Connect's system notifies you if a claim contains an error or cannot be processed. This system also monitors the status of the current claim and allows you to verify that a claim has been received. Gone are the days of the customary insurance company reply "We never received that claim. It must have gotten lost in the mail." The introduction and increasing popularity of electronic claim submission has revolutionized our industry in terms of the way in which we are remunerated for our services. Claims previously delayed or denied under the old system are now processed and paid expediently. The practice of submitting claims electronically significantly reduces the incumbent risk of accepting dental insurance assignment of benefits.

Claim Connect also offers insurance eligibility and benefits information for several major companies, including Met Life. Claim Connect is integrated to work with most major dental practice software programs including Eaglesoft and Dentrix. Claim Connect has the capacity to transmit electronic attachments, such as digital x-rays, through the use of FastAttach. Though our office has utilized only its free programs, Claim Connect also offers a paid service which includes claim processing and eligibility information for a more extensive network of insurance companies.

Chapter 20

Insurance Participation Decisions

Insurance Plan Types:

HMO/Capitation Plans

HMO stands for *Health Maintenance Organization*. I prefer to think of it as *Half My Overhead*, as this is about the amount these types of plans reimburse. These plans require patients to utilize a health care professional on their list of in-network providers. They do not allow any other choice or reimburse for treatment outside the offices of these network providers. Dentists providing care under these HMO plans have agreed to offer services at significantly reduced fees and have potentially invited substantially increased hassles. HMO insurances require pre-authorization and x-rays for most procedures.

Health care practitioners who become HMO providers may be required to see large volumes of patients in order to become profitable. This creates a hurried atmosphere in which patients may not be given the time and attention they desire. True to form, time constraints can invite clinical standard of care compromises many dentists are not willing to assume.

HMO plans typically reimburse on a capitation basis in which a dentist is paid a predetermined dollar amount per year to treat a patient. In a capitation payment plan, the dentist is paid the same amount each month regardless of the number of appointments or type of treatment provided. This is obviously not a system that encourages dentists to make efforts to ensure the best dental health for their patients. I am not saying that dentists participating with these plans do not make all efforts to provide the best care possible, simply that the HMO system does not reward for these efforts.

Though I do not speak for all dentists opting to participate with these plans, I am told that delayed treatment and patchwork are what is rewarded with respect to HMO treatment plans. If a particular tooth can be watched, it pays to do so. The more you treat, the less you may profit. At times, it actually costs you money to place a filling. I know this because my initiation into our profession took place over a four-year period in a HMO machine that would have made John Deere proud.

At the conclusion of my tenure in this Goliath of dentistry, I recall thinking; *I would bet that I have already seen more patients in these last four years than I will for the rest of my practice life.* I am unsure whether this assumption will prove accurate, but I cannot quite dispel it at this point in my career. We were paid to see patients and see patients we did. The more patients we saw the better, the more we actually treated the worse.

Though I did not alter my treatment plans based upon the fact that the HMO plans seemed to reward less treatment, the patients were educated by the support staff on the benefits of upgrading their treatment to better alternatives, many times not fully covered by their plans. A composite filling could be placed in lieu of an amalgam. A porcelain-fused-to-high noble metal crown was presented as an alternative to the covered benefit non-precious metal crown. Who wants a base metal crown anyway? A cast metal partial denture could be fabricated instead of the covered plastic partial flipper. Nearly the only restorative code that could not be upgraded was that for an extraction.

The treatment recommended was clearly the better alternative and that which most patients desired. It was a game and this office was playing it with skill and acumen. The patient was still receiving the ideal treatment, but it was the patient who was getting played by the insurance company. "Yes, we have got you covered. You are covered for any type of dentistry that, when presented with options, most patients would never select. Now please submit your premium."

In the unlikely event that a patient chose to purchase one of those non-precious metal crowns, it would come at a cost of $200. This amount would represent the total fee recovered for the procedure. It would be paid by the patient, not the insurance company. The HMO insurance might reimburse the practice $5/month for this client to be a patient of record in the office. No other reimbursement for the hard work supplied in providing a well-fitting restoration would be coming the way of the treating dentist. If this patient were never to set foot in the office for another 10-15 years, the doctor might then recover the cost of making this crown. If the patient were to come back for routine cleanings, the dentist would be losing money.

Consider the cost of placing a filling. When a patient elects to have an amalgam restoration placed, there is no reimbursement. That is correct, the filling is free! Five bucks a month will hardly cover placing too many of these. How does a dentist reasonably evade this? The dentist looking to profit might decide to watch areas which other dentists might fill. Is this the ideal treatment plan?

The cost structure of these plans is unrealistic and unworkable. In order to profit, costs must be controlled and reduced in some manner. An explanation I routinely provide patients is that we all as dentists have similar overheads. As would stand to reason, nearly all of us aspire to run profitable businesses. In order to do so, the money lost to deeply discounted fees will need to be recovered in some form or fashion. Most patients do not require further explanation to understand where I am going with this.

As can be surmised from my commentary, the HMO type is not my style of practice. Early in my career I was perplexed as to why a dentist would desire to operate under this philosophy. I was reminded by a colleague that, "Some people need to be surrounded by a lot of people to feel like their practices are thriving." I suppose there is some sense of security in having a guaranteed revenue stream coming from the capitation checks every month. This guarantee, however, is accompanied by the certainty of higher overhead and a mandatorily increased workload.

Fresh out of dental school I decided not to open my own practice, but to seek employment as an associate. I donned the suit and tie and drove to interviews virtually from California's border with Mexico to the northernmost beach in Los Angeles. I quickly learned that the suit was a touch extreme in SoCal, and even so was the tie. I also rapidly gathered education on the definitions associated with the alphabet soup of insurance terminology. As was the case with dental anatomy vocabulary as a first year dental student, this language was more foreign to me than the French and Spanish I had so diligently labored to fluently articulate.

With the pervasiveness of managed care dentistry in the area at the time, the vast majority of my interviews occurred in practices heavily involved with these plans. I began to detect a certain expression of satisfaction from my interviewers when my responses revealed my absence of knowledge on the subject of dental insurance. My naivety was far from being a deal breaker, as the role of a managed care associate was to pump out dentistry as fast as possible, not to run the business. In fact, the less I knew about the remuneration, the more employable I seemed to be.

I find this lack of understanding with respect to dental insurance to be widespread in most recent dental school graduates. This has been borne out through the interview process with most of the associates applying for work in my practices. Though I felt embarrassed by my total lack of familiarity with the topic during my own interviews, this is so common that it should not be a source of shame. Instead, it should be used as an opportunity to learn and position yourself ahead of others in our competitive field. Why would I have ever learned about HMOs, PPOs, Indemnity Plans and Fee-For-Service Dentistry until they affected my income? When they did, I began to study these topics as if they were an integral part of my business success. It soon became clear that they were.

As an associate, I began to negotiate to be paid a bonus on the monthly capitation checks my boss received. After all, I had bargained for a deal that would reimburse me proportionately more for greater productivity, yet that production was limited by the insulting fees the HMOs had to offer. I was the workhorse for those plans and I wanted to be paid accordingly. A cut of the monthly insurance checks would assure that I was being compensated for this increased workload. My boss eventually agreed to this deal, realizing the value in the work I was doing, even if the insurance company's reimbursement schedule did not reflect it.

No such negotiation would ever have taken place absent my investigation and study of the way in which these plans remunerate.

The same can be stated for PPO plans, and even insurance plans which do not consider themselves as managed care. It is incumbent on you as a successful business owner to become an expert in the area of dental insurance, unless of course you are among the stark minority of dentists who operate outside the strictures of this industry. Namely, you do not process dental insurance as a form of patient payment.

PPO Plans

PPO stands for *Preferred Provider Organization*. These plans encourage members to patronize health care providers within their networks in order to receive maximum benefits. PPO dental plans are widely popular among employer groups and continue to consume a greater percentage of the dental marketplace because they offer the employers a discount when selecting their plans. The insurance companies can offer discounts because their reimbursement schedules for dental procedures are typically so much lower than what the average dentist would charge.

While PPOs prefer their members to see in-network providers, many plans grant patients the same percentage level benefits even when visiting an out-of-network provider. For example, many PPO insurances cover preventative appointments at 100% whether a patient sees an in-network or out-of-network dentist. Most PPO plans are not forthcoming with this information, as it is in their interests to have their members seek services from network providers. Out-of-network providers should keep in mind that the reimbursement provided by a PPO insurance company will be based upon its UCR. This will not likely represent the entire fee for preventative services performed by an out-of-network dentist, even though the coverage level may be stated as 100%.

Other plans allow patients to patronize out-of-network providers, but the insurance companies will reimburse at a smaller percentage level and the patients are responsible for the difference. This disparity is quite common when considering restorative procedures. As an example, a patient visiting an in-network provider might receive benefits for a crown or a filling payable at 80% by the insurance company. The same service provided by an out-of-network dentist would yield only a 60% reimbursement from the insurance company.

We confirm insurance benefits for all new patients prior to their first appointment and provide disclosure of any co-payments that will be due. It is extremely important to instruct your front office staff in how to handle inquiries about insurance benefits. Probably the most frequently asked question by potential new patients is "Do you take my insurance?" Since we accept insurance from all plans that are not HMOs, we tell the patients "Yes, we process that insurance," and that we will look into their benefits before their initial appointment. If we determine that the patient will owe a co-pay when choosing to see an out-of-network dentist, we call the patient with this information prior to the primary appointment.

PPO policies and fee reimbursement amounts vary tremendously. Some PPO insurances will allow you to negotiate your fees and may increase the initial fee schedules they send to you if you take the time to make such requests. In our area, PPO plan fees reimburse about 50%-60% of my UCR. Given this huge chasm between one's actual fees and that of the PPO UCR, careful consideration must be given to whether or not to participate with such plans. A clear advantage to electing to do so is the abundance of new patients participation provides. This advantage, however, will come at a cost. The pros and cons of this decision will be discussed in a subsequent section, To PPO or Not To PPO? That Is The Question.

Indemnity Plans

Indemnity plans allow their participants to go to any health care provider they choose. These plans are not PPOs nor HMOs and do not have preferred provider networks. They are therefore not considered managed care plans, because the patients are not *managed* by the insurance companies. There is no difference in percentage or fee reimbursement regardless of which health care provider patients see. This does not mean these companies will pay your entire fee, as again, they are basing coverage on their own versions of UCR. However, these plans typically reimburse at much higher levels than PPO plans.

Indemnity plans appear to be on an inverse trajectory to that of Preferred Provider Organization plans. They are waning in popularity with employer groups because they, by definition, will cost these companies more money. These plans reimburse any dentist, so the employer cannot conserve costs by encouraging members to seek treatment from preferred providers who might offer fee reductions as an incentive.

If an employer group truly desired to practice benevolence, it would offer coverage for its employees to seek treatment from any provider they so choose. Treatment choices could be made based upon quality of care and a relationship of trust between patient and health care provider. Of the three insurance plan types mentioned thus far, indemnity plans come closest to this ideal. These plans still bear limitations, as they place restrictions on services covered and they dictate the fees that will be reimbursed. These elements leave the patient paying the difference between the dentist's fee and the insurance company's UCR.

Indemnity plans are great for the practicing dentist. You will most commonly receive close to your entire fee because you are not signed on to an agreement defining your fee schedule. You will be able to treat any patient possessing one of these plans because a patient is not restricted to see a doctor on a designated list. Therefore, potential new patients on indemnity plans are open to seek treatment on the open market, allowing you to compete for them through exercising your competitive advantage. The only constraints you may encounter are that of services the insurance company deems to be *not a covered benefit*, and the sometimes hefty copayment a patient may owe when the plan's UCR falls short of reality.

Direct Reimbursement/Fee-For-Service Plans

One rung up the ladder from the Indemnity Plan rests the Direct Reimbursement/Fee-For-Service Plan. As the name implies, this type of plan pays the dentist for services rendered. The American Dental Association defines a Direct Reimbursement Plan as: "A self-funded dental benefits plan that reimburses patients according to *dollars spent* on dental care, not type of treatment received." The ADA also offers the related definition, "Direct Reimbursement is a self-funded group dental plan in which the employee is reimbursed based upon a percentage of dollars spent for dental care provided, and which allows employees to seek treatment from the dentist of their choice." [30] My definition of a Direct Reimbursement Plan is, "The type of dental insurance plan dentists wish covered all their patients."

Direct reimbursement plans allow the patient complete freedom to choose any dentist, regardless of cost structure. These plans are obviously not considered managed care plans. Instead of paying monthly insurance premiums for all of their employees, including those who never visit the dentist, employers simply pay a percentage of actual treatment received. Moreover, employers are removed from the potential responsibility of influencing treatment decisions via plan selection or sponsorship.

The clear advantage of the Direct Reimbursement Plan is the liberty it affords the patient to seek a health care provider relationship based upon trust. Patients are free to select unrestricted, ideal treatment options as they deem appropriate, without concern for insurance limitations. This puts an onus of accountability on the dentist to be trustworthy and driven by the desire to provide optimal health, rather than by any monetary gain. This obligation is present independent of the strictures of any dental insurance dictate, but some might argue that the fee plans keep dentists accountable. We have an enormous responsibility as health care providers, one different from any other form of employment. We have all agreed to make every effort to adhere to the highest clinical standards which help to assure patient health. Presumably we do not require the external forces of a for-profit insurance company to enforce this commitment.

In the mid to late 90's there was a movement in Southern California to dramatically expand the utilization of Direct Reimbursement Dental Plans. Groups of dentists would assemble and offer their own form of these plans to employer groups. Some dentists on the lecture circuit would encourage individual dentists on a grass roots movement to solicit large corporations to select these plans for their employees. As is the case with most small business owners, dentists were busy doing the business of dentistry, not that of petitioning companies for justice in their field. This combined with the reality that the large employer groups were in the business of profitability and the fate of these plans was predictable.

The unfortunate truth about health insurance, including dental insurance, is that plans resembling the Direct Reimbursement/Fee-For-Service paradigm are rapidly becoming extinct in the marketplace. Employer cost control efforts, coupled with the rising cost of health care, are stifling attempts made by dentists to ensure deregulation of our industry. Though there are a select few on the lecture circuit who continue to maintain that the insurance independent practice is achievable, these practices remain the overwhelming minority. Most practices continue to operate under the constraints of insurance companies which, unbeknownst to most of our patients, may not at times hold the patient's health as first priority.

To PPO or Not to PPO? That is the Question.

My immediate answer to this question is "Don't do it!" I would rather not have you work for the insurance companies and accept a mere 50% of your fee. However, I have experience both working as a PPO provider and as an independent dentist not participating in any PPO networks. I acknowledge that there are some benefits to being an in-network provider, especially when you are starting a dental practice from scratch. Namely, you open your practice up to an immediate list of potential new patients. The upfront marketing cost to enlist these new patients is zero, but the cost from fee reductions will be evident after treatment has begun. I have had success through initially participating with these plans when my practices were in their infancy, then terminating my enrollment after having established a substantial patient base.

When choosing to participate in PPO networks, request fee schedules, policies, number of participants in your area and applications from a large number of insurance companies. Compare the fee schedules and policies to determine which companies would be the most beneficial to you. When I review applications, far and away the most important element of concern for me is the actual fee schedule. Regardless of the number of potential patients a particular PPO plan may insure, it will not be worth the cost of participating if the fees are unreasonable. In fact, it may actually cost you money to treat these patients. Many times I am called to control my emotions when I learn what some of these plans deem as the reimbursable value of my work.

This is another time when consulting with colleagues in your area is beneficial in helping determine which insurance plans are offered by various local companies. As an example, if MasterCard operates just down the street from your office and insures many thousands of employees through a Cigna PPO, it would behoove you to look into participation with this plan. You might also inquire of area dentists as to which insurance plans come accompanied with the greatest degree of aggravation. This is an often ignored yet highly important decisive factor, considering the cost related to chasing down your money. If, for example, a particular insurance plan that has a local track record of delaying payment is offered to the employees of a major company in your area, it may not be worth taking on this substantial employer group. If your area competition is less than forthcoming with the information you desire, the dental insurance benefits provided are readily accessible via the HR departments of these local companies.

When deciding to participate with PPO plans in a new practice, I would suggest choosing five to seven of the larger insurance companies insuring a sizeable number of members in your area. You can add more networks later if your business is not growing as you would like. Given the difficulty involved in transitioning off insurance networks and the risk of patient loss when you discontinue participation, do not initially enroll your practice in every insurance plan available. It can take several months for a general termination process, but it may actually be much longer before the PPO plan's book of preferred providers and online directory no longer lists you as a participating doctor. Even when you follow every cancellation protocol to the letter, the mammoth insurance company's left hand rarely knows what the right hand is doing.

Though the fee schedule is of paramount importance, your decision as to which insurances to join should not be based solely on their rates of reimbursement. An insurance company that pays at a slightly lower rate, but provides instant access to benefits and processes claims quickly may result in being more beneficial than a company that has a slightly higher fee schedule. This is particularly salient when the higher payer consistently denies claims and requires climbing a phone tree to the moon. When paying employees to spend valuable time researching benefits, contacting insurance supervisors and re-submitting claims, the cost of participation can quickly become preventative.

A well-guarded secret of the managed care insurance industry is that many of these plans will allow you to negotiate for higher fees when they are properly motivated. If you have chosen to participate as an in-network provider with an insurance company that allows negotiation of fees, by all means, do not ignore this opportunity. Some insurance companies allow you to re-submit your fees and renegotiate your fee schedule once or twice a year. Do not merely negotiate when you initiate the contract. Make a note on your calendar to actively renegotiate fees as often as possible.

An insurance company's primary incentive for negotiating fees is consistent with the most basic business principle of Economics101, supply versus demand. Of course these insurance companies do not want to increase their reimbursement for you, any more than you want to reduce your fees to some substandard level for them. The reality is that these companies set their fees at a level which is most profitable for them, yet continues to supply the greatest number of willing participants, i.e., participating dentists. Your fee schedule has been set at a level reflecting the quality of care in your office, has ideally been selected based upon a scientific fee analyzer and purportedly will allow your business to profit.

Insurance companies are commonly inspired to negotiate their fee schedules when very few dentists are available on their list of in-network providers. When marketing their particular plans to potential employer groups, they are at a disadvantage when they have a limited number of doctors for their employees to patronize. They will therefore incentivize area dentists to join their plans by offering higher fee reimbursement than other Preferred Provider Networks. I have witnessed this played out to the greatest degree with dental specialists. As there are considerably fewer specialists in our profession than general dentists, insurance companies are prompted more regularly to enlist the services of at least one in-network specialist for any given area. The savviest specialists are frequently able to command fees approximating, if not equaling, their own.

General dentists operating in smaller towns seem to have the greatest success with PPO fee negotiation. Again, it is a simple supply/demand issue. The fewer willing participants in your area, the greater the likelihood the insurance company will be amenable to courting your services. It should be noted, however, that even the big city docs will find success in this if the proper time is allocated to the process. You may not have because you do not ask.

Edward M. Logan, DDS

Participation in Managed Care Dentistry

Participation in managed care dentistry is simply one form of dental treatment delivery. In and of itself, managed care participation is not bad or evil. I am not intending to disparage those who elect to practice in this manner. If benevolence is the motivation, it stands as noble. Alternative methods of serving those in need might be providing dentistry to the poor and underserved through missionary work or inner city volunteering. A dentist may choose to provide services free of charge on a case-by-case basis, identifying those in greatest need. There are also a number of nationally sponsored charitable programs in which dentists may choose to participate.

If, however, the most substantial profitability of the practice is the driving factor, I am not sure if managed care dentistry is the avenue leading one to this end. While revenues may increase through enhanced managed care participation, we need to always be mindful of overhead expansion as well. Since profit is a measure of monies-in versus monies-out, we need to choose which variable we wish to manipulate most. If one does not mind working as much and as hard as possible, the increase in the monies-in value will likely outpace that of the monies going out. If, however, one is more similar to Owen Wilson's character in *You, Me and Dupree*, one's work ethic might reflect Dupree's job interview response, "I'm not gonna be your workhorse."

The managed care scenario in which I found myself entangled early in my career offered me a level of business acumen I would likely never have acquired in a lifetime of fee-for-service dentistry. My boss was an excellent dentist, one to be admired. His skills and clinical competency, buffeted by countless hours of continuing education and dedication to the highest standards in dentistry, set him apart from any I knew in our region. Given his accolades and abilities, I was perplexed as to why he would elect to participate with all these HMO and PPO plans, while maintaining a staff of over 20 employees. One day I asked him, "Why don't you just keep all of your indemnity charts and fire all of us? You could have the ideal operation that everyone on the lecture circuit touts as the dream practice." That was my way. His was another way.

The most amusing story I have heard about an HMO dental practice was recently related to me by my dental assistant. She told me that when she started in dentistry, she worked in one such office. A mere two weeks into her employment, an OSHA meeting was scheduled for 5 p.m. after the office had closed for the day. As soon as the front door was locked to patients, the back door was opened to her co-workers fleeing to the liquor store. The mission was to quickly sequester cigarettes and beer, even liquor, which was going to be required to tolerate the Charlie Brown monotone OSHA presentation. So, in the midst of this sterilization lecture provided within the confines of a health professional's office, cigarette smoke filled the air and mixed drinks flowed amid these health care providers. I was left to wonder what my dental assistant must have been thinking during her youthful initiation into our profession. Then the thought crossed my mind, *I wonder if she would prefer that my practice were more like that one?*

Discontinuing Membership with an Insurance Company

If you choose to enroll as an in-network provider for a large number of insurance plans to initially build your patient base, be mindful of the potential for patient misgivings when you elect to terminate your status. Following the unanticipated rapidity of growth in my current practice, I decided to discontinue participation in all of the eight PPO plans in which I had originally enlisted. While I do not regret or discourage this election, be informed that some patients will feel betrayed by this decision. I was accused by one patient of bait-and-switch tactics when I withdrew from his PPO network. Bait-and-switch is something I despise in business and that which I strive never to exemplify in my own.

The process of informing patients of your decision to no longer participate as an in-network provider with their insurance plans has to be handled with care. Your staff needs to be understanding of your patients' concerns while encouraging them to stay with your practice. If a patient decides to leave the practice for an in-network provider, make sure the patient knows that the door is always open to return to your office. I am happy to report that the same patient accusing me of bait-and-switch tactics returned to our practice after having tried another office. He explained that his return was the result of our not making him feel guilty about his decision to leave, and our informing him that we would welcome him back if ever he should choose to return.

It is incumbent on you to set your practice apart from the others in all ways possible. Therefore, when you have achieved insurance independence, your patients should be able to recognize the difference when electing to seek treatment from another provider who happens to be in their insurance network. I am reminded of a quote from a colleague reflecting his confidence and certainty that, "They all come back sooner or later." Though I am not convinced of the inclusive nature of his statement, many patients will return if you have done your job properly. While there will always be those whose decisions are made on price alone, it is your responsibility to create value for those who use this as their measuring rod.

Make every effort not to be discouraged by those who suggest you have no chance in this business outside participation in these managed care plans. Dentists operating in congested population areas will hear these mutterings much more commonly than those in smaller communities. I was initially dismayed to learn from a close friend that the people inhabiting the city in which I was to start my new practice were completely reliant on health care providers participating in-network with their insurance plans. Though my friend was not at all off base with this statement, I was able to forge a fee-for-service practice in the midst of this predominate PPO affiliation. In fact, we are the only practice of over a dozen dentists in our one square mile enclave operating outside the strictures of any PPO plan. I have rarely found it beneficial to heed the advice of those spouting negativity. You can do it just like I did. You just have to be willing to search out the ways to do it better than your competition.

Marketing Your Practice for Success

Chapter 21

Creating a Powerful Marketing Plan

When I started my third dental practice from scratch, there were only two other dentists in the neighborhoods surrounding my office. There was only one house across the street from the office. I chose the location because of the huge potential I saw for demographic growth. Two years later there were eight dental offices and hundreds of new homes in the community.

One dentist opened up within a stone's throw of my back door. I have never met her. There is apparently no reason for her to come over and introduce herself, and no expectation on my part that she would ever do so. This is a highly competitive market and your ability to stand out and become recognizable contributes largely to the level of success of your business. The degree to which you are able to make your services more desirable than those of the surrounding dentists is an important determinant to the growth of your practice.

Countless *experts* in the field of dental practice marketing contend that your competition is not from other dentists but from the other goods and services a patient can elect to purchase. People can choose to buy a new car, boat or house. They can buy expensive clothing, jewelry or accessories. Maybe they will take another vacation, a cruise perhaps. The truth is, however, you *are* competing with the other dentists for all the potential new patients. It is critical to your success that you do this better than the other dentists around you. You must establish and maintain a steady flow of new patients in order to support the production of a new or growing dental practice. Clearly, you have to get them in before you can compete for their disposable income.

The initial and continued success of a dental practice will be largely determined by the success of its marketing plan. If there is no plan, there will likely be no business. Although cash may be tight in the beginning, an intelligent budget plan will necessarily include a judicial amount of money earmarked for marketing. Some pundits contend that an allotment of roughly 4% of a dental practice's collections should be assigned to marketing its services. The ideal percentage allocated to a new business will be greater than that value, considering that initial revenues will be limited, and marketing from ground zero will assume a much greater role.

The following excerpt from a McGill Advisory newsletter article on dental practice marketing suggests different allocations of collections percentage to marketing based upon a practice's busyness:

> A written marketing plan must be developed to boost new patient flow. The amount of time, energy and money devoted to marketing must be inversely proportional to the doctor's level of optimal capacity. For example, if the doctor is operating near 100% of optimal capacity (busy as she wants to be doing the type of dentistry she wants to do), a marketing budget of only 1% of practice collections may be just fine. If the doctor is operating at only 80-90% of optimal capacity, 2-3% of collections should be devoted to marketing. For those operating at 70-80% of capacity, 3-4% of practice collections should be allocated to marketing. Those who are operating below 70% of optimal capacity should be spending 4-6% of collections on marketing in order to boost practice production. [31]

Relying solely on becoming a network provider for multiple PPO plans while failing to institute any paid marketing will cost you more over time in light of the long-term discounts (sometimes over 50%) that the PPO patient receives. While the initial outlay of cash for marketing may seem more daunting than simply accepting lower fees, your return on investment (ROI) from marketing projects can be much more profitable than becoming a network dentist for every PPO under the sun. I have never been a fan of the philosophy that it is better to have a chair filled with a partial pay (PPO) patient than to have an empty chair. While I am admittedly in the minority concerning my beliefs on this topic, I simply account for the costs of labor, be them financial, toil and liability. I would rather make all efforts to seat a fee-for-service patient in the operatory and assume the cost to get that patient there.

In the early years of your practice, it may seem like the majority of your time away from work will be spent working on marketing your business. The more talented entrepreneurs will be constantly searching for new and better ways to promote their businesses. It will pay to be diligent in this endeavor during the initial growth phase of your practice, permitting you to more quickly realize business solvency and practice sustenance. The more rapidly you approach this level, the greater stress relief you are afforded by ensuring that you get to keep some of the money funneling through your business. After all, though it is rewarding to provide your patients exceptional dentistry and your staff a living, the goal of any for-profit business is to ultimately do just that, profit.

Initially, the majority of these efforts will fall on your shoulders. Until you are able to impart your knowledge and desire to a motivated, skilled staff member, the time and energy expense will be primarily yours. The rewards for these efforts are extraordinary, however. The idea is to get to a place of freedom from the need to do any of these things any longer. When you do, it means your practice is operating at optimal capacity and you are treating patients who have been all your own from the very beginning.

Though I certainly spent innumerable hours promoting my practices via these external means during their early stages, those times now seem like distant memories. One of the objectives of this book is to help escort you down this path more efficiently, by removing the trial and error obstacles I encountered along the way. By concentrating your efforts on only those marketing campaigns proven to remit the greatest return on investment, you will reach business security much more rapidly than the majority of your peers.

Tracking Return on Investment (ROI)

Within your marketing plan, ensure the implementation of a system for identifying specifically which marketing efforts are worthwhile and which need to be redesigned or replaced. This is best handled through the analysis of referral reports and a spreadsheet of marketing expenditures. Again, it is imperative to inquire and record how each individual new patient first learned of your office. This information will allow you to calculate a highly accurate determination of each marketing effort's return on investment.

The ROI is the most valuable tracking mechanism we have to ascertain the most profitable ways in which we should spend our hard-earned money. Although most patients consult multiple sources before deciding to schedule an appointment, we record only one referral source for each new patient. Determining exactly who or what inspired each individual patient to select your practice is imperative to the accurate calculation of return on investment data for your marketing efforts. This in turn will allow you to ascertain which protocol is working and which is clearly ineffective, and to redefine your efforts accordingly. This not only saves you money in terms of failed advertising campaigns, but can bring great profit by dialing in those specific marketing ventures yielding the greatest returns.

It will not always be easy to assign the appropriate referral source to each new patient. When queried, many people cannot even recall with certainty how they learned of your practice. Therefore it is mandatory that your staff is trained and educated on the importance of accurately defining this piece of information. There is an art to subtly guiding the patient down the path to recollection of which particular individual or piece of marketing material drew first attention to your business. No one wants to be made to feel unimportant or used, and this feeling may be even more poignant on the first visit. "I'm here, who cares how I discovered this place? I'm important, aren't I?" Such are thoughts that may arise when a new client is pressed for this information. We gently offer, "We would just like to know so we can thank the person for referring you to our office." While this is true, we also truly value the data this information can provide to enhance the profitability of our business.

Keep in mind that return on investment numbers can sometimes be deceiving. At times it takes a deeper look into the numbers to determine the true value of your marketing investment. We once spent hundreds of dollars mailing glossy color postcards to thousands of homes. One of these postcards secured us a patient who eventually scheduled treatment for five implants, an implant bridge and five separate crowns. He also became a preventative maintenance patient for life. We obviously made out pretty well on that postcard mailer in terms of return on investment. However, he was the only patient responding to this offer to call and schedule an appointment. Was repeating this postcard mailer something that made sense for our practice? Even though we made thousands of dollars the first time we did it, I determined that the campaign was a failure and did not warrant repeating.

The Ideal Marketing Plan

Your goal should be to establish a multi-layered marketing approach. This plan of attack will include internal marketing efforts to encourage patients to appoint for treatment, remain patients of record in your office, think of you when they are away from your office and refer others for the same great service they have received. It will incorporate external marketing efforts to attract new patients via new resident mailers, small publication advertisements, repeated exposure through the use of street level signs, an Internet presence and community service participation. These after-hours endeavors will encourage prospective patients to take that crucial step of contacting your office to schedule an appointment. Make your practice stand out from the rest.

The following chapters outline ideas for internal and external marketing, as well as methods for designing and maintaining a website that ranks highly with search engines. This information is useful whether you are a dentist just beginning a scratch practice or one who has been in practice for years but still desires to attract new patients. My desire is that these chapters will help you develop a successful marketing strategy for your business, ideally before your doors are ever opened to the public. Let's get started creating your ideal marketing plan!

Chapter 22

Internal Marketing Efforts

The Importance of Recalls

A good recall system is critical to the health of your practice. Patients should not leave your office before scheduling their next appointment. We schedule the recall appointment at checkout, having patients who are uncomfortable providing an email address complete their own recall postcards with name, address and appointment time information. Receiving a postcard scripted in their own handwriting entices patients to take greater notice of it in their stack of mail. We send this postcard a month prior to the scheduled recall, providing patients ample time to recollect the appointment and re-schedule if necessary. Patients who elect to call to make an appointment are still required to fill out a postcard. The mailing of this postcard one month prior to the expected recall date ensures that a patient's recall will not fall through the cracks and reminds the patient to call to appoint.

For those patients willing to provide email addresses, which are most, we forego the recall postcard in favor of the more cost-effective method of sending email reminders. We send these reminders both one month and two days in advance of the scheduled appointments. We also request that patients confirm receipt of these reminders. This helps to ensure against the relatively common excuse, "I never received that postcard." This electronic communication also relieves us of the fiscal burden of purchasing, stamping and mailing postcards to thousands of patients. Many patients now elect to have their appointment reminder texted to them on their handheld devices as well.

When initially invited to schedule their recall appointments, patients may state that they have no idea what they will be doing in six months and will call at that time to schedule. Gently persuade patients to schedule an appointment, letting them know that they can always call to re-schedule if the time proves inconvenient. Advise them that they will receive a postcard or an email reminder of the appointment one month in advance, allowing sufficient time to re-schedule if necessary. Highlight the benefit of greater time of day choices if an appointment is scheduled in advance. Inform them that when delaying scheduling, the earliest and latest appointment times of the day will not likely be available. Most patients seamlessly become accustomed to the idea of scheduling these appointments in advance.

My patients leave the office with a reminder sticker to attach to their home calendar. My office manager also calls two days prior to remind patients of their appointments. These redundant reminders help patients avoid forgetting their appointments and provide more certainty to your schedule. Keep in mind that when patients become expectant of this reminder phone call, they may rely on it and assume they do not have an appointment unless your staff calls to confirm it. When your practice utilizes the reminder sticker, recall postcard, email and phone call, a patient cannot reasonably claim to have forgotten about the appointment.

Running an overdue recall report at least twice a year helps to ensure no patient gets left behind. Slow times (often during February and September) provide ideal opportunities to run this report. Identify from this report patients who have neither scheduled a recall appointment nor been seen in your office for over seven months. Mail these patients an additional postcard apprising them that it is time for their recall appointment. When it is clear that patients have not scheduled due to cost restrictions, additional incentives can be provided in these mailers as well. At the beginning of the year include a note to take advantage of their replenished insurance benefits. Toward the end of the year the note can instruct patients to be sure to use this year's insurance and flexible spending accounts (FSA) benefits before they expire.

If the new patient is the lifeblood of a dental practice, then the recall patient is the heart pumping that blood through the system. There is a point at which there are sufficient patients in the practice to sustain it nearly entirely through recalls. At this point, with a controlled overhead, very little dental treatment outside preventative care should be required to keep the practice afloat. This is not to say that the practice profit will be maximized without other dentistry being delivered, but a well-run business should in this case be able to pay the bills. This is critical in slow times and in the unfortunate experience of an economic downturn.

The relevance of an exceptionally managed recall system is immeasurable to the success of your practice. Every new patient has likely come by means of a sizable investment of practice funds. Once you have the patient, it would be frivolous to let that investment fade away. Patients have selected your office for a reason. By and large they want to come back and remain in your practice family. By all means, make it easy for them to do so. You can and should remove all the difficulty, effort and uncertainty that normally accompany scheduling a recall appointment so many months in advance. The most successful businesses are those that leave nothing to chance. Eliminate the hurdles and your practice will be off and running.

Patient Reminders

As a practice matures, a pattern develops exposing productivity peaks and valleys in the business cycle. January commonly supplies the practice a selection of patients having postponed treatment awaiting new insurance and FSA benefits. The year's first month additionally welcomes the initiation of dental treatment by patients having made New Year's resolutions for better health. The schedule in March and April is often booked with patients enjoying Spring Break, though I can think of more entertaining ways of doing so.

The typical dental practice operatory is occupied during the summer months with patients appreciating free time provided by school closures or vacation days from work. Activity in the dental office peaks again at year's end via patient efforts to maximize those valued insurance and FSA benefits prior to expiration. February, September and October can therefore be left to assume the role of the disrespected months of the dental practice business cycle. As outlined in the section detailing the recall program, periods of practice deceleration can be exploited by mailing reminders to patients overdue for recall appointments.

These months not only provide the ideal opportunity to take

vacation time, but also to reach out to patients having fallen through the cracks during the busier months. We mail overdue recall postcard reminders and treatment discount offers during periods just preceding our notoriously sluggish months. This treatment discount offers 15% off the patient's payment responsibility for treatment begun prior to the end of a predictably unproductive month. This offer does not typically produce an overwhelming rush of patients, but for the very reasonable expense of postcards and postage, you can minimize the empty operatory condition associated with dental practice slow times and cover your expenses.

Mailing postcards in early November reminding patients to maximize their dental insurance benefits prior to expiration is a highly rewarding business investment. November and December are frenetic months for most people and providing them an additional reminder to care for their oral health is often beneficial at this time. Given that most current forms of daily communication is technical in nature, a well-appointed postcard mailer can attract the attention necessary to encourage patients of record back into your office for care. Of course, the ease of use, economy and immediacy of email reminders is a reliable alternative to patient reminder postcards.

New Patient Referral Programs

According to Chrisad (www.chrisad.com), a leading dental marketing company, there are two vastly different types of new patients who enter your practice: The patient obtained through some form of directed marketing effort and the one contacting your practice in response to the referral of a friend, colleague or family member. [32] Chrisad identifies these dramatically different types of people as the *Referral Patient* and the *Marketing Patient*. Typically, the best patients will be those that have been referred by another patient. These patients have chosen you specifically on the kind words and recommendation of a family member, neighbor or co-worker, and enter your office positive about services they have yet to receive. People tend to trust those close to them, and after having been witness to so many glowing reviews about you, they are generally willing to extend you that same level of trust.

As is the case with so many business principles, perhaps you do not have because you do not ask. Every dental marketing program available emphasizes the importance of requesting referrals from patients and rewarding them for obliging. Referrals will ultimately be the most cost-effective avenue by which you will attract new patients. The primary obstacle to establishing a successful referral program is the discomfort involved in taking the needed step of asking for these referrals. The entire staff needs to be secure with the idea of requesting referrals when opportunities arise.

Remind the staff that your desire is to provide quality, gentle dental care for as many of those in your community as possible. Asking for referrals is an ideal way to make this happen, not just a means to increase the practice revenues. Obviously, the extent to which you actually deliver on that desire will largely determine a staff member's motivation to help bring on new clientele and a patient's desire to refer others to your office.

Is it really possible to ask a patient for referrals without making yourself into the dreaded used car salesman? Opportunities to request referrals abound within your printed materials and in your casual conversations with patients. In nearly every newsletter we include a simple statement thanking patients for their continued referrals, as well as a request to inform their friends and family members about our practice. New patients receive an information packet including a brief letter thanking them for joining our practice, and asking them to tell others about the service they received. This packet also contains business cards and assorted giveaway items. These subtle reminders take root over time, remove the hurdle of inhibition and quite often blossom into those invaluable new patient referrals.

Routine conversations with patients often provide great opportunities to encourage them to apprise their friends and loved ones of your practice. Commonly, you will hear patients describe a neighbor seeking a dentist for her children, a family member avoiding the dentist out of fear of embarrassment or a co-worker desiring a dentist with convenient hours. Your staff should be ready to assist by providing a business card or a suggestion to refer their friend, neighbor, co-worker or family member to your office. The front office staff should also capitalize on this opportunity to assist in scheduling the potential patient, before the kind thought is lost to the demands of the day once the patient exits your office.

Some offices encourage team participation by offering incentives to staff members based upon the number of new patient referrals secured. One approach is to provide your staff coupon cards to distribute to patients of record. This coupon outlines a special offer for a new patient, such as *$25 Off Your Initial Appointment, Free Exam and X-rays* or *Free Teeth Whitening*. Staff members initial their coupons and receive a bonus for each new patient responding to this promotion. Staff members can either disseminate their coupons to current patients for distribution to friends and family members, or hand them out like business cards when in a social setting.

There are many avenues to thank and reward patients who help build your practice by referring new patients. Your dental software should provide a report identifying the particular source from which each new patient learned of your office. We run this report every month, allowing us to express our gratitude for personal referrals in a timely manner. Referring patients often appreciate a personalized, hand-written thank you note and the occasional small gift expressing your gratitude.

When I started out in business, I personally inked a letter to every new patient communicating my appreciation for the trust being placed in me. I recall attending a networking seminar at the time in which a self-proclaimed *life coach* admitted to mailing a note to every new client containing merely the phrase "I like you." Though I still find this very odd, I assume the goal was to reach out to new customers and instill a feeling of business personalization. As time wore on and new patient numbers grew, I found it difficult to keep up with these hand-written letters. While the personal approach is likely the most rewarding, a standardized, type-written letter will accomplish roughly the same goal.

The simplest idea for a thank you gift is a coupon for $25-$50 off the referring patient's next dental procedure. I have a number of patients who refer in order to fund their veneer piggy banks, to be emptied into the efforts of future cosmetic dentistry. In the past, I have sent movie tickets or restaurant gift certificates as well. I have been cautious to avoid implementing a system in which it appears that I am paying patients for their referrals. However, I do think it is important to acknowledge the effort a patient has taken to spread the word about my practice.

If you notice certain patients making large numbers of referrals, be sure to thank them whenever they are in your office, and consider sending individualized gifts to let them know you appreciate their referrals. Taking the time to personally thank patients for referrals assures them that you value the time they take to tell others about your practice. If you would like help remembering to thank a patient for referring someone to your practice, your office manager can make a note on the daily schedule whenever a referring patient has an appointment. Some offices offer promotions rewarding a large prize (such as free whitening or a weekend getaway) to the patient who has referred the most patients within an established time period.

Keep in mind that most of the patients who refer routinely to your office are doing so not because of your effective modes of bribery, but because they truly appreciate the intangibles your practice has to offer. They enjoy the guest mentality offered by doctor and staff and the warm, inviting office atmosphere you have taken pains to establish. They value the way in which you provide comfortable dentistry, take time to answer their questions and outline what is to take place in advance. Most of all, they respect the way you relate to them and establish yourself as a trustworthy, caring and likable person. These people cannot be bribed and their referrals are not for sale. I am reminded of an elderly man in my practice who continues to be a steady source of newly referred patients. He routinely rejects any form of gratitude we extend to him, even that in the form of credit to his account. "I don't want your money," he says. We would all be so lucky as to have a practice made up entirely of patients like this one.

Even with the greatest referral programs in place, you will find that some patients just naturally gravitate toward referring others to you, while other patients do not. As is the case with 20% of the patient population being responsible for 80% of the cavities, the discouraging truth is that only a mere 10% of your practice population will refer on a routine basis. When I sold my last dental practice, I decided to perform a rudimentary study on the degree of loyalty of my practice family. Perusing the records, I found that less than 20% of my patients had ever referred a single patient and fewer than 15% had referred multiple times. In an effort to restore my wounded pride, I convinced myself that our practice had done everything imaginable to become an office of compassion, concern and exceptional dental care. I still adhere to those credos today. While I do believe that it is possible for you to outpace those statistics, I find that the distinct minority of people ever actually consider referring.

The rapid pace of our society can impose limitations on our thoughts as they relate to the needs of others. Although your patients may truly adore your staff, appreciate your honesty and value the excellent clinical dentistry they receive, the thought to tell someone else about their dentist may never cross their minds. Do not take this personally. Though this is part of human nature, a selection of your patients will rise to the call, making up for those who love you but forget about you as soon as your office door closes behind them. Female patients are more likely to tell their friends and neighbors about your practice, especially if you are good with children. We have been touched to see young children telling their friends about us at school. It is a true compliment indeed to receive a referral and we are sure to convey to our referring patients the level of sincere appreciation we have for them.

Given the disparity between the referred patient and the patient obtained through marketing, it behooves you to focus your efforts on solidifying your practice with the former. While the marketing patient can present feeling marketed, the referred patient arrives feeling welcomed. Where the marketing patient may levy a wall of distrust, the referred patient embraces you like an extension of the family. I am still at times amazed by how relaxed and accepting is the atmosphere during the new patient exam of a referred patient. This is the stress-free, trusting environment for which you have been striving all along. The referred patient is therefore your platinum patient. The goal should be to move your business in the direction of an eventual referrals-only practice.

Newsletters

Given that the primary goal of your internal marketing campaign should be to establish the allure of your existing patient population, publishing a quarterly office newsletter helps position your practice at the forefront of patients' minds. The newsletter can serve as a timely reminder of the appointment your patients need to schedule or provide a springboard for treatment they would like to pursue. A personalized newsletter additionally ensures that your readers know you care about patient education. Our patients comment frequently that they thoroughly enjoy our newsletters and routinely mention specific articles in the most recent edition.

Each newsletter we produce contains the following:

- A staff member or patient biographical profile
- An article about the importance of maintaining dental hygiene or the role good hygiene plays in overall health
- An appetizing recipe, many times provided by an existing patient or staff member
- An article specific to a procedure we desire to market
- A statement thanking patients for their continued referrals
- A personal note from the doctor, most often health educational in nature.

The biographical profile section routinely draws the most patient feedback. Though we like to feature a staff member at times to help personalize our practice, we find that the recognition of a particular patient for outstanding achievements or unusual anecdotes garners the greatest reader interest. A recent newsletter article highlighted a patient with Cystic Fibrosis (CF). Our patient has been battling this disease and its conditions for over forty years, a feat in itself, considering the rapidity with which this insidious malady claims the lives of its victims. Over the years, not only has he been the recipient of a double lung transplant, he has also maintained an active lifestyle, competing in the Transplant Olympics on an annual basis. This perseverant individual earns a living through motivational speaking, often employing humor to suggest the levity of his situation.

Detailing his story, and with his consent of course, our newsletter introduced this patient with CF to our patients of record. During the weeks following this newsletter's publication, we received multiple affirmative comments regarding his account. One patient was so encouraged and motivated by his narrative that she sent my office an email expressing her gratitude. I, in turn, forwarded the content of her comments along to our featured patient. His response to me brought the article's impact full circle, "Wow! he exclaimed. Thanks Dr. Logan. That just made my whole day!"

We also use the newsletter as an opportunity to mention new rewards programs for referring patients and to encourage patients to take advantage of their insurance benefits and schedule treatment. Our newsletters are only one page, front and back, allowing our readers to devour them rapidly. We design the newsletter to be eye-catching and reader-friendly. Regardless of what is actually in your newsletter, the main goal is to keep your practice in front of your patients. We have found the quarterly newsletter to provide one of the most cost-effective ways of achieving this goal.

Newsletter articles can be exploited in other arenas as well. When added to your website throughout the year, these articles provide fresh content which encourages the search engines to take recognition of your site once again. This results in the additional benefit of a higher ranking for your practice website associated with potential patient searches. Newsletter articles can be posted in online directories or on your practice's blog, creating still greater visibility for your practice in cyberspace. Local newspapers may publish a submitted article as a press release if the information is informative and newsworthy. At times we have modified our newsletters to be used as marketing pieces for health fairs or schools, and as advertising flyers to solicit new patients. Your internal marketing newsletter now becomes a source of external marketing as well.

We have recently begun to offer an email newsletter to save on the cost of printing, postage and stuffing envelopes. While it may be a good idea to offer patients the option of receiving the newsletter by email, printed newsletters will garner more attention than yet another email, which could easily be buried in the spam folder. The printed newsletter, especially one containing a tasty recipe or helpful article, will at the very least be perused, while the email newsletter may be deleted before it is ever opened. To avoid its immediate relegation to the trash folder, we request permission to send our newsletter via email when obtaining email addresses from patients.

Assuming you can get the email newsletter under the eyes of your patients, benefits for its use abound. The ease of creating and posting an email newsletter through the use of online templates adds to its attractiveness. Patients enjoy the crispness of color and picture clarity that the emails provide. An additional benefit of using this format is the ability to track page views with our online analytics. We are thereby able to visualize how many patients are actually reading our newsletters.

It is possible to create and maintain a newsletter on your own, but it requires a staff member comfortable with graphic design and skilled in creative writing. Given the importance of these quarterly newsletters to the effective internal marketing campaign of your practice, do not allow the absence of a staff member possessing these qualifications dissuade you from pursuing this endeavor. There are companies available to dentists that specialize in providing this particular type of service. The rewards of this investment, though often going unnoticed, will sustain your practice by maintaining connection with your loyal patient base.

Giveaways

Personalized promotional products help to keep your practice at the forefront of patients' minds. The variety of products available is abundant, while the cost of these various selections can vacillate dramatically. A personalized toothbrush is the obvious first choice in a giveaway product for dentists. Quality and durability of toothbrush imprinting varies significantly. This is important because your name, phone number and possible website address need to remain visible for the life of the toothbrush in order for this to remain a viable marketing expense. Ensure high quality before purchasing by testing samples from a variety of vendors to locate the lasting personalized imprint you desire. We have experienced good results ordering toothbrushes through Elite Dental (1-888-228-7706).

My hygienist continues to pester me about buying floss to hand out to all our patients at their recall appointments. I have been able to resist her not so subtle promptings to this point, but my armor is wearing thin. I have maintained that, "People can buy their own floss. The likelihood is very high that they are not going to use it anyway. The floss will just pile up in their bathroom drawers. It might at least retain some benefit if we could imprint each strand of floss with our contact information."

Of course, my hygienist believes that her patients would floss their teeth more often if we facilitated the process by providing the floss for them. She is probably right, but I tend to align myself with the jovial remarks of a patient to whom she related our friendly banter. Responding to my reluctance to shell out floss to everyone happening into my office, he offered, "That's funny! I'll bet Dr. Logan is thinking, 'Where does it all end?'" He was right. I believe this gentleman owned a small business just as I did.

Marketing companies abound willing to sell you everything under the sun, imprinting your name and phone number and assuring that their junkets will command an onslaught of new patients. In reality, most of these junkets are just that, junk. There are those, however, that remain in eyeshot of your patients on a daily basis, reminding them of your existence and of their continued need for your services. Being highly selective with what our office doles out to patients, we have decided upon a number of giveaway items that have resulted in high levels of patient appreciation, utility and demand.

In the past I have given out a diversity of marketing items, each attaining a varying level of success. The refrigerator magnet is always in high demand, and there it is, hanging on the fridge. Studies have placed the average American hand on the refrigerator door no less than 27 times per day. At roughly 25 cents a pop, that is less than a penny per daily view of your dental practice's name, phone number and website address. I can think of worse ways to spend my marketing dollars.

I have a friend and colleague from dental school with whom I travelled to Europe for the first time. European by descent, he had great familiarity with the culture and intricacies of travel abroad. I deferred to his lead and we hit five countries in eight days. Midway through the trip I found myself in the South of France in the beautiful seaside city of Nice. We were housed by my colleague's friends in a modest apartment overlooking the Mediterranean Sea. It turned out that one of my new acquaintances was my colleague's patient from the United States, and her husband was born and raised in France. The story of how the couple met was quite interesting, but almost equally as noteworthy was the manner in which she first encountered my friend, her dentist. "How did you guys meet?" I queried.

"Well, I moved across the country and settled in a new apartment," she offered. "Hanging on the fridge was a magnet with his name and practice phone number on it, apparently left behind by the former tenants. I knew I would need a new dentist, so I just left it up there. One day I had a toothache and decided to call and make an appointment. I was enticed by his European mentality and we became fast friends."

This was all good fortune for me. Thanks to that little refrigerator magnet, I was now experiencing the beauty and culture of the Cote d'Azur at the hands of two local tour guides. The free room with a view did not hurt my cause too much either.

On a more local note, my practice as recently as last week grew by one new patient who viewed our magnet on a client's refrigerator. This new patient is a cat sitter and apparently performs her duties within her client's homes. Using the website address listed on our magnet, she performed thorough research into her options for cosmetic dentistry. She is now preparing for the treatment accompanying a very large esthetic case. Though the formerly described magnet offered a bit more excitement, the latter provided substantial benefits as well.

Taking into consideration that the majority of adults begin their days with a hot cup of coffee, I had coffee mugs imprinted with my practice logo, name and phone number. Only the referring patients were the lucky beneficiaries of this gift. I cannot accurately speak to the success of this wayward giveaway program. It is sufficient to say, however, that a number of these remaining mugs keep my own coffee warm many mornings, at home and at the office. On occasion I encounter one when opening the cabinet door in a relative's house. I am pretty certain that this was not the return on investment I was anticipating when I first implemented the program.

In contrast to the coffee mugs, we currently offer two giveaway items that seem to fly off the shelf. Both items are affixed to a refrigerator magnet, assuring us redundant visibility throughout the day. Our grocery list giveaway is nothing more than a note pad containing our contact information. When hung on the fridge, this serves as a handy tablet for detailing supermarket needs. In similar fashion, our dry-erase board giveaway, in the shape of an oversized tooth, provides families opportunities to outline personal reminders, or simply to draw pictures if they so choose. While both items are in high demand, we find that the dry-erase boards attract the attention of the pre-teens the most. The grocery lists are most popular with those that do the shopping. These giveaways are cost-conservative, highly effective, loved by patients and a form of internal marketing that reaffirms that you are thinking about your patients' needs.

In order to more directly market the esthetic dentistry segment of my practice, I created and distributed my own cosmetic dentistry brochure. The professionally designed layout contains multiple *Before and After* photographs of patient cases completed in my office. The selected pictorials demonstrate a variety of esthetic improvement options as they relate to various procedures. The accompanying descriptions educate patients on what could potentially be applied to help improve their particular situations. As dentists, we have this dentistry to offer. Our patients need to be made aware that we are capable of providing it, and convinced that we are highly skilled in its delivery. This professional marketing piece has been instrumental in encouraging patients to accept cosmetic treatment plans.

The cosmetic dentistry brochure is an effective advertising tool when utilized in an assortment of fashions. At times we employ this as our new resident mailer, positioning it in scores of households of potential new patients, many of whom may express an interest in cosmetic dentistry. In our office, you will find these brochures in clear plastic stands within patient eyeshot in each operatory, at the front desk and in the reception area. We offer them to patients when describing possible smile enhancement procedures, and provide them for people who casually inquire about appearance-related improvements when scheduling recall visits. If your goal is to establish your office as the practice supplying your region with the greatest volume of esthetic dentistry, a top quality cosmetic dentistry brochure will help escort you down this path.

Upon completion of a rewarding cosmetic case, I mount a patient's *Before and After* photographs in a custom designed cardboard frame. We mail this pictorial reminder to the patient's workplace, in order to potentially capture the attention of co-workers if the patient is amenable to this option. Most patients are very appreciative of this gesture, and many take the time to call and thank me for the thought. This is again one more internal marketing effort expressing your continued concern for your patients. This, of course, in addition to providing floss threaders and proxy brushes that my hygienist ultimately convinced me to dispense. Where does it all end?

Incentive Programs

Helping children look forward to a visit to your office will greatly increase patient flow. Hiring staff members who are friendly and comfortable with children is an essential first step, but it is also wise to establish an incentive program for children. Kids respond positively to motivational programs rewarding them for a specific behavior or accomplishment. Our office has a No Cavity Club designed to reward patients ages 12 and under who receive a cavity-free checkup. These patients are awarded recognition certificates and their names are entered into a drawing. Each month one winner is rewarded two movie tickets. Every year, one lucky winner receives a video game console which is the current in vogue model. Not to be overlooked is the dentist's toy box that nearly every adult remembers from youth. All kids up to the age of too cool love to dive into the treasure chest that awaits them following a successful visit to the dentist.

Given their heavy reliance on referrals and young patient population, orthodontists are in even greater need of developing incentive programs. One local orthodontist gives kids three chances to win each time they visit the office. Children enter their names into three different prize jars: one for wearing the t-shirt they received at their first visit, one for good dental hygiene and one for having no disturbance of the orthodontic appliances. A winner is picked from each jar every month and given gift certificates to local fast food restaurants or movie theaters.

Another approach is to offer dollars as an incentive to patients. These dollars can be turned in to the office store to purchase toys, gift cards and novelty items. This incentive also works well for adult orthodontic patients who enjoy spending their dollars on music, electronics or restaurant certificates.

Our practice offers a teeth whitening incentive program to all adult patients. We entitle this objective the *Lifetime Whitening Program*. For a low enrollment fee, roughly half that of my standard rate for full mouth whitening, patients receive custom upper and lower trays and a starter kit of whitening gel. Provided they remain patients in good standing, they receive free whitening gel at each six-month recall visit.

To be considered in good standing, patients are required to provide at least two days notice of cancellation and maintain the timeliness of their six-month recall appointments without fail. This incentive program has served to markedly reduce no-shows and cancellations while increasing recall appointment scheduling and maintenance. Patients love this enticement for the free whitening product, while we love it for the free patients.

Everyone loves free! No matter what products or services you elect to give away or what incentives you decide to offer, your patients will appreciate you for your efforts. Some of these items and promotions have been shown to clearly outpace the rest in terms of their return on investment for the business owner. The goal should be to find and determine those giveaways and incentives which, while highly appealing to your clientele, are also quite attractive to your bottom line.

Will the *Real* Internal Marketing Please Stand Up?

Perception is Reality

While scheduling recalls and treatment appointments, requesting referrals, publishing newsletters, offering giveaways and incentive programs and providing patient reminders all carry value, it is the little things in internal marketing that can push your practice to the next level. Spanning from office atmosphere to staff friendliness, patients take account of all the experiences they perceive. As we should all be aware in business, perception is reality.

Your office environment affords patients their initial impression of your practice philosophy and an insight into your perceived commitment to quality. A professional décor is no less important to a patient's view of reality than all the high-tech equipment you have at the ready to care for treatment needs. The aura you create by voiding the roofing warranty to install skylights, or insisting that walls be leveled to incorporate abundant windows serves to relax patients in a stressful environment. One dentist I know offers wine to his patients to help mitigate this anxiety. We have probably all had patients who took care of this part on their own before arriving at the dentist's office! Nonetheless, you will be rewarded handsomely for taking measures to ensure comfort and instill a sense of calm in the often apprehensive dental patient.

The Comforts of Home

As a means of relaxation, we offer virtual reality glasses allowing patients to view their favorite DVDs during dental treatment. While occluding the sound and vision of the distressing procedure, the VR glasses provide the perception that the patient is somewhere more appealing. These glasses have been shown to significantly reduce the blood pressure of an anxious patient. Massage pads retailing at an affordable $40 can be affixed to dental chairs, and activated to apply warmth while relieving the tension in tight muscles. Ignoring the belief that caffeine can elevate blood pressure, I am aware of at least one dentist in Seattle operating a full-service espresso business in the reception area. The last I heard, patients still formed a line extending out the door of her office, anticipating that fix from Seattle's Best.

Controlling Dental Office Odors

Many patients indicate the smell emanating from the dental office environment as the primary deterrent to timely care. In an effort to combat that repulsion, we have offered home-baked bread prepared right in the office. The only problem we experienced with this endeavor was our inability to prevent the doctor's staff adjacent my office from devouring all our bread. It seems the smell was so appealing that it created too big a distraction for his employees, forcing them to concentrate solely on surviving until lunch hour. Other effective methods of controlling the odors arising from chemicals employed in dentistry are the strategic placement of potpourri arrangements in leaf form or heated liquid in a ceramic burner. Glade Plug-Ins or Air Wick Scented Oil Warmers are highly effective, convenient options as well. With proper planning, you can transform the Pavlovian negativity associated with the stench of dental offices into an appealing, positive motivation for patients to return to your practice.

The Guest Mentality

Though these hooks can be extremely effective in encouraging patients to remain patrons for life, most internal marketing is esoteric in nature, speaks to the human element and does not cost a penny. People tend to appreciate such things as a friendly staff, a timely appointment, a positive response to their needs and desires, the accurate calculation of the bill on the first attempt and the existence of convenient and available parking. Staff members displaying name recognition, conveying concern and extending the hospitality befitting a friend or guest will draw your patient population closer to your practice.

A Caring Doctor

A caring and considerate doctor, especially one who does not hurt patients, will forge the greatest impact on a patient's perception of the overall office appeal. A dentist can impart good will simply by listening to patients, learning about their lives, demonstrating value in them, establishing trust, identifying common ground and providing honesty and well-timed humor. Dentists can score points by accurately diagnosing and effectively solving issues of dental pain, providing and standing behind exceptional dentistry, not aggressively selling treatment plans on the first visit and under-promising and over-delivering.

It's All about Trust

In the end, a patient's decision to schedule proposed treatment is all about trust. This trust relationship begins well before the patient ever enters your office door. It begins with the initial exposure a patient has to your practice, whether in the form of a postcard mailer or by way of referral from a friend or family member. It continues to develop through the new patient phone call and expands via the guest mentality your staff extends upon arrival. The relationship grows with the gentleness and concern afforded by your hygienist and progresses further by means of displaying your own honesty and integrity. This bond matures over time through the consistent care and attention imparted by your staff and the painless, quality dentistry you reliably provide.

You can employ the best treatment plan coordinator in the world, but it is ultimately the doctor who is responsible for convincing the patient of the necessity for treatment. The dentist is the office staff member most trained and knowledgeable in the importance of oral health care procedures. This is not to overlook that many practices successfully schedule dentistry based solely upon the salesmanship of the treatment plan coordinator. It is to say, however, that these practices will never be as productive as they could be with a doctor who educates, inspires and elicits the trust of the clientele.

One way to cultivate this trust is to be wary of handing the new patient an overzealous treatment plan on the initial visit. While we are obligated to diagnose and present all oral health needs to any patient seeking our expertise by way of a comprehensive exam, certain procedures can obviously be prioritized over others. Nurturing a trusting relationship over time seems to result in the greatest cosmetic dentistry and comprehensive treatment plans being accepted. Most people take some time to develop trust, and they quite often require multiple six-month recall appointments before they are ready to sign up for those beautiful veneers you have awaiting them. Do not oversell them. The fact that they are in your chair is evidence that they want to trust you. Give them every reason to do so. With time, they will be requesting the treatment from you, their new friend.

This principle of establishing trust eclipses every other form of internal marketing you can extend your patients. This is the real internal marketing. The attractiveness of this form of marketing is that its effects are consistent no matter what type of practice you have chosen to operate. The real beauty, of course, is that the fiscal cost of this manner of marketing is zero.

Chapter 23

External Marketing Efforts

In contrast to internal marketing efforts, external marketing focuses on attracting the attention of potential new patients by means beyond the walls of your office. While internal marketing concentrates on wowing existing patients in hopes of retaining them for life, external marketing attempts to secure patients from the general population by appealing to their perception of inherent needs. Internal marketing efforts are typically much less expensive than those of external marketing, and your practice goal should be to eventually achieve 100% reliance on internal marketing. Early on and quite possibly for the life of your practice, however, external marketing will be absolutely essential to realizing your business potential. As your practice matures, the one external marketing campaign you should maintain is your Internet presence. The expense for this should only be eliminated if your practice is in no further need of new patients.

When considering how long it will take your practice to succeed, you must first define for yourself what success means. Easier it is, I believe, to gauge how long it will take before you are assured that your practice will not fail. One afternoon while making the ends meet as an associate, I asked my employing dentist how long it typically takes to achieve that level of sustenance in a new practice. After pondering for a moment, she expressed that three years is a good measuring stick for practice maturity. "One day you look around and you have enough practice inertia and patient volume to sustain you," she offered. That magical three-year period turned out to be accurate for me each time I endeavored to grow a business from scratch. Though growing pains are assured along the way, the feeling of security realized when you find yourself gainfully employed by your practice makes every effort worthwhile.

New Resident Mailers

In the not so distant past when it came to the discussion of return on investment for external marketing campaigns, the new resident mailer program had no rival. Recently, however, with the increasing popularity of Internet utilization for the selection of new health care providers and everything else under the sun, the ROI from the direct mail approach has assumed the position of runner-up. Money properly spent on practice website recognition and search engine optimization presents the potential to return multiples previously unseen for the lifetime of your practice.

This is not to say that an intelligently managed new resident mailer program cannot add significantly to your bottom line. While the majority of our new patient influx is currently generated through referrals, convenient location and Internet marketing, we continue to capitalize on the assured return of monthly new resident mailers when necessary. During the first three years of each of my practices, I relied heavily upon new resident mailers. Currently, I fall back on them for promoting new associate dentists and during times of stagnation in the business cycle.

The principle behind this program is that undoubtedly there will be some number of new residents moving into the zip codes surrounding your practice every month. Your ability to effectively capture their attention with well-appointed marketing pieces can substantially increase the lifeblood volume of your practice. A large number of companies exist with the sole intent to compile and retail the name and address data of these new residents. When initiating your new resident mailer program, you will need to define your target audience and assess staff availability and aptitude to complete any of the necessary tasks relating to the campaign. Decisions must be made concerning what type of mailing house to employ, what your advertisement will highlight, whether you wish to extend a discount offer and how broad a radius in square miles or zip codes to which you will send the mailer?

How do you choose an address list company?

Your initial decision will be that of selecting a company from which you will purchase the lists of addresses. This is no simple task considering the innumerable mailing houses willing to sell you these lists. There are many varying ways in which to compile new resident data, and therefore vastly differing success rates for these various companies. Of course, the customer service can vary substantially as well. The steepest hurdle I needed to clear when initiating this campaign in my first practice was finding one of these companies that would remain in operation longer than three months. It seemed that no employee retained the position for any time period greater than was required to secure another job. I cannot say that I blame these cold-callers, however. I do not think too many people aspire to land one of these posts as their final occupational resting place.

I recall thinking I had hit the jackpot when I was finally able to speak to the same representative, Albert, for nearly six months of dealings with one particular company. I was so enamored with this that I even referred to this company, and specifically to Albert, a colleague who was looking to distribute new resident mailers. My friend was able to seamlessly establish contact with Albert, just as I told him he would be. A few weeks later I asked him how things were going with the new resident mailer campaign. He informed me of his repeatedly unsuccessful attempts at securing a return phone call from Albert. In fact, it appeared as if Albert was no longer in the mailing house business. Apparently none of the discount pricing my friend had negotiated with Albert had been recorded either. Consequently, this doctor became hardened toward the notion of squandering the valuable time necessary to implement a new resident mailer program, and eventually scrapped the idea altogether.

For our most recent new resident mailer campaign, we researched and tested multiple companies providing new resident addresses before ultimately selecting InfoUSA (www.infoUSA.com). This company is customer friendly, provides online reports and ordering and achieves the fewest returned items resulting from inaccurate addresses. Every company will produce some erroneous addresses, but when using InfoUSA less than ten percent of our mailers are returned as undeliverable. InfoUSA's rates are higher than some of the other companies we have used, but significant discounts are available if you buy addresses in bulk. A bulk of 5,000 or 10,000 addresses can be purchased for use within the year at a 25% rebate to purchasing addresses on a monthly basis.

Many mailing houses not only supply the address information, but also offer design, labeling and distribution services as well. Electing to have the mailing house direct this entire process will conserve time and energy, but will substantially limit your input and increase your fiscal expense. With the use of Microsoft Publisher and a local printer, we have been able to design our own postcards and flyers. If you do not have an employee capable of managing this project, there are many graphic designers and marketing companies willing to assist you. We perform all labeling and addressing within our office. This maximizes staff time when patients fail an appointment or when there is an opening in the schedule. Given that we only mail 300-500 pieces a month, this is not a difficult task to accomplish.

While I have been extremely fortunate in my practices to have employed a staff member whose capabilities extended far beyond that of the traditional dental office employee, I recognize that this is a rarity. It is a true blend of art and science that makes an ad pop; grabbing the attention of potential new patients in the fleeting moments you are able to retain their interest. It is also a unique pairing that permits the doctor and staff member to work together to artistically craft a marketing piece with not only an attractive appearance, but also a grammatically correct text. I find this to be the primary reason why many dentists elect to avoid this type of marketing, while others decide to hire a firm to do the work for them.

Should you send a postcard, flyer or letter as the new resident mailer?

Your next imperative is selecting the particular mailer format you wish to employ, be it a letter, a postcard or a flyer. If you choose a document requiring an envelope, I highly recommend handwritten addresses in order to increase the likelihood that the envelope will be opened. The appearance of personalization seems to elicit a greater call to action than a standardized, bulk labeling. Although I am acutely aware of what the company intends when I receive a hand-addressed mailer, I am still guilty of surrendering to intrigue and opening the letter anyway.

Marketing firms know that this element of human nature is difficult to resist and they implement this technique with enormous success. Handwritten addresses will obviously cost more to employ, but the increased rate of return with this form of direct mail more than absorbs the additional expense. One way to allay this cost is to take advantage of a form of mechanical handwriting that simulates the style of an actual handwritten address. Most all-inclusive mailing houses offer this technique as a service to their customers.

There is research to support a better response when no return address is listed. Often a recipient will discard a mailer if it appears to be from a doctor's office with which there is no established relationship. The obvious advantages of enveloping your message are that you can add more information and include more than one item in the envelope. The clear disadvantage is that all of your carefully-crafted information is enclosed in an envelope which requires the potential customer to first open before it can be viewed. Applying the techniques mentioned above will ensure greater viewership of your marketing piece. Our experience has revealed that envelopes are opened with greatest regularity when labeled as follows, listed greatest to least:

- Actual handwritten mailing address with no return address
- Mechanical handwritten mailing address with no return address
- Actual handwritten address with a return address
- Mechanical handwritten address with a return address
- Printed label with no return address
- Printed label with a return address

If you choose to use the following labeling: *Or Current Resident* or *Bulk Sort*, you may as well forget about it.

Of course, the obstacle of an unopened envelope can be eliminated altogether by imprinting your message on a postcard instead. Although there is no guarantee that your postcard will be regarded, greater exposure is ensured as the communication is not shrouded in a covering that must first be removed. Distributing postcards is a great overhead control method as well, as it naturally reduces the costs of printing and postage.

As it is sometimes difficult to relate adequate information on the standard 4x6 inch postcard, you may consider utilizing an enhanced version. While larger postcards demand postage identical to that of a letter, they may still be a better value when factoring in higher printing costs and the expense of the envelopes. Oversized postcards provide the best chance that new residents will notice them. Postcards regularly enlist greater readership than other forms of direct mail as well.

What should you highlight in your new resident mailer?

Of paramount importance is the decision of what to highlight in your advertisement. Clearly the most reliable points of emphasis are those things considered to be of benefit to the potential new patient. We commonly incorporate the heading, *Benefits to You*, in the text of our mailers. These benefits are really what people are looking for when they peruse an ad, are they not? Why not boldly emphasize them, minimizing reader search time and reducing the likelihood of an immediate jump shot of your flyer into the trash can? In fact, what often yields the greatest success is a flyer composed entirely of Benefits to You.

Anything that makes your office unique or valuable to the patient will command a second look, a filing away for later use or possibly even an immediate phone call to your office. Your primary goal is to provide the potential patient the impetus to make contact with your practice through this mailer. Be sure to embolden your office phone number, website and email address to facilitate this process for them. This seemingly self-evident piece of information is amazingly often ignored in the marketing pieces I receive and on the websites I explore. I always think, *They want me to be able to contact them, don't they?*

These benefits must appeal to desires that patients have for themselves and not merely list services you provide. Benefits in my practice might be represented as follows:

- Open early mornings, evenings and through the lunch hour so you will not be required to miss work.
- Virtual reality glasses to take your eyes, ears and mind off the dentistry.

- Up to 12 months interest-free payment plans so you will not need to tie up a credit card.
- Air-abrasion technology for shot-free, drill-free, pain-free dentistry.
- Punctual appointments so as not to waste your valuable time.

The topic of exactly what to incorporate into your new resident mailer is one of heated debate. Countless marketing firms exist specifically to assist you with this dilemma. Books have been written on the topic, and much research has been done to reveal how best to indoctrinate your message into the minds of its readers. Having studied much of the literature relating to this subject, I have incorporated many different techniques to wow my targets.

The trial and error with respect to my new resident mailer campaigns has been an initiation by fire. The reward from this process has been a uniquely crafted marketing piece which I have employed with a high degree of success through many years and in multiple practices. I alter this piece and distribute it in varied formats to affect a desired response, based upon the time of year and current state of the practice. I am confident that we have the most effective wording, content and design because we painstakingly track the return on investment from each of our marketing efforts. An example of our new resident mailer can be accessed through the Practice Management Resources for Dentists section at the end of this book.

Keeping in mind that the average time a viewer holds a direct mailing piece in hand is as few as five seconds, your message needs to instantly elicit desire, emotion and action. The Madow Brothers (Dr. David Madow and Dr. Richard Madow) suggest designing a flyer with a mock $1,000,000 bill stapled to it. [33] They also indicate that using an attached Band-Aid or Post-It note with handwriting in blue ink are effective methods for new resident mailers. [34] The idea is to immediately grab the reader's attention, forcing your potential patient to read on. The Madows offer new resident mailing services through their company, Promail. I have found many of the Madows' services to be highly beneficial to the success of all three of my scratch practices. You may learn more about them by visiting www.madow.com.

My goal when opening mail is to get it all off my desk and into the trash can as quickly as possible. I hit an unfortunate road block in these efforts when I encounter a bill, or regrettably, the marketing piece that forces me to read on. Since most advertisements are unsuccessful in disrupting the standard path of letter opener to waste basket, it is clearly imperative that the message be properly portrayed if you stand any chance of gaining the reader as a valued patient in your practice.

Getting your message across can be achieved through expressing perceived patient benefits offered in your practice which set you apart from your competition. A doctor's broad experience in cosmetic dentistry, a practice's care for the entire family, consumer friendly hours, acceptance of in-network insurance benefits, convenient location and adequate parking are all welcomed perks to an interested client.

One way to impart the advantages of joining your practice is to let your patients do the talking for you through patient testimonials. We have received an especially good response to a flyer containing quotes about our office from patients of record. These quotes highlighted pain-free dentistry, short wait times, friendly and professional staff members and a comfortable environment for the entire family. These are things that nearly everyone seeking dental care is hoping to find. Allowing your patients' testimonials to ease the anxiety while attesting to the very benefits you wish to convey, provides the ideal avenue through which to obtain new patients.

Should you offer discounts or coupons in the new resident mailer?

Over time you may find that different forms of advertising will meet your needs better than others, depending upon the maturity of your practice and the degree to which you feel the necessity to discount your services. While a provider's benevolence is the most ideal motivation to extend to one's patients reduced-fee dentistry, the desire to grow one's practice tends to overwhelm even that at times. Most marketing firms strongly encourage including some type of offer within direct mail advertisements as the most reliable method of increasing reader response and advertiser return on investment. While it is true that extending an offer to potential patients will encourage them to move more quickly to the telephone, doing so always comes at a cost.

I have experimented with so many forms of direct mail marketing that I have firsthand knowledge of the benefits and detriments providing an offer can carry. In marketing my first practice I used a one page flyer enclosed in a hand-addressed envelope with no return address. The flyer strongly alluded to our practice's ability to provide numerous benefits to its reader. At the bottom of the flyer was a life-sized simulation of a bank check made payable to Dr. Logan's office, in the amount of one free exam and four bitewing x-rays. Accompanied by the usual disclaimers, this check entitled the new patient to this free visit when presented at the initial appointment in our office.

This flyer with associated bank check was extremely popular and initiated an influx of new patient phone calls. We seemed to have ideally crafted the most effective new resident mailer available. We had discovered the most foolproof way to encourage a recipient to actually open the envelope as opposed to discarding it immediately into the trash. This format seemingly provided us the inroads necessary to attract the insurance-independent, quality-driven new patient to our practice. Openings in our schedule were being replaced by initial exam appointments. We were encouraged that these complimentary assessments would soon lead to profitability through scheduled treatment. That may have happened had the patients actually shown up for their initial exam appointments.

It turned out that patients placed no value in these free services. I suppose the thought was that if it can be given away for nothing, then perhaps it is worth nothing. When check-toting patients did happen to find their way into our office, they appeared to be shopping us for other free services or conducting price comparisons to our competitors. If ultimately we were lucky enough to appoint one of these visitors for treatment, it was a toss-up as to whether the patient would actually show up for the scheduled dentistry.

If you want to fill your chairs, do not mind working overtime and are not concerned about people shopping you, then the offers are for you. Given that most dentists do provide discounted dentistry offers in their direct mail marketing, you will need to continually increase the value of your offer in order to compete. Though not inclusively, I have found that most people selecting your office based upon the promise of reduced-fee dentistry alone are not the loyal patients for which a successful practice thirsts. Coupon offers can be initially beneficial to help fill an empty practice in its infancy. However, when you are able, you should consider leaving these offers to those dentists less selective about what form their practice will ultimately assume.

How broad of a radius should the new resident mailer cover?

Another decision facing you early on is how broad a geographic radius to which you wish to distribute your mailer. When opening my current office several years ago, there were only two competing dentists in my immediate area. I chose to incorporate an extended mailing radius in an attempt to secure business from a larger population of potential new patients. As greater numbers of dentists set up shop in our area, I tightened the radius to roughly five square miles around the office and then to three square miles. My office is located in the heart of several new neighborhoods so I could reduce my radius while still reaching many homes. An office located in the middle of a large business district would require a larger radius to experience success.

Patients with multiple dental office options near their homes or businesses are less likely to drive long distances to take a seat in your operatory. This is by no means an inclusive principle, as every dentist will have numerous patients over the years who are loyal followers irrespective of the distance travelled. This is especially true in the profession of dentistry, wherein anxious patients seek a comfort level, after which having found, they will look no further. Notwithstanding, it becomes unreasonable to invest in external marketing to such a limited audience. This rule can be profitably broken when it comes to promoting your unique services and distinctive office environment through Internet marketing, reaching a nearly limitless population.

Mailings to new residents and current residents within a certain demographic can be a valuable niche marketing effort as well. The listing service we use allows us to define household criteria for the addresses we purchase. Selecting these parameters makes it possible to direct specialized marketing campaigns to specific groups of residents. For instance, I send a full color cosmetic dentistry brochure to high income residents within a broader radius of my office. A dentist looking to increase the pediatric population of the practice can directly mail to households with at least two children. For those desiring to expand their removable prosthodontics business, mailing a denture and implant brochure to residents over 55 years of age may yield positive returns.

When is the ideal time of year for direct mail and how often should you send each mailer?

I have created for my practice a marketing calendar which breaks out on a monthly basis those campaigns and promotions best run at various times of the year. The marketing calendar addresses the ideal times of year for direct mail marketing and the times during which you are less likely to receive a high return on investment from direct mail. The primary time to avoid using mailings spans from mid-November through the end of the year, as this is an extremely frenzied time for mailboxes and for their owners. For those people moving into a new area during these hectic months, finding a new dentist will not be one of their highest priorities. The number of families moving during the summer months is much greater than at any other time, because households commonly attempt to avoid breaking up a school year whenever possible. This is clearly a more advantageous time to initiate a new resident mailer program.

Most address lists are very current and include families having just moved the previous month. I have experimented with sending advertisements out immediately to these new residents. The advantage to direct mail marketing to households within their first month of moving is that you may be the first dentist to reach out to them. However, new residents are so overwhelmed within the first month or two of moving that selecting a dentist is never the central concern unless they are experiencing dental pain. A more profitable allotment of resources may be to delay distributing your mailers until one month has elapsed following receipt of the address list.

Disagreement exists over how often a marketer should send a new resident the same advertisement. Most marketing companies recommend mailing each new resident an advertisement at least three to five times to achieve redundant exposure. If you advertise in other manners reaching this same population, you will be able to reduce the frequency with which you send out your marketing piece. We employ a local company that distributes flyers to everyone within a ten mile radius of our office every eight weeks. We also advertise in our neighborhood's local magazine, so we do not find it necessary to send out our mailers with such frequency. No marketer can ever know for certain which particular advertisement or repetition of such actually converted the potential patient into a patient of record. Most patients are not even sure of their specific referral source. The idea is that in one way or another, it is incumbent on us to get our business in the minds of our potential patient population. Redundant marketing has been shown to be a highly effective means by which to achieve this goal.

Telephone Book Advertising

Advertising in the phone book is one of the most expensive marketing investments you can make, and positions your promotional dollar in the most competitive landscape available. Three major directories compete within our local market alone, each containing multiple large advertisements from competing dentists vying for new patients. Challenging the competition in this area would require the dedication of copious marketing resources, with little assurance of doing more than recovering our investment. We have chosen rather to devote this capital to Internet advertising and internal marketing efforts, two areas that have consistently yielded a much greater return on investment.

Telephone book directories are becoming a decreasingly valuable source of information for consumers. That notwithstanding, within a day of canceling our advertisement for the coming year's phone directory, we scheduled two new patients who found us in the phone book and who later appointed for large treatment plans. Advertising decisions are not always simple and you will never have a crystal ball to predict where your marketing dollars will make the greatest impact. This again underscores the importance of tracking the specific returns of each marketing effort, in order to make informed decisions about the positioning of your marketing dollar.

A moment of professional scrutiny stands out in my mind from years ago, after finally having made the decision to cancel my Yellow Pages ad once and for all. A local colleague expressed her amazement at my resolution in front of her staff. With mouth agape and eyes wide open she offered, "Ed Logan doesn't even have a Yellow Pages ad! How is he going to get any new patients?" That rings so amusing to me in this day and age. My thoughts were to the contrary, *Why would you waste so much money on an ad that gets lost in the competition, and then in the trash? How are **you** going to get any new patients?* The telephone book ad salesman displayed the same shock and informed me that I would not get any new patients if I did not have some visibility in the phone book. As close as I get now to the Yellow Pages is advertising in their Internet version, www.yellowpages.com. I still find some value there because people are currently searching for providers on their computers and handhelds, not in their telephone books.

Newspaper and Local Publication Advertising

Over the years I have chosen to dedicate fewer and fewer resources to advertising by means of the printed press. Local newspaper and magazine advertising costs are often high and do not affect the same response as that of Internet marketing. The local rag is taking the route of the telephone directory in its waning popularity, as seemingly everything can now be found online. Recently, several large newspapers have decided to stop the presses altogether and provide all of their articles online.

The most recent example is that of the *Seattle Post Intelligencer*, a newspaper first capturing my attention during my initial year of dental school in the Great Northwest. The *P-I*, as it was called, provided a city landmark with its spinning globe high atop the banks of Elliot Bay. I am unsure whether the globe has yet stopped rotating, but unfortunately for the *P-I*, the printing presses have. The Internet Revolution has finally begun to swallow up even the most stalwart of industries, the printed press. This will become an increasingly prevalent phenomenon over the coming years as a swelling volume of consumers adopt the Internet as their main source of garnering information.

Newspaper advertising can still be a good source of attracting older patients still dedicated to reading their daily papers, and who do not spend hours online each day. Niche marketing to denture or implant patients can be successful in newspapers or local publications, but test your market with a smaller ad first to determine if there will be any response.

If you are able to find a publication which will publish advertorials, you can attempt to lay claim to the title *expert in the field* by submitting articles related to dental health or cosmetic dentistry. This can serve the same purpose as becoming the television pundit in the area of dentistry. There is typically no cost to you when a paper decides to publish your advertorial. Editorials are read five times more often than advertisements, so you gain value by positioning your ad within an editorial. The real hurdle, once again, is getting people to pick up and read the newspaper. As with so many other print ads, your advertorial would find greater value if it were positioned online.

Many neighborhoods, suburbs and burrows publish their own newsletters and magazines. This can be an affordably priced way to advertise your business. We have had varied results with this type of advertising. The neighborhood surrounding our practice distributes a high quality, color newsletter to every home owner and business in the community. The advertising costs are reasonable, particularly considering that the ad is in full color. We typically receive a handful of new patient inquiries in response to this ad each time it is run. As the number of competing dentists entering the neighborhood has increased, the value of this advertisement has decreased. New patients who list a referral source other than the community newsletter often mention also having viewed our ad in this neighborhood publication, and that it served to remind them to schedule an appointment. You can thus take advantage of the minimal cost of such local advertising to increase the redundant exposure and name recognition of your practice.

The one advertising project that proved completely ineffective was a six-month ad we ran with a local publishing company that distributed magazines to other area neighborhoods. The cost again was reasonable, though we were required to agree to a six-month commitment. We did not receive one phone call or inquiry from this advertisement. I think it was around that time that I decided to pass on most any form of external print advertising to market my practice. When a salesperson calls my office in attempt to gain my business marketing dollars via any particular form of print media, I have my staff inform the representative, "No thank you. Dr. Logan is no longer doing any print advertising." I think this sounds a lot better than if I were to take the call and suggest, "Why would I want to throw my money away like that?"

Though I grew up in an age when the newspaper was the primary written means by which information was disseminated to the public on a daily basis, I for one was never a big fan of this form of media. As a kid I remember my dad and older brother thumbing through the paper each morning in attempts to ascertain how many games out of first place the beloved baseball Cardinals remained. I personally hated the way the paper felt in my hands, folding over on itself as I turned its pages, leaving behind its impression of ink on my fingertips. As the younger brother I tried to play along. What I really wanted to do was go outside and shoot some hoops.

It is interesting to envision the not-so-distant future when those reading this manuscript will not be able to identify with that story at all. The newspaper will soon be a relic, and most forms of print media will be completely extinct. This idea may seem unreasonable now, or maybe even a bit ridiculous. That is what they said, however, about Copernicus when he postulated that the earth revolved around the sun. I just had to Google that to make sure it was accurate!

Network Marketing

Professional networking is not nearly as integral for the general dentist as it is for specialists whose businesses rely heavily upon referrals. Dental specialists are required to dedicate a good portion of their marketing efforts to creating and sustaining referral relationships. For the general dentist, a good reputation and relationship with area specialists can lead to cross-referring. This is particularly true with orthodontists, who may treat a young person for the first time, often before the child has established a relationship with a general dentist. This is less applicable to endodontists and oral surgeons, who many times might treat individuals seeking only emergency care. A patient involved with a periodontist typically already claims a general dentist, who in most cases has referred the patient to the specialist.

This is not to suggest that establishing camaraderie with these specialists is of no benefit to the general dentist. Being highly regarded among your peers can only serve to advance your cause in terms of positioning yourself in the minds of the dental community. I was honored to receive recognition in the online and print publication of *USA'S Top Dentists*. This is a list of dentists voted by the specialists in their communities to be worthy of this categorization. Initially skeptical of the actual weight this listing carried, I was pleased when an acquaintance emailed me that she was proud to know one of the area's top dentists.

Effective network marketing can be initiated through an office Open House, in which your new practice is revealed to any invited general dentists and specialists, and to the public at large. This is often a good opportunity to inform the local media, encouraging them to cover the event in their publications and on their news broadcasts. This can serve as virtually free advertising and you should take maximum advantage of this opportunity. It can realistically only serve in this form as a onetime event. Our local Chamber of Commerce participates in these occasions, offering a ribbon cutting ceremony and providing an article about each new business in its monthly publication.

Although a true Grand Opening Open House is a solo occurrence for your business, seasonal and annual gatherings sponsored by your practice can positively impact your image in the community. A local colleague opens her office to invited guests each fall for a Luau Party. As dentists and specialists are encouraged to drop by, this serves as an excellent chance to get to know other colleagues in your community in a more relaxed environment. This event follows the annual Summer Fest put on by her practice. This is an outdoor festival which caters to children and offers a petting zoo, rides, games and prizes. While it may be difficult to assess exactly how many new patients one will secure from this type of effort, it is yet another means by which to advance the name recognition of your practice.

At one point in my career I thought it would be a good idea to market the availability of my cosmetic dentistry services to the patients of local plastic surgeons. The avenue to these potential clients went through the cosmetic surgeons themselves, of course. Several of these doctors agreed to meet with me in their offices for a brief discussion about what I had in mind. Sitting across from them in their consultation rooms, I found myself wondering if the surgeons might be restraining themselves from asking me that notable question from the TV show *Nip Tuck*, "Tell me what you don't like about yourself."

Instead, what they really wanted to know was, *What's in this for me?* I began with my ideas about placing my cosmetic dentistry brochures, *Before and After* photographs and business cards in their new patient bags and perhaps even as displays on their countertops. They countered with the suggestion that I do the same for them. Most of the surgeons were quite resistant to the idea, as they viewed my services as direct competition to their own. Why would they want to encourage their patients to spend their disposable income on cosmetic dentistry as opposed to cosmetic surgery? It was interesting to see how certain surgeons turned the table and began marketing to me, outlining exactly what they could provide for my clientele. One surgeon even shared some extremely revealing B*efore and After* photographs of surgeries I had no idea even existed. I knew then that I had made a good decision by not choosing to become a plastic surgeon.

Suffice it to say, this endeavor never really materialized the way I had envisioned. I decided to purvey my message to a slightly less invasive crowd, that of the day spa and beauty salon industry. I figured these business owners would be more inviting to my proposed objective. Having gained approval to place a cosmetic dentistry display on the front desk of a popular local spa, I felt confident that my efforts would finally pay dividends. Less than a month later I noticed that my display had been replaced by that of a competing local dentist, who apparently presented an offer more appealing than my own. Janet Jackson's lyric "What have you done for me lately," played in my mind.

Another form of networking is through groups designed specifically to fill this need. Business networking groups such as Business Network International (www.bni.com) and Leads Club (www.leadsclub.com) are composed of community business owners hoping to market their products and services to other members within the group. Each group typically limits its membership to one business type per area. Therefore, you may be able to obtain exclusivity in the group with respect to the field of dentistry.

Other groups such as the Rotary Club and Lion's Club exist with a more informal attitude toward business marketing, but offer the entrepreneur an opportunity to connect with others in the community. One group that assembles locally is entitled The New Dentists' Group. Early in my career this group allowed me to get to know a number of my peers in the area and ultimately establish some lasting friendships. I was even fortunate enough to take advantage of a business opportunity for my new practice through another member of this group.

Of course, friends and family are great sources of network marketing for your business. Assuming these relationships are intact, you should take full advantage of the word of mouth these people can provide your practice. Some of these relatives and friends may work for large firms and can be helpful in terms of marketing your practice through the Human Relations departments of their companies. If you attended college or graduate school in the area in which you practice, you can alert your former educators of the opening of your new practice and the welcoming of new patients. Certain family members and friends will rise above the rest and tell all their friends and co-workers about you and your dental practice. My mom, who has always been my biggest advocate, has referred several patients who travel two hours from their hometown to come to my office. Invite as much of this discussion as possible, for these close relationships can speak more to your true character and reputation than any piece of advertising literature can ever do.

Booth and Convention Advertising

Opportunities abound to market your practice through booth displays at area conventions, expos, health fairs and educational events. Many large businesses sponsor annual health care days in which providers hoping to secure the business of company employees can provide an exhibit. We have had great success offering one such display at MasterCard, whose headquarters is positioned just around the corner from our office.

The most cost-effective way to engage in these events is to purchase a display table and take some time in arranging marketing materials for expos of this nature. These materials might include *Before and After* photographs of completed cosmetic dentistry cases, a flyer composed of appealing patient testimonials, brochures relating to popular dental procedures and information on patient financing. Promotional offers or coupons can be distributed as well.

Other more sophisticated technologies may be employed to provide streaming video of the doctor describing the office philosophy, a virtual tour of the office or compelling photos of beautiful esthetic dentistry results. Video footage of patient testimonials is highly impactful as well. A laptop can be positioned to allow curious passers-by to cruise your practice website. Depending upon the particular type of target audience, you can modify your basic display to impart the message desired. In all cases, be sure to make available multiple forms of contact information for potential patients to easily carry away with them.

There are somewhat less conventional methods by which to network market your practice as well. One such opportunity that comes to mind is a community business Halloween extravaganza that took place in our area in which each vendor was expected to provide free goods to the neighborhood children. We were solicited to purchase space upon which we could assemble a booth display and market our business on site. I am still confused as to what compelled me to participate in this event. Given the driving need to attract new patients to pay off the loan on my beautifully appointed new office, I suppose I felt convinced that this would offer wide exposure of the new business to the residents of the community. I surmised as well that this effort might draw new families to our practice via its directed focus on the children.

What this event actually turned out to be was an opportunity for us to dole out hundreds of free toothbrushes, pieces of sugar-free candy, coloring books, magnets, toys and whatever else we had decided to purchase for this event. Hardly a parent stopped for more than the brief time required to dip a hand into our jack-o-lantern toy box before emerging with yet another six bucks of free plunder.

The real entertainment, however, came from the many vendors choosing to dress up in Halloween costumes to amuse the children. My loving wife was one of these good sports, as she showed up in an archived Halloween party, live-sized pumpkin outfit. This particular pumpkin, however, was resting atop a mantle of Go-Go boots and black tights. Though I thought she looked very cute, her slightly more skeptical older sister offered, "You must really love him." While Katie's ensemble did not exactly attract the new family business for which we had hoped, it did manage to garner the attention of the local firemen positioned directly behind our booth. I am happy to say that years later my practice is currently home to several of our community's loyal firefighters.

Door-to-Door Marketing

Dentists operating practices in their infancies may need to take what might be considered extreme measures in order to obtain extreme results. I am reminded of a dental school instructor who related the story of a husband and wife dental team recently graduated from professional school. He proudly suggested that this couple had it right when they decided to spend their idle time knocking on doors in attempts to gain the business of their neighbors. I found it less than glamorous at most, but was nonetheless impressed at the commitment these two displayed in growing their shared practice. In the beginning, when time is your most available commodity, you may choose to market your services by any means necessary.

A slightly less invasive mode of reaching out to your neighbors is the individual placement of your marketing flyer on the windshields of vehicles parked in business lots. You may elect to do this throughout the residential streets as well, but will be doing so at the elevated risk of being identified by neighbors peering out their windows. You can be a much stealthier flyer-dropper in the colossal Wal-Mart parking lot.

I found it rather amusing after opening a practice in a planned residential community when I was presented with the option of hiring a group of ladies whose business it was to hand deliver marketing pieces to each neighborhood resident. The only thing required of me was to provide the advertisement and cut them a check each month. They even offered me exclusivity in terms of my profession. I am still the only dentist they allow to advertise on their route. They actually walk around from house to house and affix a bag of marketing materials to the handle of each door. This has remained an incredibly affordable and effective means by which to market my practice to my target audience. Though it may be difficult to find, if you can identify a local business such as the Bag Ladies, I would highly recommend utilizing its services.

Community Service and Charity Auctions

Be prepared for patients to frequently request your participation in charity auctions and sponsorship events. Your clients will often ask you to sponsor little league teams and golf tournaments, and to contribute services to various auction events. We make donation decisions on a case-by-case basis and often contribute a free whitening product to charity auctions. These auctions provide the opportunity to market your business for the cost of the product donated. We have not gained more than a handful of patients from these auctions and sponsorships, so your primary goal in this area should be community improvement, not marketing.

Very commonly a donation is requested by adult patients to support a particular charity project or fundraising drive pursued by one of their children. If the child is old enough, I typically encourage the parents to have their kids ask me personally. I cannot say no to the kids. I believe this also gives the kids an opportunity to gain experience and knowledge in what it is like to earn something. I was quite impressed with one of my early teenage patients who recently requested that I help sponsor her school's track team. "Of course I will," I said. *And thank you for asking*, I thought.

The month of February serves as National Dental Hygiene Month and offers you the opportunity to bring your practice to the public. Many pre-schools and elementary schools may request your presence during this month to provide education to their students on oral hygiene and how to develop good dental habits. We have taken advantage of these invitations in the past by having staff members give fun presentations to the kids while encouraging child participation. Children really enjoy these demonstrations and are usually full of entertaining questions. Sometimes very insightful inquiries are offered as well. I recall one such event that I directed in which a child queried, "Do people grow new teeth when they lose them like sharks do?"

Your dental assistant and hygienist can invite one child to come up front and stand in between them. Each grasping opposite ends of a long piece of yarn, they can *floss* the kid as if they were flossing a tooth, thus demonstrating proper flossing technique. Kids enjoy the display of larger than life x-rays on a video screen and viewing slideshows of some of your not so threatening *Before and After* photographs. It is also fun for the children to hold the oversized mouth of plastic teeth and practice brushing them with a monster-sized toothbrush. I have even allowed the kids to pass around gold crowns, and they always seem to find that to be pretty cool.

In advance of these presentations we put together goodie bags for the kids to take home with them. Each bag contains a variety of items they may find enjoyable, most of which are inscribed with our contact information. We have had good success with distributing customized coloring books with dental-related pictures for the kids to artistically enhance. A toothbrush, refrigerator magnet, dry-erase board and assorted toys all make it into the bag as well. Many of these items can be used interchangeably with other marketing endeavors you pursue. While marketing your practice is one goal of these presentations, bringing kids to the realization that dentistry does not have to be something they dread is often very rewarding as well.

Sponsoring a coat drive is a unique way to request patient involvement in your community service efforts. In our area the winters can get a bit nippy and many less fortunate people are left to suffer without adequate clothing. We advertise to our patients that we are collecting coats to be donated to the community shelters serving the indigent and encourage them to bring in anything they will not need during the winter months. Many patients are happy to help and also pleased to see that we are trying to make a difference as well.

Community service efforts are more about serving the community than serving your business. Very often this benevolence is rewarding to you in areas separate from your practice, though quite commonly comes back around to supplement your business life as well. Many times newspaper organizations or online publications will pick up on the story of your community service endeavors and provide free advertising to your practice. This will be in the form of editorials, so you will not be required to do any of the marketing work either.

Additional forms of community service include serving as the dentist for area amateur or professional sports teams. A good friend and practicing optometrist had the opportunity to serve as the contracted eye specialist to the San Diego Chargers pro football team. He and two other doctors provided examinations and eye care for the players, and thereby received some pretty ideal seating at Qualcomm Stadium on Sundays. My similar involvement came in the form of serving as resident dentist to the San Diego Charger Cheerleaders. I am unsure if anyone would actually consider these things to be the sacrifice of community service, but I will list them here nonetheless.

Radio, Television, Billboard and Banner Advertising

There are certainly more costly forms of external marketing that you can employ in attempts to advance your business. Positioning your message in front of many thousands of people can be achieved through utilizing various types of mass media. Though typically reserved for larger segments of Corporate America with fattened marketing budgets, a dentist will always be permitted to throw some cash in the ring and make a bet that this just might work to turn a profit. The primary obstacle to profitability, however, is the limited revenue potential of our small business model versus the overwhelming costs associated with coordinating such a media event. Obviously when marketing overhead is increased so significantly, the return on investment will track inversely.

Radio advertising was once one of the most effective methods of disseminating information about a business. Almost everyone listened to the radio, and by necessity, begrudgingly absorbed the commercials between songs or talk segments as well. With the increasing popularity of satellite radio, however, the need to waste time stomaching an advertisement segment once every three songs has been eliminated. Though commercial radio stations continue to serve a large percentage of the market, listeners maintain the option of channel surfing in search of their favorite songs or content.

Despite my perception that terrestrial radio was quickly becoming a dinosaur, I was somehow persuaded to give radio advertising a shot. This required handing over a large quantity of my hard-earned money to the radio station, of course. In return I was offered the gamble that flooding the airwaves with my name and practice information would in turn flood my office with new patients. Unfortunately for me, I wound up on the losing end of this wager. In an effort to steer you clear from this marketing pitfall, I have detailed my experience with radio advertising in the chapter, Mistakes I Have Made.

Television advertising provides the obvious advantage of employing visual media to advance an image-based message to your audience. If you are hoping to increase the volume of esthetic dentistry performed in your practice, or if you consider your practice to be primarily a cosmetic dentistry business, TV commercials may be for you. Patients welcome the ability to envision what their smiles might look like in the *After* photographs.

You can also use this opportunity to take the patient on a visual tour of your office, similar to the way this is done for prospective buyers hoping to purchase a new home. Potential patients may be put at ease when seeing and hearing the dentist warmly and calmly relating how gentle and caring the entire office staff is known to be. Keep in mind, however, that television advertising is also becoming increasingly easy to ignore with the widespread use of the DVR. Most DVR owners intentionally delay watching a program until ample time has elapsed, ensuring evasion of the commercial blocks altogether.

Creating such an image for patients through producing a television commercial is, however, a colossal undertaking in terms of time and expense. As if funding the final wrap of the actual spot is not enough, the cost related to purchasing air time during which to run your visual masterpiece is yet another unwelcome surprise. Regrettably, I am all too familiar with this process because I allowed myself to be taken down that road one time too many. My first-hand knowledge of television advertising is also discussed in the chapter, Mistakes I Have Made. I hope you are able to learn from my mistakes and only employ the select marketing campaigns which I have found to provide the greatest return on investment. The results I achieved marketing via mass media have positioned radio and television advertising outside the boundaries of this restricted category.

Despite my negativity with respect to television advertising in dentistry, some dentists have achieved great success through television by becoming recognized as experts in the field. A more realistic avenue to television marketing success may be to enlist a local news channel to run a story about your office, highlighting a unique service you have to offer the community. This may take some time and effort to coordinate, but this labor just might pay great dividends.

I am reminded of a dental school classmate who was fortunate enough to assume the role of expert dentist on a solo spot for one news channel, and apparently her practice phone line has been ringing ever since. Certain television and radio stations may be amenable to procuring your services to host a weekly or monthly health care forum in which dental and medical professionals respond to inquiries from the general public. Positioning yourself as the local expert in your field can potentially yield appealing returns.

Depending upon state and local regulations, billboard advertising may be an available marketing option to you as well. As is the case with other forms of mass marketing, these ads are likely to set you back a pretty penny. Though I have had no experience in purchasing one of these eye sores, I know health care providers who have. One chiropractor comes to mind whose billboard ad consisted of a larger than life picture of himself which more resembled Lucifer than a nice, comforting care giver. Unfortunately for him, this picture that he probably paid so exorbitantly to display to thousands did not do him justice. The display came to be known as the *Devil on the Billboard*. While I am pretty sure that is not exactly what this chiropractor had in mind when he purchased the ad, I somehow cannot extricate this image from my mind when I think of billboard advertising.

The take home point may be that if you decide to market your practice through the forum of mass media, realize that the image the ad portrays will be one that sticks with you for years to come. When one of my buddies suggested that I market my practice by plastering my face on the sides of the local city buses, I resisted by considering the consequences of potentially becoming known as the *Devil on the Red Line*.

One final form of mass marketing that always intrigued me was that of banner ads being flown behind small aircraft above the beach. Of course, I recognize that this type of advertising is limited in geography to areas approximating large bodies of water. When I was first starting in practice and a bit younger, I lived and practiced in a beach community in Southern California. On the weekends we would go to the beach and I would always take note of these banner ads flying high above, and then look up and down the beach in an attempt to estimate the number of potential eyes viewing these messages. While I should have been relaxing at the beach or catching the next wave, I could not shake my entrepreneurial instinct to market my business. After all, my office was just down the street. Certainly these thousands of people were in need of a good dentist, right?

Though I never actually took the initiative to purchase one of these ads, I always wondered what would have been its potential. While the idea of an airplane supported banner ad displaying my name above the Pacific Ocean appealed to my ego, I am pretty sure that its return on investment would have proved slightly less appealing. This type of marketing to the masses may not have a suitable place in dentistry in terms of bringing value to the business. Mass marketing is better suited for big companies who can afford to absorb the costs incumbent with the associated ego boost. Having said that, I do on occasion wonder what would be the cost to hang my name above the left field wall at Busch Stadium for fellow Cardinal fans to admire!

The Real External Marketing

Though external marketing by its very nature may appear to be much more dynamic than the passive forms of internal marketing previously detailed, its greatest value may lie in its subtlety. When you start a practice, there will be many marketing companies encouraging you to spend fortunes to design your logo and business card. They purport that therein rests your identity. While this notion may border on the extreme, it is important to develop your practice personality and impart it to the general public. You can therefore establish your individuality and promote the unique characteristics that set you apart from your competition. Consider the message you want to relate about your practice. Bear in mind that the most effective message may be to convey the *Benefits to You* that your office provides.

The real external marketing is contained in the things that can also be considered internal sources of marketing as well. Though your business cards will most certainly make their way out the practice door and into the community, you will definitely use your business cards inside the office as well. Your practice logo will not only be imprinted on these business cards, but also affixed to the business stationary which speaks about your office everywhere it lands. The same consideration you gave your business card design should also be granted to the creation of your practice logo and tag line. In lieu of hiring an expensive marketing firm to assist with such design decisions, you can opt to do this yourself with the help of software programs and online services such as Vista Print (www.VistaPrint.com). This website allows you to design and print your business cards for an extremely reasonable price.

Building signage is such an important marketing display as it is clearly a demonstration of your internal and external practice identity. As our website is our most effective source of marketing, we have chosen to post the website address on our building sign. In fact, the entire building sign consists of the capitalized link, WWW.DOCLOGAN.

COM. Because the sign is actually on the building, one might consider this a source of internal marketing. Because the website is actually external, the sign also clearly serves as an external marketing source. In fact, any signage on the premises will assume this dual identity and thus serve this twofold purpose. Lawn banners can be employed from time to time to affect this impression as well. If you operate a practice in a stand-alone building, your yard sign is a permanent fixture serving as a constant source of internal and external marketing of your practice image. Carefully consider what you want this image to be.

Given my practice focus on providing dentistry in the most esthetic fashion possible, I have elected to employ the descriptive heading, *Artistry in Dentistry*. This caption is imprinted on my business cards and office stationary, and utilized on our websites as well. The graphic design logo of a painter's palate with a toothbrush dissecting it is positioned beside this subtitle wherever it is inscribed. I cannot count the number of comments and compliments I have received regarding this graphic expression. Identify something that defines you and be creative. Give people a reason to remember you and your practice.

Marketing Calendar

We have discovered great value in the design and utilization of a marketing calendar delineating various campaigns we anticipate implementing throughout the year. Some advantages of scripting such a well-conceived plan are: accountability in adhering to marketing goals, ability to track marketing campaign progress and accumulation of valuable return on investment data. Practices implementing such a plan are much more likely to maximize the profit from their marketing budgets and increase their abilities to ensure a steady stream of new patients. An example of our marketing calendar can be accessed through the Practice Management Resources for Dentists section at the end of this book.

Internet Marketing

When I first began in dentistry, the Internet as we know it today did not exist. I recall my brother's summation of the World Wide Web in its infancy, "It's like a big mall with a bunch of stores and no merchandise in them." In other words, the Internet was open for your perusal, but it was far from being open for business. Doctors graduating from dental school today may find this type of business environment difficult to fathom. Within the last decade, the Internet Revolution has transformed the way business is transacted worldwide, and dental professionals who elect to ignore this trend will find their businesses being left behind.

The topic of external marketing took on an entirely different appearance at the time I opened my first practice than is currently the case. Prior to the late 1990's, there was no literature concerning, or consultants advocating, Internet marketing for the dental professional. The new resident mailer was considered best in show when it came to driving new patient traffic to your office. Practice management consultants instructed us to mail postcards to zip codes up to two hours away, in order to establish our identity as *The* dentist to see. The following chart outlines an ADA study of the referral sources of new patients to general dental practices in 1999, thus confirming the absence of Internet marketing during this era:

Sources and Mean Percentage of New Patients Referred to New General Practitioners, 1999

Referral Source	New Patients Referred (%)
Patients	55.7
Direct Mail/Commercial Advertising	12.3
Other	9.8
Capitation or Closed Panel Contracts	6.5
Specialists	5.9
Other Professionals (for example, physicians)	4.2
Other General Practitioners	4.3
Dental Referral Service	1.5

www.ada.org/prof/resources/pubs/dbguide/newdent/considerations.asp, Copyright © 1999, American Dental Association. All rights reserved. Reprinted by permission.

While I never actually captured any long-distance patients from my new resident mailers, just last week I treated a new patient who found me through a Google search and drove 45 minutes to my office. Imagine how many dental practices there were between my office and this patient's home? This patient chose my practice as a result of my #1 ranking with Google for her specific search query. When she visited my website, she was intrigued by the *Benefits to You* page and impressed with the *Before and After* Cosmetic Photo Gallery. She was convinced that no further searching was necessary and that ours would be the dental office for her. This scenario has played itself out in my practice many times over, since I invested the time and resources necessary to position my website at the top of the chain in terms of competing dentists in my area.

Although your website is truly a form of external marketing, I dedicate its own section here because of its importance to your success in business. Apart from internal marketing efforts, it can stand alone as the only marketing element necessary to sustain your business into the future. Younger generations of doctors will migrate naturally to Internet marketing campaigns, while those starting practices before the Internet (BI) may find they need slightly more education on the intricacies of this form of business promotion. Though this type of marketing has been around for little more than ten years, we can wager with certainty that it will rule its domain for many decades to come. It is never too late to begin the process of capturing the deluge of potential new patients that Internet marketing can supply your practice.

This section will introduce you to the critical information that people in the industry are not telling you about how to establish your practice as the one patients will choose when searching online for a dentist. Though many companies purport to offer this service, no one can guarantee you the top listing with the search engines. Nonetheless, my goal is to provide the knowledge you need to create and optimize a website that will position your practice in front of the greatest number of potential new patients as possible. Being #1 in searches is not merely about providing the best content, or copy, for your website. It is also about including the proper keywords and phrases, title tags and description tags and designing a site that maintains authority by receiving plentiful website links.

The following chapters on website design, search engine optimization and social media marketing are not meant to serve as an expert opinion on the topics covered. Instead, I am attempting to explain this material in a language which can be understood by professionals who are involved in careers outside the specialties of computers, technology and the Internet. I have sifted through countless articles on the subject and consulted several Internet optimization specialists. I am a dentist, not an Internet guru. However, as a dentist, I am uniquely qualified to convey my experience with respect to how Internet marketing can benefit the dental practice and explain these things in terms that do not require technical expertise. Be sure to take advantage of the Internet Glossary at the end of this book whenever you require clarification on any of these terms.

These chapters will communicate the critical information I have found extremely useful in promoting my websites and increasing my online presence over the last decade. Application of these principles has allowed my websites to consistently place in the top three results on Google and Yahoo! in searches for a dentist in my area. These rankings have proved invaluable to the growth of my practice in this technology-driven age. This section concludes with a discussion of the importance of active involvement in social media in order to elevate your online presence to the next level. If you take away only one thing from this book, mastery of Internet marketing in your business should be it. Doing so will assure your practice a steady stream of new patients, both in good economic times and bad.

Chapter 24

Designing a First-Class Website

Does a Dentist Really Need a Website?

I recognized the value of maintaining a quality website for my dental practice very soon after starting my own business. I was the first among my dental school roommates to launch a site and thereby earned the nickname, *DotCom*. Most of my dental school friends have followed suit and added their own practice websites in recent years, adding great value to their practices. I am still often asked if creating a dental practice website and devoting the search engine optimization efforts needed to increase its online presence are worth the investment. My answer is a resounding, "Yes!" My practice referral source statistics consistently point to Internet marketing as the leading source of new patients to my practice. It is not uncommon for patients to inform us that they made an appointment simply because our website was the first they encountered when searching online for a dentist.

The process of creating a website can seem a bit daunting when getting started and is replete with initial questions: How do I find a good web designer? What is the average cost of a quality dental website? How can I be sure my website will appear high in online searches for a local dentist? How much will I need to pay for Internet marketing and optimization? Will the return on investment make the process worthwhile? As I reveal the answers to these questions, you will, no doubt, more clearly appreciate the value of the Internet in taking your practice to the next level!

Selecting a Web Designer

While some dentists possess a thirst for technical knowledge and have honed the ability to design and code their own websites, in most cases, outside help is required. Hiring an experienced and competent web designer is vital to creating a website that will appear high in online searches while delivering quality content. The ideal web designer will be familiar with the coding and creation process of designing a website, as well as the intricacies involved in search engine optimization (SEO).

Search engine optimization refers to techniques used to enhance a website's performance in search engine results, such as those on Google or Yahoo!. The more optimized your website, the higher will be its ranking in a Google search or a search on any of the major search engines. SEO encompasses both website design and external factors such as building up links to a website. Since the degree to which your website becomes visible to the public directly hinges upon its level of optimization with the search engines, much of this chapter on website design outlines ways in which to best optimize your site. It is a mistake (and unfortunately one that I have made) to assume that every web designer knows how to maximally optimize your site. It is therefore imperative for you to dedicate ample time to selecting a web designer who can provide the end product quality, as well as the search engine optimization, your website requires.

Some designers will claim that optimization is not the role of a designer and that you will need to hire an additional company to help you increase the visibility of your site in online searches. Other designers may boast a vast knowledge of SEO but are not current with the most recent changes in how search engines rank sites. While it may be necessary to hire a company to enhance your optimization efforts after your website is launched, there are key ingredients that require inclusion during the initial design of the website. These important components of a well-optimized site will be discussed further. Given the disparity among web designers' understanding of how to make a site highly visible in online searches, it is incumbent upon you to have a familiarity with this information prior to choosing a web designer.

It is the understood role of the website designer, not the dentist, to be familiar with the needs of a website. However, I have learned by my own experience and similar experiences related by my colleagues, that it is useful to have a general knowledge of this information when choosing a designer and when looking to expand your website's presence online. When you venture blindly into this process, you risk having to pay someone to re-design or enhance your site at a later date. Including these crucial items in the original design and expense will spare you limitless frustration and ensure a higher return on investment.

Some of the major dental industry website designers include TNT Dental, Prosites, Televox, Sesame Communications and Einstein Dental. I was able to lower my costs by using a local web designer for the creation of both of my websites, so I have no personal experience with any of the aforementioned companies. I began my search for a web designer by asking colleagues for recommendations and reviewing the portfolios of several web designers who I was considering. Designers typically have their own website with links to the sites they have created. It is important to contact the owners of other sites the designer has created and inquire about their experience with this designer. This is the same reference checking technique any employer would use when considering a candidate for employment. Bear in mind that any designer's portfolio most likely showcases web designs that were created for satisfied customers.

When requesting an estimate, point the designer to several existing websites that most closely resemble what you desire for your end product. Ask your potential website designer the following questions:

- What is the overall cost of the project?

- When can the designer begin the project and how long will it take to complete?

- Will the designer write any of the content or should all content be provided by your office? I later discuss the importance of unique content and not hiring a designer who will create a copy-cat site.

- What is the hourly cost to make changes and enhancements to the site once it is complete? As I discuss in more detail later, you should routinely add new *Before and After* pictures and fresh content to help your site continue to be recognized by search engines. Therefore, before choosing a designer you need to gain a realistic expectation of the ongoing costs of updating your website.

- What techniques will be employed to ensure your website will have good visibility in online searches? The information in the next chapter will outline key terms that a competent web designer should use when discussing optimization.

- What does the designer do to stay abreast of the latest trends in SEO? Does the designer attend seminars, research online, subscribe to newsletters or self-educate? Be aware that some designers do virtually no research, so make use of your questions to ferret out the pretenders.

- Will the site be designed with a Content Management System (CMS) that will facilitate your own additions? This is beneficial in allowing you to make simple updates to your website without paying a web designer for each change or requiring you to learn complicated coding.

- Will the site be designed in compliance with W3C? This is a list of regulations developed by the World Wide Web Consortium that will help your website be viewed properly by all browsers and devices.

- Does the designer provide a contract with a completion date?

- How is payment handled? Do not pay for the entire site up front. Unfortunately, some designers become less motivated after payment is received.

- Under our arrangement, who owns the domain name and website? The answer should be that you would own both.

Choosing a Website Host

In order to publish a website online, you need a web host. The web host stores all the pages of your website and makes them available to computers connected to the Internet. Web designers often offer hosting themselves or suggest a company with which they have a working relationship to host your website. Designers' web hosting preferences are based upon the ease with which they can access and make changes to the site and which scripting languages are supported by the host. Your web designer should be able to guide you in your hosting decision, but it is good to be informed in this selection. If you decide to manage some of the updates to the website without enlisting a web designer, ensure that the web host provides easy access to a user-friendly control panel with editing options.

Web hosts often offer several plan options depending upon your website's needs. The premium packages offer unlimited disk space and bandwidth, as well as more email accounts and email storage than a typical dental office would require. The greatest variables among these companies are their customer service, statistical reports, data back-up procedures, hidden fees, ease of transfer and upload speeds. Also, some webhosts are not able to run multimedia video and audio streams. This is not a problem for a text and photo only site, but is a consideration for those sites that run streaming audio or video.

Hosting prices and contracts vary, but you should be able to hire a reliable host for around $100/year. Depending upon the web host, you will typically be required to sign a 3, 6, 9, 12 or 24 month contract. Many hosts offer business plans in which you can host multiple sites for one low monthly price. My particular plan allows me to host up to six sites for a total cost of $8.95/month.

Two important considerations in selecting a web host are the amount of downtime a web host experiences and the website speed. It may prove difficult to get a straight and accurate answer on the average amount of downtime a web host experiences, but online reviews from customers can let you know if this is a significant problem. Another consideration that has increased in importance recently is the website speed. Overall website speed is a result of the design of the site as well as the speed provided by the web host. Google has stated that website speed is now an important factor in its search engine ranking formulation.

If you are considering several options, conduct online research of user reviews. There are several helpful web hosting company comparison sources online, including www.TopTenReviews.com, www.webhostinggeeks.com and www.clickfire.com. These sites offer reviews of the major web hosts. TopTenReviews provides a helpful comparison chart. Some of the major players in web hosting are BlueHost, InMotion, Global, GoDaddy and Yahoo!. When reading reviews, pay particular attention to comments regarding customer service, outage periods, upload times, hidden fees and data back-up. Hidden fees can be particularly problematic when some hosting companies purport an overall low monthly fee, but nickel and dime you without permission for a laundry list of *additions*. Many of the better web hosts include these additions in their base pricing. Research will reveal that no web hosting company has perfect reviews. Just as a disgruntled dental patient is much more likely to take the time to write a review, the same is true of an unhappy web host client. Every web host I examined received at least a few bad reviews. Check with your colleagues for recommendations as well.

As a result of copious research on web hosting companies, I recently switched my business websites to InMotion Hosting and my experience has been very positive. Multiple review sites posted numerous overwhelmingly positive reviews, especially in regard to InMotion's customer service and straightforward fees. Even this company received a handful of negative reviews, but as one reviewer stated, "Even Jesus gets bad reviews from some people." InMotion's business plans allow you to host anywhere from 6-16 websites on the same account, depending upon the plan you purchase. InMotion's customer service representatives can be easily reached by phone, email or live chat. In switching over three sites and designing one new site, I have had to make use of InMotion's support team quite often. InMotion's speed of response and commitment to problem resolution more than meets my needs. The control panel provided makes it easy for me to make basic changes to my websites with very little knowledge of coding. I was able to add a WordPress blog to my website with one easy step through a program InMotion provides.

Important Components of a Successful Website

The specific criteria used by search engines to analyze and rank your website's relevance continually change. Successful web designers and search engine marketers stay current with the latest trends in search engine ranking and re-design their strategies to capitalize on these trends. At times these efforts force search engines to re-think how to ascertain which websites are truly relevant to their searchers. The following information outlines some of the key components needed to make a website more visible in online searches and more helpful to potential patients who find your website. You may choose to have a copy writer or web designer write all of your content, but it is still important to be familiar with these concepts in order to ensure their inclusion into your website. This is not an exhaustive list, but includes what I have found through extensive study and personal experience to be the most essential features of a quality website.

Searchable Domain Name

A domain name is the name of your website, for example, www.theaustindentist.com. Whenever possible, choose a domain name that contains the main search terms used to find your service. If your practice is located in Denver, first determine if www.denverdentist.com is available. You may need to experiment with variations of the name, but try to stay as close as you can to a searchable name. For a list of available domain names, check out www.whois.net or www.godaddy.com, where you can register your domain name as well.

Depending upon the competition in your area, it may be difficult to find a name that contains searchable terms. You may be forced to settle on a site that ends in .net instead of .com to find a domain name that contains the terms you desire. Using a .net ending does not negatively affect your visibility when someone is browsing search engines. However, when people type your website name directly from memory they may assume an ending of .com and therefore be directed to a different site. Unfortunately for the .nets, this happens more often than one might think. If selecting a domain name with searchable terms is not an option, your next consideration should be to choose a name that is easy to remember.

I designed my first website, www.DocLogan.com, before I realized the value of using searchable keywords in my domain name. It would appear that I did not follow my own advice, and should consider changing the name of my website. Since my site has been live for over a decade and has built a large number of links to its content, I have not changed the name. On the positive side, my patients find it easy to remember my website's name and often share it with others when referring them to my practice. The simplicity of the name also allows drive-by motorists who take note of the website address on my signage to easily recall my domain name once they arrive home. Had I chosen a more searchable domain name, I may have unknowingly chosen a name too similar to other dentists in my area and thereby driven potential patients to those dentists' sites accidentally.

Domain names can be registered for less than $10/year. Your web designer can handle registration for you, but it is typically cheaper and safer to register your domain on your own. Some web designers will register a domain in their name, not their client's name. The domain name ownership should be in your name! You may consider purchasing several domain names for future development of mini-websites, niche marketing websites or sites that re-direct traffic to your main website. There are several benefits to owning multiple domain names and maintaining more than one website, which I later discuss in greater detail. Some dentists purchase a large number of domains in order to defend against their competition purchasing high quality names. Lore has it that one particular dentist owns more than 250 domain names.

Quality Home Page

The home page is the main hub of your website and provides searchers their first impression of your website and your practice. Whenever someone directly types in your website address, your home page is what will appear. The vast majority of potential patients who find your site online will enter through the home page. The need for a quality home page is obvious. You never get a second chance to make a good first impression. Searchers typically give a new website just a few seconds to catch their attention and keep them on the site. If they cannot find what they need quickly or are turned off by an unprofessional presentation, searchers will hit the back button and go to the next site in their search query results. Home page content is also very important to search engine rankings. This page of a website is typically the one most examined by search engines to determine your website's relevance to searchers.

Being recognized and ranked highly by search engines should not be your only goal when designing a site. All of your search engine optimization efforts may be in vain if you do not provide a high quality site with relevant information that will make your reader respond. A common mistake is to so fill your website with keywords that the site lacks substance and flair. Since most online searchers will not spend very long on your site, it is imperative to highlight on the home page why a searcher should become a patient in your practice. Just as in other areas of marketing, remember that potential new patients want to know how your office can benefit them. Take the opportunity to offer information on what sets you apart and how your office provides excellent patient care. If you offer convenient hours, sedation dentistry, patient financing and a warm, inviting atmosphere, by all means broadcast these benefits on your homepage!

What should be included on a home page?

Contact information – We include contact information on every page of our websites, but this information should certainly be readily available on the home page as well. A Contact Us link to another page is helpful, but you must ensure that the display of your street address and phone number can be easily found on your home page. This allows the searcher/potential new patient to know you practice in the local area and to contact you immediately if pressed for time. For optimization purposes, try to include your address in the top one-third of the page and in the footer.

High quality images of the dentist and/or patients – The home page is a great place to display a warm, friendly picture of a smiling dentist. My front office staff has recounted many stories of new patients calling to schedule who specifically mention seeing my picture and thinking I looked like I would not hurt them. If you wish to grow the family aspect of your practice, a picture of a smiling dentist with a young patient leaves a lasting impression. Pictures of patients with beautiful smiles created in your office can enhance your cosmetic dentistry practice goals. While some websites display *Before and After* images of patients on the home page, I would caution against posting any overly graphic photos of a frightening dentition. Save these pictures for the *Before and After* gallery. Smiling, happy faces of satisfied customers typically engender the most good will from viewers. A colorful patient testimonial alongside one of these cheerful faces further drives home the point that you are the dentist to see.

Searchable content – The home page of your website is an ideal place to include keywords that might be used to search for a local dentist or for specific dental services such as Invisalign or dental implants. If you are an oral surgeon in San Diego, for example, your home page should contain the phrase *San Diego oral surgeon*, preferably near the top of the page and repeated in another location on the page. These terms can be used as anchor text for links to other pages of your website that discuss these services in further detail. Anchor text and its importance will be defined in a subsequent section.

Easy Navigation – While this concept applies to the design of the entire site, it is especially important that a website visitor can quickly establish how to move about your site from the home page. This is typically accomplished through tabs to other pages contained either at the top of each page or in the left-hand column. Research has shown that the left-hand side of a web page is where the eye typically travels first. Navigation bars on the left are helpful for this reason, but be sure to order them in importance and ensure that the most important page links appear above the fold. Many viewers are so time-pressed that they will not even scroll down to assess the remaining links.

Reasons a Patient Should Come to Your Office – The home page may be the only one a potential new patient visits. Take the opportunity to highlight the benefits your office offers. This can be done in a separate Benefits to You page as well, but the main points need to be highlighted on the home page. Brainstorm what patients in your area find most important in a dental office. Do they need a convenient location near home and work? Do they need convenient hours because they live in a commuter area? Is the area comprised of young families searching for a dentist who can care for the needs of every family member? Do you practice in a highly technical area with customers who would appreciate references to the latest technologies our profession has to offer? Is your practice located in an area with a large number of elderly patients who may be seeking implants and dentures?

Original and Link-Worthy Content

While search engines' techniques for ranking the importance of websites are in a constant state of flux, the one constant is the importance of high quality content! Search engines are looking for sites full of text, pictures, graphics and videos. Your site is more likely to be recognized as substantial if it is full of rich content describing your particular area of expertise. It is tempting to skimp on your budget and produce a small website with few pages and very little content. This approach will leave your website buried low in the rankings, receiving merely cursory glances from patients searching for a new dentist.

Numerous companies specialize in producing dental websites. Some boast of low fees and quick turn-around times. It will be detrimental, however, to hire these companies if their speed and low fees come as a result of using a template containing very little unique content. Search engines penalize sites if the overall content is a duplicate of other dental websites, with only the dentist's name and location being changed. While it is more time-consuming and expensive, *you must ensure that your site contains original content that cannot be found on other sites*! This not only helps your search engine optimization efforts, but also allows you to present your unique traits and benefits to attract more patients. With all that you have to do in any given day, writing content for your website may not be high on your list of priorities. If you do not have the time or desire to create much of the content yourself, you will need to enlist a staff member, copy writer or web designer to write original content for you. One cannot overemphasize the importance of original content on your website in order to avoid search engine penalties for duplicate content. Falling prey to this lackadaisical approach is tantamount to not having a website at all.

Another important factor is to provide content to which people would choose to link or that they may desire to bookmark. A website that is designed with basic information about the office and contact information does not attract many natural links. Consider adding a dental health articles section in which you explain basic oral health and dental procedures. Include information on children's dental health and consider adding children's activities that might draw links from teachers' resources. These additional web pages will draw more traffic to your site, create a greater number of valuable keywords and provide more relevant content that the general public may choose to bookmark or link to on their own blogs or websites. The great significance of links to your website is discussed in the search engine optimization section. Listed below are several websites that make good use of dental guides:

www.prestonwooddental.com
www.dentalgentlecare.com
www.commerceparkdental.com

While many searchers will select the first dentist to appear in their online search findings, some patients *shop* for dentists online. These shoppers quite commonly compare your website to those of several other dentists before arriving at a decision. Sometimes their final decision is based upon the overall appearance of your site even more than the content. Inform your web designer that you desire a visually appealing website that provides the same comforting appearance you wish to convey in your office.

Keyword Density

Keywords and key phrases are used by search engines to determine if the content on a website is relevant to what the searcher desires. When creating content for your website, begin the process by brainstorming a long list of keywords and keyword phrases that might be used to find a local dentist. Include specific services for which dental shoppers might search as well. You can begin this process by requesting ideas from your staff, friends and family by simply asking the question, "What words would you enter into a search engine query to find a local dentist?" A somewhat less techie way to ask this question might be, "What would you type into Google to find a dentist?" You may be surprised by how many different routes people take to find the same information. Searchers looking for a San Diego dentist might choose any of the following: *San Diego dentist, San Diego CA dentist, dentist in San Diego, 92130 dentist, best dentist in San Diego, dentist for my kids in San Diego*, etc. Examine your list of brainstormed keywords and attempt to work the most popular phrases into the content, title tags and description tags of your website. Title tags and description tags are discussed in greater detail later in this section.

Google provides a free Keyword Tool, located at https://adwords.

google.com/select/KeywordToolExternal, which can be a wealthy source of ideas for keywords to include in your content. This free tool allows you to enter several keywords or keyword phrases and assess how many times those words were searched locally on Google within the past month. It also provides an estimate of how much competition you would have if you chose those keywords in a pay per click campaign with Google. While this information does not directly translate to organic results competition for those words, it gives an overall indication of the difficulty you might encounter attempting to rank highly for specific terms. This tool also provides a list of similar keywords for your consideration, as well as their competition levels and search query numbers for the past month. Google's Webmaster Tools provides a list of the keywords Google has found on your website, in order of frequency. The list presents individual words, not key phrases. Your city name and names of surrounding communities you serve should appear in the first ten to twenty keywords on this list. The word *dentist* should mandatorily appear in the top ten as well.

Your practice location is one of the most important keyword phrases to display throughout your site. This can easily be accomplished with an address block as well as a phrase built into the banner of each page. An example of this phrase might be, *Family and Cosmetic Dentist serving the St. Charles, O'Fallon, St. Peters and Wentzville areas*. If your patients commute from multiple cities, be sure to include those cities in your content, in addition to the city in which you practice. When considering content for your website, work in the location name whenever possible. For example, instead of including, *Call or drop by our office to learn more*, include, *Call or drop by our Seattle dental office to learn more*.

Look for opportunities to mention your location within Meet the Dentist and Staff Bio sections as well. If your home page contains a video message or a link to an introductory biographical article about you, introduce it with *Meet Ann Arbor Family and Cosmetic Dentist Dr. Jane Doe*. Incorporating your location into the practice name, for example, *Winghaven Pediatric Dentistry*, makes it considerably easier to work in the location reference within your content. A colleague had an extremely informative orthodontic website that attracted the attention of searchers throughout the country to its informational articles. Unfortunately, the site did not contain enough references to her location and therefore did not attract the volume of new patients she desired.

Be sure to include the plural version of dentist in some of your content, as a patient may search for San Diego *dentists* rather than San Diego *dentist*. Take caution with your placement of keywords, making sure not to overdo it and fill your page merely with keywords. Most search engines recognize this as deception and will ignore your site altogether. You certainly do not want to be black listed from Google. Also, a website full of keywords will not provide the information searchers desire and will quickly lose the interest of the reader/potential new patient. Keywords and key phrases should be worked naturally into the overall content of each page. This may be easier said than done, but with a little practice it becomes second nature. Keep in mind that you can and should add new keywords to your content at a later time through additions to your website.

Niche Marketing and Long Tail Keywords

If you practice in a metropolitan area with a highly competitive market, it may be difficult to index highly for a keyword phrase containing *Your City dentist*. While this is a goal you should continue to pursue, it is important to add long tail keywords to your pages as well. A long tail keyword is a more detailed phrase that may be entered when a patient is searching for a dentist. It will be easier for your website to rank highly in a long tail keyword search, such as *dentist using Cerec in San Diego*, than it will be to rank highly for the more simplistic search, *San Diego dentist*. These longer and more specific keyword phrases will not be searched as often, but since a smaller number of sites will be relevantly indexed for this phrase, your site has a much higher chance of appearing on the first page of results. Another benefit is that patients who use these more specific terms are typically more certain of what they desire and more likely to be converted into new patients when finding your website. The Google Keyword Tool is an outstanding means by which to assist you with ideas of long tail keywords to include in your website's content.

It seems at times awkward to work these longer phrases into your regular text, it is important that they appear as content throughout your website. Long tail keywords can be smoothly included in a Dental Articles page, a Frequently Asked Question section, blog posts on specific procedures and techniques, a Benefits to You section and separate pages highlighting some of the unique technologies and features of your practice. Many dental websites have descriptive pages for each procedure offered, including information on why a particular procedure may be needed and how it is performed. These pages provide a great source of long tail keywords. If there is a particular procedure for which you wish to increase visibility, be sure to include a reference to it on your home page as well.

Posting articles relevant to dentistry on your website provides an abundant source of keywords and key phrases. Simply worded articles about dental procedures and cosmetic dentistry can be useful in attracting new patients. Remember to reference your location within these articles as well. Another avenue for providing useful information while adding keywords to a website is a FAQ (Frequently Asked Questions) section with answers to common questions such as:

- Do you accept my insurance?
- Does your office offer financing?
- How often should I get a dental cleaning?
- What can I do about my fear of the dentist?
- How do I prepare my child for a dental visit?
- When should my child first see the dentist?
- What treatment do you offer for sensitive teeth?
- Does your office provide an in-office denture lab?
- Does your office use Cerec technology?
- Are you a provider of Invisalign?

Meta Tags

Meta Tags are pieces of coding information inserted by a web designer into the head section of a website page. Other than the Meta tag known as a title tag, this information is invisible to someone browsing a website, but Meta tags provide important information to search engines. The web designer should add these tags when coding your website, but some designers leave this space blank or provide the same text for every title tag or description tag. This is a waste of a valuable resource! Dentists can gain a huge advantage over their competition when designing a website, simply by establishing some familiarity with the significance of these Meta tags.

The most important Meta tags are title tags and description tags. In a listing of search results, the title tag will appear as the blue underlined text that is clicked to go to a website. Often, the description tag is the text that follows and gives a short summary of the site. The following example displays the title tag as the underlined information and the meta description tag as the descriptive text below it:

O'Fallon Missouri **Dentist** - Dr. Edward Logan DDS
Dr. Logan offers pain-free *dentistry* for the entire family and cosmetic *dentistry* for the smile you've always wanted. Located in the WingHaven area of O'Fallon, MO.

A title tag refers to the brief wording used to describe a web page. Title tags are coded into every page of a website. When you are online, title tags are displayed as the first line at the top of your Internet browser, just above the toolbars. Google displays the first 60-70 characters of a title tag, while Yahoo! may display up to 120 characters. A title tag can read as one long phrase or be divided by hyphens or a pipe bar in order to display several different key phrases.

Title tags give searchers their first impression of your website and will help determine whether it is worthwhile to click through to your site. This important tool is sometimes ignored by designers who choose to use the domain name as the title tag on each page. This is wasting valuable real estate! Google's Webmaster Tools section discusses the importance of using different title tags on each page. In my research, I have found that title tags are among the top three most important factors for search engine optimization. The other two important components are links to your website and keyword rich content.

Web designers with knowledge of search engine optimization will understand the importance of title tags and will add unique title tags within the coding of each page. When I was in the market for a new web designer, one of the first things I researched in their portfolios was whether their websites made proper use of title tags. Again, each page of your website should have a different title tag! This also provides an enormous opportunity to add in several variations of keywords.

Title tags should describe what the page is about and contain keywords or phrases that may be used to search for your services. If your website contains a page describing Invisalign, then your title tag should reference your location and Invisalign. Reference your keyword brainstorming list and include some of these phrases in your title tags. It is important to include your name and practice name in some of the title tags as well, as many searchers will look for you by name.

An example of this would be an Ann Arbor family and cosmetic dentist whose site contains separate pages on multiple dental procedures. The following title tags could be used in association with those pages:

Home Page: Ann Arbor Family and Cosmetic Dentist – Dr. John Doe

Page on Cosmetic Dentistry: Cosmetic Dentist in Ann Arbor, MI – Veneers, Implants, Teeth Whitening

Page on Invisalign: Ann Arbor Dentist – Invisalign provider – Dr. John Doe

Web Page with Testimonials: Best Dentist in Ann Arbor – Dr. John Doe

Ideally, other title tags throughout this website would make reference to procedures Dr. Doe provides, as well as a variation of other location references. The location references should include mention of other local communities to market to patients residing in these areas. An example of the display of a title tag in search results is shown in the next section on description tags.

Meta description tags are the snippets of information displayed beneath your website listing in search results. Once heralded as a great source for keywords to optimize your search engine efforts, Meta description tags are no longer as widely used by search engines to rank sites. However, having your web designer complete this information affords you the opportunity to determine the website description searchers will see. Even though Meta description tags do not play as great of a role in search engine rankings, they do provide the best opportunity to inform searchers that your site is relevant to their needs.

Since searchers will be presented with several results per page, having clear Meta description tags can encourage them to click on your website before others. There is a limited amount of information you can fit into these tags so ensure that it immediately tells searchers what they want to know, primarily your location and line of business. For my business, I include that I am a family and cosmetic dentist in O'Fallon, Missouri. I also include a message that serves to put fearful patients at ease, as in the Meta description tag example listed above.

Each page of your website can have a different Meta description tag. Every page's Meta description tag and title tag should be assessed together to ensure that at least one of those tags on each page will contain a reference to your location. If the Meta description tag is left blank, search engines will scan your site and choose what they think may be relevant to display as the description of your website. Search engines may choose to do this even if your tags are filled in, but most often they choose to use the tag you provided. Regardless of your particular skills in writing content, I am quite certain that you are more capable of describing your dental practice than someone working for Google or Yahoo!.

Search Engine Optimized Design

My original website was designed in 1999 using the latest technology available at the time. Despite my initial efforts to drive more traffic to the site and improve its rankings on the major search engines, my website remained buried several pages deep in the search listings. I made some headway with my efforts, but was not satisfied with the results. After consulting a patient who had considerable experience in search engine optimization, I decided to re-design my site. An examination of the underlying structure of my original site revealed that the site was created with frames that were making it difficult for search engine robots and spiders to crawl across the site. Within weeks of updating the overall design, my site began to appear high in searches for a dentist in my area. If you have an older website that is not providing you with the leads you desire, look into updating the site's format.

A website's compatibility with multiple browsers and hand-held devices is also important. Many of today's online searches are being conducted through the use of a cell phone or PDA. Your website's appearance may vary depending upon what device or browser is used to view it. Your website should be designed with W3C compliance in mind in order to be viewed correctly on a variety of browsers and devices. You can learn more about W3C compliance at www.W3.org. Your web designer should know about these requirements and design your site in accordance with them.

A Call to Action or a *Contact Us* Option

A large number of online searches for a local dentist take place during non-business hours, as potential patients are home from work and recalling that they need to find a new dentist. When potential new patients visit your site during non-business hours, afford them the opportunity to contact you through your website. Providing a potential patient the ability to *act now* significantly increases your chance of converting the searcher into a patient of record. This can be accomplished quite simply by including a Contact Us section that encourages patients to email you with an appointment request or inquiry. Include a cautionary statement that email is not considered a secure form of communication and should not be used to share personal health information. If you choose to publicly display your email address on your website you will receive more Spam emails, but I have not found this to be a substantial issue.

You may choose to create a contact or scheduling form that can be completed and submitted on your website. This allows patients the ability to contact you while not revealing your email address to potential spammers. Some consultants encourage the use of articles relevant to dentistry to capture a potential patient's attention. A portion of these articles are displayed on your website, but the reader is required to provide a name and email address in order to receive the entire article. An opt-in feature can be added to your site in which a pop-up box appears requesting a name and email address for further communication as someone navigates away from your site. These pop-up boxes are often ignored, so if you choose to use them you should also afford other opportunities for someone to contact you by email.

Providing electronic new patient forms and an online scheduler serves to capture new patients as well. Several companies, including www.SecureDentalForms.com, www.SubmitPatientForms.com and www.PatientForms.com, offer secure patient registration and health history forms that can be completed and submitted online. This allows dental offices to validate insurance information in advance without subjecting a customer to a lengthy list of questions during the initial new patient phone call. Receiving the health history prior to the initial visit allows dentists to prepare for patients who may require pre-medication. If you operate a practice in an area heavily populated with people working in Information Technology, such as San Francisco or Austin, this type of service may be even more beneficial in attracting new patients. You can also provide patient forms for download on your website to circumvent security issues, but this does not capture the searching new patient like a submitted form does.

Basic contact information should be visible on every page of a dental practice website. This allows a potential patient who enters the website through any given page the ability to reach for the phone and contact you quickly. Searchers may be directed to a page on your website that highlights the value of veneers, rather than entering your website's home page. Make it easy for them to contact your office immediately.

Anchor Text (FIX)

Anchor text is the use of descriptive wording to indicate what a link to another page describes. An example of this kind of link appears in the following sentence: *Dr. Doe provides cosmetic dentistry, as well as general dentistry*. In this example, *cosmetic dentistry* is considered the anchor text and viewers are able to click on those words to be taken to a page on the website that highlights cosmetic dentistry. Anchor text is used by search engines to determine what the website or webpage being linked to is about. Descriptive keywords should be chosen to clarify the link, rather than the generic *click here*. Search engines view link descriptions as more valuable because they define link content and establish link relevance to a searcher's needs. This is yet another occasion when lazy website design can limit your visibility. Take advantage of this knowledge and optimize your site wherever possible. The use of carefully selected anchor text is an important piece of your optimization puzzle.

Optimized Pictures and Video

The adage, "A picture is worth a thousand words" holds true in the arena of dental office website design. The importance of *Before and After* patient photos was previously discussed in the section on what to include on a website's home page, but those pictures need to be optimized to garner attention from the search engines. Search engines cannot see the photo or video when crawling a website, so the name of those files is one of the only pieces of information they have to determine importance and relevance. Most picture and video files are automatically assigned a generic numerical title, but the title of an online photo or video is used by search engines to determine whether that item is relevant to a searcher. Photos and videos should be named with keywords in mind. For example, a picture of a patient displaying beautiful new veneers could be named "St. Louis dental veneers." Using keywords in the text near the image or in an image caption also allows search engines to ascertain what the image is about. Using the aforementioned anchor text to link back to a photo elsewhere on your website may provide more search engine relevancy for that image as well.

Benefits You Provide

Outlining what sets you apart from the competition does not necessarily lead to better search engine optimization. However, it is important to quickly establish to potential new patients that they can now end their search for a new dentist and appoint with your office. In the case of dentistry or orthodontics, *Before and After* photographs and patient testimonials should always be included on your website. Include as many varying cases as possible to maximize the chance that potential patients will recognize a problem similar to their own and witness how you resolved it into a beautiful smile. This style of marketing increases the likelihood that patients will enter your office already sold on your abilities.

Meet the Staff

Our website statistics consistently point to our Meet the Staff page as the one most popular with searchers. Pictures and brief bios of the dentist and staff members can make potential patients feel at ease before they walk into the door. They may discover a common interest or hobby with one of the staff members and feel more connected even prior to meeting the staff. Most often, people just want to visualize a warm, caring environment that can most easily be expressed through smiling faces. These smiles, of course, need to include that of the dentist as well as the staff.

Sitemap

A Sitemap is a list of all the pages on your website. Creating a Sitemap and submitting it to the major search engines is one of the most efficient ways to initiate search engines crawling and indexing of all the pages of your website. This Sitemap lets Google and other search engines know about pages and URLs on your site that they may otherwise overlook. If you have a relatively small site (less than ten pages), a Sitemap will not be as important, but it is a simple step in the right direction.

Assure that your web designer includes a Sitemap in the design of your website. A brief Internet search will point you where to go to submit your Sitemap to the major search engines. Google, Yahoo! and Bing will all require you to create an account with them before submitting a Sitemap. If your website designer did not include a Sitemap in the original design of your website, there are numerous free Sitemap generator tools available online. The Sitemap generator found at www.xml-sitemaps.com provides a user-friendly tool for creating a Sitemap.

Website Statistics/Analytics

Most webhosts supply website statistics as part of your hosting fee. Even if your web host offers its own statistics, it may still a good idea to take advantage of Google Analytics' free service. Analytics is simply installed by copying a code provided by Google into the coding of every page you wish to monitor. Google Analytics allows you to monitor a wide variety of statistics on traffic sources, how your visitors interact with your site and the location of your visitors. It displays which keywords or referral sources are being used to find your site in searches and presents information on how long the visitors stayed on your site and how many pages were visited. Analytics provides you rich insight into areas of strength and weakness in your website's optimization.

Google Webmaster Tools is an additional free service that tracks top search queries, links to your website and crawl errors. Google Webmaster Tools can be added with a one step verification process. The diagnostics section of Webmaster Tools lists suggestions on how to create better title tags and Meta description tags. It examines the Meta tags you have on your site and displays whether any title or description tags are missing, duplicated, too long or too short. Google Webmaster Tools also demonstrates whether there are any problems with crawling your website or following links within your website. These two programs combine to tell you just about anything you would like to know about how people find and interact with your website.

Blog

I will discuss the benefits and implementation of a blog in greater detail later, but a blog incorporated into your website is an excellent way to provide updated content on a regular basis. Search engines give more frequent attention to websites that add content regularly. A blog is a simple means by which to add this content without having to enlist the help of a web designer with coding knowledge. Employing a user-friendly blogging service such as Google Blogger or WordPress, front office staff members or the dentist can easily manage adding new information and articles to the blog on a weekly or monthly basis.

Should Your Practice Have More than One Website?

If you are new to the Internet marketing world and do not have a website, you may be feeling a little overwhelmed after reading about the important components of website design and optimization. You may even be a little frustrated that I would pose the question of creating more than one website while you are lamenting over all the work that one site can require. Take heart, it is not necessary for you to do all of these things at once. Optimization is a continual process. Please do not avoid implementing a website because it appears like too much work! Get out there and get your feet wet and see how providing a website for your customers can benefit your business. If you have yet to establish a website, or you have thus far not begun the optimization process for the one that you do have, I would recommend focusing on your original site first before considering the addition of another site.

For those of you who already have a well-optimized website and steps in place to continue the optimization process, an additional practice website focusing on a niche market may serve you well. A dentist who practices in multiple locations is a prime candidate for multiple websites which highlight each geographical region. Dentists who provide both family and cosmetic dentistry may find having a site dedicated to each of these areas quite useful. Patients seeking a dentist for the entire family will gravitate toward the dentist's site that displays pictures of children, answers frequently asked questions about children's hygiene and highlights the comprehensive nature of the practice. Those looking for high quality cosmetic dentistry will be more interested in a site demonstrating a dentist's expertise in this area through the use of *Before and After* case photographs, patient testimonials, videos and credentials.

Establishing more than one website can provide the following:

- An opportunity to cross-link between multiple sites to help build links for SEO,

- The possibility of lowering the rankings of your competition's websites by appearing as the first two or three sites in major searches for dentists in your area,

- The ability to include more content about specific services or features you provide without overwhelming visitors with a crowded website and

- A niche marketing opportunity to highlight your expertise in cosmetic dentistry, Invisalign, 6 Month Braces, periodontal surgery, implants or dentures.

When designing a secondary website, do not make the mistake of copying any content from the original site! The magical brains behind the major search engines' robots and spiders can recognize duplicate content and search engines will penalize a site if it is believed to be a copycat. It is acceptable to use some of the same photos, but they should be saved using different file names in order to avoid the appearance of duplicate content.

Chapter 25

Getting Your Website Recognized (Search Engine Optimization)

What is Search Engine Optimization and Why Do You Need It?

As defined in the chapter on Website Design, search engine optimization (SEO) refers to techniques used to enhance a website's performance in search engine results, such as those on Google or Yahoo!. Again, the more optimized your website, the higher will be its ranking in a Google search or a search on any of the major search engines. SEO encompasses both website design and external factors such as building up links to a website.

In the previous chapter, I outlined the most important factors within the design and maintenance of a website which yield outstanding search engine performance. Now I will highlight steps to promote your properly designed website so that search engines will find it quickly and rank it highly when a potential patient is searching for a local dentist. By adhering to the following protocol, you will position your website to appear above your competitors when someone is searching online for dental services.

My initial practice website ranked quite highly for several years, but eventually became buried within the search engine results when competitors began to enter the Internet marketing space. I then decided to revamp my site with a commitment to search engine optimization. My website now consistently appears in the top three organic (non-purchased) results for a dentist in my area. Search engines change the formula they use to classify and index websites on a regular basis. It is therefore mandatory for a web designer to keep current with these changes in order to maintain a website's position at the front of the pack. Remember, search engine optimization is always a work in progress.

Google devours an overwhelming portion of the search engine pie, accounting for the vast majority of daily searches. Much of the material in this section highlights ways to enhance website rankings with Google. Within the search engine hierarchy, Yahoo! slots in at second place, though its slice of the pie pales in comparison to that of Google. Microsoft's re-designed search engine, Bing, comes in at a distant third, while Ask and AOL trail much further behind and round out the top five.

When a user enters text into the search bar of any of the three major search engines and submits the search, a search engine results page (SERP) is displayed. When someone is searching for a local business such as a dental practice, the SERP will commonly display three different types of search results in the following order:

- Sponsored Listings - These listings appear at the top, side and bottom of the results page. Businesses pay to have these ads displayed.

- Local Business Listings - Businesses claim these listings with the search engines. These listings are displayed with maps and appear more commonly when a location is included in the search terms entered.

- Organic Listings - These listings occur naturally as a result of a website's ability to be recognized by the search engines by a particular search term. Organic listings are not purchased and do not result from businesses signing up for local business listings with the search engines. The goal of search engine optimization for your dental website is to appear high in organic results when a potential patient is searching for a new dentist.

One may question why a book on dental practice growth and management would devote so many pages to information on website design and search engine optimization. After all, would this information not be better handled by professionals? My desire with its inclusion is to educate dentists and encourage wise decisions on how to move forward with Internet marketing. While the majority of dentists will require professional help with these efforts, a dental professional armed with this knowledge will be enabled to monitor website design and implementation and ensure high visibility for the practice website. The resulting high ranking of a well-optimized website will pay outstanding dividends to the growth and success of your practice.

Will You Require Professional SEO Assistance?

If you are able to hire a web designer well-versed in search engine optimization, you will need to do less to get your website recognized. However, do not expect to simply follow all of the right protocol with respect to designing a quality website and then sit back and hope that search engines, and therefore potential patients, will find your site. Even if your site begins to rank highly, it will not maintain this high ranking unless you keep up your optimization efforts.

The importance of appearing on the first page of search engine results was highlighted in iProspect's 2006 Search Engine User Behavior Study of 2,639 Internet users. [35] The study's results revealed that 62% of users stated that they do not look past page one for results. Over 90% of users reported that they never look past the first three pages for results. As this study bears out, if your website is not appearing on the first page of results, it is highly unlikely to be found by potential patients.

Internet marketing is becoming a fiercely competitive industry and it is a challenge to stay abreast of the ever-changing protocols used by search engines to rank websites. As recently as last year, wholesale changes occurred with respect to the manner in which search engines index major social media outlets such as Facebook and Twitter. Microsoft redeveloped its search engine and introduced Bing. Yahoo! and Microsoft announced a merger to enhance their efforts in paid advertising. Google began to personalize search results based upon a searcher's web history. In April 2010, Google enhanced its Local Business Center, changing the name to Google Places and offering businesses greater opportunities for promotion. Google also announced that website speed was an important factor in its consideration of website ranking. These are merely a few among many examples highlighting the importance of keeping current with changes in the search engine world, and thereby maintaining practice website relevance and visibility.

With this continual flux of information, it may appear that your only option for optimization is to seek professional help. As soon as your website is live, you may be inundated with emails and phone calls from companies purporting to specialize in website optimization. This is especially true if an email contact is listed on your website. Many of the emails you receive will be spam and even those coming from legitimate companies may be rife with poor English, as some of the companies or employees are based outside the United States. These emails and phone calls will be filled with promises such as, "We can guarantee top placement on Google."

Fees and services vary widely among optimization companies so it is wise to obtain multiple quotes. Consulting companies typically offer a menu of choices and you can select the areas in which you feel you need the most help. For instance, you can hire a company to submit your website to search engines, set up pay-per-click advertising, research keyword competition in your area and find useful links for your particular site. Many companies will require a commitment for a certain length of time, as search engine optimization does not happen overnight. Be cautious in committing to a long-term contract with a company that has not been personally recommended to you. Consult with colleagues for referrals to quality Internet optimization companies, request estimates from at least three different companies and research online for reviews of each company.

Unfortunately, there are some shady SEO practices and consultants. In particular, you should be wary of companies that claim to guarantee top placements on search engines. There is no way to guarantee this legitimately. Also, avoid companies that will auto-submit your website to thousands of directories and search engines and companies that mention link exchange programs. Google's Webmaster Central Forum outlines several tips for increasing your awareness of unethical SEO practices. Several of Google's key points are outlined below:

- Be skeptical of unsolicited emails from SEO companies,

- Do not believe claims to a special relationship with Google or the ability to guarantee a first place ranking on Google,

- Make companies explain exactly what they are doing to increase your SEO and what your money is being spent on. Be wary of companies that offer to submit your site to thousands of search engines or take part in link popularity schemes,

- Ask specifically about the use of doorway pages or shadow domains which could get your site penalized and

- Perform online research and look for reviews on the SEO companies you are considering. [36]

I currently practice in a mid-sized local market and employ a business manager to keep up with developments in the Internet marketing space. I have therefore been able to avoid hiring a company to manage my Internet marketing and optimization. I consider myself extremely fortunate to have an amazingly talented and intelligent staff member capable of staying abreast of these trends. I realize that it is rare to find an employee so skilled in the intricacies of managing the Internet presence of a dental practice.

For those doctors not so fortunate, I would highly encourage hiring a professional. Likewise, if you practice in a metropolitan area such as Dallas, you may require more assistance from a professional in implementing an SEO strategy. Remember, optimization is always a work in progress. If you do not have a staff member who can regularly work toward keeping your website at the top of search engine rankings, you would be well advised to hire an outside company to perform this task.

You may choose to blend your knowledge of Internet optimization with that of a professional. When re-designing my website, I enlisted the services of a local Internet specialist to re-engineer the site and begin the search engine optimization process. One year later, we added an additional website focusing on esthetic dentistry. We applied the information garnered through the restructuring of our original website to the development of the new site.

Search Engine Optimization Checklist

After you have launched a well-planned website full of keywords, well-defined tags, quality content and a searchable framework, you need a clear attack plan for getting your website recognized. Below is a summary checklist of how to start and maintain optimization of your site within search engines. Each of these topics is further explained following the checklist. All applications on the checklist can be performed for you by a consulting company if you elect not to spend your time on these items. The most important aspect of optimization is building links to your website!

- Submit your website to the major search engines: Google, Yahoo! and Bing. This is a very simple process using the following links:

  Google: http://www.google.com/addurl/
  Yahoo!: https://siteexplorer.search.yahoo.com/mysites
  Bing: http://www.bing.com/docs/submit.aspx

- Submit your Sitemap to these search engines as well. This will require establishing a member account with each search engine. Member accounts will allow you access to statistical information on your site's performance from each of these search engines as well.

- Sign up for local business listings on major search engines using the following links:

  Google: www.google.com/local/add
  Yahoo!: http://listings.local.yahoo.com
  Bing: https://ssl.bing.com/listings/ListingCenter.aspx

- Research possible sites which can link to your website. Link-building is always a fluid event and needs to be a continuous activity.

- Research online directories such as www.TheDentistSearch.com, which appear high in keyword searches for a local dentist.

- Highly visible directories will charge a monthly fee. These directories will not only provide a link to your website, but also serve to increase your overall presence online. Patients may find your practice directly through one of these sources.

- Submit articles and press releases to online sources such as http://www.ezinearticles.com, making sure to link to your website when allowed.

- Consider starting a pay per click campaign with the major search engines. If your practice is in a particularly competitive market this will be expensive.

- Continue to update the content on your website, possibly through the addition of articles or patient case descriptions and pictures.

- Monitor your website statistics on a monthly basis to determine what is working and what needs restructuring.

- Perform your own research on a regular basis to determine where your websites and social media accounts are appearing in searches for a dentist in your area.

- Examine social media marketing avenues through a blog, Facebook, Twitter, MySpace, Mixx, Reddit, Digg and YouTube.

- Submit your blog feed to blog directories which will provide links to your blog and website.

- Post comments on dental-related blogs and general answer forums, always providing a link back to your website.

Submission of URL and Sitemap to the Major Search Engines

Submitting your website URL, or web address, to the major search engines is a simple process that should be done as soon as your site has been completed. URL is an acronym for *Uniform Resource Locator*. It is similar to a domain name, but used specifically in reference to a web page's address. While a website only has one domain name, it will have multiple URLs pointing to different pages on that site. For example, www.TheDentistSearch.com/add_office.htm is a URL for a certain page within the domain name www.TheDentistSearch.com, which is also a URL.

This submission does not require the expertise of a search engine optimization consultant, as it merely requires completing the URL request page for each of the search engines. Links to the major search engines can be found in the SEO checklist. Currently, there exist a large number of smaller search engines, with new search engines being designed and added regularly. If you focus on submitting to the major search engines and providing all the key ingredients of a searchable website, the smaller search engines will find you as well.

If your website contains a Sitemap, the Sitemap file should also be submitted to the major search engines. This allows the search engines a quick roadmap to finding all the pages on your website. You will need to create a free account with each of the three major search engines before submitting your Sitemap. Google and Bing require you to establish a Webmaster Tools account with them in order to submit a Sitemap. Yahoo! requires you to create a Site Explorer account before submitting a Sitemap. Update and resubmit your Sitemap whenever new pages are added to your website.

Local Business Listings/Google Maps

Some websites and search engines offer free local business listings. Local business listings are generally displayed as the first results after sponsored listings when someone searches for a local business. The most important local business listing to seek is with Google Places, formerly known as Google Local Business Center. One of the first steps a dental office should make in enhancing online presence is either to establish a Google Places account or to claim an existing listing that Google has created. You can get started at www.google.com/local/add. The local business center allows you to feature extensive information about your business, including a link to your website, status updates, coupons, business details, photos and a video.

A recent redesign of the way Google delivers local search results has put a greater emphasis on the Google Places' local listings, as they now appear immediately following the sponsored listings. A Google Map including these listings also appears in the right-hand column, giving searchers the opportunity to scan to find the closest dentist to their home or work location. Google Maps includes listings for businesses which have signed up for a Google Places Page. It also includes businesses which have not signed up, but which post business information on multiple sites that Google examines for relevancy. It is possible that Google will have multiple accounts created for one office if it has found variations in business name or address existing online. Duplicate listings have a negative effect and can be penalized by Google so if you discover multiple listings for your businesses, take steps to delete them.

Google's algorithm for deciding where to rank businesses on Google Maps is a bit of a mystery and Google makes attempts to keep it that way. Factors that may contribute to a higher ranking on Google Maps include: consistent business information found on multiple websites and directories throughout the web, a number of customer reviews on sites such as www.insiderpages.com and www.citysearch.com, a complete and accurate profile with Google Places, address information displayed within the first one-third of a website and a central location within your city. When adding your business information anywhere online, make sure to type the address the same way each time, including abbreviations!

Yahoo! also offers a free local business listing which can include your business name, contact information, website address, business hours and products and services. You can visit its local business center at http://listings.local.yahoo.com. Bing offers a similar local business listing with the ability to include contact information, office hours, photos, payment methods, services provided and a brief description of your practice.

Links, Links and More Links

In researching website search engine optimization, every article I encounter points to having numerous quality links as the most important factor in achieving high search rankings! A website backlink, or inbound link, is quite simply a link from another website or web page to a page on your website. Search engines view backlinks as an indication that others have found the content on your website to be worthwhile. A link can be described as a vote of confidence in your website. Remember, your website should contain content that would attract others to link to it. Providing valuable content for which consumers may be searching facilitates link building to the pages within your site.

Expanding the number of links to your website should be a continual process achieved by researching possible quality link sources and adding link-worthy content. Your goal should be to build links to all the pages within your website, not just to the home page. A common mistake is to share only the URL to the home page of your website. A better practice is to share a link to pages within your website or blog, writing a description of the information on that page. In analyzing the quality of a website, search engines look for a large number of links to pages throughout a website, not just to the home page.

Building a large number of links to your site can be time consuming. Many companies offer this service, but beware of a large number of scams and ineffective practices within this sector of the industry. Practices such as link-farming can cause you to backslide in your optimization efforts, as the major search engines will penalize your website for these practices. Each search engine has different and ever-changing practices for how they assign importance to links. These practices depend upon numerous factors beyond the understanding a dentist typically requires in order to enhance a website's ranking. This process reminds me of the seemingly random way in which a credit reporting agency arrives at an individual's credit score.

The most valuable links are those relevant to your subject matter and those appearing on a page with a high Page Rank. Page Rank is an indicator that Google uses to quantify its perceived importance of a particular web page. Page Rank is becoming devalued over time, but it is still considered when indexing sites. Your website will even gain some improvement in SEO from less relevant sites which link to you, so brainstorm every possible avenue for links and do not hesitate to ask friends to link to your site. Your website statistics should demonstrate which links are regularly providing traffic to your site.

Be cautious about the links that you post on your own site. Ensure that the links are to relevant websites, not just to promote your friends. Two-way links (also known as reciprocal links) which link from your site to another site and from that site back to yours are not as helpful in increasing your website ranking. Many web directories offer free submission as long as you provide a reciprocal link to their directory. While you will get some benefit from this type of reciprocal linking, it may be only marginal.

The following pages will discuss several options for building links to your practice website. Creating these links can help to increase your website's ranking in search engines, drive direct traffic to your website, increase your overall online presence to ensure that patients can find you online and bring about patient referrals. While I will be discussing each of these arenas in terms of their provision of links, many of these sites are helpful in and of themselves in attracting patients to your practice.

Nofollow Tag

Before discussing where to look to build links to your website, I need to discuss an important term. Nofollow is a coding tag used by some websites to indicate to search engines that they should not use the links provided there for purposes of ranking websites. A dofollow link is one that does not contain the nofollow tag and therefore does not influence search engines to ignore it. The use of the nofollow tag by bookmarking, review and news sharing sites has increased as these sites grapple with spammers and users whose sole purpose it to promote their own site. A link with a nofollow attribute is not as valuable in building up a website's SEO, but may still provide other value.

From my research, it appears that each of the major search engines deals with the nofollow tag slightly differently. Google does not use these links for indexing or ranking, but may recognize the link if the page is already indexed. Yahoo! does not use the link for its ranking, but will index the web page once it has found it through a nofollow link. Bing does not use the link in its ranking formulas either, but it is unknown if it follows the link and then indexes the page. Ask ignores the nofollow tag altogether and considers the nofollow link as it would a dofollow link.

Some of the websites listed below do make use of the nofollow tag, as is indicated in several places. The bigger social media bookmarking sites, such as Digg, Delicious and Mixx, all use the nofollow tag. Some of the telephone directory websites and review sites, such as Yellowpages.com and Yelp.com, use the nofollow tag as well. However, some searchers go directly to these sites to find local businesses, so they may provide value beyond the website link. The major social media networks, such as Facebook and Twitter, use the nofollow tag on all outbound links from their sites. Of course, participation in Facebook and Twitter provides its own set of optimization benefits regardless of the nofollow tags.

There remain benefits to sharing a link to your website on sites that use the nofollow tag, especially if you are sharing a blog entry or web page that contains information for which others may be searching on these sites. Searchers who find relevant information on your website will be more likely to share a link to your site elsewhere, possibly in an environment without the nofollow tag. The ideal, yet time-consuming way to share links to your website in any arena is to look for natural opportunities when you are making use of these sites for other reasons.

The utilization of the nofollow tag is an ever-changing discipline, so I am hesitant to define here which sites do and which do not use the nofollow tag. An attempt to do so would be outdated almost instantly. You can find lists of websites that utilize the nofollow tag by performing an online search for this topic. There are also several blog entries containing lists of dofollow links. I use a tool for Firefox called SearchStatus which I have set to highlight all of the nofollow links on a website in order to alert me to the use of this tag.

Links through Online Web Directories

One way to build up links is to submit your URL to online web directories. You may not get much in direct traffic from these directories, but their links to your site can improve your website's indexing on the major search engines. While a small number of these directories will list your site free of charge, most require a reciprocal link for this free service.

Most directories require a paid submission with fees ranging from $5- $299. When submitting to one of these directories, make sure to find the most relevant category under which to list your website and begin the submission process from that page. The major directories will advise you that your payment does not necessarily guarantee that your site will be included in their directory. The fee is to examine your site and decide if it fits within their directory goals. This process of paying for a review rather than paying for a link is more attractive to the major search engines. If you follow each directory's instructions and submit a quality dental practice website, the chances of inclusion are extremely high for these paid reviews. If your practice is in a highly competitive market, it may be necessary to pay for inclusion in these more expensive directories. A small market practice may have great results while not being included in the major directories.

The big four online business directories are as follows:

- Yahoo! Business Directory (dir.yahoo.com) – Requires a yearly fee of $299. Provides numerous links to your website and is highly regarded by search engines when indexing sites.

- Best of the Web (botw.org) – Requires a yearly fee of $99.95. Best of the Web typically provides numerous links to your website as well.

- Business.com – Requires a yearly fee of $299. This directory is highly regarded by the search engines and may provide numerous links to your site.

- DMOZ Open Directory Project (dmoz.org) – This is a free directory that is very highly regarded by the search engines. However, it has been estimated that less than ten percent of the submissions are accepted. Follow its directions carefully to increase your chances of being included. Once you have submitted your website, there is nothing further you can do to follow-up or monitor whether your site has been examined.

Some of the smaller, less expensive web directories can provide valuable links to increase your optimization as well. I have experienced particular success with the directories listed below. The pricing was current at the end of 2009:

- Seoma.net – For a one-time fee of $15, Seoma will provide an anchor texted link to your site. After you sign up for the first submission, Seoma typically offers a discount on additional URL listings.

- InCrawler.com – Provides a basic and premium listing option. The basic option costs $24.95 and will be reviewed within seven days. The premium listing costs $49.95, is reviewed within three days and will appear above other listings.

- JoeAnt.com – Requires a one-time fee of $39.95 and promises to review your site for inclusion within two days.

- DrQuery.com – Requires a one-time fee of $9.95 and guarantees a review within 48 hours.

- Turnpike.net – Free service and the links are recognized by Yahoo! and Google.

- Hotfrog.com – Provides a free business listing, along with a link to your website.

Links through Dentistry Specific Directories

Several online directories specific to dentistry provide a search service for patients to find a local dentist or dental specialist. Unlike regular web directories, your website will receive *direct* traffic from these dental specific directories, and therefore your practice will receive direct traffic as well in the form of new patients. A few of these directories will offer a free listing, though these free listings usually do not provide a link to your website. Most directories charge a monthly fee for a business listing with a website link. This fee can range from $10/month to several hundred dollars per month.

Obviously, the most beneficial listings are those on directories that appear high in searches for your relevant keywords. These directories are usually more expensive because they are paying for their own marketing and SEO. Even directories that do not appear high in searches may be beneficial to your overall ranking if they provide a dofollow link to your practice's website for a nominal fee. Examples of some of the more relevant dentistry specific directories are as follows:

TheDentistSearch.com – This directory of United States dentists allows searchers to locate a dentist by zip code or city name and by specialty. Dentists can participate at three different levels with the lowest level costing just $10/year. At the highest level, for $99/year a dentist's listing includes practice name, dentist's name, address, phone number, office hours, procedures, a paragraph about the dentist's office, a dofollow link to the dentist's website and an opportunity to contact the dentist by email. Participating dentists are offered member's only discounts from several dental industry vendors, including discounts on dental software and toothbrushes. Members also have the opportunity to submit an article to the directory's blog. The blog article can contain links back to the dentist's own website.

DoctorOogle.com – This directory of dentists provides a review section in which patients can grade the dentist on five criteria (facilities, service, painless, results and cost). Patients are also afforded the opportunity to script a paragraph detailing their experience in the practice. In order for the reviews to be publicly available, dentists are required to have paid for an open listing or the searcher must pay a $14.95 lifetime membership fee. Dentists who pay for a listing can post pictures, articles, case descriptions and information about their practice. New patients can fill out an online appointment request form which is emailed to the dentist. Prices for an open listing vary by region, but in my suburban market it costs $70/month for a listing.

EveryDentist.com – This directory allows potential patients to search for a dentist by location, specialty or dentist's name and offers three levels of listing. A basic listing with name, address and phone number is provided free of charge. A listing that provides a link to a dentist's website costs $8/month. An enhanced listing which provides contact information, a website link, a map of the office location, office hours and an online contact form costs $35/month.

Links through Online Review Sites

Recently, there has been an increase in the number of websites that provide reviews of local businesses. On these sites, patients are given the opportunity to write a brief review of their experience in a local dental office. Google combines reviews from several sources, including Insider Pages and City Search, when displaying offices that have signed up through Google Places. These listings often appear as the first free, or non-sponsored, results next to a Google Map when a location-specific search is entered for a dentist. There is speculation that businesses with more reviews rank more highly on Google Maps.

It may feel somewhat awkward asking patients for reviews and you certainly do not want to request one from every patient who walks into your office. Guide your front office staff in asking for online reviews from established patients who have made a generous number of compliments. Make an effort to facilitate the process for a patient to write a review. After patients have agreed to write a review, my office emails them a link to the review page and instructions. The link takes them directly to my page on the review site so that they can begin the review process immediately without having to hunt around for my company.

A friend and colleague who practices in a tech-savvy area apprised me that his staff is never required to request online reviews. In his city, patients simply make this effort as part of their daily routine. My friend may argue that if I had his personality, I would not be required to ask for reviews either!

New patients who have read these positive reviews often enter our office with these accolades in mind. This benefit is tantamount to a patient being referred by another patient. The actions and attitudes of these patients, though marketed, more resemble the previously defined *Referred Patient* than they do the *Marketing Patient*. The following review sites appear high in many searches for a local dentist:

- InsiderPages.com – nofollow link
- CitySearch.com – nofollow link
- MerchantCircle.com – dofollow link
- Yahoo!Local.com – dofollow link
- GoogleMaps.com – dofollow link
- Yelp.com – dofollow link

One concern with using review sites to promote your practice is the possibility of negative reviews. Each review site handles the removal of negative reviews differently and may require significant substantiation that the review is false or malicious before permitting its removal. Some sites require removal of the entire office listing, including the positive reviews, in order to remove the negative review. It is common knowledge that people who are unhappy with a service are more likely to take the time to post a review than are those who are thrilled with the service they have received. However, if you are confident in the work you perform and how your office treats patients, I do not consider it necessary to live in fear of the possibility of a negative review.

We resist the temptation to request reviews from our entire patient population. Our policy is to specifically ask patients who have made positive comments during their visits and who already make the effort to refer other patients to us. Even with this selection process, an unhappy patient might seek out an avenue for posting a negative review. Patients finding you through an online review site are the most likely to go back to that site to post a negative review if their experience was not positive. I have signed up for a free service through Google called Google Alerts to stay abreast of when my name or practice name is appearing online. This provides the opportunity to quickly counter a negative review. Fortunately, I have yet to be required to take this action. You can sign up at www.google.com/alerts to be emailed on a daily or weekly basis whenever Google has found a new posting with your name online.

You have several options when receiving a negative review. The first step is to look into the review site's policy on removal of negative reviews and contact the website about the possibility of removing that review. Another possibility is to comment on a review. If this is an option, only take this action if you can do so in a positive manner, while keeping your temper in check. If you choose to comment on a negative review, refrain from sharing personal anecdotes about that patient's experience and choose instead to make a statement representing your desire to make every patient's experience a positive one.

When a negative review exists online, in particular if it is appearing high in search engine results for a dentist in your area, you may need to boost your online presence in other ways with the goal of pushing that site's reviews further down the list of search results. The best way to counteract a negative review is to overwhelm it with all the positive reviews your practice receives. Most logical people will see the inconsistency in the negative review, and likely attribute it to an unreasonable patient or disregard it altogether.

Links through Article Submission and Press Releases

Greater Internet visibility and website links are available when you post articles of interest and press releases online. Some e-zine article and press release sites allow you to post articles cost-free, provided that you follow its content and linking guidelines. This presents a great avenue for submitting articles about advances in dental technology that provide for less anxious dental appointments and smile reconstruction. You may choose to write an article mentioning a local charity drive you are sponsoring or a new creative promotion you are offering. When writing an article or press release, ensure that the information provided is truly news-worthy. An article or press release written solely as marketing hype will be rejected.

Anchor text, an integral component of website design, is also an important element to include in these articles or press releases. Each website has different rules and allowances regarding the use of anchor text and linking. Sign each article with your name and website. This will provide a link back to your site. Other websites or bloggers may choose to link to your article or your site if the content is helpful to them. Some article sites to consider are: www.ezinearticles.com, www.goarticles.com, www.PRWeb.com and www.free-press-release.com. PRWeb charges a fee for press releases, but offers more optimization than the free services. You can gain valuable information on ways in which to format a press release at www.PRWeb.com.

Links through Bookmarking and News Sites

The Internet is replete with social bookmarking sites, as well as article and news sharing sites. The purpose of these sites is to provide users a place to bookmark and share websites, articles and news pieces they have found interesting. Each site operates through differing formats, though many of them seem very similar. You may find several of these sites to be useful in performing online research. It is not the goal of these websites to be used to optimize other websites and suspicious activity that appears to be a veiled attempt at promotion may be penalized.

While these sites provide linking opportunities to the content found on your website and blog, your approach should be to add value to the sharing community that is using these sites to increase their knowledge and enjoyment. If you simply sign in once to post a link to your website or to every page of your site, your benefit will diminish. This is a time-consuming process that requires building links over time. I would recommend focusing on the major players first and visiting the smaller sites if you find time at a later date. Ideally, you will find a handful of bookmarking and article sharing sites that will help you outside of your SEO goals as well.

When sharing your URL and website information on one of these sites, provide an accurate account of what the web page is about using keywords, but avoiding their overuse. Use descriptive wording that makes contextual sense, particularly in the title which may be used as anchor text for the link to your website. Remember to share links to multiple pages throughout your website, not just to the home page. Sharing links to pages containing information that consumers may be seeking (like children's dental health and cosmetic dentistry) is more likely to benefit your website optimization efforts.

An online search for bookmarking sites will return an extensive list. Since many of these websites now use the nofollow tag, committing valuable time submitting your website link to each of these sites may not prove fruitful. Bear in mind, this is not the intended purpose of these sites so your efforts may even be penalized or ignored. I have found value in submitting links to pages within my websites and blog to Mixx.com, Digg.com and Reddit.com, even though they employ the nofollow tag. The following sites do not currently use the nofollow tag: Propeller.com, Technorati.com, Searchles.com and Folkd.com.

Links through Question and Answer Forums

The major Q and A forums are Yahoo! Answers (www.answers.yahoo.com), Wiki Answers (www.wiki.answers.com) and Askville (www.askville.amazon.com), though there are countless others. These types of websites often allow you to post answers to questions, along with a link to your site, either in your signature or source list. Since these websites are global in nature, the chances of a local searcher discovering your answer and thereby deciding to appoint as a new patient in your practice are similar to those of winning the lottery. While these websites can serve to increase your overall online presence, their main benefit is in their potential to provide links to your website. You may find useful information on these sites as well. Personally, I have posted a variety of questions and received overall helpful information on these forums. However, you may be surprised by how many offensive and uneducated answers appear.

Answer forum websites typically require membership and some level of participation before allowing you to post a URL link. When building up your participation level, you do not need to focus solely on answering dental-related questions. If you are an avid runner or golfer, seek out questions concerning these disciplines. If you are a pundit in another topic or hobby, you may choose to answer those questions as well. However, a link to your dental practice website placed in the sources section when answering a question about golfing has the chance of being removed and possibly penalized, so save your linking for more relevant topics.

URL links are typically posted within the sources section, but certain websites permit you to post a URL within the context of your answer. This process can cannibalize your time and is certainly not the place to start your optimization and link building efforts. If you choose to participate in these types of forums, I recommend initiating the process with a single website in order to build up your participation level and establish the ability to post URL links. Yahoo!Answers seems to dominate the industry and questions here are often indexed and may rank highly in searches.

Links through Blog Comments

Posting comments on blogs can provide an easy opportunity for links to a website. Most blog comment formats allow for a link within your profile information. The comment is displayed with your name and a link to your website. Relevant comments made on dental-related blogs are typically the most helpful, but comments on unrelated blogs may still provide valuable website links. If you commonly read blogs or online articles, take a few minutes to leave a pertinent comment which will enhance the blog and thereby provide a link to your website.

Increasing Your Online Presence through Telephone Directory Websites

Each of the leading national telephone directories has its own website equivalent. The major players in telephone directory websites are www.superpages.com, www.yellowpages.com and www.switchboard.com. Costs and advantages of paid advertising on these sites vary by region and company. Most of the links provided by telephone directory websites are tagged as nofollow, so they will not add greatly to your website's ranking. However, they may be beneficial in attracting patients who go directly to these sites rather than perform online searches to find local businesses.

One could argue (and believe me the sales reps from these companies will argue) that you should have a paid listing with these companies. I have found the cost of being on page one of these directories to be too cost-prohibitive in my area. The quoted cost to my practice is higher because I choose not to advertise in the local telephone book publication. I do subscribe, however, at a lower monthly rate and realize a small amount of consistent website traffic from this listing. Each year, a handful of new patients to my practice list it as a referral source as well.

I recently decided to cancel my listings on some of the major phone directory websites, as I received only a minimal number of new patients from these sources. I had subscribed at the lowest level so I cannot attest to whether a greater expenditure would have yielded enhanced results.

Pay Per Click Advertising versus Organic Search Results

Organic, or natural, search results are free listings of websites that appear after a search because of their relevance to the words typed into the search bar. These listings come as a result of the search engines deeming them as most worthwhile for the searcher's interest. All information outlined in this chapter to this point has been in the context of increasing your online presence in organic search results. Organic listings often appear after the paid sponsored listings when a search is entered, yet commonly attract the most attention from searchers.

In contrast to organic search results, pay per click campaigns charge advertisers a previously budgeted amount each time a searcher clicks on or views an advertisement. This click will take the searcher directly to your website. Most companies offering pay per click advertising allow advertisers to pay either based upon clicks through to their website or based upon the number of impressions, which is the number of times an ad is viewed. Pay per click advertisements appear at the top, side and bottom of the search results page and are listed as sponsored results. Though the placement of these ads is designed to catch the eye, the literature confirms that most searchers completely ignore these sponsored sections and are drawn instead to the organic search results listings.

Eightfold Logic, a web analytics company that focuses on search results statistics, issued findings of an overall analysis of the greater than 5,000 websites it tracks. [37] This report found that searchers are 8.5 times more likely to click on an organic search result than on a pay per click ad when searching for the same keywords. Greater than 80% of the search engine marketing budgets of the websites studied was spent on pay per click campaigns, while just over 10% was spent on organic search engine optimization. The results of this study clearly display the backward logic employed by most companies when allocating funds to improve Internet visibility. More information regarding similar studies and Eightfold Logic's analytics packages can be found at www.EightfoldLogic.com.

Experienced Internet searchers know that sponsored listings are paid advertisements. Sponsored listings, therefore, can be viewed by some as less trustworthy than organic listings. Numerous studies have shown that up to 85% of users completely ignore the sponsored listings. Considering this overwhelming percentage, it may behoove companies to spend more of their marketing dollars on enhancing organic search results, and less perhaps on paid advertising.

While increasing your website's organic search engine rankings is the most important vehicle to achieving Internet marketing success, pay per click advertising may be beneficial in the elementary stages of building your online presence. It can take months for your well-optimized website to climb in organic search engine rankings. A pay per click campaign may help attract new patients while your efforts to optimize your website are gaining traction. If your initial budget is limited, pay per click campaigns permit you to start online advertising with no long-term contract or significant up-front expense. Pay per click campaigns can also be beneficial for advertising a limited time discount or special event in your office. A truncated campaign can also be employed to encourage patients to take advantage of year-end insurance benefits or summertime appointment availability for children.

Each of the major search engines provides pay per click services. The overall system varies among providers, but they all allow you to select a daily or monthly budget, a maximum amount you are willing to pay per click or impression and which keywords you want to trigger your advertisement. Each pay per click company offers helpful instruction tools which explain how to get started with pay per click advertising on its search engine. There are no long-term contracts and you can increase your allotment or cancel at any time.

If you elect to hire a company to manage your pay per click campaign, your cost per click will be greater than if you choose to supervise this portion of your Internet advertising on your own. These management companies may mandate a much higher budget than a practice in a smaller market will ever need. A more conservative approach in terms of time and expense is to manage your pay per click campaigns in house. After the initial learning process, a smaller amount of time is required to monitor and maintain these programs.

Initially, you may need to experiment with the maximum pay per click bid and your monthly budget allotments in order to ensure adequate visibility. The search engines can provide you an estimate of how much a particular keyword or phrase should cost. When getting started with pay per click, we established our bid in accordance with that estimate. Fear of spending too much money in any given month caused us to initially set our maximum bid too low. Our insufficient maximum bid and monthly budget was causing our ad not to run at all, or to appear lower within the advertised section. We increased our maximum bid and monthly budget to generate more traffic, yet avoided increasing our true overall cost by never exceeding our monthly budget.

Information about the major search engines' pay per click campaign programs is available as follows:

Company Name	Campaign Name	URL
Google	Ad Words	http://adwords.google.com
Yahoo!*	Yahoo! Sponsored Search	http://searchmarketing.yahoo.com
Bing	Microsoft Advertising	http://adcenter.microsoft.com
Ask	Ask Sponsored Listings	http://sponsoredlistings.ask.com

*Yahoo! and Microsoft have recently formed an alliance to manage both of their advertising campaigns through the Microsoft adCenter. The timeline for this merger is still unknown, though they hope to have the transition complete before the holiday season of 2010. The Yahoo! link provided above may direct you to Microsoft's adCenter.

Some of the major search engines' programs allow your ads to be run on their content networks. The content network is a series of websites that allow sponsored listings to be run on their sites. Google's content network includes About.com, nytimes.com and FoodNetwork.com. If you choose to allow your ads to run on these content network sites, the ads will appear on pages with content that may not have any relevance to dentistry. You can establish a separate maximum bid for content network ads and to some degree control the geographical regions in which they are shown. Running content network ads has not yielded a significant volume of new patients in my practice. Most of our patients find us through performing a search on a major search engine.

The importance of long tail keywords also applies to keywords chosen for pay per click advertising. If you practice in a market with heightened competition for keywords for a local dentist, adding more long tail keywords to the list of words that will trigger your ads may become necessary. Selecting *broad match* with Google or *advanced match* with Yahoo! will cause your ad to appear in searches for keywords that are similar, but not exactly specific, to the keywords you have chosen. This practice requires monitoring to assure that you are not paying for irrelevant clicks. When opting in for the broader match options, utilizing the *negative match* or *exclusions* feature helps to filter out words that you desire not to trigger your ads.

Google's Keyword Tool can help you determine which keywords might be valuable to include in a pay per click campaign and which keywords will provide strong competition. A similar tool has been designed by www.KeywordSpy.com. Through a free trial, you can search by domain name or keyword to learn more about keyword competition in your area. KeywordSpy reports keyword specific data regarding overall monthly search volume, number of pay per click clients and ads competing for each keyword, average cost-per-click for a keyword, number of websites competing for organic placement for each keyword and a list of related keywords. KeywordSpy even displays the actual ads being used for specific keywords, and offers a paid membership that includes more advanced research and continual tracking of your competition.

Each pay per click campaign distributor provides statistics on which keywords are triggering your ads, the average position in which your ads appear and which keywords are leading to click-throughs. Website statistics also provide insight into whether a pay per click campaign is leading traffic to your website and what these searchers do once on your website. What is difficult to measure is the return on investment generated from these types of campaigns, since ROI is based upon acquiring new patients who appoint for treatment. For e-commerce companies selling products directly on their website, it is much easier to assess the ROI of these campaigns. As dentists, our patients more typically report, "I found you online," rather than, "I clicked on your pay per click ad while searching for the keywords *Denver dentist*."

One approach to determining the benefit of pay per click campaigns is directing your pay per click ads to a specific landing page of your website or to a secondary website which displays a different phone number than your main line. If your office has a rollover line or more than one phone line, you could direct the searchers who land on this page to call the secondary number. Phone calls that go directly to this secondary number will most likely be attributable to your pay per click campaign.

Since pay per click campaigns allow you to pause or cancel your campaigns at any time, it may be useful to test their benefit by running the ads for a month and then freezing the campaign for a month. If during the paused month your website statistics and new patient referral reports show a significant drop in traffic to your site and decrease in the number of new patients from Internet searches, you can assume that the pay per click campaign had been beneficial. You may choose to re-initiate these campaigns immediately or continue to monitor your website traffic and new patient appointments while your campaign is paused. We recently froze our pay per click campaigns. My primary website has continued to experience an increase in traffic even while the pay per click campaign has been inactive. This is likely the result of my accelerated efforts in social media marketing and link building.

Even if you elect to take part in a pay per click campaign, it is imperative that your efforts to optimize your website remain a continual process. Ultimately, continued efforts to optimize your website through content and link building, which boost your organic search results ranking, may prove to be a better long-term investment than pay per click advertising. Actively pursue the goal of increasing your website's organic results ranking. Consider using pay per click to supplement visibility in times when your website is not appearing on the first page of results.

Website Updates and Monitoring

Adding fresh content, in the form of quotes, articles, pictures and supplementary pages will cause the search engines to take greater notice of your website. Search engines track how frequently a website's content changes in order to determine how often the search engine should examine the site. After having implemented all the strategies previously outlined, you would be remiss to ignore the necessity to add new content on a regular basis. New *Before and After* photographs, quotes from satisfied customers and articles from your most recent newsletter provide the easiest format for adding new content. If you have a Dental Health Guide section, consider adding new articles on a regular basis.

Adding fresh content through incorporating a blog into your website domain can enhance your optimization efforts tremendously. Updating your blog on a regular basis promotes more frequent crawling and indexing of your website by the search engines as well as more searchable content for your site. As in other areas of your website, new content options for your blog may include posting *Before and After* photos, patient testimonials and newsletter articles. While these items can be incorporated into your blog, ensure that you promote them on other pages of your website as well.

Research Your Appearance in Search Engine Results

Periodically, I perform searches for a dentist in my area on Yahoo! and Google to ascertain where my websites are placing in search results. I experiment with a variety of terms that may be employed by a user searching for a dentist in my area. This simple research technique, along with the review of my website statistics and Google Webmaster Tools account, provide the data I need to make decisions on improvements and additions to my websites.

To sustain the optimization of your website, adding fresh content and monitoring your website's presence in the major search engines needs to be performed on a regular basis. The difference between being #1 and #5 in relevant keyword searches is dramatic. We routinely have patients specifically tell us that they chose our practice because our website appeared first when they searched for a dentist. When we took a reprieve from website optimization and focused on other projects in the office, my website soon began dropping in the rankings and new patient phone calls stalled significantly. The principle cannot be overemphasized that optimization is not a one-and-done event.

Chapter 26

Social Media Marketing

What is Social Media?
The term Social Media is broadly used to define websites that exchange information while interacting with the user and allowing the user to interact with others. There are multiple genres within the general definition of social media including:
- Blogs
- Forums. These fit within the broadest definitions of social media and were the beginning of the social media trend. The forums on DentalTown.com are a great resource for dentists.
- Social Network Websites. Examples are Facebook, Twitter and MySpace.
- Social Business Network Websites. Examples are ZoomInfo and LindkedIn.
- Social News Websites. Examples are Digg, Reddit and Mixx.
- Social Bookmarking Websites. Examples are Delicious, Technorati and StumbleUpon. These sites allow you to bookmark articles of interest.
- Photo and Video Sharing Websites. Examples are Flickr, Vimeo and YouTube.

Can Social Media Participation Benefit Your Dental Practice?
I often hear business owners utter the following objections to and inquiries about social media as it relates to their trade: "I don't have time to mess with social media!" "How is social media really going to help

my practice?" "Isn't Facebook just for teenagers?" "Will anyone really care about my status updates or tweets?" "How would I adequately establish a true measure of the return on investment from social media marketing?" "Could social media venues damage my credibility in some way?" There are many justifications offered to avoid exploring what social media can do to promote a dental practice. Personally, I have asked most of the questions listed above and avoided entering the social media circus until recently. My foray into social media for my practice has already begun to reap rewards, so I encourage you to put aside your reservations and read on.

Once you have an established website and are making efforts to increase its search engine optimization, social media is the next step in enhancing your online visibility and increasing the optimization of your dental practice website. Some of these sites can offer more than just marketing opportunities. They may provide a rich source of articles, comments and posts that can assist you with decisions relating to the operation of your dental practice. With so many avenues to explore, social media can be an overwhelming time siphon if you fail to start simply and maintain reasonable goals. However, the benefits of free marketing, links to your website, frequent communication with current patients and the ability for patients to share about your office with their peers make exploring social media worthwhile for dentists.

Social media participation allows you to interact with your patients and potential new patients on a daily or weekly basis rather than merely when they visit your website. If you have an Internet-savvy staff member managing these efforts, your practice will realize even greater benefits. Do not expect that your initial social media efforts will be met with a deluge of new patients beating down your office door. Your social media goals must include retaining patients, affording patients the ability to share about you with others, making patients feel more a part of your dental family by interacting with you online and keeping your practice and your patients' dental needs at the forefront of their minds. It may take a few weeks or even months before you realize your first new patient appointing as a direct result of social media marketing. However, the internal marketing connections made through social media can be extremely valuable even though they are impossible to quantify with precision.

Where Should You Begin with Social Media?

It is easy to become overwhelmed by the vast opportunities awaiting you in the arenas of social media and Internet marketing. Try not to believe it mandatory to participate in every possible avenue and therefore feel that you lack adequate time to do any of it. My business manager fell prey to this trap upon initiating our social media marketing campaign. Her crowded schedule did not permit the exploration and maximization of all the options available with social media. She found it best to start with one or two outlets with which she had the most comfort and concentrate on building those first. This approach helped her avoid the pitfalls of giving cursory attention to all of the social media sources, becoming inundated and quitting.

Maintaining social media efforts can require plentiful time and should be entered into with a plan of action. Do not expect to get any benefit if you set up a Facebook page, ask patients to become fans, post a couple comments and then sit back and become complacent. Likewise, with Twitter, you will need to actively tweet, follow others and interact with them there. We have found following dentists on Twitter to be highly beneficial and more professional than less sophisticated methods of tweeting. Following patients on Twitter has also yielded positive results. A current patient recently tweeted, "I love that my dentist is on Twitter!" You may find yourself more comfortable participating in a business network such as LinkedIn rather than tweeting. Determine where you are most at ease participating and jump in.

Much of the roadmap to Internet optimization and social media participation outlined in this text results from strategies that have worked in my practice. The path I followed to increase my online presence began with establishing a practice website and working to enhance it. An additional website was then added to focus on my cosmetic dentistry cases. After instigating a plan to maintain my search engine optimization efforts, I began writing a blog which is now incorporated into my primary website.

I then established a Facebook business page and a Twitter account. Recently, I explored the options available through social news and bookmarking sites by signing up for free accounts with the major sites and posting links to articles on my blogs and websites there. I follow certain topics such as dental health and exercise on these bookmarking sites as well. These articles become sources to share on my blog, in patient e-newsletters and through Twitter and Facebook. I have become more active on the forums at DentalTown and have found useful information for managing and promoting my dental practice. I also maintain a LinkedIn, HotFrog and ZoomInfo account.

My business manager keeps me current with my social media trends. Social media can be a huge time vacuum and I would much rather be active outdoors and with my family than sitting in front of a computer all day. We sometimes joke that I am a "rock-star" since I have a personal assistant helping me with my social media efforts. This good fortune has allowed me to delve more deeply into the domain of social media than pursuing it on my own would have permitted. My business manager helps brain-storm, create and edit content for the patient blog, updates for Facebook and tweets for Twitter. She keeps up with local events and researches articles that may be of interest to my patients. While it is not absolutely necessary to have a staff member do this for you, it can serve to keep an employee productive during slow times in the office or when patients fail appointments.

Out-sourcing your social media marketing by hiring a company to manage it for you is an option for the busy dental practice. However, this seems to run contrary to the entire purpose of social media, which is to personally interact with others. My strong opinion is that social media should be supervised within your office. Patients are choosing to interact with *you*, not a consulting company, through these sources. It may be beneficial to seek assistance in establishing your goals and personalizing the look of your social media accounts, but these things can all be handled rather easily and efficiently on your own.

More and more large corporations are hiring for the position of Social Media Director. CEOs and upper-level managers of these companies are commonly active on social media networks and use them to communicate with their clientele. It is now common to see such established companies as American Airlines and CNBC advertising their presence on Facebook and Twitter and inviting you to become a fan and to follow them. Clearly, the highly compensated marketing directors of these major corporations have identified value in this space and are unwilling to leave a significant return on investment on the table. You would be wise as a health care professional to follow their lead.

To maximize the benefits of social media, it is important to be active on most of these outlets at least on a weekly basis. Our weekly to-do calendar includes the following:

- Post one or two blog entries on the patient blog. Respond to comments on the blog. Submit new blog articles to directories and social media sites.

- Post three or more tweets. Ideally post once a day. Search for local Twitter users to follow. Respond to interactions on Twitter.

- Post two or three Facebook updates. Respond to interactions on Facebook.

- Scan our subscribed blogs and forums and make comments accordingly. You can spend countless hours here, but you need not. This can be done during down time or when searching for information to share in a newsletter or on your blog.

- Search Digg, Reddit and Mixx for articles that may be helpful to our patients or to us in terms of managing the practice.

- Maintain a list of items to include in our monthly patient e-newsletter.

Keep in mind that all these things do not necessarily get accomplished each week, but the list is a good reminder of the importance of keeping things current. The first three items are of highest priority, as blogs, Facebook and Twitter accounts quickly become irrelevant if not kept up to date. Initially, it may feel like you are laboring to brainstorm a relevant tweet or status update, but it will soon become habitual and you will find yourself thinking, *That would make a great tweet.*

Blogging

Writing a blog can provide myriad benefits to your practice including:

- Providing dental health information and updates to your current patients,

- Attracting new patients who find your blog in Internet searches or who have been referred to your blog by a current patient,

- Providing links to articles on your website,

- Providing fresh content to your website when the blog has been incorporated into your website domain and

- Creating an opportunity for your followers on social media outlets such as Facebook and Twitter to learn more about you when you post a link to your new blog entry.

Maintaining blogs is a simple and free way to expand your web presence. There are numerous free options for blogging, but the most common venues are Google Blogger, WordPress and TypePad. All of Google Blogger's features are free, while WordPress and TypePad provide a free basic service with paid upgrades for greater customization. You can accomplish most of what is necessary through WordPress' free service, but TypePad's service is very limited, offering only one template choice. TypePad's paid upgrade is available for only $4.95/month, making it a worthwhile consideration.

When searching online for blog service recommendations, you will encounter diehard fans of each of these three major blog services. You will also discover loyalists to other lesser known blogging services, such as LiveJournal. The following chart demonstrates basic information regarding the three most used blogging services:

Blogging Services	WordPress	TypePad	Google Blogger
Free Services	Offers most of its services free of charge	Very limited free service	All services are free
Paid Upgrades	Video, additional storage and templates	$4.95/month for unlimited storage and extra features	
Statistics	Large variety of statistics provided	TopTenReview considers Type Pad to have the best statistics available	Must add 3rd Party option for statistics
Ease of Use	Fairly easy for a beginner to initiate, offers advanced features	Overall, simple to use with some advanced features	Very simple to set up
Customer Support	Accepts emails	Accepts emails	Does not accept emails
Help Options	FAQ, Forums and Tutorials	FAQ, Forums and Tutorials	FAQ, Forums and Tutorials
Submissions	Google and Technorati	Google, Technorati and FeedBurner	Google
Unique Features	Can create an entire website	Photo Album Gallery	Simple to install AdSense

My main practice website has incorporated a WordPress blog. I was able to add the blog component through WordPress to my website on my own through the use of the control panel provided by my web host. WordPress offers more options to those with extensive website coding knowledge, but also provides many simple features to incorporate for those who work outside the I.T. industry. I have found it difficult to navigate at times, primarily because of the vast options available to enhance a WordPress blog. However, once you learn the basics, it is relatively easy to maintain and customize your WordPress blog.

WordPress is extremely popular, and therefore many online resources are available to help if you encounter uncertainty. Another unique feature of WordPress is that it allows you to design an entire website using its software.

What Should Your Blog Include?

Your blog can be a combination of information for current patients and marketing to new patients. Use your blog to establish your expertise, but also to show your personality. Avoid establishing a tone of preaching dental health, as this may frighten potential patients who may deem you unapproachable or expect to be met with lectures when entering your office. It is important to write with your reader in mind, remembering that most people viewing your blog did not attend dental school and are more interested in health tips than detailed information about teeth.

A dental blog should include general health and dental health articles, as well as patient testimonials. Since the topic of dentistry is not quite as exciting for outsiders, we realize that few people will be quick to follow a blog comprised solely of dental practice promotion and dental health snippets. For a broader appeal, consider including healthy recipes, health and wellness tips, cartoons or funny stories and details of activities in the local area. I recently posted a blog entry about holiday activities in my area. This provided great keywords for the surrounding cities, increased traffic to my blog and consequently to my practice website.

Though dentists may find it easier to write blog entries about dental health and local activities than about self-promotion, blogs must contain both types of entries in order to be effective. We reference a list of benefits to patients and unique features of our office to serve as a springboard for ideas inspiring practice promotion blog entries. We have found it useful to maintain a list of patient frequently asked questions as a source for blog postings as well.

You can involve your patients by asking them for input on what type of blog entries might interest them. Patients may enjoy contributing recipes and event ideas. Consider featuring a new cosmetic case description and patient testimonial alongside *Before and After* photos once each month. One of our most popular newsletter features is a patient profile. This idea can be incorporated into a blog as well. If you already offer a patient newsletter or e-newsletter, you have ready-made blog topics. Examine your newsletter archive and begin to post relevant articles from former issues. Establish Google Alerts (www.google.com/alerts) on phrases such as *dental hygiene* and *dental health*. These alerts will provide references as fodder for new blog topics and articles to which you may link in a blog entry.

Moderating Blog Comments

Blogging services provide the ability to moderate comments and to install an anti-spam tool. I highly recommend that you install an anti-spam comments tool such as Akismet and approve all comments before permitting them to be published. The vast majority of comments I have received have been spam efforts to provide a link to another site. Some of these are quite obvious as they contain random numbers and letters and are most likely automatically generated. Other comments are disguised as more natural. I received one comment on a short blog entry regarding the location of my patient e-newsletter archive which stated, "I usually don't comment, but your amazing writing led me to want to comment." This comment was posted on a three sentence blog entry pointing patients to my e-newsletter archive; not exactly my best piece of creative writing. Other comments are blatantly rude and most likely posted by some bored soul with too much time and too little social life.

I have chosen to moderate all comments before publishing them. Certain blogging services offer the ability to permit all comments from a previously approved blogger to be published immediately. I avoid this approach as someone can easily make a positive, on topic comment on the first post and then attempt to slip through a link or inappropriate comment in the next post. Moderating comments is an efficient process of reading the comment and then choosing to publish, delete or label it as spam. Your blog is a professional outlet and moderating comments will help you to maintain your professionalism.

Cross-Promoting Your Blog, Website and Social Media Efforts

You can link easily to your blog from your website, but a better choice is to add the blog to the website domain. If you blog regularly, this will provide fresh content on your website and encourage the search engines to crawl and take note of your site more often. If a searcher enters your site through the blog page, there will be easy access to the rest of your website and all that you have to offer patients. An integrated blog provides the searcher/potential new patient immediate access to your site without having to hunt around for the link.

Dentists taking advantage of free social media marketing opportunities such as Facebook and Twitter should alert fans, friends and followers of the new blog and link to it from these social media sites. Plug-in options that can be added to your blog allow you to do this automatically. Updates will be sent to Twitter and Facebook notifying your followers of a new blog entry. The more you take advantage of automatic updates like these, the less time will be required in keeping these sources current. From a time-management perspective, this principle cannot be overemphasized.

Take advantage of linking through your blog to articles on your website and social media memberships. If your blog is not integrated within your website, include a link to your site in an important links section on your blog and in your profile. It is also worthwhile to link to articles or cases highlighted on your website using anchor text. The major networking sites will create a box to add to your blog indicating that you have an account with them and how to find you there. A blog can include an option to display your latest activity on Twitter and Facebook.

WordPress' default setting is set to block your blog and links shared within it from search engines. If you have a WordPress blog, one of your first steps is to adjust this setting. Go to *Settings*, choose *Privacy* and select *I would like my blog to be visible to everyone, including search engines* (such as Google, Bing and Technorati) *and archivers*.

While I have accounts established with most of the major social media sites, I elect not to inundate my patients with a barrage of requests to *Link with me here*, and *Follow me here*. I simply utilize the back of my business card to introduce my Facebook and Twitter information, as well as the web address of my patient blog. My e-newsletters often highlight blog entries and invite patients to join me on Facebook and Twitter. My website displays my Facebook and Twitter status with links to become a fan and to follow me. I have a sign in my waiting room informing patients of my Facebook and Twitter accounts, as well as my blog.

What is an RSS Feed?

If you are taking the time to write a blog, make sure that readers can easily choose to follow it by subscribing to an RSS feed of your blog. RSS stands for *Real Simple Syndication*, and allows readers to subscribe to your blog postings. Subscribers to your RSS feed will receive a list of your latest blog entries when viewing their RSS reader. RSS readers, such as Bloglines, MyYahoo and Google Reader allow their users to follow the headlines of many sites and blogs in one place. Rather than being obligated to visit each individual site or blog, users can scan their reader listings for any interesting articles they may want to peruse. When establishing your blog, be sure to prominently display how readers can subscribe to your RSS feed. Depending upon which blogging service you use, you may need to add an RSS subscribe feature.

There are a variety of options for allowing readers to share your blog posts with others. WordPress has numerous plug-ins that provide a bar with share buttons which can be included at the end of each blog posting. Readers can click on *Email* or *Favorites* or a variety of icons representing the major players in social media to share the article. *Add This* and *AddtoAny* are two of the more popular options for providing a share button. Explore all options to facilitate the process for readers to follow your blog posts and share them with others.

Submitting your blog's RSS feed to blog directories is a valuable step in optimizing your blog and website. You may not experience a large number of local readers (or a large number of any readers) subscribing to your blog as a result, but these submissions provide links to your blog, and therefore to your website, if your blog is part of your website domain. You can submit your blog's RSS feed to a variety of free websites. For a list of these websites, most of them free, visit http://www.masternewmedia.org/rss/top55/.

Facebook

Facebook now purports to serve over 500 million users. Greater than half of these users are logged into Facebook each day. The fastest growing demographic on Facebook is 55 years and older, dispelling the contention that Facebook is merely for today's youth. My 88-year-old grandmother recently skewed these demographics northward when she established a profile on Facebook.

Each day over 10 million users become fans of one of the businesses supporting a page on Facebook. Most likely, you are among the 500 million users familiar with Facebook, but you may not know how to harness its power to benefit your dental practice. The following section outlines the basics of how to capitalize on the Facebook platform to grow your dental practice. It may be a considerable oversight in today's technology-driven society to leave such an abundant marketing resource untapped. I can imagine no more cost-effective way to reach such a substantial target population. A return on investment is almost assured, as the investment component of this equation is limited to the small amount of labor you invest in its maintenance.

Benefits of a Facebook Business Page

Facebook offers three platforms: a personal profile in which you become *friends* with others on Facebook, a business page in which Facebook users can become *fans* of your business and a group page. It is possible to maintain both a personal profile and a business page, but I have adopted only the business page format for the following reasons:

- A business fan page more easily maintains a professional platform. I considered that establishing a personal profile may require me to accept my patients' friend requests, and monitor closely what friends outside my dental practice posted on my wall. Personal pages can take such a relaxed tone, sometimes bordering on the unprofessional. By supporting only a business page, I have more confidence that my friends and acquaintances will observe professionalism.

- There is no guilt in promoting your business on a fan page. Maintaining a profile with *friends* can engender discomfort when using status updates to spread the word about one's business. On a business page, those who follow you (your fans) have chosen to follow your business and are happy to receive these kinds of status updates. If they are not, they can discontinue their fan status.

- This format is available to the general public, even to those without a Facebook account. My business page on Facebook is found at www.facebook.com/ofallondentist, which can be accessed by the general public, even those who do not have a Facebook account. In order to interact or leave comments on a business page, the user is required to establish an account. However, anyone can read the content on your page without signing in to an account.

- Facebook allows businesses to choose a vanity URL. Once you have established 25 fans, the Facebook fan page platform allows you to create a *vanity URL*. My URL, www.facebook.com/ofallondentist, is considered a vanity URL because it facilitates directing others to my Facebook page. As soon as you achieve 25 fans, be sure to sign up for a vanity URL, preferably one that identifies your location. Be deliberate when selecting your vanity URL, as you will not be allowed to change it.

- Search engines are now indexing Facebook pages. Google has begun to include Facebook fan pages in search results for local businesses. Search engines collect information from websites across the Internet and index, or list, sites that are relevant to a searcher's request. Search engine indexing of Facebook pages affords tremendous optimization advantages. This is particularly true for those who ensure that business pages and status updates contain numerous local and industry-specific keywords.

- An unlimited number of fans can be updated all at once. A business fan page is allowed an unlimited number of followers and is capable of sending updates to all of its followers simultaneously through a status update.

The one business page disadvantage, though not meriting reconsideration of the fan page platform, is that you can only interact with your fans on your page. You cannot post anything to your fans' Facebook walls. However, you can send individual fans a private message through Facebook.

Facebook Basics

Though the basic elements of Facebook are common knowledge to many, I define them here for those not yet involved in social media. A Facebook status update is used to share whatever you wish with your friends (in the case of a personal profile) or fans (on a business page). These status updates become a part of your fans' *news feed*. Therefore, when they log in to Facebook they will see all of the recent activity and status updates on their friends' and fans' pages within this feed.

We try to update our status two or three times each week and take this opportunity to share about a new blog entry or an interesting article. We do not strictly post articles and updates relating to dental health, but include a variety of topics that may be appealing to others. We provide information about local events and personal thoughts on things such as our weather, professional sports teams, healthy living and holiday plans. We also try to ask questions to generate some discussion and interaction on the page.

A standard Facebook fan page contains six tabs. The *wall* displays your status updates, as well as comments your fans have made on these updates. The Info tab allows you to post your contact information, as well as links to your website. The Photos tab allows you to post pictures of your office and staff. You can also post *Before and After* photos of patients here, but be sure to obtain written permission before doing so. Under the Reviews tab, your fans can write a review of your office. You can delete this tab if you are concerned about negative reviews. Under the Discussions tab, you can initiate a topic for your fans to discuss. Lastly, the Links tab will keep track of any links to other websites that you have posted within your status updates. You can choose to delete the Photos, Reviews, Discussions and Links tabs. Facebook also allows the easy addition of tabs for sharing Events, Notes and Videos.

The appearance of fan pages can be customized through thousands of Facebook applications found at www.facebook.com/apps. There is even an option to add website coding to your Facebook page in order to customize the look. While you can invest appreciable time experimenting with these applications to customize your page and create a more worthwhile experience for your fans, do not feel compelled to immediately do so. The abundant options should not intimidate you nor prevent you from taking the first step of simply creating a business page that can be customized later if you so choose. As with all applications of social media in your practice, try not to succumb to paralysis through analysis. Simply get your page live and learn how to maximize its presence over time.

New Patients through Facebook Participation

Not long after establishing our Facebook fan page, we began to receive very positive feedback from patients who visited our Facebook page and became fans. Many patients have a Facebook profile, making it easy for them to become fans of our page. Updates appearing in our fans' news feeds keep our practice and their dental care needs more at the forefront of their mind. Participation in Facebook and other social media outlets allows patients to see the dentist in another light and perhaps to view our profession with reduced levels of anxiety. Our updates and article links provide easy opportunities for patients to share with others about our practice.

The search engine indexing of our Facebook fan page has served to enhance practice visibility among potential new patients. We have additionally realized an increased volume of traffic to the dental practice websites and blogs from links posted on Facebook. The *Info* section on Facebook allows you to post links to multiple websites, and these links consistently drive new traffic to my websites each month. Each time we write a new blog article for patients, we post an update with a link to the new entry as well. We have started very simply with Facebook, creating a basic fan page and informing patients how to access it. Through a very minor investment of time, our office has already greeted a handful of new patients having found us on Facebook.

Twitter

Twitter allows users to share whatever they would like in 140 characters or less. Twitter provides many of the same benefits as Facebook, albeit in a simpler, more expedient fashion. For a dental practice, Twitter can be used to remind patients that annual dental insurance benefits will be expiring soon or that parents should make appointments now for their children's Spring Break. Dentists who offer new patient discounts or teeth whitening specials can highlight these campaigns on Twitter through a special offer code. Twitter also affords the ability to share brief dental health tips and dental facts. As with Facebook, Twitter can be used to deliver information and to provide a link to your latest blog entry as well. Twitter permits you to share your personality and interests, helping to demonstrate that dentists are not the sadists they are often portrayed to be in movies.

The Basics of Twitter

Twitter is simple to use and an account can be maintained with relatively little time invested. Through minimal research and experimentation, you can quickly learn the basics of Twitter. If you are unfamiliar with Twitter, the following basic information will provide an overview of the protocol for getting started on Twitter. Establishing an account is simple and merely requires the input of a real name, user name, email address and password. Twitter allows you to add a photo, choose a template background or use your website as a background, add a link to your website and write a short biographical paragraph. The following chart displays the basic functions available when using Twitter, with each concept being explained in greater detail after the chart:

Twitter Function	**Definition**
Tweet	140 character message posted to your page
@	Used before a Twitter user name to interact with that user. The @ function is also used to keep track of references to you.
RT	Retweet - Referencing a copied tweet from another user
Follow	Used to receive a Twitter user's tweets in your updates
Stream	A list of tweets from users you have chosen to follow
#	Hashtag - Included before a word to help searchers keep track of references to a particular topic
Direct Message	Allows you to send a 140 character private message

The centerpiece of Twitter is called the *Tweet*, which is a statement composed of up to 140 characters. A tweet can include links to other websites or blogs, pictures or videos, provided that it is kept within the 140 character maximum. Twitter also provides a Direct Message link through which you can send a 140 character private message to another Twitter member. Direct messages are often used as a thank you and first contact with someone who has chosen to follow you on Twitter.

Many Twitter users employ a standard initial greeting direct message to send to all of their followers. It may state something similar to the following: "Thanks for the follow. Let me know if you have any questions about your dental health." While this standardized greeting allows you the opportunity to express thanks, it can create an awkward situation when being unknowingly sent to the wrong person. After following another dentist on Twitter, I received a direct message offering me $100 off a dental procedure in his Georgia dental office. No thanks.

Twitter allows you to reply to a tweet by simply clicking *Reply* next to the particular tweet. This will insert the @ symbol before the person's Twitter name and provide space for you to type your message after it. For instance, if you wish to respond to a question that AskDrLynch posted as one of his tweets, you would simply click *Reply* next to that tweet. Twitter will fill in @AskDrLynch and you then type your response after that. The benefit of the @ function is that it allows you to easily follow every reference in which someone has replied to you, re-tweeted your message or directly entered your Twitter name into a tweet. Simply click on "@Mentions" on your Twitter home page in order to view any references made to you.

If you would like to *retweet* another user's posting so that your Twitter followers can see that tweet, click *Retweet* which appears as a choice immediately after the tweet when the mouse hovers over it. This retweet will now appear in the tweet stream of all of your followers with a note above it showing that it has been retweeted by you. In the past, Twitter inserted "RT" in front of any retweets and some users still use RT when quoting another tweet. Twitter keeps record of the tweets you have retweeted as well as your tweets that have been retweeted by others. You can access this information by clicking on *Retweets* toward the top of your Twitter home page.

Twitter makes it easy to follow other users through a *Follow* icon found at the top left-hand corner of a user's page. You can search for Twitter users through the *Find People* function located at the top right-hand corner of the page. The *Search* box located at the top of each Twitter page can be used to search for specific words or topics that have been mentioned in tweets by others. The *Search* box is useful in finding local Twitter users when searching for location specific terms. For a more advanced search by location or keyword, go to http://search.twitter.com/advanced.

Another way to locate Twitter users you may wish to follow is to review the followers and following lists of other local Twitter users. In order to help others find your Twitter account, you will need to follow local Twitter users. This alerts them to your existence in this domain as well. I follow local businesses in order to keep abreast of local activities and discounts, but also to alert their social media coordinator of my existence. Following a local charity and mentioning it in a tweet earned our practice a new patient when a charity employee replied to us on Twitter that she was seeking a new dentist.

In terms of business promotion, your goal through using Twitter should be to attract local followers who may be in need of a new dentist. Many social media gurus recommend searching for and following all local Twitter users. While this is probably an intelligent business approach, I am less than comfortable following random people in my area who are using Twitter socially, and perhaps imparting the wrong impression. Keep in mind that you should not feel compelled to participate in social media in any way that makes you uneasy, even if the experts recommend it.

When you choose to follow someone, the tweet updates from that user's account will stream in a reverse chronological order on your Twitter home page. Be warned that some users like to tweet a lot! You may choose to un-follow someone at any time if your list of tweets becomes dominated by a user you are not sufficiently interested in following.

When others choose to follow us, we typically run a brief check of their recent tweets and bio information before deciding whether to reciprocate and follow them. It is important to take this step in verifying another Twitter user's content, as choosing to follow someone denotes a certain level of trust in that person. Other Twitter users can easily view who you have chosen to follow.

TrueTwit offers a validation service that requires users to enter two words in order to validate that an account is being maintained by a human, not a machine. You can elect to block a follower as well by selecting *Block* after clicking on the sunshine icon found to the right of a follower's name in your followers' list. Unfortunately, there are Twitter users who post illicit material and will ask you to view their explicit videos. The *Block* function can be employed in certain situations to maintain the professionalism of your Twitter account.

Unless you have set up a privacy barrier against access to your tweets, the information contained in tweets is open to the public without requiring a membership account. Therefore, if you tweet something, anyone can read it. For example, if you want to follow Lance Armstrong's or Alyssa Milano's frequent updates of what they are doing at any particular hour, simply go to www.twitter.com/lancearmstrong or www.twitter.com/alyssa_milano. It is not necessary for you to establish an account with Twitter in order to read their tweets. When using Twitter to promote your business, there is no reason to choose to privately protect your tweets.

Twitter Applications

If you become active in social media, free applications available through companies such as HootSuite, TweetDeck, UberTwitter and EchoFon can provide a format for keeping current with everything. HootSuite is currently free, although its website does mention investigating paid plans. Using HootSuite, you can create a list of tweets and a schedule for posting them to your Twitter account. This automates the process of posting frequent tweets. HootSuite also offers a way to manage the delivery of the stream of tweets from your followers and provides assistance in managing Facebook pages and LinkedIn accounts as well. HootSuite provides a URL shrinker which allows you to share an article or web page which have website addresses too lengthy to include within a 140 character tweet.

TweetDeck also offers tools to manage your Twitter, Facebook, MySpace and LinkedIn accounts. TweetDeck allows you to choose topics you would like to follow in *real-time* and use its service to record and share videos. A service like TweetDeck can help save time if you become highly active on Twitter. All on a single page, you can view the tweets stream of your followers, direct messages, mentions of you and recommendations for other Twitter users you may want to follow. Both HootSuite and TweetDeck are free and offer iPhone applications. EchoFon offers an application to manage your Twitter account from your iPhone, while UberTwitter allows BlackBerry users to do the same.

These sites are just a small representation of what is available to assist in the management of social media activity. Again, the sheer volume of opportunities can prove overwhelming and thwart a dentist's desire to enter this circus, but Twitter can be started and maintained quite easily and efficiently. Though your Twitter account can be managed simply, the more time you dedicate to it, the greater its potential benefits to your practice. As advised with Facebook, start out with a simple Twitter account and grow it from there as time permits.

Get Started Today and Realize the Benefits of Twitter

It may require some time with Twitter to build up a group of users who choose to *Follow* your updates. However, since your Twitter page and updates are accessible to anyone and indexed by search engines, your number of followers is not a direct reflection of how often your tweets are viewed. Having a large number of followers living outside your state carries little benefit for a local dental practice. We have primarily used Twitter to share interesting health-related articles and inform others about our blogs, Facebook page and websites. There is often valuable information to be discovered through following other local Twitter users. Garnering information about freeway bottlenecks and thereby avoiding potential traffic jams is always a nice perk when running slightly late for work.

Though our time invested in Twitter has been minimal, our practice has already realized its value. Recently, a patient following us on Twitter appointed for veneers and then shared a follow-up tweet about her positive experience in our office. While I am uncertain as to whether my Twitter presence was what brought her to the tipping point of making the appointment for treatment, I do believe it helped keep the idea in the forefront of her mind. Another patient contacted us through Twitter just this morning, indicating her need of a new dentist and inquiring about our practice location.

Late in 2009, Google and Microsoft compensated Twitter for the right to index tweets in their search engine results. This new trend may prove very beneficial to local businesses choosing to utilize Twitter, as their keyword specific tweets might soon attract attention in searches. To capitalize on the search engine indexing of tweets, be sure to include enough location-specific tweets to increase the possibility that your Twitter page will appear in searches for a local dentist.

Twitter recently launched a Promoted Tweets Program in which businesses can pay to have their tweets appear in relevant searches on Twitter. At the time this book went to press, the Promoted Tweet Program was in its infancy and few details had been disclosed. Twitter is also now considering adding a paid service to commercial Twitter accounts which will analyze the traffic to their Twitter pages.

Bookmarking and Social Media News Sites

Bookmarking sites such as Delicious.com and StumbleUpon.com offer the opportunity to build links to your website, share your website link with their users and use the bookmarks for your own personal needs. The same benefits are found in sharing your website URL on article sites such as Digg.com, Mixx.com and Reddit.com. Remember, the use of the nofollow tag on most of these sites results in a diminished value for the link. However, these sites provide other value by sharing your information with their community of users, some of whom may choose to link to you elsewhere without a nofollow tag. Since each search engine treats this tag differently, there is speculation that even nofollow links can help build your optimization efforts. A large number of social media bookmarks to a website lends it credibility.

We utilize bookmarking and news sharing sites to save and share interesting articles with colleagues and patients who might find this information helpful. When we encounter an article answering a question a patient has posed in the office, we can quickly forward the article to the patient's email address. These websites can be accessed from any computer, unlike the bookmarks section of your Internet provider which may only be accessed via your home computer. An additional benefit of these sites is the content they provide for blog entries and patient newsletters.

Photo and Video Sharing Sites

Photo and video sharing websites such as Flikr and YouTube offer the opportunity to easily and quickly share case photos and patient testimonial videos. Always obtain written consent from any patient whose image you would like to use online. Any modern camcorder can be used to capture patient testimonials, a Frequently Asked Questions segment with the dentist, an office tour or an educational video. Simple editing will be all that is needed if the process is kept simple by merely interviewing a patient or having the dentist answer a series of relevant questions. These videos can be shared within minutes on YouTube, GoogleVideo, Yahoo!Video and Truve. A link to the video or the video itself can be placed on the home page of your website or in a patient benefits or testimonial area.

If you have yet to immerse yourself in social media, filming a *Meet the Dentist* video and uploading it to YouTube is a great way to dip your toe in the water. Embed this video in your website's homepage and add it to your Google Local Business Places account for display with your Google Maps' listing. The video does not require Hollywood professionalism, but jittery camera shoots and poor lighting should be avoided. Consider having your office staff film the video or contact the audio visual department of a local university and inquire as to whether a student is in need of a project. If you have the money in your budget, a local video production company can offer a professional end product and guidance on how to submit the video and post it to your site.

The company SmileReminder offers a product called vSling, which positions a camera to capture testimonials when patients come in for their appointments. These videos are uploaded to a website on which the dentist can view and select which videos to distribute to the major online video sites. Arguably, a dentist could accomplish all of this in house if staff members are capable of handling the filming and distribution process. However, it may be easier and less awkward to request a patient review if you have a system in place which does not require the participation of a staff member in the filming process. I find patients to be considerably less comfortable smiling for the camera when my dental assistant is standing there staring at them.

While many dentists have joined the video bandwagon, most videos do not get a large number of views on the more popular sites such as YouTube. A patient testimonial or dental office tour does not carry the attractiveness of a funny video in terms of its ability to go viral. *David After the Dentist* has been viewed over 77,000,0000 times on YouTube. One YouTube commenter calculated that corporately the world has spent over 109 years viewing David's reaction to dental anesthesia. David's personal video has been re-mixed several times and has launched its own blog. Little David's two minute video is the first to appear in a search for *dentist* on YouTube. Your video about cosmetic dentistry may only be viewed hundreds of times or even less than that. Nonetheless, one viewing of a patient testimonial video that convinces a patient to appoint for veneers or implants can quickly make the inexpensive video process return the investment.

Streaming a video on your website not only establishes the impression that you are an expert in the field, but also advances your optimization efforts. Since Google may rank sites that have YouTube videos running on them higher than those that do not, it behooves you to invest the minimal time necessary to get a video live on your website. Ensure that the text description and title of your video both make adequate use of keywords that may be entered into a search query to find a local dentist. Search engines cannot read the content of the video itself so care must be taken when naming the video and providing a text description. Providing videos further increases your recognition with the search engines, augmenting your ranking versus your competition that chooses to ignore this optimization effort.

Business Networking Sites

Another medium for expanding your dental practice's online presence is through business networking sites such as LinkedIn. While I have not maximized the potential of these sites, my websites do receive regular traffic from my participation on LinkedIn. Establishing a profile page on LinkedIn is a simple process, requiring very little time. Be sure to include links to all your websites, as this is the means by which to attract customers from these business networking sites.

Edward M. Logan, DDS

MerchantCircle and CitySearch have recently modified their review sites to allow members of the local business community to interact with one another through these sites as well.

Chapter 27

Internet Toolbox

There are numerous websites and Internet tools which I have found to be especially helpful when researching how to optimize my websites. Many of these resources have been mentioned previously within the context of what they provide, but the following list groups these resources together for easy reference:

Google's Goods

The superpower known as Google offers a variety of tools and tips for optimizing your website, as well as for growing and monitoring your online presence. When establishing a Google account, which simply involves signing up, a vast array of resources is available to you:

- *Google Webmaster Tools* allows you to submit your Sitemap, analyze your website's use of title and description tags, learn where your website ranks for certain keyword searches, examine your website's keyword density, determine which websites are linking to your site, locate crawl errors and view how fast your web pages load.

- *Google Analytics* provides an array of statistics displaying how searchers are finding your site and what they do once they arrive. Google Analytics demonstrates which referral sources and keywords are bringing searchers to your site, which search engines are being used to find your site, how many times a page has been viewed, the geographical region of your visitors and which browser your visitors use. If your web host does not provide statistics, Google Analytics can serve as your website's only source of statistics. However, I recommend using Google Analytics along with another statistical measure, as Google seems to overlook a substantial amount of my website traffic. Google Analytics must be added to the coding of every page on your website that you wish to analyze.

- *Google Places* (previously known as Local Business Center) allows you to submit your business information in order to receive a listing on Google Maps. Google Places listings provide the option of submitting your location, website, email address, blog link, business hours, insurance and payment information, specialty, Facebook and Twitter pages, education information, years in practice, photos, a video and a short description of your business. Google Places now offers the opportunity for businesses to provide a 160 character status update as well. Google Places tracks reviews from several sources, including InsiderPages and CitySearch. One of your first steps in enhancing your online presence should be to sign up for a Google Places listing.

- *Google Alerts* gives you the opportunity to be notified by email of the latest relevant results for a word or phrase you have chosen. These alerts can be emailed to you as soon as a reference is found, once a day or once a week. I have set up alerts for different variations of my name in order to monitor reviews about me and to see where Google is finding me. Google Alerts can be used to provide information for blog posts, tweets, status updates or patient e-newsletters by setting up a weekly alert for topics such as Children's Dental Health.

- *Google Blogger* is free blogging software that is easy to use.

- *Google Reader* allows you to track blog subscriptions and read the latest updates from your favorite blogs.

- *Google Blog Search* provides a search tool to identify blogs on topics that interest you.

Google also provides numerous other resources available to anyone with an established Google account. *Google Mail* (also known as *Gmail*) provides an email program. *Google Earth* is a fun tool for exploring the world. *Google Health* provides a place to monitor your personal medical records online. Google has tools for creating websites and online groups as well. A recent online list identified more than 250 Google services, so what has been discussed here is merely a brush stroke on Google's broad palate of benefits.

SEOBook.com

SEOBook has designed several helpful tools for analyzing how search engines view a website. The tool I have used most often is the Spider Test Tool (http://tools.seobook.com/general/spider-test/). This test displays a web page's title tags, Meta description, keyword tags, html coding, keyword density and links to the web page. It provides links to view Google's latest cached copy of that web page, as well as how many pages of the site are indexed by Google. There is a link to Yahoo!'s Site Explorer statistics which shows the number of links to the website and how many pages of the site are indexed by Yahoo!. Links to Bing's and Ask's listings of indexed pages are provided as well.

SEOBook contains a blog and short video tutorial that will be valuable to anyone initiating the website optimization process. A free membership provides additional tools, a beginner's guide to SEO and a compilation of interviews with SEO specialists. SEOBook's *Rank Checker Tool*, available with your free membership, allows you to search a website's ranking on Yahoo! and Google for keywords and phrases that you choose. This powerful tool enables you to search multiple sites and keywords at the same time. SEOBook also offers a paid membership which provides videos, training modules and a community forum.

KeywordSpy.com

Through a free membership, Keyword Spy allows users to research organic and pay per click competition by keyword and domain name. When searching a keyword, you will receive detailed results on how many companies are competing for that keyword in the organic and pay per click markets. A keyword query will provide a visualization of the actual ads being run for that keyword, as well as a listing of the domain names and pay per click budgets of the companies behind those advertisements. This allows you to analyze your competition before deciding upon keywords to include in your website content and pay per click campaigns.

When searching by domain name, Keyword Spy delivers a report with a list of keywords for which a site is being ranked, where the site ranks and the number of times that keyword is searched each month. Keyword Spy allows you to analyze your organic competition through a list of websites using similar keywords. For those websites that participate in a pay per click campaign, Keyword Spy provides results on the pay per click ads and keywords being used by that domain. With a free trial, you will not receive a full list of organic keywords or competitors, but you will receive a large number of results. A paid membership costs $89.95/month and allows members to continually track keywords.

DentalTown.com

Within the past year, I have increased my participation in the forums on DentalTown, and have found them to be a great source of information about virtually every aspect of running a dental practice. DentalTown contains message boards on nearly every imaginable subject within dentistry, including practice management, marketing, insurance billing, imaging, labs, endodontics, restorative dentistry, prosthodontics, periodontics, orthodontics, practice transitions and office design. DentalTown purports to have over 70,000 members, providing a unique community of dentists whose experience is helpful in answering almost any question.

SearchStatus Tool

The SearchStatus Tool, accessed via www.quirk.biz/searchstatus, is a free download for use with the Internet browser Mozilla Firefox. When browsing online, it allows you at a glance to see the Google Page Rank and Alexa Ranking (a value derived in part from the amount of traffic to a website) of any web page you visit. Other options include highlighting nofollow links and keywords, reporting on the number and types of links on a page and providing the title, description and keyword tags. You may choose to view the domain ownership information, Sitemap, number of pages indexed by the major search engines and keyword density.

Search Engine Optimization Blogs

The following is a short list of blogs that I have found useful when researching how to optimize my websites:

- www.SearchEngineJournal.com
- www.eConsultancy.com/blog
- www.SEOmoz.org/blog
- www.SEOChat.com
- www.searchengineguide.com

Chapter 28

Internet Glossary

Anchor Text - Text used to describe what a link to another web page is about. This text is clickable, leading the user to another web page. Anchor text should be descriptive, using keywords that illustrate what the page is about rather than using generic text such as "click here."

Description Tag - A Meta tag component which is coded into the head section of a web page and invisible to the reader. The description tag provides an opportunity to describe in more detail what a web page is about. Description tag information is usually displayed after the title tag in a display of search engine query results.

DoFollow - A link that does not contain the nofollow tag, thereby encouraging search engines to follow the link and use it in determining ranking and relevance of the linked website.

Domain Name - The name of a website. For instance, the dental directory, The Dentist Search, has a domain name of www.TheDentistSearch.com.

Home Page - A website's primary page which appears when a domain name is entered. The home page serves to greet the reader and lay the foundation for the rest of the site.

HTML - Hypertext Markup Language – The most common website coding language used to design a website.

Keyword - Words used by a web searcher to gather information. Dental website content should contain the keywords that might be used to locate a local dentist. Search engines scan web pages to determine whether they contain the words being used by the searcher in order to provide relevant results.

Link - Also referred to as a hyperlink, web link, inbound link, inlink or back link. Clicking a link provides a way to direct a reader to another website. Links are typically in blue underlined text to indicate that the text can be clicked.

NoFollow - A coding attribute given to some links indicating to search engines that the link should not be used when determining a website's importance or ranking. It is simply advising the search engine to not follow the link. Each search engine handles this advice differently.

Organic Search Results - Search engine results that occur naturally owing to the optimization of a website. Organic results are not purchased and are typically displayed after sponsored listings.

PageRank (PR) - A Google patented algorithm used to determine the overall importance of a web page. Google uses over 200 indicators to establish a website's PageRank. PageRank was formerly a highly important component of SEO, with links from pages with higher Page Ranks being deemed more valuable.

Pay Per Click (PPC) - Paid advertising campaigns offered by the major search engines in exchange for sponsored listing results. The name is derived from the fact that advertisers pay each time a searcher clicks on their ad and is directed to their website.

RSS Feed - Really Simple Syndication - Allows the updates and information on a blog or website to be shared. Readers and blog directories may subscribe to a blog's RSS feed in order to receive notifications of new entries.

Search Engine - A website that collects, analyzes and displays information from web pages throughout the Internet when a user performs a search. The major search engines are Google, Yahoo! and Bing.

Search Engine Marketing (SEM) - A broader term than SEO, used to indicate the inclusion of practices such as pay per click campaign marketing and paid inclusion into directories.

Search Engine Optimization (SEO) - The process of designing and updating a website in order to promote its visibility on search engines. SEO involves more than the design of a website and includes important dynamics such as building up links to a website from other websites.

Search Engine Results Pages (SERP) - Pages of website listings that result when someone performs a search query. The vast majority of searchers do not look past page one of the SERP to find a website that matches their query.

Search Query - When a user types keywords into a search engine to find a product or service online. In laymen's terms, "What you type into Google when you are trying to find something." A search query results in a listing of websites that may contain the relevant information being searched.

Social Media - Websites that provide information while interacting with the user and allowing the user to interact with others. Social media encompasses multiple different genres, including social bookmarking, informational forums, video and picture sharing sites, blogs, personal and business networks.

Title Tag - An important Meta tag coded into the head section of every page of a website. Title tags are displayed in search results as the clickable text used to access a website. Establishing unique title tags which describe the content of every page of a website is important for search engine optimization.

URL - Uniform Resource Locator - It is similar to a domain name, but used specifically in reference to a web page's address. While a website only has one domain name, it will have multiple URLs pointing to different pages on that site. For example, www.TheDentistSearch.com/add_office.htm is a URL for a certain page within the domain name www.TheDentistSearch.com, which is also a URL.

Can You Really Do This?

Chapter 29

A Success Story

Several years ago a friend and colleague was wrapping up his tour of duty as a dental Naval Officer aboard a ship in the South Pacific. I continue to share with my patients his stories of providing dentistry to shipmates while sailing the high seas. The primary antagonist to ideal dental care was not the nervous, fidgety patient; it was the degree of pitch and roll of the swaying tide. "One hand on the rail to hold myself steady and one hand on the forceps!" was the method described for tooth extraction aboard the ship. My patients seem to relax a bit when they realize that their procedure will instead be performed on *terra firma*.

After completing his responsibilities with the Navy, Dr. HD as we will refer to him, took some time to consider where best to open his dental practice. The results of his research landed him in Austin, TX. The capitol of Texas happens to fit many of the ideal demographic criteria previously outlined in this book. Following a brief stint working as an associate, Dr. HD was ready to pursue life as a business owner and private practitioner. He chose to lease an existing dental office suite with completed tenant improvements, though one in dire need of a facelift. This meant that the exiting dentist had in place all the necessary essentials to operating a dental practice. However, Dr. HD desired to personalize this office to better represent his style of practice.

This is an ideal setting in which to start a business from scratch. The upfront cost is minimal, depending upon your sense of style. Dr. HD opted to replace the linoleum flooring with stained concrete. He leveled the antique cabinetry and upgraded to a more current standard.

Other modifications were made to the operatories, the drywall corridors, the reception area, the office furniture and finally, the paint scheme. The formerly weathered office environment now took the form of a brand new, state-of-the-art dental practice. While his investment was not negligible, it was much more reasonable than had he purchased an existing practice. The intelligent application of expense to office atmosphere details that seem so important to the patient but less so to many dentists, positioned his practice for success.

Another attentive decision this new business owner made was in selecting a location. His new office site assured plenty of visibility and drive-by traffic from a substantial commercial and residential population. Redundant signage allowed these potential patients to realize there was a new dentist in town, and that perhaps they should give him a try. Dr. HD knew from the successful experience of the previous dentist that this was a great place for a dental practice. The former tenant had grown such a thriving business that he was required to move his practice to a larger suite with more operatories.

Initially equipping two operatories with the ability to build out two more when justified, Dr. HD limited his expense while building his practice. He exercised overhead control by hiring one superhero staff member with whom he had previously worked. Wonder Woman served as receptionist, treatment plan coordinator, collection agency, supply manager and dental assistant. Dr. HD further managed his payroll by performing the roles of dentist and hygienist.

Dr. HD fulfilled his role of MBA Dentist by learning all the appropriate ways in which to market and advertise his services. He took full advantage of the technologically savvy nature of his patient demographics by maximizing exposure on patient review websites such as www.DoctorOogle.com. He added his practice to the online directory of dentists, www.TheDentistSearch.com, selecting a Gold Listing and thereby positioning his practice above all the other general dentists listed in Austin. His intelligently named, well-appropriated website maintained high rankings with the search engines.

Dr. HD thoroughly researched dental equipment and supplies in periodicals such as *Clinicians Report* and attended seminars which provided him the material and supply checklist, *Cutting-Edge Products for Clinical Excellence*, prior to outfitting his office. The knowledge he gained permitted Dr. HD to purchase items at a reasonable cost which other clinicians have determined to be of superior quality. This background research eliminated much of the trial and error waste that most dentists experience on a daily basis.

Dr. HD performed an array of dental procedures in his office that many general dentists may refer to specialists. This allowed Dr. HD not only to attract new patients through an expanded procedure mix, but also to place productive procedures on the schedule in lieu of empty time slots. Since he was trained to do these procedures, he had the available time and his patients needed them, it made sense to do so. It is common knowledge in the industry that most patients do not welcome having to leave your office in order to have dental procedures performed. You are convenient for them, they trust you and they have chosen you. When dentists can treat to the standard of care a complex of procedures in house, patients are highly appreciative.

Dr. HD implemented and adhered to cost control strategies that were second to none. He effectively managed his schedule through clinical and front office time and efficiency protocol. He avoided the mistakes I made by rejecting high dollar marketing techniques such as radio and television advertising. He retained local companies for computer installation and maintenance, equipment purchase and monthly supply provisions.

Dr. HD's practice was slow to grow in the first six months, but began to improve by the end of its inaugural year. Gradually, he added staff members and before long, a hygienist. Reaching this milestone was a great victory in itself, as few of us as general practitioners have signed up to play dental hygienist. Patient by patient, Dr. HD's practice grew. It seemed as though every other month he would call to inform me of his hiring of yet another employee. Then there was the need to equip another operatory, then another. Before long, one more part-time hygienist was required.

In less than four years, Dr. HD's practice had outgrown its confines and called him to seek space with double the square footage. Once again applying the fundamentals for choosing a location, he discovered a commercial condo for sale which boasted a stunning view of downtown Austin. With the capital earned through the success of Dr. HD's initial practice, he was able to apply a large down payment to the purchase of this beautiful space. With the suite build-out now nearing completion, Dr. HD is scheduled to treat his first patient in the new complex next month. I am confident that through the reapplication of his template for success, Dr. HD will continue producing, as he does in his current practice, in the top one percent of practices nationwide.

Perhaps more important than any other element to this new business owner's success was the manner in which he talked to his patients. Not only did Dr. HD insist that his staff members provide five-star customer service, he easily became the doctor his patients could trust. With a tone absent dominance, he listened and addressed patient concerns with care, concern and integrity. When you talk to this doctor, it is easy to tell he is a good man. He is soft-spoken, down-to-earth and does not esteem himself higher than others. Patients get a sense of his honesty and do not feel sold, much less swindled.

Dr. HD amassed a collection of anecdotes on his naval tours around the world, and man can he spin a story! I imagine that many of Dr. HD's patients leave his office feeling as if they have just spent time in the bowels of a Navy vessel. Though I have never sat in on one of his consults, I sometimes wonder how he ever gets any work done. Most people like to be engaged in entertaining conversation, particularly when they are anxious and apprehensive. Since our line of work embodies those feelings, this skill has served him well in forming relationships in his practice. What most patients tend to remember has little to do with your clinical expertise and much more to do with your likeability.

Dr. HD and I have been friends a very long time. We knew each other when I was in between practices and he was on sabbatical after completing his military obligation. I had recently sold my first practice and was taking a break of my own. Though still in my early thirties, I jokingly told my friends that I was retired. Both deliberating our next career move and still single, we had the freedom to move about as we pleased. Now, so many years later and in the throes of running private practices, we often reflect on the days when life was a little less stressful.

My parents built a house on a small private lake as they neared retirement. Though in their sixties and still working, Dr. HD and I were afforded the opportunity to relax and enjoy the property while my parents punched the clock. We would float around the lake on rafts, enjoying a beer or two and soaking up the sun as they were earning the mortgage. Though the feeling of guilt passed over us as my parents rolled off to work, it did not seem to linger long. We often nostalgically look back on that period of freedom as our *Six Months of Saturdays*.

Though the shine finally began to wear off that apple as the funds retreated from our bank accounts, we never regretted that period of mid-life retirement that dentistry afforded us. While it is important to apply the principles outlined in the template for growth and success of your practice, it is also valuable to take some time to appreciate the fruits of your labor. After all our years of training, deferred gratification and efforts to build successful practices, we are fortunate to belong to a profession that affords us the ability to do just that. I do not take time often enough to count my blessings.

Closing

For the majority of us, we made a decision when we were young to pursue a profession which we deemed noble, challenging and potentially rewarding. We studied hard for many years, assuming risks and financial obligations, and thus deferring gratification for a period much longer than that of most of our contemporaries. With the greatest risk comes the greatest reward, and through the most diligent efforts often comes the highest level of satisfaction. We have invested so much; we want to enjoy our chosen profession. Unfortunately, many dentists find themselves reeling in debt, frustration and the inability to control their futures. These doctors need to be wary of those aspiring to take advantage of their discontent and perceived helplessness.

There are approaches proven to enhance the control practitioners wield over their careers, their practices and their futures. A template for growth and success of your new or existing practice can be implemented toward this end. Cost control and overhead limiting measures can be instituted to reposition the reigns of your business back into your hands. The likelihood for practice growth to the level of sustenance can be greatly increased by proper and consistent application of the practice management techniques and marketing campaigns outlined in this book. We should be mindful of the fact that our chosen occupation does not need to define us as people. Dentistry is what we do; it does not have to become our identities. Therefore, dentistry can truly be a means to an end, not the end in itself.

Practice Management Resources for Dentists

The following helpful items are available for purchase through our website at www.DentistrysBusinessSecrets.com. For your convenience, we have packaged all of these items on a single compact disc. After purchasing this CD, you are free to download and reproduce the forms, mailers and brochures for the purposes of your dental practice. We are confident that the following tools included on the CD will allow for immediate implementation into your practice, thereby reducing staff costs and doctor labor while increasing your bottom line:

DENTAL INSURANCE BROCHURE FOR PATIENTS

PATIENT CONSENT FORMS

SMILE EVALUATION FORM

NEW PATIENT FORMS

NEW PATIENT LETTER

FINANCIAL ARRANGEMENT FORM

EMPLOYEE MANUAL

CANCELLATION POLICY

THANK YOU FOR REFERRAL LETTERS – PATIENT AND SPECIALIST

INSURANCE BENEFITS CHECKLIST

LIFETIME WHITENING FLYER

QUESTIONS TO ASK IN AN INTERVIEW

QUESTIONS TO ASK REFERENCES

NEW RESIDENT MAILER

TREATMENT DISCOUNT POSTCARDS

MARKETING CALENDAR

11 QUESTIONS TO ASK YOUR WEBSITE DESIGNER

WHAT SHOULD BE INCLUDED ON YOUR WEBSITE'S HOME PAGE?

SEARCH ENGINE OPTIMIZATION CHECKLIST

WEEKLY TO-DO CALENDAR FOR SOCIAL MEDIA EFFORTS

INTERNET TOOLBOX

CONTACT INFORMATION FOR DENTAL PRACTICE BUSINESS RESOURCES

References

[1] United States Department of Labor, Bureau of Labor Statistics. (2009). *Occupational Outlook Handbook* (2008-09 ed.). Retrieved from http://www.bls.gov/oco/ocos074.htm

[2] U.S. Department of Labor, Bureau of Labor Statistics. (2007). *Occupational Outlook Handbook.* (2006-07 ed.). Retrieved from http://www.bls.gov/oco/ocos072.htm

[3] Kennedy, M. (2009). Finding an Associate-We're Your Tipping Point, *ETS Dental Industry Insights, 12,* 2.

[4] The McGill Advisory. (2009). *Set 2010 Practice Fees as Part of Your Practice Budget Process,* 24 (11) , 3-4. Reprinted with permission.

[5] The McGill Advisory. (2008). *Financial Crisis Spells End to the Consumer Spending Era: How to Run a Profitable Practice Now,* 23 (10), 1-2. Reprinted with permission.

[6] Kennedy, M. (2009). Finding an Associate-We're Your Tipping Point, *ETS Dental Industry Insights, 12,* 1.

[7] List of available seminars by CR Foundation retrieved from http://www.cliniciansreport.org.

[8] List of available clinicians reports retrieved from http://www.cliniciansreport.org.

[9] Udell Webb Leadership, LLC. (2004) *Customized Fee Analyzer*

Companion Guide: Unlock the Secrets of UCR. 2-5. Copyright © 2004 Saint George, UT.

[10] Some content in the section, How Often Should You Raise Your Fees?, has been adapted from The McGill Advisory. (2005). *Doctors Surveyed on Raising Fees; What Should You Do for 2006?* 20 (12) , 1-2.

[11] United States Department of Labor, Bureau of Labor Statistics. (2010). *Occupational Outlook Handbook.* (2010-11 ed.). Retrieved from http://www.bls.gov/oco/ocos097.htm.

[12] United States Department of Labor, Bureau of Labor Statistics. (2010). *Occupational Outlook Handbook.* (2010-11 ed.). Retrieved from http://www.bls.gov/oco/ocos097.htm.

[13] United States Department of Labor, Bureau of Labor Statistics. (2010). *Occupational Outlook Handbook.* (2010-11 ed.). Retrieved from http://www.bls.gov/oco/ocos097.htm.

[14] The McGill Advisory. (2007). *Use Technology to Improve the Dental Hiring Process*, (11), 3-4. Reprinted with permission.

[15] Orent, T. (1998). *The Anatomy of a Smile Analysis, or, Getting to Yes, Fast!* p. 10.

[16] Orent, T. (1998). *The Anatomy of a Smile Analysis, or, Getting to Yes, Fast!* p. 14.

[17] Orent, T. (1998). *The Anatomy of a Smile Analysis, or, Getting to Yes, Fast!* p. 10.

[18] Oakes, W. (1992). *The Profitable Dentist,* p. 37. New Albany, IN. Reprinted with permission.

[19] Jameson C. (1996). Scheduling for productivity, profitability and stress control. *JADA 127*(12) 1777-82. Copyright© 1996 American Dental Association. All rights reserved. Excerpted by permission.

[20] Blanchard, K. and Johnson, S. (2000). Harper Collins Entertainment

[21] The McGill Advisory. (2008). Effective Time Management—Ten Steps to Improve Productivity and Reduce Stress, 23 (10). 4, 8. Reprinted with permission.

[22] Bender, Weltman, Thomas, Perry and Co, PC, Certified Public Accountants, (2008). *Dental Statistics for the Year Ended 2008.* 6-7.

[23] Lehman, J. (2008) *The Frugal Millionaires.* Seattle, WA: Mentor Press LLC.

[24] Orent, T. (1998). *The Anatomy of a Smile Analysis, or, Getting to Yes, Fast!* p. 17.

[25] Orent, T. (1998). *The Anatomy of a Smile Analysis, or, Getting to Yes, Fast!* p. 18.

[26] Gladwell, M. (2005). *Blink, The Power of Thinking Without Thinking*, Hachette Audio.

[27] Levinson, W. (1997). Physician-patient communication: The relationship with malpractice claims among primary care physicians and surgeons. *Journal of the American Medical Association. 277.* (7), 553-559.

[28] Ambady, N. et al. (2002). Surgeons' tone of voice: A clue to malpractice history. *Surgery.* 5-9.

[29] Interview with Jeffrey Allen and Alice Burkin by Berkeley Rice. (2000) How Plaintiff's Lawyers Pick Their Targets. *Medical Economics.* April 24, 2000.

[30] ADA Website Fact Sheet, Copyright© 2010 American Dental Association, all rights reserved, reprinted by permission. Retrieved from: http://www.ada.org/1330.aspx.

[31] The McGill Advisory. (2009). Set 2010 Fees as Part of Your Practice Budget Process. 24 (11). Reprinted with permission.

[32] Chrisad/Christensen Advertising. (1998). What's the Difference Between These Two New Patients? *Chrisad Dental Marketing News.* (winter ed.). 1-2.

[33] Promail News. (1998). The Million Dollar Grabber. (September ed.)

[34] Madow, D. (1996). How to Start the Most Successful New Patient Program EVER! pp. 9, 12.

[35] iProspect Search Engine User Behavior Study (April 2006). iProspect and Juniper Research. Retrieved from http://www.iProspect.com.

[36] Retrieved from http://www.google.com/support/webmasters/bin/answer.py?hl=en&answer=35291.

[37] Retrieved from http://www.EightfoldLogic.com.

Index

Symbols

11 questions to ask your website designer 424

A

About.com 374
Academy of Dental C.P.A.s 163
A caring doctor 290
Accounts overdue report 63
Adhesion dentistry 19
Adjustments report 63
Ad Words 374
Alexa Ranking 406
The All-in-One Dentist 83
Allowed amount 243
Alternate benefit 245
Amalgam downgrade 244
Anchor text 336, 346, 347, 368, 369, 388, 409
Artistry in Dentistry 319
Ask.com 374
Askville 369
Associate dentist 104, 164, 181
Auto-mix and fast-set materials 141

B

Backlink 359
Banner advertising 314
Basic services 242
Before and After 51, 52, 208, 210, 286, 308, 309, 310, 313, 324, 329, 335, 347, 350, 376, 377, 386, 392
Benefit amount 243
Benefits to You 298, 318, 324, 336, 341
Benefits you provide 347
Best of the Web 363
Billboard advertising 316, 317
Billing and collections report 64
Bing 348, 352, 353, 356, 358, 359, 361, 374, 388, 405, 411
BlackBerry 398
Blog 282, 332, 341, 349, 357, 360, 362, 365, 369, 370, 371, 376, 377, 381, 382, 383, 384, 385, 386, 387, 388, 389, 392, 393, 394, 400, 401, 404, 405, 407, 410
Blogging 349, 384, 385, 387, 389, 404
Bloglines 389
Bonding with your patients 214
Bookmarking sites 362, 368, 369, 381, 382, 399
Booth and convention advertising 310
Build-out 45, 48, 49, 198, 418
Business.com 363
Business loans 153, 154
Business manager 85, 95, 96, 107, 109, 355, 381, 382
Business networking sites 401

C

Call to action 296, 345
Cancellation policy 59, 423

Capitation plans 251
Care Credit 224, 231
Cathy Jameson 132
CDA 88
Charity auctions 312
Checking references 92, 104, 105
Checkout procedure 223
Choosing a contractor 47
Choosing a website host 330
Chrisad Dental Marketing 428
CitySearch 402, 404
CitySearch.com 359, 366
Claim Connect 249
Clinical efficiency and material selection 138
Clinicians Report 66, 67, 416
Collection 10, 28, 62, 64, 85, 100, 137, 225, 226, 229, 238, 239, 240, 248, 416, 418
Collection incentive plans 100
Collections 20, 21, 28, 52, 62, 64, 100, 101, 131, 163, 164, 223, 225, 229, 232, 268
The comforts of home 289
Communicating effectively 218
Community service 271, 312, 314
Complete/full mouth x-ray series 243
Computer company selection 192
Computer maintenance and repair 160
Conflict resolution 180, 181
Contact information for dental practice business resources 424
Contact Us option 345
Contractor 43, 47, 48, 49, 50, 53
Controlling dental office odors 289
Coordination of benefits 245
Co-pay 52, 85, 224, 225, 226, 227, 244, 256
Co-payment 73, 224, 226, 227, 238, 240, 244, 245
Cosmetic dentistry 18, 19, 26, 57, 65, 161, 182, 188, 208, 210, 211, 278, 285, 286, 291, 300, 302, 306, 308, 309, 310, 315, 335, 341, 342, 343, 346, 350, 369, 381, 401
Cost control 44, 83, 127, 159, 166, 169, 258, 417, 421
Cost controlling 12, 151, 152, 196
CRA Newsletter 66, 67

D

Daily reports 61, 62
Debt reduction 154, 199, 200
Deductible 199, 226, 241, 242
Delegate 143, 149, 171
Delicious 362, 379, 399
Demographic 34, 35, 46, 267, 302, 390, 415
Dental assistant 1, 44, 80, 84, 86, 87, 88, 94, 97, 103, 118, 128, 136, 139, 140, 142, 144, 167, 207, 219, 262, 263, 313, 401, 416
Dental equipment 28, 37, 38, 39, 40, 41, 45, 47, 51, 54, 55, 61, 66, 68, 134, 165, 168, 193, 198, 416
Dental equipment and supply companies 47, 61, 165
Dental equipment and supply reps 37, 39, 55
Dental hygienist 88, 89, 90, 91, 92, 93, 94, 417
Dental insurance brochure 423
Dental laboratory costs 160
Dental school xvii, 1, 2, 7, 15, 16, 17, 18, 22, 23, 24, 60, 68, 78, 83, 125, 140, 143, 147, 151, 152, 158, 169, 175, 176, 237, 253, 254, 284, 305, 312, 316, 323, 327, 386
Dental software 60, 63, 64, 224, 248, 278, 365
Dental supplies 159
DentalTown 106, 379, 382, 406
DentalTown.com 106, 379, 406
Description tag 341, 342, 344, 409
Design for ergonomics 134
Digg 357, 362, 379, 383

Digg.com 369, 399
Digital radiography 134, 135
Digital x-rays 135, 220, 249
Direct message 394, 395
Direct reimbursement plans 258
DMOZ Open Directory Project 363
DoctorOogle.com 365, 416
Dofollow link 361, 364, 365, 366
Domain name 330, 333, 334, 342, 358, 375, 405, 406, 409, 411, 412
Door-to-Door Marketing 311
Dr. Analytical 159, 199
Dr. David Madow 299
Dr. Efficiency 6, 126, 127
Dr. Gordon Christensen 66
Dr. Jumper vs. Dr. Keeper 158
Dr. Ray Bertolotti 19
Dr. Tom Orent 113, 213, 214
Dr. Woody Oakes 130

E

EchoFon 397, 398
eConsultancy.com/blog 407
Educating the patient 219
Efficiency 6, 12, 17, 18, 61, 67, 69, 70, 73, 87, 97, 125, 126, 127, 128, 131, 132, 133, 134, 135, 136, 138, 139, 140, 141, 142, 143, 146, 148, 149, 166, 167, 229, 417
Efficient communication 137
Electronic claim submission 61, 248, 249
Employee manual 107, 109, 423
E-newsletter 19
EOB 225, 228, 243, 247
Equipment 27, 28, 37, 38, 39, 40, 41, 44, 45, 47, 48, 51, 54, 55, 56, 61, 65, 66, 67, 68, 73, 133, 134, 153, 158, 159, 164, 165, 168, 189, 193, 198, 199, 220, 288, 416, 417
Equipment and supply decisions 65
Equipment choices 133
Establishing trust 213, 290, 291
Esthetic dentistry 18, 19, 65, 182, 190, 209, 210, 286, 310, 315, 355
Estimation of benefits 116
ETS Dental Industry Insights 425
External marketing 11, 34, 162, 271, 282, 293, 294, 302, 314, 318, 319, 323, 324

F

Facebook 105, 353, 357, 362, 379, 380, 381, 382, 383, 384, 388, 389, 390, 391, 392, 393, 394, 397, 398, 404
Facebook business page 381, 390
Facebook fan page 391, 392, 393
Facebook status update 392
FAQ 341, 385
Fee-for-service 26, 36, 165, 233, 254, 257, 258, 262, 264, 269
Fee-for-service plans 257
Fee schedule 69, 71, 244, 257, 259, 260, 261
Fifth Quarter Seminars Newsletter 19
Financial arrangement form 423
Five-star customer service 111, 118, 418
Fixed costs 153, 155, 157
Flexible spending account (FSA) 274, 275
Flickr 379, 400
Follow 64, 81, 92, 95, 107, 143, 183, 224, 226, 232, 239, 260, 333, 353, 363, 368, 381, 382, 383, 386, 388, 389, 390, 394, 395, 396, 397, 398, 409, 410
Forums 357, 369, 370, 379, 382, 383, 385, 406, 411
The Frugal Millionaires 183, 427

G

The Gems Guy 113
Gems Publishing, USA 113

Get Organized! 128
Getting treatment scheduled 11, 207
Giveaways 283, 286, 288
GoldAutoPilot.com 113
Google Alerts 367, 387, 404
Google Analytics 348, 403, 404
Google Blogger 349, 384, 385, 404
Google Blog Search 404
Google Earth 405
Google Health 405
Google Mail (Gmail) 405
Google Maps 358, 359, 366, 400, 404
GoogleMaps.com 366
Google Page Rank 406
Google Places 353, 358, 359, 366, 404
Google Reader 389, 404
Google's Keyword Tool 375
Google's webmaster central forum 354
GoogleVideo 400
Google Webmaster Tools 349, 377, 403
Greeting patients 85, 116
Guest mentality 113, 118, 279, 289, 290

H

Handling criticism 221
Headphones 136
Hiring 10, 47, 55, 56, 75, 83, 85, 86, 87, 88, 90, 91, 92, 94, 95, 96, 98, 105, 106, 108, 145, 155, 156, 162, 167, 223, 287, 312, 318, 328, 329, 355, 382, 416, 417, 426
Hiring mistakes 108
HMO 26, 40, 228, 251, 252, 253, 262
HMO plans 251, 252
Home page 334, 335, 336, 339, 341, 343, 346, 347, 360, 369, 395, 396, 400, 409
HootSuite 397, 398
HotFrog 364, 382
HTML (Hypertext Markup Language) 409

Hygienist incentive plans 101

I

Ideal staff 27, 75, 77, 78, 79, 80, 81, 98, 108, 162
I hate dentists 173
Improve productivity 149, 427
Inbound link 359, 410
Incentive programs 287, 288
Indemnity plan 257
Initial phone call 114, 115, 240, 241
InMotion Hosting 332
InsiderPages 404
InsiderPages.com 359, 366
Insurance 101 237, 240
Insurance benefits checklist 240, 424
Insurance benefits definitions 242
Insurance claim submission 246
Insurance levels of service 242
Insurance overdue report 63
Insurance participation 27, 35, 251
Insurance plan types 251, 257
Insurance premiums 155, 258
Interior designer 54, 55
Internal marketing 11, 50, 53, 56, 59, 62, 116, 137, 161, 207, 211, 223, 271, 273, 280, 282, 283, 286, 288, 289, 291, 293, 304, 318, 319, 324, 380
Internet glossary 325, 409
Internet marketing 11, 158, 294, 302, 305, 321, 323, 324, 325, 327, 349, 351, 353, 355, 372, 381
Internet toolbox 403, 424
The interview process 86, 90, 106, 107, 254
Investing for retirement 197
iPhone 398
iProspect 353, 428
Isolate and visualize 140
Isolating multiple quadrants 140
It's all about trust 290

J

Jamesonmanagement.com 132

K

Keyword 338, 339, 340, 342, 343, 354, 356, 373, 375, 377, 396, 399, 403, 405, 406, 407, 410
Keyword density 338, 403, 405, 407
Keyword Spy 405, 406
Keyword tags 405, 406

L

LDH 89, 90
Lifetime whitening flyer 424
Link 105, 318, 335, 337, 338, 339, 346, 347, 350, 354, 355, 356, 357, 358, 360, 361, 362, 363, 364, 365, 366, 368, 369, 370, 371, 374, 376, 384, 387, 388, 393, 394, 395, 399, 400, 404, 405, 409, 410
LinkedIn 105, 381, 382, 397, 401
Links 35, 324, 328, 329, 334, 336, 337, 338, 342, 349, 350, 351, 354, 356, 357, 358, 359, 360, 361, 362, 363, 364, 365, 366, 368, 369, 370, 371, 380, 382, 384, 388, 389, 392, 393, 395, 399, 401, 405, 406, 410, 411
Links through dentistry specific directories 364
Links through online web directories 362
Local business listings 352, 356, 358
Long tail keywords 340, 341, 374
The low overhead practice 126, 162

M

Mailing houses 295, 296, 297
Major search engines 328, 344, 348, 350, 351, 352, 356, 357, 358, 360, 361, 362, 363, 373, 374, 377, 407, 410, 411

Major services 243
Managed care dentistry 254, 262
Marketing calendar 303, 319, 424
Marketing patient 276, 280, 366
Marketing plan 96, 267, 268, 269, 271
Maximum benefit 242
Maximum capacity 6, 69, 163
McGill Advisory 21, 105, 149, 231, 268, 425, 426, 427, 428
Meet the staff 347
MerchantCircle.com 366
Meta description 342, 343, 344, 349, 405
Meta tags 341, 342, 349
Micromanage 144
Microsoft 296, 352, 353, 374, 399
Missing tooth clause 242
Mistakes I have made 8, 12, 42, 187, 315, 316
Mixx 357, 362, 379, 383
Mixx.com 369, 399
Monthly reports 62
More than one website 334, 349, 350
Morning huddle 146
Multi-tasking 86, 145
MySpace 105, 106, 357, 379, 397
MyYahoo 389

N

Negative review 367, 368
Networking gift programs 161
Network marketing 307, 308, 309
New patient 7, 12, 22, 24, 29, 35, 36, 37, 41, 58, 59, 63, 71, 85, 95, 100, 114, 115, 116, 119, 120, 129, 150, 161, 178, 188, 191, 212, 213, 223, 229, 238, 240, 241, 268, 270, 274, 275, 276, 277, 278, 280, 285, 290, 291, 294, 298, 301, 306, 308, 323, 324, 335, 336, 340, 345, 346, 370, 376, 377, 380, 388, 394, 396, 423, 428

New patient and production numbers report 63
New patient forms 115, 119, 345, 423
New patient letter 423
New patient paperwork 85, 119
The new patient phone call 114, 115, 116, 290
New patient referral programs 276
New patient volume incentive plans 100
New resident mailer 11, 286, 294, 295, 296, 298, 299, 300, 301, 302, 303, 323
Newsletters xv, xviii, 11, 280, 281, 282, 283, 288, 306, 330, 382, 388, 400, 404
Newspaper and local publication advertising 305
Niche marketing 302, 305, 334, 340, 350
Nofollow tag 361, 362, 369, 399, 409

O

Office atmosphere 27, 28, 40, 44, 45, 50, 53, 54, 71, 279, 288, 416
Office cleaning 157
Office design 10, 28, 43, 50, 51, 53, 55, 133, 406
Office environment 29, 43, 45, 49, 50, 52, 53, 56, 59, 77, 88, 98, 109, 130, 212, 220, 288, 289, 302, 416
Office hours 58, 71, 359, 365
Office manager 62, 64, 79, 84, 85, 86, 88, 102, 107, 117, 127, 128, 146, 225, 227, 229, 246, 274, 279
The One Minute Manager 144, 145
On the job training 80, 87
Open house 45, 53, 308
Optimal capacity 21, 22, 70, 178, 231, 233, 268, 269
Optimized pictures and video 347
Organic listings 352, 371, 372

Organic search results 371, 372, 376, 410
Original and link-worthy content 337
Overdue recall report 63, 64, 274

P

Page Rank 360, 406
Patient consent forms 423
Patient criteria report 64
Patient financing 230, 310, 335
Patient perceptions 182
Patient referral programs 161, 276
Patient referral report 62
Patient reminders 275, 288
Patient responsibility/due from patient 245
The patient you want to keep 179
The patient you want to lose 176, 179
Pay per click 339, 357, 371, 372, 373, 374, 375, 376, 405, 406, 410, 411
Payroll 61, 74, 83, 89, 95, 101, 114, 142, 147, 155, 156, 161, 162, 226, 240, 416
Perception is reality 173, 288
Perfect team 97
Photo and video sharing sites 400
Photo and video sharing websites 379, 400
Position your practice for success 35
Potential new patient 12, 115, 298, 335, 336, 340, 388
PPO 36, 59, 71, 73, 255, 256, 259, 260, 261, 262, 263, 264, 268, 269
PPO plans 255, 256, 260, 262, 263, 268
Practice location 10, 33, 34, 35, 42, 339, 399
Practice name 57, 58, 162, 339, 343, 365, 367
Practice opportunity 33, 37, 40, 42, 45, 50
Practice purchase 21, 198

Press release 282, 368
Preventative services 72, 242, 255
Production incentive plans 101
Professional burnout 12, 148, 174, 176, 196, 202
The Profitable Dentist newsletter 130
Promail News 428
Promoted Tweets Program 399
Promoting cosmetic dentistry 208
PRWeb.com 368
The psychology of happiness 183
The psychology of management 12, 171

Q

Quality home page 334
Quality links 359
Quarterly reports 62, 63
Question and answer forums 369
Questions to ask in an interview 424
Questions to ask references 424

R

Radio advertising 187, 188, 191, 315
Raise your fees 73, 74, 426
Rank Checker Tool 405
RDA 88
RDH 88, 90
Recalls 60, 61, 84, 273, 274, 288
Reciprocal link 361, 362
Recurring marketing expenses 157
Reddit 357, 379, 383
Reddit.com 369, 399
Reduce stress 149, 427
Referral patient 276
Referral source report 62
Resource section 8, 107
Respecting your staff 219
Résumé 102, 104, 107
Retirement 22, 99, 155, 156, 175, 197, 198, 199, 200, 202, 203, 418, 419
Return on investment (ROI) 44, 47, 53, 56, 63, 96, 164, 188, 191, 268, 269, 270, 271, 285, 288, 294, 299, 300, 303, 304, 315, 316, 317, 319, 327, 329, 375, 380, 383, 390
Retweet 394, 395
RSS (Real Simple Syndication) feed 389, 410

S

Saving 12, 61, 195, 196, 197, 200, 233
Scheduling for production 12, 20, 69, 129, 131
Scheduling quadrant dentistry 131
Scientific fee analyzer 71, 72, 261
Scratch practice 7, 24, 25, 27, 28, 29, 45, 83, 92, 94, 167, 192, 271
Scripting your communication 212
Searchable domain name 333, 334
Search engine 294, 325, 327, 328, 331, 333, 334, 335, 337, 338, 342, 343, 344, 347, 351, 352, 353, 354, 355, 356, 358, 359, 360, 367, 372, 373, 374, 376, 377, 380, 381, 391, 393, 399, 407, 409, 410, 411, 428
Searchengineguide.com 407
SearchEngineJournal.com 407
Search engine marketing (SEM) 372, 411
Search engine optimization blogs 407
Search engine optimization checklist 356, 424
Search engine optimization (SEO) 294, 325, 327, 328, 330, 335, 337, 338, 342, 344, 347, 350, 351, 352, 353, 354, 355, 356, 358, 359, 360, 361, 364, 369, 372, 380, 381, 405, 407, 410, 411, 424
Search engine optimized design 344
Search engine results 328, 351, 352, 353, 367, 377, 399, 410, 411
Search engine results page (SERP) 352, 411

Search query 324, 334, 339, 401, 411
SearchStatus 362, 406
Selecting a web designer 328
SEOBook.com 405
SEOChat.com 407
SEOmoz.org/blog 407
Signage 57, 58, 318, 319, 334, 416
Sitemap 348, 356, 357, 358, 403, 407
Six-handed dentistry 142
Smile evaluation form 119, 423
SmileReminder 400
Social bookmarking websites 379
Social business network websites 379
Social media 325, 353, 357, 362, 376, 379, 380, 381, 382, 383, 384, 387, 388, 389, 392, 393, 396, 397, 398, 399, 400, 411, 424
Social media marketing 325, 357, 376, 379, 380, 381, 382, 388
Social media news sites 399
Social network websites 379
Social news websites 379
Soft tissue management programs 211
Spider Test Tool 405
Sponsored listings 352, 358, 371, 372, 374, 410
Staff benefits 99
Staff bonus programs 99, 162
Staff management 144, 167
StumbleUpon 379, 399
Superpages.com 371
Supplies 38, 65, 84, 85, 127, 133, 159, 207, 275, 416
Switchboard.com 371

T

Teaching through technology 220
Technorati 369, 379, 385, 388
Telephone book advertising 304
Television advertising 191, 315, 316, 417
Template for growth and success 7, 8, 9, 10, 419, 421
Thank you for referral letters 424

TheDentistSearch.com 157, 356, 358, 365, 409, 412, 416
Third-party financing 224, 232, 233
The three-day workweek 147
Time and efficiency 12, 67, 125, 127, 135, 417
Title tags 324, 338, 342, 343, 349, 405, 411
Treatment coordinator 95, 207, 223, 224, 228
Treatment discount postcards 424
Treatment plan 24, 41, 63, 64, 85, 95, 167, 207, 208, 209, 210, 211, 212, 218, 219, 220, 221, 222, 223, 224, 228, 229, 253, 290, 291, 416
Treatment plan estimate 223
Treatment planning 10, 207, 211, 212, 218, 220, 229, 239
Trial and error 5, 8, 20, 29, 41, 71, 93, 139, 180, 187, 269, 299, 417
Truve 400
TVs 136
Tweet 381, 383, 394, 395, 396, 397, 398, 399
TweetDeck 397, 398
Twitter 353, 357, 362, 379, 381, 382, 383, 384, 388, 389, 393, 394, 395, 396, 397, 398, 399, 404
Two-way radios 137, 138
TypePad 384, 385

U

UberTwitter 397, 398
Udell Webb 73, 425
Uncovering practice opportunities 37
Unscheduled treatment plans report 63
URL (Uniform Resource Locator) 357, 358, 360, 362, 364, 369, 370, 374, 391, 397, 399, 411, 412
Usual, Customary and Reasonable (UCR) 72, 225, 226, 227, 228, 238, 243, 244, 245, 255, 256, 257, 426

Utilities 157

V

Variable costs 147, 158
Video marketing 188, 190, 191
Vimeo 379
Virtual reality glasses 136, 289, 298
Vista Print 318
vSling 400

W

Waiting period 242
Website design 11, 12, 325, 328, 346, 347, 349, 351, 352, 353, 368
Website statistics/analytics 348
Website updates 376
Weekly to-do calendar for social media efforts 424
What should be included on your website's home page? 424
Wiki Answers 369
WordPress 332, 349, 384, 385, 386, 388, 389

Y

Yahoo! 105, 325, 328, 332, 342, 344, 348, 351, 352, 353, 356, 358, 359, 361, 363, 364, 369, 374, 377, 405, 411
Yahoo! Answers 369
Yahoo! Business Directory 363
Yahoo!Local.com 366
Yahoo!'s Site Explorer 405
Yahoo!Video 400
Yellowpages.com 305, 362, 371
Yelp.com 362, 366
YouTube 357, 379, 400, 401

Z

ZoomInfo 379, 382

About the Author

Dr. Edward Logan is a general dentist practicing in O'Fallon, Missouri. Dr. Logan graduated from the University of Washington School of Dentistry in 1993 and has since built three successful practices from scratch, one in Southern California and two in the Midwest. Though his dental education had trained him well in the area of clinical dentistry, he had learned very little regarding how to operate a successful business. Dr. Logan therefore sought extensive training in the areas of dental practice management and marketing.

Dr. Logan has since invited health care professionals nationwide to benefit from the business knowledge he has amassed over the years through the professional resource company he owns and operates, "Business Secrets for Health Care Professionals." Dr. Logan enjoys helping practitioners achieve success in business while aligning their goals for successful living. At the forefront of this strategy is the idea that time away from work is at least as valuable as that spent in the office. Techniques for obtaining practice growth and sustenance in the most efficient manner possible are presented in an effort to provide practitioners more of this valued personal and family time. Dr. Logan and wife Katie are currently expecting their second child. They and their son Will live in O'Fallon, Missouri. Dr. Logan competes regularly in the sport of duathlon, combining running and cycling.